June 20-22, 2017
Philadelphia, PA, USA

**Association for
Computing Machinery**

Advancing Computing as a Science & Profession

IH&MMSec'17

Proceedings of the 2017 ACM Workshop on
Information Hiding and Multimedia Security

Sponsored by:
ACM SIGMM

Supported by:
Drexel University and the Isaac L. Auerbach Cybersecurity Institute

**Association for
Computing Machinery**

Advancing Computing as a Science & Profession

Printed in the USA

Preface

Welcome to the 5th ACM Workshop on Information Hiding and Multimedia Security Workshop – IH&MMSec'17 in Philadelphia, PA, held June 20-21, 2017.

In response to our call for papers, 34 excellent papers were submitted from authors throughout North America, Europe, and Asia. The best 18 of these papers were accepted (53% acceptance rate) and assembled into a strong technical program. The accepted papers cover the fields of steganography and steganalysis in digital media, multimedia forensics, digital watermarking, data hiding in natural language, deep learning approaches to both forensics and steganalysis.

We sincerely thank all the submitting authors for their contributions, and the reviewers for their invaluable help. We expect the selected papers to be of wide interest to researchers working in the field and to participants from industry and from government institutions.

The technical program also includes two invited keynote speakers. The first presentation is given by Dr. Anupam Das from Carnegie Mellon University on the topic of using motion sensors in smartphones to track users. The second presentation is given by Dr. Rachel Greenstadt from Drexel University on the topic of how stylometry and machine learning can be used to determine the author of both written documents and software.

As usual, the workshop is structured into three days with the afternoon of the second day devoted to a social event. The social event is designed to promote discussions and to help establish relationships for future collaboration among participants. Also, at the end of the second day before the start of the social event, time is reserved for a rump session during which the participants are encouraged to share their work in progress, discuss unpublished results, demo new products, and make relevant announcements.

A great team effort put together the technical program. The Program Committee assisted by 29 external reviewers provided timely and high-quality reviews. A double-blind review process was used to ensure fairness. Each paper was carefully read and appraised by at least three reviewers, however the majority of papers were reviewed by four reviewers. To let the Program Chairs select the best quality and relevant work, papers with conflicting reviews were discussed at length. We thank all participants for their help in putting together this great program.

We also thank our supporters the Isaac L. Auerbach Cybersecurity Institute and Drexel University. Great thanks are due to Michelle Wells for her invaluable help with local organization of the workshop, to Owen Mayer for his help building the conference website, and to Otto-von-Guericke University Magdeburg for hosting the conference website.

Finally, we hope that you will find this program very interesting and that you will enjoy your stay in Philadelphia, the City of Brotherly Love.

IH&MMSec'17 General Chair

Matthew C. Stamm
Drexel University, USA

IH&MMSec'17 Program Chairs

Matthias Kirchner
Binghamton University, USA

Sviatoslav Voloshynovskiy
University of Geneva, Switzerland

Table of Contents

Session: Video Steganalysis

Session: Deep Learning for Media Forensics

IH&MMSec 2017 Workshop Organization

General Chair: Matthew C. Stamm *(Drexel University, USA)*

Program Chairs: Matthias Kirchner *(SUNY Binghamton, USA)*
Sviatoslav Voloshynovskiy, *(University of Geneva, Switzerland)*

ACM Liason: Jana Dittmann (University of Magdeburg, Germany)

Steering Committee: Stefan Katzenbeisser *(TU Darmstadt, Germany)*
Jana Dittmann *(Otto-von-Guericke University Magdeburg, Germany)*
Jessica Fridrich *(SUNY Binghamton, USA)*
George Danezis *(Microsoft Research Cambridge, UK)*
Patrizio Campisi *(University of Roma TRE, Italy)*
Balakrishnan Prabhakaran *(University of Dallas, USA)*

Program Committee: Mauro Barni *(Università di Siena, Italy)*
Patrick Bas *(CNRS, University of Lille, France)*
François Cayre *(Grenoble INP, University of Grenoble Alpes, France)*
Marc Chaumont *(Université de Nîmes, France)*
Rémi Cogranne *(Université de Technologie de Troyes, France)*
Pedro Comesaña Alfaro *(University of Vigo, Spain)*
Jana Dittmann *(Otto-von-Guericke University Magdeburg, Germany)*
Wei Fan *(Dartmouth College, USA)*
Caroline Fontaine *(CNRS, France)*
Jessica Fridrich *(SUNY Binghamton, USA)*
Neil F. Johnson *(Booz Allen Hamilton, USA)*
Stefan Katzenbeisser *(TU Darmstadt, Germany)*
Andrew D. Ker *(Oxford University, UK)*
Christian Kraetzer *(University of Magdeburg, Germany)*
Qingzhong Liu *(Sam Houston State University, USA)*
Chun-Shien Lu *(Academia Sinica, Taiwan)*
Wojciech Mazurczyk *(Warsaw University of Technology, Poland)*
Fernando Pérez-González *(University of Vigo, Spain)*
Tomáš Pevný *(Czech Technical University in Prague, Czech Republic)*
Alessandro Piva *(Università degli Studi Firenze, Italy)*
William Puech *(Université de Montpellier, France)*
Thomas Schneider *(TU Darmstadt, Germany)*
Pascal Schöttle *(University of Innsbrück, Austria)*
Yun-Qing Shi *(New Jersey Institute of Technology, USA)*
Thomas Stütz *(Fachhochschule Salzburg, Austria)*
Andreas Uhl *(Universität Salzburg, Austria)*
Claus Vielhauer *(Fachhochschule Brandenburg, Germany)*
Annalisa Verdoliva *(Università degli Studi di Napoli Federico II, Italy)*
Kai Wang *(CNRS, University of Grenoble Alpes, France)*

IH&MMSec 2017 Sponsors & Supporters

Sponsors:

Supporters:

Every Move You Make: Tracking Smartphone Users through Motion Sensors

Anupam Das
Carnegie Mellon University
Pittsburgh, Pennsylvania
anupamd@cs.cmu.edu

ABSTRACT

Online users are increasingly being subjected to privacy-invasive tracking across the web for advertisement and surveillance purposes, using IP addresses, cookies, and browser fingerprinting. As web browsing activity shifts to mobile platforms such as smartphones, traditional browser fingerprinting techniques become less effective due to ephemeral IP addresses and uniform software-base. However, device fingerprinting using built-in sensors offers a new avenue for attack. In this talk, I will describe how motion sensors such as accelerometer and gyroscope, embedded in smartphones, can be exploited to track users online. Next, I will discuss the practical aspects of this attack and how it can be used to track users across different sessions under natural web browsing settings. Finally, I will talk about usable countermeasures that we have developed to protect users against such fingerprinting techniques.

CCS CONCEPTS

•**Security and privacy** →**Side-channel analysis and countermeasures;**

KEYWORDS

Device fingerprinting; motion sensors; side-channel

BIOGRAPHY

Anupam Das is a Post-Doctoral Fellow in the School of Computer Science at Carnegie Mellon University. His research interests lie in the domain of security and privacy with a focus towards designing privacy-aware systems. He received his Ph.D. in computer science in 2016 from the University of Illinois at Urbana-Champaign where he was a recipient of Fulbright Science and Technology Fellowship. Previously, he received his B.S. and M.S. in computer science and engineering from Bangladesh University of Engineering and Technology (BUET) in 2008 and 2010, respectively. He also served as a Lecturer in the Department of Computer Science and Engineering at BUET from 2008 to 2010 before being appointed as an Assistant Professor of the same department in 2010.

Information-theoretic Bounds of Resampling Forensics: New Evidence for Traces Beyond Cyclostationarity

Cecilia Pasquini
Universität Innsbruck, Austria
University of Münster, Germany
pasquini@uni-muenster.de

Rainer Böhme
Universität Innsbruck, Austria
University of Münster, Germany
rainer.boehme@uibk.ac.at

ABSTRACT

Although several methods have been proposed for the detection of resampling operations in multimedia signals and the estimation of the resampling factor, the fundamental limits for this forensic task leave open research questions. In this work, we explore the effects that a downsampling operation introduces in the statistics of a 1D signal as a function of the parameters used. We quantify the statistical distance between an original signal and its downsampled version by means of the Kullback-Leibler Divergence (KLD) in case of a wide-sense stationary 1st-order autoregressive signal model. Values of the KLD are derived for different signal parameters, resampling factors and interpolation kernels, thus predicting the achievable hypothesis distinguishability in each case. Our analysis reveals unexpected detectability in case of strong downsampling due to the local correlation structure of the original signal. Moreover, since existing detection methods generally leverage the cyclostationarity of resampled signals, we also address the case where the auto-covariance values are estimated directly by means of the sample autocovariance from the signal under investigation. Under the considered assumptions, the Wishart distribution models the sample covariance matrix of a signal segment and the KLD under different hypotheses is derived.

KEYWORDS

Signal resampling, resampling forensics, Kullback-Leibler divergence, hypothesis distinguishability.

ACM Reference format:
Cecilia Pasquini and Rainer Böhme. 2017. Information-theoretic Bounds of Resampling Forensics:
New Evidence for Traces Beyond Cyclostationarity. In *Proceedings of IH&MMSec '17, June 20–22, 2017, Philadelphia, PA, USA*, , 12 pages.
DOI: http://dx.doi.org/10.1145/3082031.3083233

1 INTRODUCTION

The detection of resampling operations in 1D and 2D signals is of great interest in multimedia forensics, as it can indicate that the object under investigation has been resized or subject to other geometric transformations (e.g., rotation in case of images). Multiple methods have been proposed for this task, relying on different rationales.

When a signal is resampled, its samples are combined by means of an interpolation kernel to obtain new signal values located in a different lattice with respect to the original ones. Commonly used kernels periodically employ the same interpolation coefficients, thus introducing into the signal periodic linear correlations. This effect is exploited by most of existing techniques, which seek for periodicities in the signal itself [22] or in a linear predictor residual [14–16, 18, 23]. In doing so, a frequency analysis is generally employed for the detection, which can also provide an (unavoidably ambiguous [14]) estimate of the resampling factor. Moreover, researchers have recently tackled the problem with different approaches, e.g., by relying on set-membership theory [24], the use of SVD decomposition [21], or the measurement of the normalized energy density [9].

In parallel, the community in multimedia forensics has started to study forensic tasks from a more fundamental perspective, with the goal of assessing the performance limits of detection techniques [1, 4, 5]. In an hypothesis testing framework, this can be interpreted as quantifying the statistical distance between hypotheses and determine under which conditions they are actually distinguishable. In [5], the Kullback-Leibler Divergence (KLD) between the distributions of the signal under investigation (or a feature representation of it) and different processing hypotheses is proposed as a distinguishability measure, and a number of practical scenarios are addressed [6]. In these works, the authors are particularly interested in the distinguishability of operator chains and they consider different combinations of quantization, noise addition, Gamma correction and second-order finite impulse response (FIR) filtering operations.

However, to the best of our knowledge, such perspective has not been adopted yet to the case of resampling detection, for which performance limits are for now empirically established by state-of-the-art techniques. In this work, we start addressing this gap by quantifying how much the statistics of a 1D downsampled signal deviates from a not downsampled one. Under certain assumptions, commonly adopted in the literature, the distribution of the signal under the hypothesis of no downsampling and the hypothesis of downsampling with a certain factor and interpolation kernel is derived. We show that it is possible to compute the KLD in each case as a function of the original signal parameters, revealing the key role of the local correlation among samples. Effects of prefiltering (i.e., the use of a linear predictor) are also studied by means of this measure. Moreover, given the role of the signal's second-order moments (variance and autocovariance) in detection techniques, the KLD analysis is extended to the distribution of standard covariance matrix estimators as a function of the number of independent observations available.

It is to be noted that this work does not propose practical detection algorithms but aims to the assessment of the theoretical difficulties encountered. At the same time, it identifies space for improvement to be filled with not yet invented detectors.

The paper is structured as follows: in Section 2 we illustrate the perspectives adopted in our work and their relationship to existing studies; in Section 3, we formulate the resampling operation and recall the periodicity properties generally exploited by existing detectors; in Section 4, we formalize the assumptions on the original signal (in accordance with previous approaches in the literature), and analyze the effects of resampling in the signal statistics. These findings are then exploited in Section 5 to formulate different hypothesis tests and evaluate hypotheses distinguishability when varying the parameters involved. Finally, Section 6 concludes the paper.

2 PROPOSED APPROACH IN RELATION TO PRIOR WORK

We now describe and motivate the main novelties characterizing our study and how they are related to previous work:

- We directly study the statistics of a segment of the 1D signal under investigation under different hypotheses, although many state-of-the-art methods perform a frequency analysis [14, 18, 23]. This is due to the fact that deterministic processing (like DFT or other transformations) cannot increase the hypothesis distinguishability in terms of KLD [3, Lemma 1]. Thus, from an information-theoretic perspective, the best choice to measure the information contained in a signal segment is to study its very distribution.
- According to assumptions already adopted in the literature [14, 16, 23], we consider the original signal as a wide sense stationary autoregressive model of the 1st order (1-AR) with Gaussian innovations. In this setting, we show how the second-order moments

are transformed by the resampling operation. In particular cases, we analytically explore the role of the correlation coefficient of the 1-AR model in the statistical properties of the resampled signal.

- State-of-the-art techniques are generally evaluated by considering equally spaced values of the resampling factor in a certain range. However, it has been shown that the effects of resampling depend on the representation of the resampling factor as ratio of coprime natural numbers, where the numerator determines the period of the periodic structures introduced. For this reason, we employ sequences of rational numbers with the same numerator in our tests, thus differentiating resampled signals with the same periodicities. Such resampling factors are used, together with the chosen interpolation kernel, to define hypothesis tests and evaluate their distinguishability in terms of KLD.
- In addition to the distribution of the signal segment, we also study the distribution of the related prediction error computed in the same location and the distribution of a standard covariance matrix estimator obtained from a number of independent observations. Hypothesis distinguishability is also evaluated in these cases.
- In our analysis, we consider 1D real-valued signals, thus not accounting for quantization effects. Future work will be devoted to deal with quantization effects in the signal under investigation, as it is explored in [20, 24].

3 PRELIMINARIES

Let $s : \mathbb{R} \longrightarrow \mathbb{R}$ represent a 1D real-valued signal. We suppose (without loss of generality) that the signal is originally sampled at integer coordinates, i.e., before resampling the values $s(n)$ with $n \in \mathbb{Z}$ are available. In this case, a resampling operation with factor ξ can be seen as a map from the integer lattice $\mathbb{Z}$ to the lattice $\xi^{-1}\mathbb{Z}$, where $\xi < 1$ corresponds to downsampling and $\xi > 1$ to upsampling. In fact, every value $s(n\xi^{-1})$ is obtained starting from the original samples $s(n)$ as

$$s(n\xi^{-1}) = \sum_{n' \in \mathbb{Z}} h(n\xi^{-1} - n')s(n') \qquad (1)$$

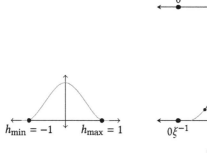
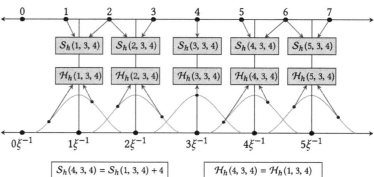

(a) Example of an interpolation kernel.

(b) Representation of the sets $\mathcal{S}_h$ and $\mathcal{H}_h$. The shifted interpolation kernel, centered at each resampled values, is plotted in red.

Figure 1: Example of resampling operation with $\xi = \frac{p}{q} = \frac{3}{4}$ and an interpolation kernel with support in $]-1, 1[$.

where $h : \mathbb{R} \longrightarrow \mathbb{R}$ is an interpolation kernel and the values $h(n\xi^{-1} - n')$ are the interpolation coefficients.

Starting from this definition, in the following section we derive the periodicity properties commonly exploited by existing detectors, and then express the resampling operation in matrix form.

3.1 Periodicity properties

Common interpolation kernels have finite support $]h_{\min}, h_{\max}[$, thus the sum in (1) is also finite. Moreover, the resampling factor ξ is in practice expressed in rational form as $\xi = \frac{p}{q}$ where p and q are coprime, and we will equivalently use the notation ξ or p/q in the following. This allows us to derive properties from (1):

- The resampled value $s((n+p)\xi^{-1})$ is obtained by combining samples whose indices are shifted by q with respect to the ones used to calculate $s(n\xi^{-1})$. In fact, we can obtain the set of values n' that are actually employed in the sum in (5) as a function of n, p and q as follows:

$$\mathcal{S}_h(n, p, q) = \left\{ n' \in \mathbb{Z} \,\middle|\, n\frac{q}{p} - n' \in]h_{\min}, h_{\max}[\right\} \qquad (2)$$

$$= \left\{ \left\lceil n\frac{q}{p} - h_{\max} \right\rceil, \left\lceil n\frac{q}{p} - h_{\max} \right\rceil + 1, \ldots, \left\lfloor n\frac{q}{p} - h_{\min} \right\rfloor \right\}.$$

It is easy to show that $\mathcal{S}_h(n+p, p, q)$ contains the very same elements of $\mathcal{S}_h(n, p, q)$ incremented by q.

- The interpolation coefficients used in the resampling operation are periodic with period p. From (1) the interpolation coefficients used for $s(n\xi^{-1})$ are given by

$$\mathcal{H}_h(n, p, q) = \left\{ h\left(n\frac{q}{p} - n' \right) \,\middle|\, n' \in \mathcal{S}_h(n, p, q) \right\} \qquad (3)$$

so that, for the previous point,

$$\mathcal{H}_h(n+p, p, q) = \left\{ h\left((n+p)\frac{q}{p} - n' \right) \,\middle|\, n' \in \mathcal{S}_h(n+p, p, q) \right\} \qquad (4)$$

$$= \left\{ h\left(n\frac{q}{p} + q - (n'+q) \right) \,\middle|\, n' \in \mathcal{S}_h(n, p, q) \right\}$$

$$= \left\{ h\left(n\frac{q}{p} - n' \right) \,\middle|\, n' \in \mathcal{S}_h(n, p, q) \right\} \equiv \mathcal{H}_h(n, p, q).$$

An example in case of $\xi = n/p = 3/4$ and an interpolation kernel with support in $]-1, 1[$ is reported in Fig. 1.

As it was first observed in [18] for the application in image forensics, this leads to periodic linear correlations in the resampled signal, which motivates the use of a linear predictor as a detection approach [14, 15, 18]. Given a set of prediction weights $\beta_{-T}, \ldots, \beta_T, \beta_0 = 1$, the prediction error

$$e(n\xi^{-1}) = \sum_{\substack{|t| \leq T \\ t \in \mathbb{Z}}} \beta_t s(n\xi^{-1} + t\xi^{-1}) \qquad (5)$$

is used as a measure of the linear correlation between the interpolated value $s(n\xi^{-1})$ and its $2T$ closest neighbors. A frequency analysis is then generally performed on $e(\cdot)$ to identify periodicities due to resampling operations.

3.2 Matrix formulation

As noted in [14], both (1) and (5) are linear combinations of the original samples $s(n)$ with coefficients that depend on ξ, h and the

β_t. Thus, it is convenient to consider the original signal as a finite vector and express the resampling operation and the prediction error computation in matrix form. Without loss of generality, we can define the vector $\mathbf{s} = [s_1, \ldots, s_N]$ where $s_n \doteq s(n)$. Fixing the interpolation kernel with finite support $h(\cdot)$ and the resampling factor $\xi = p/q$, the vector $\mathbf{s}$ can be linearly transformed according to (1) to obtain a vector $\mathbf{r} = [r_1, \ldots r_M]$ containing the resampled signal. The component r_1 is the first interpolated value that can be obtained from the samples $s(n), n \geq 1$, and r_M is the last interpolated value that can be obtained from the samples $s(n), n \leq N$. The correspondance between the indices of $\mathbf{r}$ and the multiples of ξ^{-1} in (1) depends on both the support of h and the value of ξ (for instance, in Fig. 1 we have that $r_1 = s(1\xi^{-1})$, but in case of $\xi > 1$ also $s(0)$ would be necessary to compute $s(1\xi^{-1})$, so $r_1 = s(2\xi^{-1})$), but this does not compromise the generality of our analysis.

The resampling operation can then be written as

$$\mathbf{r} = C\mathbf{s}, \qquad (6)$$

where each n-th row of the matrix C contains the values of $\mathcal{H}_h(n, p, q)$ at the locations contained in $\mathcal{S}_h(n, p, q)$. Thus, its entries depend on both ξ and h, so $C = C(\xi, h)$, and its size $M \times N$ is such that $M < N$ in case of downsampling and $M > N$ in case of upsampling, as represented in Fig. 2.

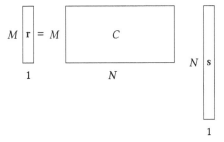

(a) Downsampling

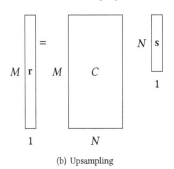

(b) Upsampling

Figure 2: Resampling matrix transformation.

Because of the previous considerations, the nonzero entries in the rows of C will be the same every p rows, but shifted by q positions to the right. For instance, for a linear interpolation kernel h and

$\xi = p/q = 3/4$, we have

$$C\left(\frac{3}{4}, h\right) = \begin{bmatrix} 2/3 & 1/3 & 0 & 0 & 0 & 0 & \cdots \\ 0 & 1/3 & 2/3 & 0 & 0 & 0 & \cdots \\ 0 & 0 & 0 & 1 & 0 & 0 & \cdots \\ 0 & 0 & 0 & 0 & 2/3 & 1/3 & \cdots \\ 0 & 0 & 0 & 0 & 0 & 1/3 & \cdots \\ \vdots & \vdots & \vdots & \vdots & \vdots & \vdots & \ddots \end{bmatrix}. \tag{7}$$

Moreover, the computation of the prediction error in (5) can be seen as a discrete convolution of the resampled signal with vector $[\beta_{-T}, \ldots, \beta_T]$. In fact, by removing the condition that $\beta_0 = 1$, the prediction error is essentially a linearly filtered version of the resampled signal and in the literature such operation is also referred to as prefiltering [23]. Then, the elements of $\mathbf{r}$ are transformed as

$$\mathbf{e} = B\mathbf{r}, \tag{8}$$

where B is a $(M - 2T) \times M$ matrix such that

$$B = \begin{bmatrix} \beta_{-T} & \cdots & \cdots & \cdots & \beta_T & 0 & \cdots & \cdots & \cdots & \cdots \\ 0 & \beta_{-T} & \cdots & \cdots & \cdots & \beta_T & 0 & \cdots & \cdots & \cdots \\ 0 & 0 & \beta_{-T} & \cdots & \cdots & \cdots & \beta_T & 0 & \cdots & \cdots \\ \vdots & \vdots & \vdots & \vdots & \vdots & \vdots & \vdots & \vdots & \vdots & \vdots \\ 0 & 0 & 0 & 0 & 0 & \beta_{-T} & \cdots & \cdots & \cdots & \beta_T \end{bmatrix} \tag{9}$$

and $\mathbf{e}$ contains $M - 2T$ samples of the prediction error corresponding to the central indices of $\mathbf{r}$.

Finally, the whole process can be summarized as

$$\mathbf{e} = A\mathbf{s}, \tag{10}$$

where $A = BC$ and $\mathbf{e} \equiv \mathbf{r}$ if no prefilter is applied.

4 ANALYSIS OF SECOND-ORDER MOMENTS AND ASSUMPTIONS ON THE SIGNAL

Several approaches rely on the assumption that the original signal is a wide sense stationary (WSS) process [14, 16, 23], i.e., the expected value $E\{s(k)\}$ and the autocovariance $E\{(s(k) - E\{s(k)\})(s(k + t) - E\{s(k + t)\})\}, \forall t \in \mathbb{Z}$, are constant over $k \in \mathbb{Z}$. This allows us to link the periodicity of the interpolation coefficients to the periodicity of second-order moments in the resulting resampled signal.

In fact, in [19] the authors show that a multirate system performing sampling rate conversion by a factor p/q on a WSS signal produces a cyclostationary signal with period $p/\gcd(p, q)$. With p and q being coprime in our case, this means that for the components of the vector $\mathbf{r}$ we have

$$\mathrm{Cov}\{r_k, r_{k+t}\} = \mathrm{Cov}\{r_{k+jp}, r_{k+jp+t}\} \tag{11}$$

for every integers j and t.

Further results have been obtained by extending the definition of both (1) and (5) to the whole real line instead of the discrete lattice $\xi^{-1}\mathbb{Z}$. In [22, 23], it is proved that the interpolated signal $s(x), x \in \mathbb{R}$, defined as in (1) is cyclostationary with period 1, i.e., the original sampling rate. The author of [14] shows that the variance of the prediction error $e(x), x \in \mathbb{R}$, is also periodic with period 1 regardless of the prediction weights, thus establishing a link between methods based on the prediction error and the ones based on a prefiltering operation like discrete differentiation [7, 11, 16].

However, the vector $\mathbf{r}$ contains only values of $s(\cdot)$ sampled at multiples of ξ^{-1}, so that the periodicity with 1 is not observable. In other words, by considering the indexing of $\mathbf{r}$, the periodicity would be non-integer with period ξ. In fact, the authors in [22, 23] denote this property as "almost cyclostationarity", referring to the fact that the available vector $\mathbf{r}$ would have non-integer periodicity ξ, in contrast with the "pure cyclostationarity" with integer period p proved in [19].

It is common in the literature to assume statistical models for the distribution of the original signal. While a white Gaussian model would not be accurate, 1D autoregressive models of first-order (1-AR) with Gaussian innovations [12] have been used to capture local correlation in 1D and 2D signals [23]. Moreover, it is also commonly assumed to deal with zero-mean signals, by implicitly supposing that the mean value can be subtracted from the signal under investigation. We can formalize these properties as:

Assumption 1. *The original signal is a WSS 1-AR model with Gaussian innovations, i.e.:*

$$s_n = \rho s_{n-1} + \varepsilon_n \tag{12}$$

where ρ is a correlation coefficient satisfying $|\rho| < 1$ and ε_n is a zero-mean Gaussian random variable with variance σ_ε^2 such that $\varepsilon_n, \varepsilon_{n'}$ are independent $\forall n, n'$.

Under Assumption 1, the covariance between samples at distance $t \in \mathbb{Z}$ is given by

$$\mathrm{Cov}\{s_n, s_{n+t}\} = \frac{\rho^{|t|}}{1 - \rho^2} \cdot \sigma_\varepsilon^2, \quad \forall n \in \mathbb{Z}, \tag{13}$$

and the covariance matrix of the vector $\mathbf{s}$ has the form

$$\Sigma_{\mathbf{s}} = \begin{bmatrix} \frac{1}{1-\rho^2}\sigma_\varepsilon^2 & \frac{\rho^1}{1-\rho^2}\sigma_\varepsilon^2 & \frac{\rho^2}{1-\rho^2}\sigma_\varepsilon^2 & \cdots & \frac{\rho^{N-1}}{1-\rho^2}\sigma_\varepsilon^2 \\ \frac{\rho^1}{1-\rho^2}\sigma_\varepsilon^2 & \frac{1}{1-\rho^2}\sigma_\varepsilon^2 & \frac{\rho^1}{1-\rho^2}\sigma_\varepsilon^2 & \cdots & \frac{\rho^{N-2}}{1-\rho^2}\sigma_\varepsilon^2 \\ \vdots & \ddots & \ddots & \ddots & \vdots \\ \frac{\rho^{N-2}}{1-\rho^2}\sigma_\varepsilon^2 & \vdots & \frac{\rho^1}{1-\rho^2}\sigma_\varepsilon^2 & \frac{1}{1-\rho^2}\sigma_\varepsilon^2 & \frac{\rho^1}{1-\rho^2}\sigma_\varepsilon^2 \\ \frac{\rho^{N-1}}{1-\rho^2}\sigma_\varepsilon^2 & \cdots & \frac{\rho^2}{1-\rho^2}\sigma_\varepsilon^2 & \frac{\rho^1}{1-\rho^2}\sigma_\varepsilon^2 & \frac{1}{1-\rho^2}\sigma_\varepsilon^2 \end{bmatrix}. \tag{14}$$

Moreover, by iterating (12) we have that each s_n is a linear combination of independent Gaussian realizations, so that every subset of samples is a multivariate normal random variable. Thus, the covariance matrix $\Sigma_{\mathbf{s}}$ completely determines the distribution of the random vector $\mathbf{s}$ and we can write

$$\mathbf{s} \sim \mathcal{N}_N(\mathbf{0}, \Sigma_{\mathbf{s}}), \tag{15}$$

where $\mathcal{N}_N(\mu, \Sigma)$ indicates an N-dimensional normal distribution with mean vector μ and covariance matrix Σ, and $\mathbf{0}$ is a vector of N zeros.

By the definition of multivariate normal distributions, the transformed vector $\mathbf{r}$ is also multivariate normal, so its distribution is again determined by its covariance matrix:

$$\mathbf{r} \sim \mathcal{N}_M(\mathbf{0}, \Sigma_{\mathbf{r}}). \tag{16}$$

The entries of $\Sigma_{\mathbf{r}}$ can be obtained by computing

$$\mathrm{Cov}\{r_k, r_{k'}\} = E\{r_k, r_{k'}\} \tag{17}$$

for two arbitrary indices $k, k' \leq M$. Considering that every r_k is the scalar product of the k-th row of C and $\mathbf{s}$, equation (17) can be expanded to obtain the following equality:

$$\Sigma_{\mathbf{r}} = C\Sigma_{\mathbf{s}}C^T. \tag{18}$$

However, in order for the multivariate normal to be non-degenerate, the covariance matrix must be positive definite. The resulting matrix $\Sigma_{\mathbf{r}} = C\Sigma_{\mathbf{s}}C^T$ preserves the positive definiteness of $\Sigma_{\mathbf{s}}$ if and only if the matrix C^T has rank equal to M [13, p. 431, Obs 7.1.8]. This can only hold in case of downsampling, while in case of upsampling C^T can have at most rank equal to $N < M$. This is crucial as in the degenerate case the multivariate normal vector does not have a density and, thus, the KLD is not defined. In our analysis we will focus on downsampling, while we leave for future work the problem of dealing with upsampling matrices.

5 HYPOTHESIS TESTS AND DISTINGUISHABILITY

A forensic analysis consists in deciding whether the signal under investigation has been resampled or not. In particular, the decision is usually made on a segment of the signal, that we can represent as a vector $\mathbf{x}$ of M contiguous samples starting at an arbitrary position. Our previous analysis now allows us to obtain information on the binary hypothesis test

$$H_0\colon \mathbf{x} \text{ has not been downsampled.} \tag{19}$$

$$H_1\colon \mathbf{x} \text{ has been downsampled}$$

$$\text{with factor } \xi \text{ and interpolation kernel } h.$$

As observed in [4], the decision between H_0 and H_1 on $\mathbf{x}$ can be taken according to the distribution of $\mathbf{x}$ itself or a related feature representation $F_{\mathbf{x}}$ defined in a certain space Ω under the two hypotheses. Then, we can define $P_0(\cdot), P_1(\cdot)$ as the distributions of $F_{\mathbf{x}}$ under H_0 and H_1, respectively. Motivated by known results in information theory, the author of [5] then suggests the use of KLD as a measure hypotheses distinguishability, which in the continuous case is defined as

$$\mathrm{KLD}(P_0, P_1) \doteq \int_{\Omega} P_0(F_{\mathbf{x}}) \log_2 \frac{P_0(F_{\mathbf{x}})}{P_1(F_{\mathbf{x}})} dF_{\mathbf{x}}, \tag{20}$$

where we consider the logarithm to the base 2, without loss of generality.

In the next subsections, we explore the behavior of the KLD for different representations $F_{\mathbf{x}}$ for which we derive P_0 and P_1. In particular, we will first focus on the use of the signal itself (Section 5.1) or a prefiltered version of it (Section 5.2), and then we consider the case where the analyst estimates the second order moments of the signal from the observations available (Section 5.3). While the first two cases result in a multivariate normal distribution of the vector $F_{\mathbf{x}}$, we will see that in the third case $F_{\mathbf{x}}$ is a matrix following a Wishart distribution.

We will suppose that Assumption 1 holds, thus relying on the analysis in Section 4. We fix $M = 30$, i.e., we evaluate the ability of taking a forensic decision on a signal segment of 30 samples. Moreover, we have selected a fixed location of the samples in the signal under investigation in such a way that, in case downsampling occurred, no original samples with indices < 1 would be necessary to obtain the resulting downsampled signal or its pre-filtered version.

Clearly, the test (19) is determined by the chosen interpolation kernel h and the resampling factor $\xi < 1$. Thus, we consider three commonly used interpolation kernels (linear, cubic, Lanczos) represented in Fig. 4. Then, we vary the value of the resampling factor ξ by considering sequences of rational numbers with the same numerator p lying in the interval $[0, 1]$. In fact, we have seen that the resampling factor is in practice expressed as a rational number p/q, so we consider the sequences

$$\xi_{1:10}^a = \left\{ \frac{2^a}{q} \; \middle| \; q = 2^a + 1, \ldots, 2^a + 10 \wedge \gcd(2^a, q) = 1 \right\}, \tag{21}$$

for $a = 0, 1, \ldots, 8$, as represented in Figure 3. By doing so, we can separately observe resampled signals with the same pure cyclostationarity. In fact, only combinations of coprime numerator and denominator are included. There is no intersection among sequences for different values of a.

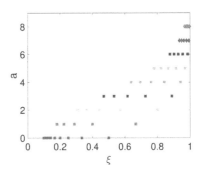

Figure 3: The sequences $\xi_{1:10}^a$ for $a = 0, \ldots 8$.

5.1 Signal distribution

We first analyze the case where the decision on $\mathbf{x}$ is taken according to the multivariate distribution of $\mathbf{x}$ itself, i.e. $F(\mathbf{x}) = \mathbf{x}$. We have already derived P_0 and P_1 in Section 4 and observed that in both cases it is a multivariate normal distribution, but with different covariance matrix. By denoting with Σ_0 and Σ_1 the covariance matrices under H_0 and H_1, we have that Σ_0 is an $M \times M$ matrix defined as in (14), thus $\Sigma_0 = \Sigma_0(\sigma_\varepsilon, \rho)$. Depending on h and ξ, the hypothesis H_1 indicates that $\mathbf{x}$ is the outcome of a resampling operation from a certain number N of original samples, so

$$\Sigma_1 = C\Sigma_0^{\mathrm{ex}}C^T, \tag{22}$$

where C is the $M \times N$ resampling matrix and Σ_0^{ex} is also defined as in (14) but has size $N \times N$, thus $\Sigma_1 = \Sigma_1(\sigma_\varepsilon, \rho, \xi, h)$.

The test (19) can then be rewritten as

$$H_0\colon \mathbf{x} \sim \mathcal{N}_M(0, \Sigma_0(\sigma_\varepsilon, \rho)). \tag{23}$$

$$H_1\colon \mathbf{x} \sim \mathcal{N}_M(0, \Sigma_1(\sigma_\varepsilon, \rho, \xi, h)).$$

In case of multivariate Gaussian, the KLD has the following expression [17]:

$$\mathrm{KLD}(\mathcal{N}_M(0, \Sigma_0), \mathcal{N}_M(0, \Sigma_1)) = \frac{1}{2}\left[\mathrm{tr}(\Sigma_1^{-1}\Sigma_0) + \log\frac{\det(\Sigma_1)}{\det(\Sigma_0)} - M\right] \tag{24}$$

In order to have a consistent evaluation, we have fixed the location of the $M = 30$ samples contained in $\mathbf{x}$ for every combination of

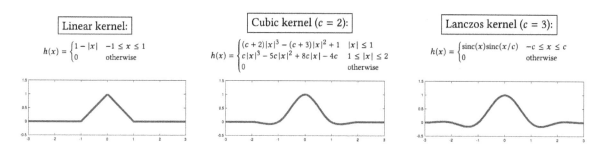

Figure 4: The three kernels used in our tests are reported.

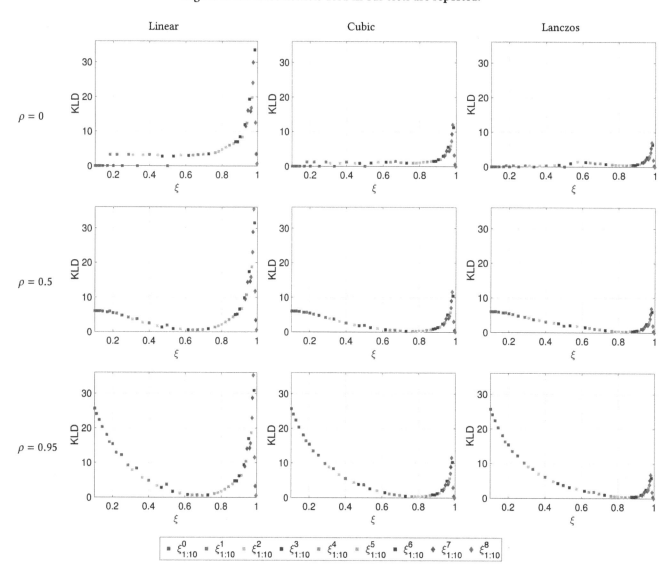

Figure 5: KLD values are reported as a function of ξ for different values of ρ (row-wise) and different interpolation kernels (column-wise). Different marks and colors indicate the different sequences $\xi^a_{1:10}$, according to the legend. The KLD in each case refers to the distributions of a M-variate vector with $M = 30$ under the two hypotheses.

h and ξ, so that N and Σ_0^{ex} are consequently determined to obtain the distribution of $\mathbf{x}$ under H_1.

From (23) we see that the test also depends on the signal parameters σ_ε, ρ and their influence on KLD should be studied. However, we can first note that the following Lemma holds:

LEMMA 5.1. *Under Assumption* (1), *given the correlation coefficient* ρ, *the resampling factor* ξ *and the interpolation kernel* h, *the measure*

$$\mathrm{KLD}(\mathcal{N}_M(0, \Sigma_0(\sigma_\varepsilon, \rho)), \mathcal{N}_M(0, \Sigma_1(\sigma_\varepsilon, \rho, \xi, h)))$$

is independent of σ_ε.

PROOF. See Appendix A.   □

It is worth recalling here that we are not considering quantization effects and this result shows that, in this setting, the variance of the original samples turns out to act as a scaling factor (i.e., it does not add nor remove information). However, this may not hold when the signal is discretized before and after the resampling operation, thus leaving as future work the task of assessing the sensitivity of such result when a more or less slight quantization is applied.

In our current study, we can then fix the parameter $\sigma_\varepsilon = 1$ and analyze the variation of ρ, ξ and h, as reported in Fig. 5. We consider $\rho = 0$ (the signal is white Gaussian noise), $\rho = 0.5$ and $\rho = 0.95$, which is adopted in [23] to represent natural images. Different sequences $\xi_{1:10}^a$ (corresponding to locations along the horizontal axis) are identified by different markers and colors.

This shows that in each plot the KLD follows a general trend, although there are oscillations due to the specific interaction between the parameters. In each case, there is a peak in the interval $[0.95, 1]$ followed by a sharp decrease towards 0 when the resampling factor approaches 1. Moreover, we notice that the linear interpolation kernel generally yields a higher KLD, while it decreases when switching to cubic and Lanczos interpolation.

However, the most interesting observation is the different behavior of the KLD when the resampling factor approaches 0 among different rows. In fact, it appears that the correlation coefficient ρ substantially influences the KLD value when downsampling is strong.

In order to examine this phenomenon, we focus on the sequence $\xi_{1:10}^0 = \{1/q, q = 2, \ldots 10\}$ (blue squares in the plots). In fact, we see that for $\rho = 0$ the KLD is always zero, while the left tail significantly increases as ρ increases.

In this case, we can explain analytically the relationship between the entries of Σ_0 and Σ_1, according to the following Lemma:

LEMMA 5.2. *Under Assumption* (1), *for every downsampling factor* $1/q, q \in \mathbb{N}^0$, *and an interpolation kernel such that* $h(0) = 1$ *and* $h(k) = 0$ *for every* $k \in \mathbb{Z}$, *the following expression holds:*

$$\Sigma_1[k, k+t] = \Sigma_0[k, k+t] \cdot \rho^{|t|(q-1)}, \quad t \in \mathbb{Z}. \tag{25}$$

PROOF. See Appendix B.   □

Note that the linear and cubic interpolation kernels analytically fulfill the requirement of the lemma, while the Lanczos kernel yields very small values at integers different than 0.

Given equation (13), we have that (25) does not depend on k but only on the lag t, so that the entries of Σ_1 are constant along each diagonal, just like it happens Σ_0. Thus, we can evaluate the

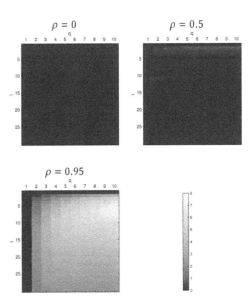

Figure 6: The quantity (6) **is plotted as a function of** q **and** t **for different values of** ρ.

absolute difference between the covariance matrix entries at the t-th diagonal under the two hypotheses as a function of q, which is given by

$$D(q, t) = \frac{\rho^{|t|}}{1 - \rho^2}(1 - \rho^{|t|(q-1)}) \tag{26}$$

In Fig. 6, we report the values of D when varying q and and t, so that each vertical bar represents the first row of the covariance matrix for a fixed q, which contains all the values appearing in Σ_1.

We observe that when $\rho = 0$, the whole covariance matrix is unaltered, thus explaining the zero values of the KLD in the first row of Fig. 5. If $\rho \neq 0$, no changes are clearly introduced when $q = 1$ and the same happens in any case when $t = 0$: the variance of samples is not modified.

It is worth considering that such kind of downsampling factors do not introduce observable periodicities in the covariance matrix, as the downsampled signal has pure cyclostationarity with period 1 (in fact, covariance matrix values are constant along diagonals). This situation has been already pointed out in the literature [18] and represents a major obstacle for existing forensic detectors based on the periodicity analysis, which (therefore) rarely address the detection of strong downsampling ($\xi < 1/2$).

However, our analysis shows that forensically useful information is still present in the signal. In this case, observe the decay of the autocovariance when t increases: expression (25) indicates that after downsampling with factor $1/q$ the autocovariance decays as the power of ρ^q instead of ρ.

5.2 Prediction error distribution

According to the formulation in Section 3, a similar analysis can be performed when the prediction error with coefficients $\beta_{-T}, \ldots, \beta_T$ is employed (i.e., when the signal is prefiltered), so to evaluate whether this operation increases the distinguishability of the null and alternative hypothesis. In this case, a transformation by means

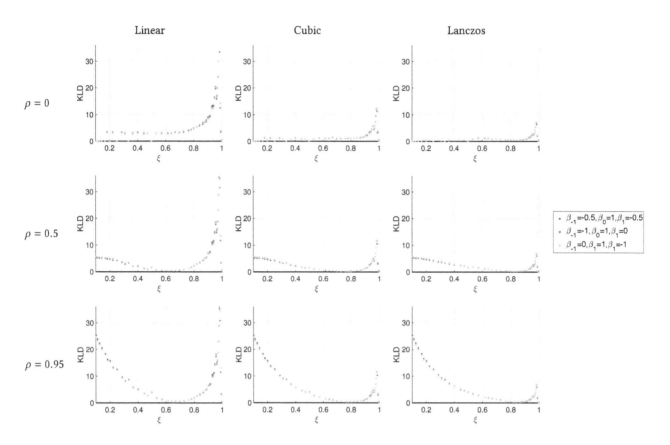

Figure 7: KLD values are reported as a function of ξ for different values of ρ (row-wise) and different interpolation kernels (column-wise). Different colors indicate different prefilters, according to the legend. The KLD in each case refers to the distributions of a M-variate vector with $M = 30$ under the two hypotheses.

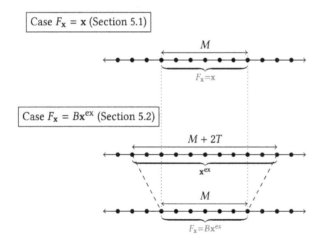

Figure 8: The figure shows the signal samples considered in the hypothesis tests of Sections 5.1 and 5.2, respectively. It can be noted that $F_\mathbf{x}$ in both cases refers to the same M locations in the signal, although $2T$ additional samples are used in the second case.

of the matrix B defined as in (9) is applied. However, it is to be noted that applying B to $\mathbf{x}$ would not increase the hypothesis distinguishability with respect to the test considered in 5.1. This is due to the result recalled in [3, Lemma 1], stating that deterministic processing of data cannot increase the KLD of between two distributions. Thus, we define $\mathbf{x}^{\text{ex}}$ as an extended version of $\mathbf{x}$ containing in the first (last) positions the T samples of the signal under investigation lying before (after) $\mathbf{x}$. Then, we consider $F_\mathbf{x} = B\mathbf{x}^{\text{ex}}$, so that the obtained vector $F_\mathbf{x}$ has length M and contains the values of the prediction error at the same locations of the values of $\mathbf{x}$, although more information is used with respect to the test in Section 5.1 (i.e., the additional samples). An illustration is given in Fig. 8.

By replicating the reasoning of Section 4, $F_\mathbf{x}$ is also a multivariate normal random vector and the covariance matrices under the two hypotheses are computed as in (22) with an additional premultiplication by B and post-multiplication by B^T. Thus, the KLD of $P_0(F_\mathbf{x})$ and $P_1(F_\mathbf{x})$ can be computed in the same way as in (5).

In Fig. 7 we report the KLD values when varying ξ and h as in Section 5.1. We considered three different kind of prefilters represented with different colors in the plots: one related to the discrete second order derivative ($\beta_{-1} = -0.5, \beta_0 = 1, \beta_1 = -0.5$) and two corresponding to discrete first order derivative, namely the backward finite difference ($\beta_{-1} = -1, \beta_0 = 1, \beta_1 = 0$) and the forward finite difference ($\beta_{-1} = 0, \beta_1 = 1, \beta_1 = -1$).

We can observe that the values resemble the ones of Fig. 5, although a direct comparison would not be fair due to the different amount of information used (cf. Fig. 8). Moreover, the different prefilters do not lead to significantly different results, except for the case of the second order derivative filter with strong downsampling. This is certainly related to the specific interaction of the prediction coefficients in β and the interpolation coefficients in C. An analytical characterization of the results reported in Fig. 7 as a function of ρ would explain the general trend observed in every plot and will be subject of future investigation. With this respect, our current conjecture is that, apart from information introduced by the additional samples, pre-filtering cannot substantially increase hypothesis distinguishability from an information-theoretic perspective, while its effect strongly depends on the decision method adopted (e.g., in [23] it proves to be crucial when performing a frequency analysis).

5.3 Autocovariance estimator distribution

As emphasized before, one of the properties exploited by many existing techniques is the periodicity of the elements of the covariance matrix Σ of $\mathbf{x}$. Moreover, we have seen in Section 5.1 that the covariance matrix can play a key role also when no periodicity is present. This calls for studying the situation where the entries of Σ are estimated starting from S realizations of $\mathbf{x}$ by means of standard estimators, like the sample covariance matrix

$$\frac{\mathbf{X}^T\mathbf{X}}{S}, \quad \mathbf{X} = \begin{bmatrix} \mathbf{x}_1^T \\ \mathbf{x}_2^T \\ \dots \\ \mathbf{x}_S^T \end{bmatrix}. \qquad (27)$$

It is to be noted that the estimation of second-order moments from the signal samples more or less implicitly happens in the majority of existing detectors: in [14] it is observed that the p-map is a simplified model for the error variance, so that every value of the prediction error is considered as an estimate of its variance at the specific location; in [23], the correlation of an image block with lag 0 is estimated before performing the frequency analysis; in [16], the autocovariance function after the Radon transform is estimated; in [11], different image rows are used to estimate the autocovariance in the horizontal direction.

A simple example is given by the case where the autocovariance function of the signal is considered as dependent only on the lag t and Cov$\{t\}$ is estimated as

$$\frac{1}{S}\sum_{i=1}^{S} s_i s_{i+t}, \qquad (28)$$

where the s_i are the samples of the zero-mean signal under investigation. Note that this is the approach adopted in [16] to estimate the autocovariance function of the Radon transform vectors. By referring to the notation in formula (27), this is equivalent to considering S consecutive M-dimensional vectors as observations and use their values to estimate the entries of Σ, as represented in Fig. 9. However, this approach is only suited for WSS processes, including not resampled signals under Assumption 1 or downsampled signals with factor $1/q$, as shown in Section 5.1.

Other practical examples are given by sequential images taken by a fixed camera (where signal segments at fixed locations and different frames can be considered as equidistributed) or a single image (where horizontal signal segments at fixed location and different rows can be considered as equidistributed over homogeneous regions, as done in [11]).

We consider the case where variances and covariances are jointly estimated from a number of observations, as summarized in formula (27). Different observations correspond here to different available multivariate vectors $\mathbf{x}_1, \dots, \mathbf{x}_S$ that are assumed drawn from the same distribution and, additionally, *independent*. Under Assumption (1) and according to the analysis in previous sections, the observations are zero-mean multivariate normal vectors with covariance matrix Σ_0 and Σ_1 in case of null and alternative hypothesis, respectively. It is known that in this case, the matrix $\mathbf{X}^T\mathbf{X}$ (also called scatter matrix) follows a M-variate Wishart distribution with S degrees of freedom [8] and scale matrix Σ_0 or Σ_1, according to the verified hypothesis. So, we can analyze the test

$$H_0: \mathbf{X}^T\mathbf{X} \sim \mathcal{W}_M(\Sigma_0(\sigma_\varepsilon, \rho), S). \qquad (29)$$
$$H_1: \mathbf{X}^T\mathbf{X} \sim \mathcal{W}_M(\Sigma_1(\sigma_\varepsilon, \rho, \xi, h), S).$$

where $\mathcal{W}_M(\Sigma, S)$ indicates a M-dimensional Wishart distribution with S degrees of freedom and scale matrix Σ, with the constraint that $S \geq M$ in order for the Wishart distribution to have a density in the space of $M \times M$ matrices [8]. The KLD between two Wishart distributions with the same number of degrees of freedom is given by [10]

$$\text{KLD}(\mathcal{W}_M(\Sigma_0, S), \mathcal{W}_M(\Sigma_1, S)) = S\left[\frac{\text{tr}(\Sigma_0^{-1}\Sigma_1) + \text{tr}(\Sigma_1^{-1}\Sigma_0)}{2} - M\right]. \qquad (30)$$

It is worth noticing that the KLD increases *linearly* with the number of observations. Similarly as in Lemma 5.1, we can prove that expression (30) does not depend on σ_ε, so we perform in Fig. 10 the same analysis as in Section 5.1. The trend observed in Fig. 10 further confirms the considerations made in Section 5.1. It is to be noted that a direct comparison of the KLD values would again be unfair, as in this case the whole matrix $\mathbf{X}$ is used, which contains a considerably higher amount of information with respect to $\mathbf{x}$. However, we can notice that the effect observed when the resampling factor approaches 0 seems to be here even amplified (see the case $\rho = 0.95$ and linear interpolation).

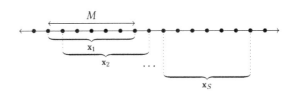

Figure 9: Example of different observations.

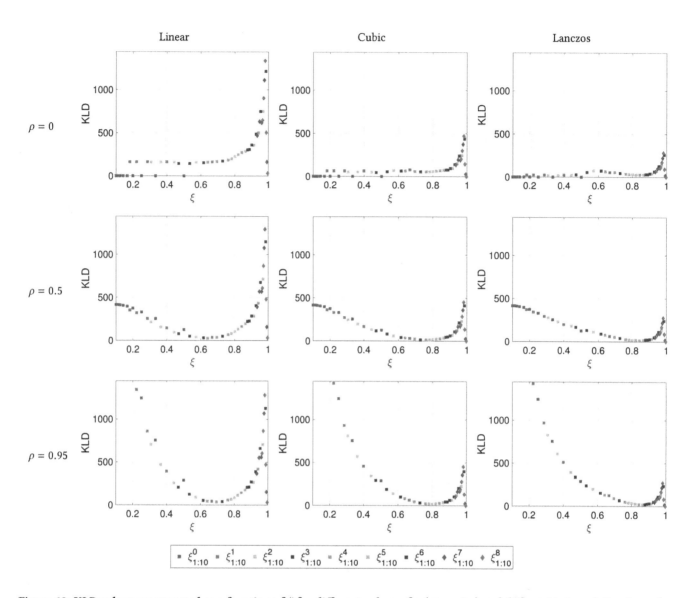

Figure 10: KLD values are reported as a function of ξ for different values of ρ (row-wise) and different interpolation kernels (column-wise). Different marks and colors indicate the different sequences $\xi_{1:10}^a$, according to the legend. The KLD in each case refers to the distributions of a $M \times M$ matrix with $M = 30$ under the two hypotheses.

6 CONCLUDING REMARKS

We have studied the statistical distance of downsampled 1D signals with respect to their non-downsampled counterparts. Under common assumptions on the original signal statistics, we have observed that all the information about a signal segment statistics is contained in its covariance matrix. This allowed us to assess the influence of both signal and resampling parameters on the distinguishability between the hypothesis of no downsampling and the hypothesis of downsampling in terms of KLD. In doing so, we have studied the distribution of the signal segment itself, of different prefiltered versions of it and also of a standard estimator of its covariance matrix.

We can first observe that the use of different interpolation kernels (namely linear, cubic, and Lanczos) does not seem to have a substantial effect on the KLD with respect to different resampling factors. However, we notice that the KLD values when the Lanczos kernel is used are upper bounded by the ones obtained with the cubic interpolation, and the same happens for cubic and linear interpolation, respectively.

When varying the resampling factor $\xi \in [0, 1]$, we can identify in each case a common trend when ξ approaches 1: the KLD increases approximately until 0.95–0.98, and then sharply drops to 0, as expected.

However, the most interesting finding is observed when the correlation coefficient ρ among consecutive original samples is modified. In fact, while the KLD behavior remains stable for ξ

approaching 1, the hypothesis distinguishability in case of strong downsampling significantly increases as ρ increases. With this respect, the choice of considering sequences of rational numbers with the same numerator (i.e., introducing the same periodicity in the resampled signal) proves to be crucial since it allows us to obtain theoretical results for specific sequences, as we did for the factors $\xi = 1/q, q \in \mathbb{N}$. In this case, we have analytically characterized the transformation of single covariance matrix entries, showing that the underlying correlation structure in the original signal plays a key role and introduces statistical distance between a non-downsampled and a downsampled signal even when *no periodicity* is introduced. This obviously calls for research on new classes of detectors which exploit these traces in real signals. For the design of practical approaches, we cannot assume the knowledge of ρ in the original signal. If and how well it can be approximated is subject to future investigations. Other issues arise for signals where ρ is spatially varying.

Also the theoretical analysis leaves room for future extensions in several directions. As mentioned, a theoretical description of different prefiltering effects on the hypothesis distinguishability as well as upsampling in general still represent open questions and would complement the present analysis. Moreover, future work will be devoted to the extension of the model to 2D signals, thus accounting for interpolation kernels and correlation structures involving both the row and column dimension. In addition, the current approach deals with continuous signals, while discretized signals should be considered in order to account for quantization effects, which cannot be avoided in practice and already proved to be a valuable help in in resampling forensics [20, 24] as well as many other forensic decision problems [2].

ACKNOWLEDGMENTS

This research was funded by Deutsche Forschungsgemeinschaft (DFG) under grant "Informationstheoretische Schranken digitaler Bildforensik" and by Archimedes Privatstiftung, Innsbruck, Austria.

A PROOF OF LEMMA 5.1

From expression (14) we have that

$$\Sigma_0(\sigma_\varepsilon, \rho) = \sigma_\varepsilon^2 \Phi_0, \quad \Phi_0 = \begin{bmatrix} \frac{1}{1-\rho^2} & \frac{\rho^1}{1-\rho^2} & \frac{\rho^2}{1-\rho^2} & \cdots & \frac{\rho^{N-1}}{1-\rho^2} \\ \frac{\rho^1}{1-\rho^2} & \frac{1}{1-\rho^2} & \frac{\rho^1}{1-\rho^2} & \cdots & \frac{\rho^{N-2}}{1-\rho^2} \\ \vdots & \ddots & \ddots & \ddots & \vdots \\ \frac{\rho^{N-2}}{1-\rho^2} & \vdots & \frac{\rho^1}{1-\rho^2} & \frac{1}{1-\rho^2} & \frac{\rho^1}{1-\rho^2} \\ \frac{\rho^{N-1}}{1-\rho^2} & \cdots & \frac{\rho^2}{1-\rho^2} & \frac{\rho^1}{1-\rho^2} & \frac{1}{1-\rho^2} \end{bmatrix},$$

(31)

so that $\Sigma_1 = C\Sigma_0^{\text{ex}}C^T = \sigma_\varepsilon^2 C\Phi_0^{\text{ex}}C^T = \sigma_\varepsilon^2 \Phi_1$, where Φ_0^{ex} is defined in the same way as Σ_0^{ex} and $\Phi_1 \doteq C\Phi_0^{\text{ex}}C^T$ does not depend on σ_ε.

We can now consider the parts of (24) that depends on σ_ε:

$$\text{tr}(\Sigma_1^{-1}\Sigma_0) = \text{tr}((\sigma_\varepsilon^2\Phi_1)^{-1}\sigma_\varepsilon^2\Phi_0) = \text{tr}\left(\frac{1}{\sigma_\varepsilon^2}\Phi_1^{-1}\sigma_\varepsilon^2\Phi_0\right) = \text{tr}\left(\Phi_1^{-1}\Phi_0\right),$$

(32)

and

$$\frac{\det(\Sigma_1)}{\det(\Sigma_0)} = \frac{\det(\sigma_\varepsilon^2\Phi_1)}{\det(\sigma_\varepsilon^2\Phi_0)} = \frac{\sigma_\varepsilon^{2M}\det(\Phi_1)}{\sigma_\varepsilon^{2M}\det(\Phi_0)} = \frac{\det(\Phi_1)}{\det(\Phi_0)}.$$

(33)

Neither (32) nor (33) depend on σ_ε, but only on ρ, and so does (24). □

B PROOF OF LEMMA 5.2

We can observe that, under the premises of the lemma, the matrix C has the form

$$C = \begin{bmatrix} 1 & \cdots & 0 & 0 & 0 & 0 & 0 & \cdots \\ 0 & \underbrace{\cdots}_{q} & 1 & 0 & 0 & 0 & 0 & \cdots \\ 0 & 0 & 0 & \underbrace{\cdots}_{q} & 1 & 0 & 0 & \cdots \\ 0 & 0 & 0 & 0 & 0 & \underbrace{\cdots}_{q} & 1 & \cdots \\ \vdots & \vdots & \vdots & \vdots & \vdots & \vdots & \vdots & \ddots \end{bmatrix}.$$

(34)

Thus, every k-th row has only one nonzero element equal to 1 at the $(q(k-1)+1)$-th column.

Coupled with (22) and (13), it means that every entry of Σ_1 is given by

$$\Sigma_1[k, k'] = \sum_{n=1}^{N} C[k, n] \sum_{n'=1}^{N} C[k', n']\Sigma_0^{\text{ex}}[n, n']$$

$$= C[k, q(k-1)+1]C[k', q(k'-1)+1]\frac{\rho^{q|k-k'|}}{1-\rho^2}$$

$$= \frac{1}{1-\rho^2}\rho^{|k-k'|q}.$$

By fixing $k' = k + t$, we have expression (25). □

REFERENCES

[1] M. Barni and B. Tondi. 2016. Source distinguishability under distortion-limited attack: an optimal transport perspective. *IEEE Transactions on Information Forensics and Security* 11, 10 (2016), 2145–2159.

[2] R. Böhme and M. Kirchner. 2016. Media Forensics. *S. Katzenbeisser and f: Petitcolas, eds., Information Hiding* (2016), 231–259.

[3] C. Cachin. 1998. An information-theoretic model for steganography. In *International Workshop on Information Hiding*. 306–318.

[4] X. Chu, Y. Chen, M. Stamm, and K.J. Ray Liu. 2016. Information theoretical limit of media forensics: the Forensicability. *IEEE Transactions on Information Forensics and Security* 11, 4 (2016), 774–788.

[5] P. Comesaña-Alfaro. 2012. Detection and information theoretic measures for quantifying the distinguishability between multimedia operator chains. In *IEEE Workshop on Informations Forensics and Security (WIFS)*. 211–216.

[6] P. Comesaña-Alfaro and F. Pèrez-Gonzàlez. 2012. Multimedia operator chain topology and ordering estimation based on detection and information theoretic tools. In *International Workshop on Digital Watermarking*. 213–227.

[7] N. Dalgaard, C. Mosquera, and F. Pèrez-Gonzàlez. 2010. On the role of differentiation for resampling detection. In *IEEE International Conference on Image Processing (ICIP)*. 1753–1756.

[8] M. L. Eaton. 2007. The Wishart distribution. *IMS Lecture Notes Monography Series. Multivariate statistics: a vector space approach* (2007).

[9] X. Feng, I. J. Cox, and G. Doërr. 2012. Normalized energy density-based forensic detection of resampled imagaes. *IEEE Transactions on Multimedia* 14, 3 (2012), 536–545.

[10] A. C. Frery, A. D. C. Nascimento, and R. J. Cintra. 2014. Analytic expressions for stochastic distances between relaxed complex Wishart distributions. *IEEE Transactions on Geoscience and Remote Sensing* 52, 2 (2014), 1213–1226.

[11] A.C. Gallagher. 2005. Detection of linear and cubic interpolation in JPEG compressed images. In *Proceedings of the 2nd Canadian Conference on Computer and Robot Vision*. 65–72.

[12] G. K. Grunwald, R. J. Hyndman, and L. Tedesco. 1995. *A unified view of linear AR(1) models*. Technical Report. Department of Statistics, University of Melbourne.

[13] R. A. Horn and C. R. Johnson. 2013. *Matrix Analysis*. Vol. Second Edition. Cambridge University Press.

[14] M. Kirchner. 2008. Fast and Reliable Resampling Detection by Spectral Analysis of Fixed Linear Predictor Residue. In *ACM Multimedia and Security Workshop (MM&Sec)*. 11–20.

[15] M. Kirchner. 2010. Linear row and column predictors for the analysis of resized images. In *ACM Multimedia and Security Workshop (MM&Sec)*. 13–18.

[16] B. Mahdian and S. Saic. 2008. Blind authentication using periodic properties of interpolation. *IEEE Transactions on Information Forensics and Security* 3, 3 (2008), 529–538.

[17] F. Nielsen and R. Nock. 2009. Clustering multivariate normal distributions. *Emerging trends in visual computing (LNCS)* (2009).

[18] A.C. Popescu and H. Farid. 2005. Exposing digital forgeries by detecting traces of resampling. *IEEE Transactions on Signal Processing* 53, 2 (2005), 758–767.

[19] V. Sathe and P. Vaidyanathan. 1993. Effects of multirate systems on the statistical properties of random signals. *IEEE Transactions on Signal Processing* 41, 1 (1993), 131.

[20] D. Vàzquez-Padìn and P. Comesaña-Alfaro. 2012. ML estimation of the resampling factor. In *IEEE International Workshop on Information Forensics and Security (WIFS)*. 205–210.

[21] D. Vàzquez-Padìn, P. Comesaña-Alfaro, and F. Pèrez-Gonzàlez. 2015. An SVD approach to forensic image resampling detection. In *European Signal Processing Conference (EUSIPCO)*. 2112–2116.

[22] D. Vàzquez-Padìn, C. Mosquera, and F. Pèrez-Gonzàlez. 2010. Two-dimensional statistical test for the presence of almost cyclostationarity on images. In *IEEE International Conference on Image Processing (ICIP)*. 1745–1748.

[23] D. Vàzquez-Padìn and F. Pèrez-Gonzàlez. 2011. Prefilter design for forensic resampling estimation. In *IEEE International Workshop on Information Forensics and Security (WIFS)*. 1–6.

[24] D. Vàzquez-Padìn and F. Pèrez-Gonzàlez. 2013. Set-membership identification of resampled signals. In *IEEE International Workshop on Information Forensics and Security (WIFS)*. 150–155.

Countering Anti-Forensics of Lateral Chromatic Aberration

Owen Mayer
Drexel University
Department of Electrical and Computer Engineering
Philadelphia, PA, USA
om82@drexel.edu

Matthew C. Stamm
Drexel University
Department of Electrical and Computer Engineering
Philadelphia, PA, USA
MStamm@coe.drexel.edu

ABSTRACT

Research has shown that lateral chromatic aberrations (LCA), an imaging fingerprint, can be anti-forensically modified to hide evidence of cut-and-paste forgery. In this paper, we propose a new technique for securing digital images against anti-forensic manipulation of LCA. To do this, we exploit resizing differences between color channels, which are induced by LCA anti-forensics, and define a feature vector to quantitatively capture these differences. Furthermore, we propose a detection method that exposes anti-forensically manipulated image patches. The technique algorithm is validated through experimental procedure, showing dependence on forgery patch size as well as anti-forensic scaling factor.

KEYWORDS

Image Forgery Detection; Anti-Forensics; Lateral Chromatic Aberration; Image Splicing; Multimedia Forensics

1 INTRODUCTION

Tampered digital images have become increasingly prevalent in today's society. Often, image forgers will manipulate the content of an image to maliciously alter its meaning. Since many facets of society rely upon authentic digital information, such as courts of law and media outlets, it necessary to ensure that images are truthful and haven't undergone manipulation. Image authenticity is verified using forensic methods that operate by detecting imperceptible traces, or fingerprints, left behind by the tampering process [16].

In response to multimedia forensics, techniques that hide or obfuscate tampering fingerprints have become common. These methods, called anti-forensics, operate by masking the traces that are inherently left behind during a tampering process. This fools forensic techniques into perceiving that a tampered image is authentic. For example, anti-forensic methods have been developed to hide traces of, median filtering [20], resampling [4, 8], JPEG compression [15], sensor noise [4], and lateral chromatic aberrations [11].

Anti-forensics, however, threaten societal confidence in both digital multimedia content and in forensic authentication algorithms. They do this by preventing multimedia content from being accurately authenticated. Therefore, it is crucial to also be able to secure images against anti-forensic methods. One way to do this is

to detect traces that are left behind by the anti-forensic processes themselves. Research has shown that many anti-forensic techniques leave behind their own traces that can be detected, such as with anti-forensic tampering of median filtering [23], resampling [13], JPEG compression [1, 10, 18], and sensor noise [5].

Research has shown that localized inconsistencies in lateral chromatic aberrations (LCA) can be used to detect cut-and-paste image forgeries [6, 12, 21], where content from one image is inserted into another image to change its meaning. LCA is an imaging trace present in optical imaging systems. It is introduced by the inability of lenses to focus all wavelengths from a single point source in a scene to a single focal point on the sensor. This manifests as imperceptible color fringes about object edges in an image. LCA patterning is also used to identify source camera model [19] and source imaging lens [22].

Work in anti-forensics, however, has shown that the chromatic aberrations in cut-and-paste forgeries can be anti-forensically altered to hide traces of manipulation [11]. Mayer and Stamm proposed an anti-forensic technique that independently scales and shifts the forged content's color channels to induce specific spatial relationships of focal points across color channels. The induced focal point relationships alters the forged LCA trace to be consistent with an authentic image. As a result, evidence of cut-and-paste manipulation are anti-forensically hidden.

In this paper, we propose a new forensic fingerprint to expose anti-forensic manipulations of lateral chromatic aberrations. Currently, there are no known forensic traces that can detect anti-forensics of LCA. Our proposed fingerprint exploits differences in resizing between color channels, which are introduced during the anti-forensic manipulation of LCA. To do this, we extract spectral properties of resampling artifacts. Then, we examine amplitude and phase angle differences across color channels at frequencies related to JPEG blocking discontinuities in precompressed images. We use these amplitude and phase angle differences to define a feature vector that captures the fingerprint of anti-forensic tampering of LCA. Furthermore, we propose a detection method to expose image regions containing anti-forensically manipulated lateral chromatic aberrations. To do this, we calculate our proposed fingerprint-feature vector in an image region, and then conduct a statistical test to determine whether the fingerprint is indicative of an anti-forensically forged region.

2 BACKGROUND

When capturing an image, light from a scene is focused onto an optical sensor using a lens. However, the refractive index of glass is dependent on wavelength of light passing through it. This causes the different wavelengths of a light ray, originating from the same point source in a scene, to be focused onto laterally offset locations

IH&MMSec '17, June 20–22, 2017, Philadelphia, PA, USA
© 2017 Copyright held by the owner/author(s). Publication rights licensed to ACM.
ACM ISBN 978-1-4503-5032-7/17/06...$15.00
DOI: http://dx.doi.org/10.1145/3082031.3083242

Owen Mayer and Matthew C. Stamm

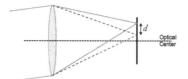

Figure 1: Ray tracing diagram of lateral chromatic aberration. The vector d shows the displacement of focal points between color channels.

on the sensor. This effect is called lateral chromatic aberration (LCA), which manifests as color fringes around object edges in an image. Fig. 1 shows a ray tracing diagram depicting LCA, which shows the red and blue components of an incoming ray of light being focused onto offset sensor locations.

Johnson and Farid developed a model to characterize the effect of LCA [6], which maps a focal point location $r = [r_x, r_y]^T$ in a reference channel to its corresponding focal point location $c = [c_x, c_y]^T$ in a comparison color channel. This mapping by the function $f(r, \theta)$ is parameterized by the tuple $\theta = [\alpha, \zeta]^T$. Johnson and Farid model LCA as a first order scaling by an expansion coefficient α, about the image's optical center $\zeta = [\zeta_x, \zeta_y]^T$, where

$$c = f(r, \theta) = \alpha(r - \zeta) + \zeta. \tag{1}$$

The comparison color channel is viewed as an expanded or contracted version of the reference color channel, with the expansion coefficient α determining the expansion/contraction scaling factor. Note that the optical center ζ need not be the image geometric center. Specification of which channels are used as reference and comparison are typically left out of notation to maintain generality, but are made explicit in the text where necessary.

The displacement vector between reference focal point r and its corresponding focal point in the comparison channel c is useful for characterizing LCA. Gloe et al. developed a method to estimate localized LCA displacement vectors in a digital image, as well as a method to estimate the LCA model tuple θ from these local displacement estimates [3]. Research has shown that localized inconsistencies of LCA displacement from the global model of displacement can be used to expose cut-and-paste image forgeries [6, 12], since the LCA displacement in the forged content is not consistent with the original image.

2.1 LCA Anti-Forensics

Work in [11] showed that the lateral chromatic aberration in a forged image region can be modified to hide traces of cut-and-paste tampering. This is accomplished by changing the LCA within the forged region to be consistent with the rest of the image. To change the LCA within the forged regions, the color channels of the forged image region are scaled and shifted, which changes the spatial relationships of focal points across color channels.

The specific scaling and shifting to be applied to the forged image region was determined so that its LCA displacements are consistent with the rest of the image. To do this, a transformation was introduced that relates the desired anti-forensicly modified focal point location in a comparison color channel c' to its current location c, such that

$$c' = \alpha_D \left(\frac{1}{\alpha_S} (c - \zeta_S) + \zeta_S - \zeta_V \right) + \zeta_V. \tag{2}$$

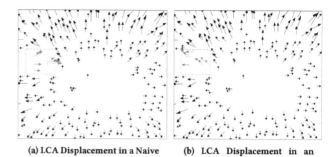

(a) LCA Displacement in a Naive Forgery

(b) LCA Displacement in an Anti-Forensic Forgery

Figure 2: LCA displacement vectors in naively forged (left), and anti-forensically forged (right) images. The LCA displacements in the forged region are highlighted in red. Vectors are scaled by a factor of 200 for display purposes.

The transformation first removes the inherent LCA parameterized by the source expansion coefficient α_S and source optical center ζ_S. Then, new focal point relationships are artificially induced by a resampling operation, parameterized by the destination image expansion coefficient α_D and virtual optical center ζ_V, a constant determined by the relationship of the forged image region to the destination optical center. The anti-forensic transformation equation can be rewritten to show that

$$c' = \frac{\alpha_D}{\alpha_S} c + K. \tag{3}$$

where K is a constant related to the scaled differences between the source and destination optical centers.

That is, the transformation that relates the comparison channel coordinates in source content c, to it's anti-forensically modified version c', is simply a geometric scaling and shift. The scaling is determined by the ratio of the in the source image expansion coefficient α_S, and destination image expansion coefficient α_D. We call this ratio the anti-forensic scaling factor.

This scaling and shift is performed via interpolated resampling [11]. The resulting anti-forensically modified forged region has LCA that matches its host image. This can be seen in Fig. 2b, which shows the LCA displacement vectors in an anti-forensically forged image region that are consistent with the destination image. Compare this with the LCA in the naively forged version, as shown in 2a, where the LCA displacement vectors in the forged region are inconsistent with the rest of the image.

3 THE LCA ANTI-FORENSICS FINGERPRINT

Anti-forensic tampering of lateral chromatic aberration poses a threat to the security of multimedia information, and therefore it is important to detect. However, no technique currently exists that is able to detect LCA anti-forensics. In this section, we propose a new fingerprint that exposes LCA anti-forensics tampering operations. Our proposed fingerprint exploits differences in resizing between color channels, which are introduced during the anti-forensic manipulation of lateral chromatic aberrations. In our model, we assume that the source image content has been compressed at some point prior to forgery and anti-forensic manipulation. Since images are commonly stored in JPEG format, it is likely that a forger will alter an image that has been compressed. We exploit distinct

Countering Anti-Forensics of Lateral Chromatic Aberration

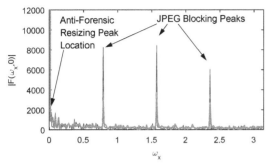

Figure 3: FFT magnitude of the resampling p-map, at $\omega_y = 0$, in an image patch where the red color channel has been anti-forensically modified.

spectral peaks that are related to JPEG blocking discontinuities, by examining amplitude and phase angle differences across color channels at these spectral peaks. The amplitude and phase differences are used as evidence of anti-forensic LCA manipulation.

Since anti-forensic LCA tampering is performed by a scaling and resampling operation, it follows that resampling detection techniques are useful for detecting anti-forensically forged images. However, the scaling factor used in LCA anti-forensics is too small to be detected by typical resampling detection methods, such as those in [7, 14]. Typically, resizing is detected using a construct called a p-map, which describes the probability that a pixel is a linear combination of its neighbors. Resizing introduces period-icity into the p-map, and the corresponding spectral peaks in the p-map FFT are used to expose resizing operations [7, 14]. However, at these small anti-forensic scaling factors, the resizing spectral peak in the resampling p-map is indiscernible from the naturally occuring low frequency content. This is seen in Fig. 3, which shows the p-map FFT of an anti-forensically tampered image region. In this figure, the anti-forensic resizing peak in the anti-forensically modified red channel is indiscernible from low-frequency content and is undetectable by traditional peak detection methods.

The effects of LCA anti-forensics, however, are apparent in the spectral peaks related to JPEG blocking discontinuities. Spectral peaks related to JPEG blocking occur in the p-map frequency domain because pixel values are not linearly predictable across JPEG blocks, and thus have a relatively low p-map value. These low p-map values occur every 8 pixels, and introduce distinct peaks in the p-map spectrum at $\omega = \frac{\pi}{4}, \frac{\pi}{2}$, and $\frac{3\pi}{4}$ [9], which can be seen in Fig. 3.

When an image channel is anti-forensically modified, the channel is slightly resized through an interpolation operation. This consequently introduces correlations, albeit slight, in pixel values across the JPEG blocking grid. As a result, the p-map deviations that are typically observed at JPEG blocking boundaries are decreased. Thus the spectral peaks related to JPEG blocking are reduced in anti-forensically modified color channels. This effect is seen in Fig. 3, which shows the p-map FFT in the x direction ($\omega_y = 0$) for three color channels, with the red channel anti-forensically modified. The JPEG spectral peaks in the anti-forensically modified red channel are small relative to the to unmodified green and blue channels.

In practice, an image is anti-forensically modified by keeping one color channel unmodified and applying the anti-forensic scaling and shifting to the remaining two color channels [11]. The unmodified

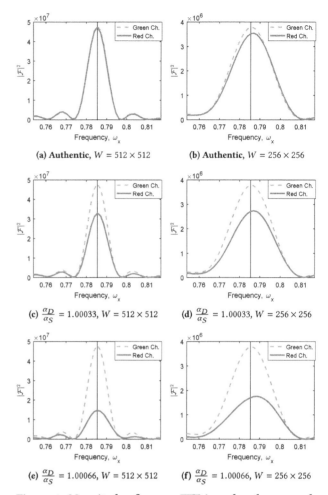

(a) Authentic, $W = 512 \times 512$

(b) Authentic, $W = 256 \times 256$

(c) $\frac{\alpha_D}{\alpha_S} = 1.00033$, $W = 512 \times 512$

(d) $\frac{\alpha_D}{\alpha_S} = 1.00033$, $W = 256 \times 256$

(e) $\frac{\alpha_D}{\alpha_S} = 1.00066$, $W = 512 \times 512$

(f) $\frac{\alpha_D}{\alpha_S} = 1.00066$, $W = 256 \times 256$

Figure 4: Magnitude of p-map FFT in red and green color channels showing the affect of LCA anti-forensics. The JPEG blocking peak at $(\omega_x, \omega_y) = (\frac{\pi}{4}, 0)$ is shown. The pre-compressed image taken by a Canon SX500-IS has an anti-forensically modified red channel using the green channel as the reference channel. Different window sizes W and anti-forensic scaling factors α_D/α_S are examined. The windowed p-maps are zero padded to 4096×4096 before taking their FFT.

color channel is called the reference channel and the modified color channels are called the comparison color channels. As a result, an anti-forensically tampered image region will have JPEG-blocking spectral peaks that are much smaller in the comparison color channels relative to the reference color channel.

The effect of LCA anti-forensics is detailed in Fig. 4, which shows the spectral p-map FFT magnitude with different anti-forensic scaling factors and different inspection window sizes. The figures show the first JPEG spectral peak in the x direction at $\omega_x = \frac{\pi}{4}$, $\omega_y = 0$ in both the red comparison channel and in the green reference channel. In authentic image regions, the spectral peak in the red (comparison) and green (reference) channels are nearly identical. The spectral peak in the comparison channel is reduced when LCA anti-forensics is applied with scaling factor 1.00033, and further reduced when the scaling factor is increased to 1.00066. Furthermore,

Owen Mayer and Matthew C. Stamm

the peak differences are much more discernible at larger window sizes of 512×512 than 256×256.

The spatial shifting of color channels during LCA anti-forensic tampering also affects the phase of the JPEG blocking grid. This manifests as phase angle differences when comparing the phase angle of the reference channel to the phase angle of the anti-forensically modified comparison channel. Fig. 5 shows phase angles in an authentic image patch and in the same image patch that has been anti-forensically modified. In the anti-forensically modified patch, the phase angles of the red comparison channel deviate from the phase angles of the green comparison channel. In the authentic image patch, the phase angles are well matched.

4 PROPOSED FINGERPRINT FEATURE VECTOR OF LCA ANTI-FORENSICS

To quantitatively capture the effects of LCA anti-forensics we define a feature vector as follows. We measure the ratio of JPEG spectral peak magnitudes between the 1) red and green channels, 2) blue and green channels, and 3) red and blue channels. In authentic image regions, it is expected that these ratios are near unity whereas in anti-forensically tampered regions these ratios deviate significantly. Since the choice of reference channel is unknown to an investigator, ratios between all three possible color channel pairs are considered. Additionally, the difference in phase angle at the JPEG spectral peaks are measured for each of the three color channel pairings. In authentic image regions, it is expected that these phase angle differences are near zero whereas in anti-forensically modified image regions these phase angle differences deviate from zero.

At a given peak location defined by frequencies ω_x and ω_y six fingerprint values are measured: three magnitude ratios and three phase angle differences. These six values are represented by the vector $\mathbf{x}\left(\omega_x, \omega_y\right)$ as follows,

$$
\mathbf{x}\left(\omega_x, \omega_y\right) = \begin{bmatrix} \left|\mathcal{F}_\mathcal{R}\left(\omega_x, \omega_y\right)\right| / \left|\mathcal{F}_\mathcal{G}\left(\omega_x, \omega_y\right)\right| \\ \left|\mathcal{F}_\mathcal{B}\left(\omega_x, \omega_y\right)\right| / \left|\mathcal{F}_\mathcal{G}\left(\omega_x, \omega_y\right)\right| \\ \left|\mathcal{F}_\mathcal{R}\left(\omega_x, \omega_y\right)\right| / \left|\mathcal{F}_\mathcal{B}\left(\omega_x, \omega_y\right)\right| \\ \angle\mathcal{F}_\mathcal{R}\left(\omega_x, \omega_y\right) - \angle\mathcal{F}_\mathcal{G}\left(\omega_x, \omega_y\right) \\ \angle\mathcal{F}_\mathcal{B}\left(\omega_x, \omega_y\right) - \angle\mathcal{F}_\mathcal{G}\left(\omega_x, \omega_y\right) \\ \angle\mathcal{F}_\mathcal{R}\left(\omega_x, \omega_y\right) - \angle\mathcal{F}_\mathcal{B}\left(\omega_x, \omega_y\right) \end{bmatrix}^\mathsf{T} . \quad (4)
$$

Here, $\left|\mathcal{F}\left(\omega_x, \omega_y\right)\right|$ is the p-map FFT magnitude at frequency (ω_x, ω_y), and $\angle\mathcal{F}\left(\omega_x, \omega_y\right)$ is the p-map FFT phase angle at frequency (ω_x, ω_y). The subscripts $\mathcal{R}$, $\mathcal{G}$ and $\mathcal{B}$ denote the red, green, and blue color channels respectively.

The fingerprint values are measured at six JPEG spectral peak frequencies $(\omega_x, \omega_y) = \left(\frac{\pi}{4}, 0\right), \left(\frac{\pi}{2}, 0\right), \left(\frac{3\pi}{4}, 0\right), \left(0, \frac{\pi}{4}\right), \left(0, \frac{\pi}{2}\right)$, and $\left(0, \frac{3\pi}{4}\right)$. This yields six vectors that are then concatenate to form the full, proposed feature vector

$$
\mathbf{X} = \left[\mathbf{x}\left(\frac{\pi}{4}, 0\right) \ \mathbf{x}\left(\frac{\pi}{2}, 0\right) \ \mathbf{x}\left(\frac{3\pi}{4}, 0\right) \ \mathbf{x}\left(0, \frac{\pi}{4}\right) \ \mathbf{x}\left(0, \frac{\pi}{2}\right) \ \mathbf{x}\left(0, \frac{3\pi}{4}\right)\right]^\mathsf{T} .
$$
(5)

The full LCA anti-forensics feature vector $\mathbf{X}$ contains 36 values, comprised of 18 spectral peak magnitude ratios and 18 phase angle differences.

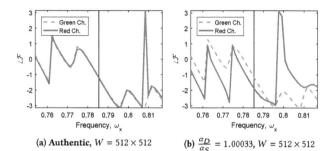

(a) Authentic, $W = 512 \times 512$ (b) $\frac{\alpha_D}{\alpha_S} = 1.00033$, $W = 512 \times 512$

Figure 5: Phase angle of p-map FFT in red (comparison) and green (reference) color channels showing the affect of LCA anti-forensics on the JPEG blocking peak at $\omega_x = \frac{\pi}{4}, \omega_y = 0$.

Examples of the fingerprint $\mathbf{X}$ are shown in Fig. 6 for authentic and anti-forensically modified image patches. Fig. 6a shows histograms of $\mathbf{X}_1 = \left|\mathcal{F}_\mathcal{R}\left(\frac{\pi}{4}, 0\right)\right| / \left|\mathcal{F}_\mathcal{G}\left(\frac{\pi}{4}, 0\right)\right|$, the first fingerprint dimension. The authentic values are distributed near unity whereas values from anti-forensic patches are typically smaller, and are easily discriminated. Fig. 6b shows a scatter plot of dimensions $\mathbf{X}_1 = \left|\mathcal{F}_\mathcal{R}\left(\frac{\pi}{4}, 0\right)\right| / \left|\mathcal{F}_\mathcal{G}\left(\frac{\pi}{4}, 0\right)\right|$ and $\mathbf{X}_{19} = \left|\mathcal{F}_\mathcal{R}\left(0, \frac{\pi}{4}\right)\right| / \left|\mathcal{F}_\mathcal{G}\left(0, \frac{\pi}{4}\right)\right|$. The use of two (and more) dimensions increases discrimination.

5 PROPOSED DETECTION METHOD

To expose image regions that have undergone LCA anti-forensic manipulation, we propose a new detection method using the fingerprint described in Sec. 4. To do this, we define a hypothesis testing problem where under the null hypothesis $\mathcal{H}_0$ the image patch has not undergone LCA anti-forensics, and under the alternative hypothesis, $\mathcal{H}_1$, the LCA in the image patch has anti-forensically modified.

$$\mathcal{H}_0 : \text{No LCA anti-forensics}$$
$$\mathcal{H}_1 : \text{LCA anti-forensics}$$

To describe patches under the null hypothesis, we build a statistical model of the LCA anti-forensic fingerprint in unmodified image regions. Fig 6a shows a histogram of $\mathbf{X}_1$, the first dimension of the fingerprint feature vector, in authentic and anti-forensically modified image patches. We observe from this histogram that $\mathbf{X}_1$ is distributed approximately Gaussian in authentic patches, with a mean near one. We model the entire fingerprint vector as a 36 dimensional random variable that is distributed Gaussian, with a mean vector $\boldsymbol{\mu}$, and covariance Σ. The probability density function $p(\mathbf{X}|\mathcal{H}_0)$ of $\mathbf{X}$ in authentic patches is as follows:

$$
p(\mathbf{X}|\mathcal{H}_0) = \frac{1}{\sqrt{(2\pi)^{36} |\Sigma|}} \exp\left(-\frac{1}{2}\left(\mathbf{X} - \boldsymbol{\mu}\right)\Sigma^{-1}\left(\mathbf{X} - \boldsymbol{\mu}\right)\right). \quad (6)
$$

The authentic distribution parameters mean, $\boldsymbol{\mu}$, and covariance, Σ, are estimated from image patches extracted from many JPEG compressed images that are known to have not been modified. Since the patch size effects the fingerprint values, as seen in Fig. 6, the authentic distribution parameters must be estimated separately for each patch/window size that is used.

The fingerprint feature vector under the alternative hypothesis depends upon the anti-forensically scaling factor. This is shown in Fig. 4. Without knowing the anti-forensic scaling factor, which

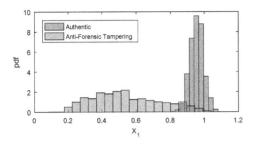

(a) Histogram of X_1

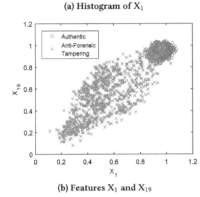

(b) Features X_1 and X_{19}

Figure 6: Histogram (top) and scatterplot (bottom) of fingerprint features X in authentic (blue) and anti-forensically modified patches (red).

requires knowledge of the source image, it is impractical to model the fingerprint feature in anti-forensically manipulated patches. As a result, we are left only to compare with authentic model. In anti-forensically forged image patches, the fingerprint feature vector deviates significantly from μ. This effect is seen in Fig. 6b, where a scatter plot of features X_1 and X_{19} shows that the fingerprint in anti-forensically modified patches deviates significantly from the fingerprint in authentic patches.

To quantify the deviations of X from the authentic model of the fingerprint feature, we use the Mahalanobis distance [17], which is as follows:

$$m = \left((X - \mu)^\top \Sigma^{-1} (X - \mu) \right)^{\frac{1}{2}} . \quad (7)$$

The distance m describes deviations of the fingerprint vector X from the authentic distribution mean μ. Importantly, the Mahalanobis distance accounts for differences in the variances of each of the fingerprint dimensions. That is, a deviation in a dimension with a small variance is more indicative of manipulation than an equivalent deviation in a dimension with a large variance. The differences in variances are normalized by the Σ^{-1} term in (7). Additionally, the Mahalanobis distance accounts for any correlations that may exist among the authentic fingerprint dimensions.

The distance m is small in authentic image patches, and large in anti-forensically tampered image patches. We use this to define a decision rule $\delta(\cdot)$ to determine if an image patch authentic or anti-forensically modified. The decision rule employs a threshold test, where distances m greater than or equal to the threshold τ reject the null hypothesis in favor of the alternative hypothesis.

$$\delta(m) = \begin{cases} \mathcal{H}_0, & m < \tau \\ \mathcal{H}_1, & m \geq \tau \end{cases} \quad (8)$$

The decision threshold τ can be varied to set the false alarm rate.

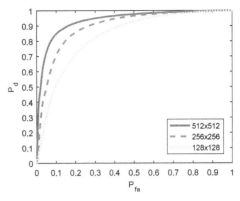

Figure 7: ROC curves of the proposed detection method on different block sizes. Forgeries were made by copying and pasting image blocks from database images, and anti-forensically modifying their LCA to hide forgery traces.

6 EXPERIMENTAL RESULTS

We conducted a series of experiments in order to evaluate the efficacy of our proposed fingerprint and proposed detection method at exposing image patches that have been manipulated by LCA anti-forensics. To do this, we started with a database of images 16961 unaltered, JPEG compressed images from the Dresden Image Database [2]. We used all images from the "Natural images" set, which were captured by 27 unique camera models and representing a diverse set of LCA expansion coefficients. We produced 20000 cut-and-paste forged images and anti-forensically tampered the forged regions to hide traces of LCA inconsistency. To make the cut-and-paste forgeries, we randomly chose a source image to cut from, and randomly chose a destination image to paste into. The source (cut) and destination (paste) locations were chosen at random, as well.

To make each forgery, a 512×512 block was cut from the source location in the source image, and pasted at the destination location in the destination image. The LCA model parameters for the destination and source images were estimated using Gloe et al.'s efficient method [3]. Finally, LCA anti-forensics was applied using Mayer and Stamm's method [11], using the green channel as the reference channel and the red and blue channels as the comparison channel.

The LCA anti-forensics fingerprint was calculated in each of the 512×512 forged image regions. Furthermore, to evaluate the effect of inspection window size, the forged image regions were segmented into 4 non-overlapping 256×256 patches, as well as 16 non-overlapping 128×128 patches and the anti-forensic fingerprint was determined for each patch. To measure the anti-forensic fingerprint, we first determined the resampling p-map FFT for each color plane in the image region, using the method described in [7]. Finally, the anti-forensics fingerprint X was determined, its distance m to the authentic model was calculated according to 7, and classification decision $\delta(m)$ rendered according to (8).

To estimate the authentic model parameters, 100000 unmodified image patches of size 512×512, 256×256, and 128×128 were chosen. The LCA anti-forensics fingerprint was measured in each of the 300000 authentic patches (100000 patches for each of 3 window sizes). At each size, 10000 patches were randomly chosen to estimate the authentic fingerprint distribution parameters mean

Owen Mayer and Matthew C. Stamm

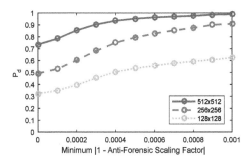

Figure 8: Probability of detection versus LCA anti-forensic scaling at a 5% false alarm rate.

μ, and covariance Σ. The remaining 90000 patches were used to determine false alarm rates at varied decision thresholds.

Fig. 7 shows the receiver operator characteristic for our proposed detection method. At a 10% false alarm rate, our method achieved a 85% positive detection rate when using a 512×512 inspection window, demonstrating that our proposed fingerprint feature vector and detection method are able to successfully expose image patches as having been manipulated with LCA anti-forensics. At a smaller window size of 256×256, our detection method achieved a 71% positive detection rate, and a 52% positive detection rate with the smallest 128×128 window. At a 5% false alarm rate, our method achieved a 73%, 50%, and 31% positive detection rate at window sizes of 512×512, 256×256, and 128×128 respectively.

Furthermore, we evaluated the effect of the scaling factor used in the LCA anti-forensic tampering process on detection performance. Fig. 8 shows the detection rates at a 5% false alarm rate as a function of anti-forensic scaling factor. For each forgery, we determined the anti-forensic scaling factor applied for each of the two comparison color channels and determined its absolute distance from 1 (no scaling). The x-axis of Fig. 8 includes all forgeries with at least one of the two anti-forensic scaling factors greater than the x axis value. This method gives a measure of "strength" of LCA anti-forensics. For example, a scaling factor value of 0.0005 indicates that at least one of the red or blue comparison channels were scaled by either greater than 1.0005, or less than 0.9995.

At a scaling factor value of 0.0005, anti-forensically tampered patches were correctly identified at a rate of 95% with a window size of 512×512, 79% with a window size of 256×256, and 53% with a window size of 128×128. At a scaling factor value of 0.001, anti-forensically tampered patches were correctly identified at a rate of 99% with a window size of 512×512, 91% with a window size of 256×256, and 62% with a window size of 128×128. This result demonstrates that the strength of the LCA anti-forensic tampering greatly effects its ability to be detected.

7 CONCLUSION

In this paper, we propose a new algorithm for securing digital images against anti-forensic manipulation of LCA. To do this, we exploit resizing differences between color channels, which are induced by LCA anti-forensics, and define a feature vector to quantitatively capture these differences. Furthermore, we propose a detection method that exposes anti-forensically manipulated image patches.

The proposed algorithm is validated through experimental procedure, showing dependence on patch size as well as anti-forensic scaling factor.

8 ACKNOWLEDGMENTS

This material is based upon work supported by the National Science Foundation under Grant No. 1553610. Any opinions, findings, and conclusions or recommendations expressed in this material are those of the authors and do not necessarily reflect the views of the National Science Foundation.

REFERENCES

[1] FONTANI, M., BONCHI, A., PIVA, A., AND BARNI, M. Countering anti-forensics by means of data fusion. In *IS&T/SPIE Electronic Imaging* (2014), International Society for Optics and Photonics, pp. 90280Z–90280Z.

[2] GLOE, T., AND BÖHME, R. The dresden image database for benchmarking digital image forensics. *Journal of Digital Forensic Practice 3*, 2-4 (2010), 150–159.

[3] GLOE, T., BOROWKA, K., AND WINKLER, A. Efficient estimation and large-scale evaluation of lateral chromatic aberration for digital image forensics. In *IS&T/SPIE Electronic Imaging* (2010), Int. Society for Optics and Photonics, pp. 7541–7547.

[4] GLOE, T., KIRCHNER, M., WINKLER, A., AND BÖHME, R. Can we trust digital image forensics? In *Proceedings of the 15th International Conference on Multimedia* (New York, NY, USA, 2007), MULTIMEDIA '07, ACM, pp. 78–86.

[5] GOLJAN, M., FRIDRICH, J., AND CHEN, M. Sensor noise camera identification: Countering counter-forensics. In *IS&T/SPIE Electronic Imaging* (2010), International Society for Optics and Photonics, pp. 75410S–75410S.

[6] JOHNSON, M. K., AND FARID, H. Exposing digital forgeries through chromatic aberration. In *Proceedings of the 8th workshop on Multimedia and security* (2006), ACM, pp. 48–55.

[7] KIRCHNER, M. Fast and reliable resampling detection by spectral analysis of fixed linear predictor residue. In *Proceedings of the 10th ACM workshop on Multimedia and security* (2008), ACM, pp. 11–20.

[8] KIRCHNER, M., AND BÖHME, R. Hiding traces of resampling in digital images. *IEEE Transactions on Information Forensics and Security 3*, 4 (2008), 582–592.

[9] KIRCHNER, M., AND GLOE, T. On resampling detection in re-compressed images. In *Information Forensics and Security, 2009. WIFS 2009. First IEEE International Workshop on* (2009), IEEE, pp. 21–25.

[10] LAI, S., AND BÖHME, R. Countering counter-forensics: The case of JPEG compression. In *Int. Workshop on Information Hiding* (2011), Springer, pp. 285–298.

[11] MAYER, O., AND STAMM, M. C. Anti-forensics of chromatic aberration. In *IS&T/SPIE Electronic Imaging* (2015), Int. Society for Optics and Photonics.

[12] MAYER, O., AND STAMM, M. C. Improved forgery detection with lateral chromatic aberration. In *2016 IEEE International Conference on Acoustics, Speech and Signal Processing (ICASSP)* (2016), IEEE, pp. 2024–2028.

[13] PENG, A., ZENG, H., LIN, X., AND KANG, X. Countering anti-forensics of image resampling. In *Image Processing (ICIP), 2015 IEEE International Conference on* (2015), IEEE, pp. 3595–3599.

[14] POPESCU, A. C., AND FARID, H. Exposing digital forgeries by detecting traces of resampling. *IEEE Transactions on signal processing 53*, 2 (2005), 758–767.

[15] STAMM, M. C., AND LIU, K. J. R. Anti-forensics of digital image compression. *IEEE Trans. Information Forensics and Security 6*, 3 (Sep. 2011), 1050 –1065.

[16] STAMM, M. C., WU, M., AND LIU, K. J. R. Information forensics: An overview of the first decade. *Access, IEEE 1* (2013), 167–200.

[17] THEODORIDIS, S., AND KOUTROUMBAS, K. Pattern recognition (4th edition), 2009.

[18] VALENZISE, G., NOBILE, V., TAGLIASACCHI, M., AND TUBARO, S. Countering JPEG anti-forensics. In *Image Processing (ICIP), 2011 18th IEEE International Conference on* (2011), IEEE, pp. 1949–1952.

[19] VAN, L. T., EMMANUEL, S., AND KANKANHALLI, M. S. Identifying source cell phone using chromatic aberration. In *Multimedia and Expo, 2007 IEEE International Conference on* (2007), IEEE, pp. 883–886.

[20] WU, Z.-H., STAMM, M. C., AND LIU, K. R. Anti-forensics of median filtering. In *Acoustics, Speech and Signal Processing (ICASSP), 2013 IEEE International Conference on* (2013), IEEE, pp. 3043–3047.

[21] YERUSHALMY, I., AND HEL-OR, H. Digital image forgery detection based on lens and sensor aberration. *International Journal of computer vision 92*, 1 (2011), 71–91.

[22] YU, J., CRAVER, S., AND LI, E. Toward the identification of DSLR lenses by chromatic aberration. In *IS&T/SPIE Electronic Imaging* (2011), International Society for Optics and Photonics, pp. 788010–788010.

[23] ZENG, H., QIN, T., KANG, X., AND LI, L. Countering anti-forensics of median filtering. In *Acoustics, Speech and Signal Processing (ICASSP), 2014 IEEE International Conference on* (2014), IEEE, pp. 2704–2708.

Modeling Attacks on Photo-ID Documents and Applying Media Forensics for the Detection of Facial Morphing

Christian Kraetzer
Dept. of Computer Science, Otto-von-
Guericke University Magdeburg
Universitaetsplatz 2,
39106 Magdeburg, Germany
kraetzer@iti.cs.uni-magdeburg.de

Andrey Makrushin
Dept. of Computer Science, Otto-von-
Guericke University Magdeburg
Universitaetsplatz 2,
39106 Magdeburg, Germany

Tom Neubert
Dept. of Computer Science, Otto-von-
Guericke University Magdeburg
Universitaetsplatz 2,
39106 Magdeburg, Germany

Mario Hildebrandt
Dept. of Computer Science, Otto-von-
Guericke University Magdeburg
Universitaetsplatz 2,
39106 Magdeburg, Germany

Jana Dittmann
Dept. of Computer Science, Otto-von-
Guericke University Magdeburg
Universitaetsplatz 2,
39106 Magdeburg, Germany

ABSTRACT

Since 2014, a novel approach to attack face image based person verification designated as face morphing attack has been actively discussed in the biometric and media forensics communities. Up until that point, modern travel documents were considered to be extremely hard to forge or to successfully manipulate. In the case of template-targeting attacks like facial morphing, the face verification process becomes vulnerable, making it a necessity to design protection mechanisms.

In this paper, a new modeling approach for face morphing attacks is introduced. We start with a life-cycle model for photo-ID documents. We extend this model by an image editing history model, allowing for a precise description of attack realizations as a foundation for performing media forensics as well as training and testing scenarios for the attack detectors. On the basis of these modeling approaches, two different realizations of the face morphing attack as well as a forensic morphing detector are implemented and evaluated. The design of the feature space for the detector is based on the idea that the blending operation in the morphing pipeline causes the reduction of face details. To quantify this reduction, we adopt features implemented in the OpenCV image processing library, namely the number of SIFT, SURF, ORB, FAST and AGAST keypoints in the face region as well as the loss of edge-information with Canny and Sobel edge operators. Our morphing detector is trained with 2000 self-acquired authentic and 2000 morphed images captured with three camera types (Canon EOS 1200D, Nikon D 3300, Nikon Coolpix A100) and tested with authentic and morphed face images from a public database.

Morphing detection accuracies of a decision tree classifier vary from **81.3%** to 98% for different training and test scenarios.

CCS CONCEPTS

• **Security and privacy** → **Security services** →
Authentication;
• **Applied computing** → **Computer forensics** →
Investigation techniques

KEYWORDS

Digital image forensics, face morphing attack detection, modeling

1 INTRODUCTION

Even though the intention of Biometrics is to generate a strong (i.e. hard to steal) link between a person and an authentication token, also biometric authentication scenarios are in the focus of various identity theft schemes. In the paper "The Magic Passport" [1], the authors present a novel identity theft scenario for face biometric that, in its potential consequences, by far outperforms simplistic presentation or spoofing attacks.

The idea of the attack is simple, yet elegant: A face morph (a combination of two or more face images) is created so that it is similar to multiple real persons, e.g. Alice (an accomplice that has so far been innocent) and Mallory (a wanted criminal). If a photo-ID document is created on the basis of this photograph, the document could successfully be used by Alice as well as by Mallory. Summarizing the consequences of such an attack, Ferrara et al. in [1] point out that the potential attack outcome could be a 'clean', authentic and perfectly regular passport, issued by official authorities, for a wanted criminal (e.g.

Mallory). This document will therefore pass all optical and electronic authenticity and integrity checks.

Currently, virtually no security mechanisms for detecting this novel kind of attack seem to be foreseen in many document generation processes in many countries (incl. the passport application procedures in U.S.A., India and many European countries such as France and Germany).

Our contributions can be summarized as follows:

(i) We propose a novel **life-cycle model for photo-ID documents** that foresees the integration of media forensics into the document creation and -usage phases. The model let us describe and compare different attacks on photo-ID documents and highlights the severity of the face morphing attack.

(ii) We also introduce a novel **image editing history model to describe face morphing attacks** in details. The model allows for a systematic and fine-granular description of attack realizations and traces or image anomalies resulting from editing operations. Moreover, the model helps to derive requirements for forensic morphing detectors. It is used in the paper to define and describe the classes used for the empirical tests.

With contributions (i) and (ii) we intend to provide the community with means to perform the methodological work required to enable the usage of detectors for face morphing attack in field application versions of detectors (e.g. to be used for document application processes or in document usage).

(iii) **We implement and evaluate a morphing attack detector**, based on a feature set derived from existing OpenCV image analysis methods (keypoints- and edge-based trackers). Two different realizations (Attack Type I (complete morphs; warping&blending of the complete image) and Attack Type II (splicing morphs; warping&blending of the face region in the image)) are implemented on the public Utrecht Face DB (http://pics.psych.stir.ac.uk/2D_face_sets.htm). Using WEKAs J48 classifier (a pruned C4.5 decision tree [2], [3]), our detector shows for two different training and scenarios detection accuracies of 81.3% to 98% without anti-forensics and still significant results for tests with 8 different post-processing methods (6 legitimate and 2 illegitimate).

Hereafter, the paper is structured as follows: Section 2 gives an overview on face morphing attacks and targeted forensic detectors for this threat. In Section 3, the novel life-cycle model for photo-ID documents is presented and several attacks (including the face morphing attack) are modeled and compared. In Section 4, a model of the image editing history is introduced to extend the document life-cycle model which allows for a systematic analysis of forensically usable artifacts. Section 5 introduces the design of our morphing detector and Section 6 discusses the goals, setup, performance measures and results of our morphing detection experiment. Section 7 concludes the paper with a summary and future work.

2 STATE OF THE ART IN FORENSICS ON FACE MORPHING ATTACKS

Ferrara et al. [1] introduced a novel morphing attack to show the vulnerability of identity verification based on photo-ID documents, but proposed no security mechanism to resist this attack. Moreover, the only one exemplary realization of the morphing attack was demonstrated, namely a manual generation of morphed faces with GIMP/GAP (www.gimp.org) resulting in a low number of generated morphs. However, this publication showed that the media forensic detection of facial morphs is an important, yet unsolved task.

To confirm the relevance of this attack, Ferrara et al. in [4] evaluate the performance of three automatic face recognition (AFR) systems to reject morphings. The evaluation results of these systems are alarming, because the tested systems are not able to differentiate between morphings and genuine faces. Additionally, the authors evaluate the human performance to match faces in original and morphed images. In many cases, the testees decide that morphed and original faces images represent the same person.

An approach for the automatic generation of visually faultless facial morphs is presented in [5]. The automatic generation of morphs allows the creation of abundant experimental data, which is essential for the training of forensic morph detectors. The quality of morphs is evaluated in a subjective human experiment and with an AFR system. The human experiment demonstrated that the human ability to distinguish between morphed and genuine face images is close to random guessing. The matching scores resulting from the AFR test demonstrated that Alice and Mallory would be successfully verified against the morphed image. The authors also propose an approach to automatically detect morphs making use of Benford features derived from quantized DCT coefficients of JPEG images. It was demonstrated that the feature distributions are significantly different for genuine images and automatically generated morphs.

In [6], we benchmark the approach from [5] using the StirTrace (https://sourceforge.net/projects/stirtrace) to simulate different post-processing approaches to challenge media forensic detectors. There are 3940 morphed images were generated with 2 different approaches. Based on this data set, 86614 samples were generated to evaluate the influence of image processing on the detector and the face matcher performance, determining the impact of the processing on the quality of the forgeries. The results show that the anomaly detection performance for different types of processing can be differentiated into good (e.g. cropping), partially critical (e.g. rotation) and critical results (e.g. additive noise). For the biometric matcher, the influence of the processing is marginal.

Another recent effort to withstand the morphing attack is reported in [7]. The morph detection approach is based on binarized statistical image features used in conjunction with a linear SVM. In [8] the authors have evaluated the vulnerability of two different face recognition systems with respect to scanned morph face images. Gomez-Barrero et al. present in their paper

[9] a framework for the evaluation of the vulnerability of biometric system to morphing attacks. The analysis implies that biometric systems providing are vulnerable to different kind of attacks, depending on the verification threshold and the shape of the match score distributions.

The Biometrics community also acknowledges the challenge imposed by face morphing attacks. In the well-known "Face Verification Contest ongoing" (FVCongoing), recently a new challenge "Face Morphing Challenge" was issued, looking at the effects of image morphing on face recognition accuracy (see https://biolab.csr.unibo.it/FVCOnGoing/UI/Form/BenchmarkAre as/BenchmarkAreaFMC.aspx).

Beyond these specific papers on face morphing detection there exist large numbers of publications on image forensics. These can be grouped into two classes: on one hand the papers that look into detector designs for other specific image forensic investigations, like e.g. copy-move forgery detection, and on the other hand the papers looking into the modeling of media forensic processes.

For the first class, survey documents like [10] or [11] try to provide a comprehensive overview of approaches. One prominent example paper from the latter class is [12], where the authors look into a model for determining manipulation histories for images in multiple parenting relationships, i.e. for detection compositions combining parts from different images. Despite the fact that it is not directly transferable to the problem of face morphing detection, this modeling motivates the work on the image editing history presented in this paper.

Despite the research existing in this field (the few targeted face morphing attack detection papers as well as the universal image forensics publications) there exists, to the best of our knowledge, right now no publication that precisely models the problem imposed by face morphing attacks OR proposes a systematic, generalized solution strategy for addressing this threat. With the modeling work proposed in this paper it is intended to provide some first steps towards better process designs as well as establish some best practices for the evaluation of face morphing attack detectors.

3 LIFE-CYCLE MODEL - DOCUMENTS FOR PHOTO-BASED ID VERIFICATION

In order to understand the severity of face morphing attacks, it has to be put in contrast to other attacks on photo-ID documents. In this chapter, we introduce a generalized life-cycle model that is valid for a wide range of (paper as well as RFID-enabled) documents including passports (eMRTDs), national ID cards, drivers' licenses, company IDs, etc.

3.1 Formal description of the life-cycle model

The generalized process for generation and usage of a face-image based authentication token can be reduced to three core steps: Image data acquisition, Document generation and Document usage (see Figure 1(a)).

In Step 1, the face image is newly generated or acquired for re-usage.

In Step 2, a person applies for a document and all administrative and authentication steps that are necessary for the commissioning of the document creation are performed by a corresponding authority. Furthermore, the document is created and picked up by or delivered to the applicant.

In Step 3, the document is used in authentication scenarios like border control, authentication at the desk of a car rental agency, etc.

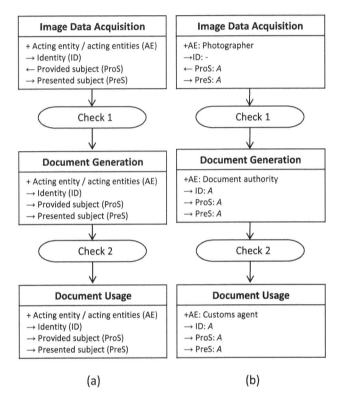

Figure 1: (a) the generalized life-cycle of a photo-ID document and (b) a standard document use-case without attack

All three steps can be characterized by a the following four-tuple data set: the acting entity (*AE*; a person, group of persons or in some cases also automated processes) performing the necessary operations in the step, the identity (*ID*) assigned to the document (e.g. a passport number linked to a citizen of a country), the provided subject (*ProS*; equivalent to the intended validity set for the image or document under consideration; traditionally this set contains exactly one person, but in the case of the specific attacks discussed below several persons can be engaged) and the presented subject (*PreS*). While the *AE* and the *ID* are self-explanatory, the specification of subjects requires additional explanation. In the case of a morphing attack there is a document that could be successfully used/provided by two (or more) subjects (*ProS*), but contains only one *ID* and can at one point of time (e.g. a check at a border control station) be only presented by one subject (*PreS*). The need for this split will be substantiated in examples presented in Section 3.

In Figure 1 and Figure 2, the arrows in front of the *ID*, *PreS* and *ProS* elements of the tuple indicate whether they are an input ($\rightarrow$) or output ($\leftarrow$) at this point.

Besides the steps and the entities, the model includes a third important component - the Checks that connect two steps in the pipeline. In these checks, various document-specific characteristics are evaluated, including, amongst others, authenticity (document as well as entity authenticity, the latter including a comparison of *ID*, *ProS* and *PreS*) and integrity checks as well as tests on compliance to standards. In these Checks, **media forensic considerations are mostly neglected so far**, even though most of the example processes discussed in this paper already contain automated check components that could strongly benefit from media forensic detectors. Addressing this gap and providing a strong motivation for the improvement of the Checks already in place by adding media forensic detectors is one of the goals of this paper.

In Figure 1(b), the legitimate document usage is shown representing a first exemplary document life-cycle use-case. In Step 1, the applicant Alice (*A*) asks a photographer to produce a face image for the purpose of applying for a document (e.g. a passport). For this use-case, the corresponding tuple is: (*AE*: photographer; input *ID*: - (none; Alice does not have to authenticate herself); output *ProS*: *A* (the photographer assumes that Alice intends to apply for a document and takes the photo); input *PreS*: *A* (Alice is photographed)).

Prior to the commissioning the document that *A* applies for in Step 2, the passport authority verifies in Check 1 that all process requirements are met. Currently, such a check contain the following components: Alice is authenticated using an already existing *ID* document (e.g. old passport, national identity card or birth certificate), the face on the image is verified against the presented face (i.e. *ProS* and *PreS* are compared) and the image properties are checked against the technical requirements of the document issuing authority (e.g. compliance to ICAO standards for eMRTD images [13]). If the check is successful, in Step 2, the photograph is accepted by the authorities for document generation. Notice that this submission is strongly regulated in each country. Therefore, both digital and analogue submissions (the latter in form of a developed, hardcopy photograph) have to be foreseen. On the basis of the face image and the additional ID information provided, the document generation is commissioned. The corresponding tuple for describing this step is: (*AE*: authority; input *ID*: *A*; input *ProS*: *A* (by issuing the document, the authority intends to create a biunique identification token), input *PreS*: *A*).

Prior to document usage (e.g. for authentication of *A*), the document is checked in Check 2. Such checks verify the document integrity ("Does it look tampered?") as well as additional characteristics ("Is the document still valid?", etc). If positive, the document is used, e.g. by a border control agent, for

authenticating the presenting person. The corresponding tuple for describing this step is: (*AE*: customs agent; input *ID*: *A*, input *ProS*: *A*; input *PreS*: *A*).

Since the last three elements in the tuple for Step 3 point to the same value, this is the case of legitimate document usage.

In the following section, the document life-cycle modeling approach is used to describe and compare different attacks on photo-ID documents. It shows that the current realizations of Check 1 and Check 2 are sufficient to handle the established threats like presentation attacks, but are ill-designed to handle face morphing attacks. The clear message of our paper is that media forensics methods must be integrated into the established processes to enable a higher level of protection also including this novel threat.

3.2 Attack comparison using the document life-cycle model

Here, we formally describe and compare different attack scenarios to show that the current realizations of Checks 1 and 2 may be sufficient to handle the established threats like presentation attacks, but are ill-designed to handle the face morphing attack. Figure 2 shows three examples: simplistic presentation attack, document tampering and face morphing attack. Our clear message is that media forensics methods must be integrated into the established process of personal identity verification to enable a higher level of protection also covering this novel threat.

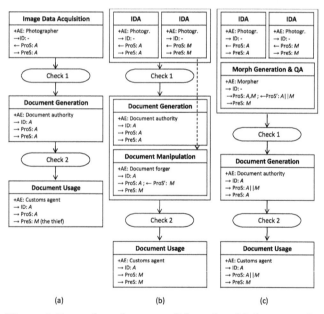

Figure 2: Exemplary document life-cycles: (a) document is stolen and presented by the thief; (b) document is modified by a forger; (c) face morphing attack

In Figure 2(a), an example of presentation attack is shown. Here, a thief Mallory (*M*) steals the passport from its owner Alice (*A*) and shows it at a border control. Even this simplistic presentation attack [14] might succeed if *A* and *M* look similar and personal details in the document are not contradictory. The model of this attack is similar to the legitimate document usage presented in Section 3.1 except for Step 3. The tuples for Steps 1 and 2 as well as for Checks 1 and 2 are identical. In Step 3, the tuple in this attack scenario reads: (*AE*: customs agent; input *ID*: *A*, input *ProS*: *A*; input *PreS*: *M*). The outcome of Check 2 is that no anomaly for the document could be found (i.e. the document was created by an authorized entity and was not tampered), the *ID* matches the provided subject (*ProS*), but *ProS* does not match the presented subject (*PreS*). If this mismatch was not detected by the *AE* in Check 2, *M* could successfully use the document for illicit authentication.

Figure 2(b) shows an attack scenario, where an existing passport is modified by a forger. After the photos of *A* and *M* are taken in two parallel image data acquisition (IDA) operations, the forger takes a valid passport from *A* and replaces the image in the document with a photo of *M*. Admittedly, this is a very unlikely scenario for modern day ICAO compliant travel documents, but for other photo-ID documents, e.g. company ID cards, this might still be a valid attack. As shown in Figure 2, the "Document generation" step in the pipeline is extended by the "Document Manipulation" step. As a result, the corresponding modeling of the attack is identical to the previous two examples for Step 1 and Check 1. For Step 2, the two specific tuples have to be created. The first one is identical to the one from the previous examples, while the second one describes the extension of this step by forging: (*AE*: document forger; input *ID*: *A*, input *ProS*: *A*, output *ProS'*: *M*; input *PreS*: *M*). The forger transfers *ProS* to *ProS'* by replacing the photograph. After this manipulation, the *ID* and *ProS* show a mismatch, i.e. the document was tampered. In Check 2, the documents integrity check should detect the tampering, otherwise *M* could successfully use the document for illicit authentication in Step 3, since the acting entity in this step (e.g. a customs agent) compares *ProS* and *PreS* and trusts in *ID*.

In Figure 2(c), a face morphing attack is shown. In contrast to all previous examples, Step 1 is extended by an illegitimate addition - the morph generation and the morph quality assurance (QA). The tuples for both sub-steps in the new Step 1 are: for the photographer taking the photos of *A* and *M* (*AE*: photographer; input *ID*: - ; input *ProS*: *A,M*; output *PreS*: *A,M*) and for the morpher (*AE*: morpher; input *ID*: - ; input *ProS*: *A,M*; output *ProS'*: *A||M*; *PreS*: *M*). The photographer takes pictures of two persons (Alice (*A*; an innocent accomplice) and Mallory (*M*; assumedly a wanted criminal who wants a new document that can be used e.g. to cross a border; '*A,M*' in Figure 2) in two parallel IDAs. The morpher creates one face image from two inputs ('*A||M*' in Figure 2). The output image is visually as well as biometrically similar to *A* and *M* and is used by (previously innocent) accomplice *A* to apply for a new passport. If Check 1 does not detect the face morphing operation (i.e. a suitable media forensic detector as discussed in Section 5 is missing), a valid document is generated in Step 2 described by the following tuple: (*AE*: authority; input *ID*: *A*; input *ProS*: *A||M* (the intention of this attack is to create a document that can be used either by *A* or *M*), input *PreS*: *A* (since *M* is assumedly a wanted criminal,

she asks *A* to do the application and document pick-up)). Check 2 performs the same operations as in the previous examples. If no traces of the morphing operation are found (i.e. a suitable media forensic detector is missing), *M* could successfully use the document for illicit authentication in Step 3. Indeed, the acting entity in this step notices that *PreS=M* is a sub-set in *ProS=A||M* (i.e. Mallorys face and the morph are similar enough) and trusts in *ID=A* (which is a (previously) innocent person that should not raise any alarm in this check).

Notice that it might be relevant to distinguish between Alice being a cooperating accomplice (*A_cooperating*) or an innocent victim of an ID theft attempt by face morphing attack (*A_innocent*). This would have consequences for the image data acquisition step and might influence the quality of the morphs. In case of a cooperating accomplice, the photos for *M* and *A_cooperating* could be taken with the same camera, at the same location and identical environmental conditions, while for *A_innocent* the camera, etc. might strongly differ. In our paper this distinction is not necessary.

The difference of the face morphing attacks to the other attacks is that the attack happens before the document generation step and that it enables the (presumably criminal) attacker to obtain a 'clean', valid and un-tampered document issued by the official authority.

In the following section the modeling of face morphing performed here is used as the basis for the in-depth analysis of two different attack realizations and potential media forensic traces that could be used to design and implement media forensic detectors for Checks 1 and 2.

4 IMAGE EDITING HISTORY MODEL – POTENTIAL FORENSIC TRACES

The life-cycle model of photo-ID documents provide us with the idea at which places the forensic checks should be applied to prevent attacks, but does not give any information about which particular forensic checks are required. In order to make a link between a particular type of attack on photo-ID documents and media forensics approaches required at Checks 1 and 2 to prevent the attack, we introduce the image editing history model.

The image editing history model formally describes a current state of a face image by:

1) describing the sequence of editing operations applied to the original camera image to obtain the current image, and

2) aggregating knowledge about which traces are left behind in the image after applying each particular edition operation.

If the editing history of an image is known, the image can be analyzed for artifacts revealing the knowledge about which artifacts are produced by which sequence of editing operations. The aggregated knowledge gives a clue about which traces should be looked for in an image with the unknown editing history to reveal the presence or absence of particular image editing operations in its editing history. Here, the editing history model should support us in making a decision whether a face image is authentic or tampered.

4.1 Formal description of the editing history

The image editing history is represented by a path in the full-connected directed graph with two specific nodes denoting the original (I_0) and the current state of an image I_n (see Figure 3). Other nodes correspond to image states after particular image editing operations. The current image results from the propagation of the original image through the intermediate nodes, one in each layer. The set of image editing operations in each layer is the same. Besides all relevant editing operations, the set includes an 'no op' operation to model the case of no image editing. An edge represents the parameters of the consecutive editing operation. Notice that parameters can also include another image for e.g. *splicing* operations. Formally, a current image is given by the following recursion: I_n = (I_{n-1}, editing operation: E_n, parameters: p_n), I_0 = original image.

Another important component of our model is the set of traces or artifacts that can be found in an image: T = {T_i, i=1..k}.

In order to better describe the relation between an editing operation and traces in the image, we specify our model by introducing three attributes of each editing operation: *preserved*, *altered* and *acquired* characteristics, or more specifically, traces. For instance *cropping* preserves camera-imposed fingerprints and the content of an image, changes the image dimensions and adds no new traces. Camera fingerprint as a trace is considered to be an element in T.

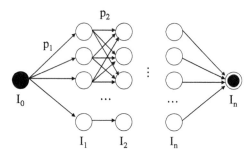

Figure 3: The descriptive image editing history model

The set of image editing operations is divided into the subsets of legitimate and illegitimate operations. We consider an image to be authentic if only legitimate image editing operations are presented in its editing history. A single illegitimate operation in a path makes an image non-authentic. Detecting a non-authentic face image should raise an alarm in Checks as described in Section 4. For the sake of this paper, it is assumed that the set of legitimate operations includes exactly those operations that are foreseen in the ICAO standard for a face image [13] intended to be used in passport generation. These operations are: *cropping, scaling, rotation, down-sampling, white*

balance adjustment, ICC color management transformation, and exactly one *compression* operation.

Each successive operation may destroy traces of previous operations. In the absence of anti-forensics, the illegitimate editing presumably happens at the last step resulting in the fact that the current image contains corresponding traces. However, the traces of illegitimate image editing may be disguised by subsequent legitimate image editing (anti-forensics). For our model, it means that the illegitimate operation becomes more distant from the current state in the editing history and therefore harder to detect. Moreover, one illegitimate operation might compensate the effect of another illegitimate operation so that no traces are left behind, for instance image blurring followed by image sharpening.

An example of a trace left behind by a camera is the color filter array (CFA) interpolation pattern [15], which is either completely or partially destroyed after any illegitimate image editing (as well as some legitimate operations). Therefore, the revealed CFA interpolation pattern indicates the authenticity of an image. The absence of CFA interpolation pattern, however, does not imply non-authenticity of an image. The inconsistent CFA interpolation pattern undoubtedly indicates image *splicing* or copy-move forgery.

By introducing our image history editing model, we want to motivate researchers to use this formalism to gather knowledge about which traces are caused (or destroyed) by which editing operations (or sequences of editing operation).

4.2 Integration to the document life-cycle model

In Figure 4, it is shown how the image editing history model is integrated into the document life-cycle considerations. It is used in Check 1 (and Check 2 as well) to prepare the systematic generation of the classification models required by media forensic detectors at this point.

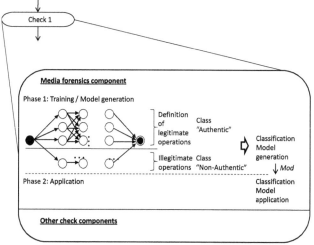

Figure 4: Using the image editing history model within a check routine in the document life-cycle

In Phase 1, the requirements for classification models are carefully defined and corresponding training sets are created. On this basis, the *classification model generation* process produces the classification model *Mod*. In Phase 2, the classification model *Mod* is applied to verify the suitability of the image in Check 1 and the authenticity and integrity of the document in Check 2.

4.3 The editing history of a morphed image

Since morphing can be created in many different ways, there is no one unified image editing history representing morphing attack. In this paper, we focus on two exemplary realizations of a morphing attack: Attack Type I (*warping&blending* the complete image) and Attack Type II (*warping&blending* the face region in the image). These morphing strategies are referred to as complete morph and splicing morph in [5]. The examples of morphed images are illustrated in Figure 5.

The morphing pipeline of the Attack Type I is comprised of five consecutive steps:
1) localization of facial landmarks,
2) blending of landmarks,
3) triangulation based on average landmarks,
4) affine warping of image triangles and
5) alpha-blending of warped images.

Let I^A and I^M be original images, the morphed face image (FM) is then described by the following editing history:

$$FM^{AM} = FM^{MA} = ((I^A, \textit{warping}, \textit{triangles}^A \rightarrow \textit{triangles}^{AM}),$$
$$\textit{blending}, (I^M, \textit{warping}, \textit{triangles}^M \rightarrow \textit{triangles}^{AM}))$$

The relevant editing operation in the image editing history are *warping* and *blending*. The morphed image created by Attack Type I often contain 'ghosting' artifacts resulting from *blending* of not perfectly aligned face regions as well as interpolation artifacts resulting from *warping*. Moreover, *blending* leads to image smoothing and reduction of face details.

The Attack Type II is designed to avoid 'ghosting' artifacts. Here, the *splicing* operation is included in the morphing pipeline. Hence, the pipeline comprises six steps:
1) localization of facial landmarks,
2) cropping of the face region,
3) triangulation based on landmarks,
4) affine warping of image triangles in the face region,
5) alpha-blending of warped face regions and
6) insertion of the blended face into one of the original images.

Formally, the morphed images FM^{AM} and FM^{MA} generated from images I^A and I^M are described by the following editing history:

$$FM^{AM} = (I^A, \textit{splicing},$$
$$((I^A, \textit{cropping}, \textit{landmarks}^A), \textit{blending},$$
$$((I^M, \textit{cropping}, \textit{landmarks}^M), \textit{warping}, \textit{triangles}^M \rightarrow \textit{triangles}^A)))$$
$$FM^{MA} = (I^M, \textit{splicing},$$
$$((I^M, \textit{cropping}, \textit{landmarks}^M), \textit{blending},$$
$$((I^A, \textit{cropping}, \textit{landmarks}^A), \textit{warping}, \textit{triangles}^A \rightarrow \textit{triangles}^M)))$$

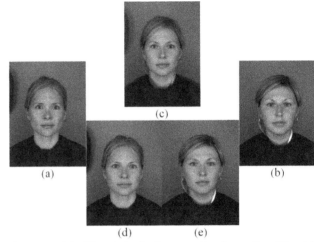

Figure 5: (a), (b) original photographs from the Utrecht ECVP data set; (c) Attack Type I; (d), (e) Attack Type II

From the perspective of image forensics, the latter type of morphing does not differ from image *splicing*. The resulting image bears the characteristics of the original image in the background and the new characteristics of the 'synthetically' generated (here: morphed) face region in the foreground. The reduction of image details still occurs (like in Attack Type I), but only in the face region.

All in all, there are three clues for detecting morphed images created by Attacks Type I and Type II. The first clue is 'ghosting' artifacts which are abundantly presented in the hair region for the Attack Type I and occasionally presented in the eye regions for the Attack Type II. The second clue is the inconsistency between foreground and background regions for the Attack Type II. The third clue is the reduction of image details in the whole image for the Attack Type I and in the face region for the Attack Type II.

In our experiments we rely on the third clue, namely the reduction of image details in the face region as a trace of *blending* operation. This trace is uniform for both types of attack.

5 DESIGN OF OUR MORPHING DETECTOR

The design of the feature space for the morphing detector is based on the idea that the *blending* operation in the morphing pipeline causes the reduction of face details. We quantify this reduction by the number of keypoints in the face region, assuming that the number of keypoints becomes lower after *blending*.

As pre-processing, prior to feature extraction, the face area is segmented as a convex hull of the 68 facial landmarks localized with the *shape_predictor* class from the *dlib* programming library version 19.2 (http://dlib.net/).

The keypoints are the corners extracted by the following algorithms:

1) Scale Invariant Feature Transform (SIFT) [16],

2) Speed Up Robust Feature (SURF) [17],

3) Oriented BRIEF (ORB) [18],

4) Features from Accelerated Segment Test (FAST) [19] and

5) Adaptive and Generic Accelerated Segment Test AGAST [20].

We are using several keypoint detectors, because we assume that the impact of blending operation is different for each detector, some of them should react more sensible to blending operations than others. Due to this, it is likely that more feature detectors deliver more accurate results.

Out next assumption is that the number of edges in the face region becomes lower after *blending*. Therefore, we also count the number of edge pixels after applying the following edge detectors:

6) CannyEdge [21],

7) SobelX [22] and

8) SobelY [22].

We chose the CannyEdge and Sobel operators because they are well known and should have a sensible reaction for image processing techniques, especially for blending operations.

For extracting these eight features, we use functions that are implemented in the *OpenCV* programming library version 3.0 with contributions (http://opencv.org/). We normalize the number of detected keypoints and edge pixels for every feature with the natural logarithm of the face pixels because the number of detected keypoints and edges increases non-linearly with the face size.

Furthermore, we assume that the JPEG compression applied to authentic images will lead to higher reduction of details than that applied to morphed images. This is why we build a lossy self-reference of each sample by applying JPEG compression with the quality set to 75%. Then, the same features are extracted from the face region of the compressed image. In order to quantify the quality loss, we introduce next eight features representing the difference between features extracted from the original image and features extracted from the lossy image. The resulting feature space has 16 dimensions.

To perform the training and testing of our classification model, we using the J48 decision tree (a pruned C4.5 decision tree [2]) from the open source data mining suite WEKA version 3.8.0 with default parameterization [3].

6 EVALUATION

The presentation of the evaluation is split in this paper into the evaluation goals, the setup, a definition of performance measures and the presentation of the classification results.

6.1 Evaluation goals

In order to evaluate the potential impact of introducing media forensic detectors in Check 1 or Check 2 to search for artifacts created in images by morphing operations, a set of experiments is performed for two exemplarily attack realizations. We define four evaluation goals:

G_1: The accuracy estimation of the initial detector (i.e. combination of feature space and classifier) for two exemplary attack realizations by stratified cross-validation on our proprietary dataset

G_2: Estimation of the generalization ability of our classification model trained for the detector in G_1 by testing it with a large dataset derived from a publicly available database of face images

G_3: Estimation of the impact of legitimate post-processing operations (including passport scaling) on the detector performance

G_4: Estimation of the impact of illegitimate post-processing operations (anti-forensics) on the detector performance

The goal G_1 represents a test in which the detector is tested under perfect "laboratory" conditions. The goals G_2, G_3 and G_4 are intended to reproduce more realistic conditions with different training and test sets (G_2) with addition of six exemplarily selected post-processing operations that are allowed by the ICAO standard [13] (G_3) as well as with addition of two exemplarily selected illegitimate operations (G_4).

6.2 Evaluation setup

For our evaluations goals G_1-G_4, we apply supervised learning to train a two-class classification model *Mod* for detecting morphed images (here images that show traces of *blending* operations in their editing history). The first class "Authentic" includes 1000 face images of 50 different persons (20 face images each) that were acquired in our laboratory and were not modified. The images were taken with different cameras and parameters (see Table 1). For each of the three camera models we used two different instances.

Table 1: Cameras and acquisition parameters used for the training data for G1-G4 (*NL = Nikkor Lens)

Camera (lens)	Resolution	ISO-value
2x Canon EOS 1200D	2304x3456	100, 400
(EF 50mm f/2.5 Compact Macro)	1728x2592	100, 400
2x Nikon D 3300	2000x2992	100, 400
(NL*: AF-S50mmf/1.8G)		
2x Nikon Coolpix A100	1704x2272	125, 400
	1200x1600	125, 400

The second class "Morphing" includes 1000 morphed face images of two different types, namely 335 images for the Attack Type I and 665 images for the Attack Type II. The higher number of samples for the latter is explained by the fact that for a pair of original images one morphed image can be created for the Attack Type I and two morphed images for the Attack Type II. We keep equal numbers of training samples in classes "Authentic" and "Morphing" to train the unbiased classifier.

Considering the pair of images I^A and I^M from the class "Authentic" as a source for morphing, the formal description of morphed images $FM^{morphed,I,AM}$, $FM^{morphed,II,AM}$ and $FM^{morphed,II,MA}$ is given in accordance with our image editing history model as follows:

$FM^{morphed,I}$ = $FM^{morphed,I,AM}$ = $FM^{morphed,I,MA}$ = ((I^A, *warping*, triangles^A), *blending*, (I^M, *warping*, triangles^M))

$FM^{morphed,II,AM}$ = (I^A, *splicing*,
((I^A, *cropping*, landmarks^A), *blending*,
((I^M, *cropping*, landmarks^M), *warping*, triangles^M→triangles^A)))

$FM^{morphed,II,MA}$ = (I^M, *splicing*,
((I^M, *cropping*, landmarks^M), *blending*,
((I^A, *cropping*, landmarks^A), *warping*, triangles^A→triangles^M)))

We double the number of training samples in both classes by adding the same images scaled to the passport format. The passport scaling includes the following steps: face detection, cropping of the face region and scaling to 413x531 pixels. The face region is detected using Viola-Jones face detector [23] from the OpenCV programming library. The applied Haar-cascade is *haarcascade_frontalface_default*. The formal description of the resulting images $I^{authentic,Passport}$, $FM^{morphed,I,Passport}$, $FM^{morphed,II,AM,Passport}$ and $FM^{morphed,II,MA,Passport}$ is given in accordance with our image editing history model as follows:

$I^{authentic,Passport}$ = (($I^{authentic}$, *cropping*, face_box), *scale*, 413x531)

$FM^{morphed,I,Passport}$ = (($FM^{morphed,I}$, *cropping*, face_box), *scale*, 413x531)

$FM^{morphed,II,AM,Passport}$ = (($FM^{morphed,II,AM}$, *cropping*, face_box), *scale*, 413x531)

$FM^{morphed,II,MA,Passport}$ = (($FM^{morphed,II,MA}$, *cropping*, face_box), *scale*, 413x531)

Hence, the classification model used for our evaluation goals (G_1-G_4) is trained based on 2000 "Authentic" samples and 2000 "Morphing" samples (1000 camera-native and 1000 passport-specific image scales in each class).

Passport-scaled images are included into the training set to better fit the real-world requirements (i.e. application for a passport or its usage). The camera-native images represent the expected input at Check 1 while the passport-specific images represent the expected input at Check 2 for the face morphing attack scenario described in Figure 2(c). We assume that the classification model *Mod* is more robust for detection of morphed images even after the image quality loss caused by passport scaling which is one of the most severe, legitimate editing operations during the creation of a face image based authentication token like a passport.

In order to evaluate our classification model, we perform two tests (T_1 and T_2) using the J48 decision tree (see Section 5) from the open source data mining suite WEKA version 3.8.0 with default parameterization [3].

The evaluation goal G_1 is addressed in T_1 that is based on 10-fold cross-validation to evaluate the reference classification accuracy, achieved by applying *Mod* to our set of face images. The second test T_2 addresses evaluation goals G_2, G_3 and G_4 to determine whether the model generalizes well with the test data of different origin. To this end, three test datasets (TDS) were generated based on Utrecht ECVP (http://pics.psych.stir.ac.uk/2D_face_sets.htm) face dataset:

TDS^{authentic}: 75 non-smiling Utrecht genuine face images

TDS^{morphed,I}: 1326 AttackType I morphs created from TDS^{authentic}

TDS^{morphed,II}: 2614 AttackType II morphs created from TDS^{authentic}

The initial image editing history of these images is the same as the history of the images used for the training of the model *Mod* without passport scaling. In addition, we simulate legitimate post-processing usually performed by photographers (*scaling, cropping, rotation, passport-scaling*; G_3) as well as selected anti-forensic post-processing (*unsharp masking, median filtering*; G_4). We apply post-processing (using StirTrace version 4.0; https://sourceforge.net/projects/stirtrace) to the test datasets to see whether the created artifacts have an influence on the detection performance. Notice that, except for the passport-scaling, post-processing was not included in training, to mimic a detection scenario that is closer to anomaly detection than classical supervised classification. Table 2 shows the parameters.

Table 2: StirTrace parameters (post-processing for G_3 and G_4)

Applied post-processing	Parameters
Scaling	75%, 110%
Cropping	75%
Rotation	4°, -3°
Passport-scaling	413x531
Median filtering	3x3 kernel size
Unsharp masking	5x5 kernel size

6.3 Performance measures

The standard performance measures for two-class classification systems are false positive rate (FPR) and false negative rate (FNR) which are also referred to as *error of the first kind* and *error of the second kind* respectively. For our detection system, we interpret "positive" as "authentic" and "negative" as "morphed". Therefore, the FPR represents the likelihood of classifying a morphed image as an authentic image and the FNR represents the likelihood of classifying an authentic image as a morphed image. We also report the complementary values, namely TPR = 1 − FNR as the likelihood of correctly classifying authentic images and TNR = 1 − FPR as the likelihood of correctly classifying morphed images. The combination of FPR and FNR (or its complementary value TPR) completely describes detection performance of a system. We also report the classification accuracy as the likelihood of making correct decision regardless of image class.

6.4 Classification results

In the first test T_1, we evaluate the reference detection performance of our model *Mod* with 10-fold cross-validation (G_1). The results are presented in Table 3. As can be read from the table, the TPR is equal to 90.1% while FPR is equal to 7.1%. The classification accuracy of *Mod* is 91.5%. Notice that T_1 gives no insight into the generalization performance of *Mod*.

Table 3: Results of the first test T_1, 10-fold cross-validation for the classification model *Mod* with the J48 classifier (G_1)

		Classified as:	
		Authentic	Morphing
Ground Truth:	Authentic	**90.1%** (TPR)	9.9% (FNR)
	Morphing	7.1% (FPR)	**92.9%** (TNR)

The evaluation goals G_2- G_4 are addressed together in the second test T_2. The results of the test are presented in Table 4.

For G_2, considering authentic instances TDS^{authentic}, the TPR is equal to 81.3%. For the sets of morphed images TDS^{morphed,I} and TDS^{morphed,II} the FPR values are equal to 10% and 2 % respectively. Even though these results are slightly worse than the results achieved for G_1, we state that our morphing detector can generalize to some extent.

After legitimate post-processing operations (G_3), the TPR values dramatically decrease except for the case of *down-scaling*. Here, the TPR increases from 81.3% (without post-processing) to 84%. Surprisingly, the FPR values also decrease except for the case of *up-scaling*. Here, the FPR values of TDS^{morphed,I} and TDS^{morphed,II} increase from 10% to 12% and from 2% to 4.7% respectively. Generally, the relatively low TPR and FPR values in the experiment for G_3 indicate that our classifier tends to classify most of the input images as morphs meaning that the considered post-processing operations has the similar effect on the extracted features as morphing.

Two illegitimate post-processing operations (G_4) have different effect on classification performance of *Mod*. After applying *median* filtering, TPR as well as FPR values

dramatically decrease. The TPR decreases from 81.3% (without post-processing) to 44% while FPR values of TDS^{morphed,I} and TDS^{morphed,II} decrease from 10% to 2.1% and from 2% to 1.2% respectively. Here, the same conclusion can be made as for the legitimate post-processing, namely our classifier tends to classify most of the input images as morphs. Indeed, *median filtering* blurs the images and this effect is nearly the same to *blending* in morphed images. The number of keypoints and edges decreases so that authentic images are often classified as morphed images. In contrast, after applying *unsharp masking*, TPR as well as FPR values dramatically increase. The TPR increases from 81.3% (without post-processing) to 95% while FPR values of TDS^{morphed,I} and TDS^{morphed,II} increase from 10% to 53.4% and from 2% to 15.6% respectively. This implies that our classifier tends to classify most of the input images as authentic images. It can be explained by the fact that due to the artificially generated sharpness effect, the number of keypoints and edges increases so that morphed images are often classified as authentic images.

Table 4: Results of the second test T_2 for the classification model *Mod* with the J48 classifier (G_2, G_3, G_4); correct decisions are highlighted in bold

Evaluation Goal	Test data sets	Post-processing (parameter)	Classification results for *Mod*	
			authentic	morphed
G_2	TDS^{authentic}	-	**81.3%**	18.7%
	TDS^{morphed,I}		10.0%	**90.0%**
	TDS^{morphed,II}		2.0%	**98.0%**
G_3	TDS^{authentic}	Passport Scale (413x516)	**68.0%**	32.0%
	TDS^{morphed,I}		8.9%	**91.1%**
	TDS^{morphed,II}		0.7%	**99.3%**
	TDS^{authentic}	Cropping (75%)	46.7%	53.3%
	TDS^{morphed,I}		0.8%	**99.2%**
	TDS^{morphed,II}		0.01%	**99.9%**
	TDS^{authentic}	Scaling (75%)	**84.0%**	16.0%
	TDS^{morphed,I}		8.2%	**91.8%**
	TDS^{morphed,II}		0.8%	**99.2%**
	TDS^{authentic}	Scaling (110%)	**78.7%**	21.3%
	TDS^{morphed,I}		12%	**88.0%**
	TDS^{morphed,II}		4.7%	**95.3%**
	TDS^{authentic}	Rotation (-3°)	**65.3%**	34.7%
	TDS^{morphed,I}		3.0%	**97.0%**
	TDS^{morphed,II}		0.9%	**99.1%**
	TDS^{authentic}	Rotation (4°)	**60.0%**	40.0%
	TDS^{morphed,I}		3.0%	**97.0%**
	TDS^{morphed,II}		1.4%	**98.6%**
G_4	TDS^{authentic}	Median (3x3)	44.0%	56.0%
	TDS^{morphed,I}		2.1%	**97.9%**
	TDS^{morphed,II}		1.2%	**98.8%**
	TDS^{authentic}	Unsharp Masking (5x5)	**95.0%**	5.0%
	TDS^{morphed,I}		53.4%	**46.6%**
	TDS^{morphed,II}		15.6%	**84.4%**

7 SUMMARY, CONCLUSION AND FUTURE WORK

The main contribution of our paper is a novel and relevant method for modeling the application context of face morphing attacks and designing the appropriate media forensic detectors. The introduced life-cycle model for photo-ID documents is used to describe and compare different attack classes and to highlight the severity of the threat imposed by face morphing attacks. Furthermore, it allows for defining the requirements for document checking. Our model of the morphing attack shows that the threat can be reduced by preventing a user from submitting images into Document Generation processes. We recommend that the photographs are taken by officers at the application desk, which is common practice in some countries, but requires changes in other national legislations. Another recommendation is to apply media forensic detectors within the Document Generation and Document Usage processes (Check 1 and 2 respectively).

Our second contribution is the image editing history model that allows for a formal, systematic and fine-granular description of morphing attack realizations and also allows for depicting traces or image anomalies resulting from image editing operations. We use this model to compare different face morphing attack realizations and to derive the engineering requirement for morphing detectors.

Summarizing the test results of the empirical evaluations presented in the precious section it can be said that all applied post-processing techniques have an influence on classification results, especially the selected anti-forensic approaches: *unsharp masking* and *median filtering*. Nonetheless, our morphing detection approach yields accurate results and is robust to legitimate post-processing.

Summarizing the results of our four evaluation goals, it can be mentioned that the tests with the stratified cross-validation (G_1) as well as the tests with training and testing on independent image sets from completely different sources (G_2) show very high average detection performances. A certain degree of robustness of our morphing detector to legitimate post-processing operations is demonstrated (G_3). For the illegitimate post-processing operations and counter-forensics, the evaluation goal (G_4) can be considered to be partially fulfilled.

As one step in future work, the re-design of the media forensic detectors as a two-stage process would strongly benefit the system performance. In the first step, specific operations in the image editing history would have to be detected to allow for the selection of optimized face morph attack detection models in the second step. One example of operations that could be covered in the first step would be a detection of *passport-scaling* as used within this paper, which would allow to select for stage 2 models that are trained on either original-sized or passport-scaled images (as assumed inputs for Check 1 and Check 2 respectively). A more significant first stage analysis would determine whether the image used for the application is a scan or original image (esp. for Check 1) because the scanning process has significant impact to all image statistics and would therefore require separately trained models.

The results presented signify that the used feature space is sub-optimal to cover the *blending* accurately. Hence, additional feature design considerations are required to increase the detection performance. Besides using extended feature spaces the classification scheme should be modified (or extended). In this first approach the distribution of errors is balanced between the two classes during the training of the classifier. This inevitably results in a large number of authentic images being classified as potentially morphed images, which currently renders the detection method useless for any practical use in forensics. However, some classifiers, such as WEKA's J48 implementation [3], provide class membership probabilities for each processed feature vector. This would allow for determining Likelyhood Ratios (see e.g. [24]) which are increasingly used in forensic sciences and help to express uncertainties in binary decisions. Here, the membership for each class is treated as disjunct hypotheses. Based on the determined Likelihood Ratio the detectors might be tuned to alert the operator only if a pre-defined threshold of certainty is achieved and thus reducing the false alarm rate by accepting an increased miss rate. In order to determine such a threshold, it is necessary to analyze the predicted class probabilities in future work. Based on a preliminary analysis of the prediction probabilities in a tenfold stratified cross-validation we can assume that an extension of the feature space and a combination with other detector is still necessary in order to improve the accuracy of the detection.

Additionally, besides the *blending*, further operations that are relevant for face morphing attacks have to be identified and covered in future feature space designs. An example is the *interpolation* that arises during the geometry correction (*warping*). Additionally, *splicing* operation detection might be used reveal traces of face morphing attacks.

A further example for an important operation that would have to be covered in future research is *print and scan* operations. In many countries worldwide these play an important role in document application and creation processes. Additionally, they have a severe impact to images undergoing these operations, making forensic analyses on manipulations that might have occurred to the images prior to the printing even harder. Therefore, they would have to be evaluated on one hand as a legitimate pre-processing operation that has to be compensated for in the Checks (similar to the passport scale discussed above) and on the other hand as a blind (untargeted or context insensitive) anti-forensics method – similar to the Stirtrace operations considered within this paper.

Besides these blind methods, future research will have to look also in considerations on targeted anti-forensics (attack that know the feature space used in the detector).

In general every new feature space / detector for face morphing attacks should be evaluated using the methodology introduced here, precisely modeling the image manipulation history for the data used and looking into the robustness to legitimate operations and counter-forensics (blind as well as targeted) as well as the fragility against morphing traces.

It is obvious that such only such methodological work together with tests on a much wider scale are necessary to enable the usage of detectors in field application versions of Check 1 and 2.

ACKNOWLEDGMENTS

The work in this paper has been funded in part by the German Federal Ministry of Education and Research (BMBF) through the research programme ANANAS under the contract no. FKZ: 16KIS0509K. We wish to thank our colleague Robert Altschaffel for the discussions on modeling concepts that contributed to our work in sections 3 and 5 of this paper. We would like to thank our anonymous reviewers for their input, which helped shaping this paper.

REFERENCES

[1] M. Ferrara, A. Franco, D. Maltoni. 2014. The magic passport. In *Proc. IEEE Int. Joint Conf. on Biometrics*. IEEE, pp. 1-7.

[2] Ross Quinlan. 1993. *C4.5: Programs for Machine Learning*. Morgan Kaufmann Publishers, San Mateo, CA.

[3] M. Hall, E. Frank, G. Holmes, B. Pfahringer, P. Reutemann, I.H. Witten. 2009. The WEKA data mining software: An update. In *SIGKDD Explorations* 11(1), pp. 10-18.

[4] M. Ferrara, A. Franco, D. Maltoni. 2016. On the Effects of Image Alterations on Face Recognition Accuracy. *Face Recognition Across the Electromagnetic Spectrum*, T. Bourlai (Ed.). Springer, pp. 195-222.

[5] A. Makrushin, T. Neubert and J. Dittmann. 2017. Automatic Generation and Detection of Visually Faultless Facial Morphs. In *Proc. 12th international Conference on Computer Vision Theory and Applications*, February 2017.

[6] M. Hildebrandt, T. Neubert, A. Makrushin, J. Dittmann. 2017. Benchmarking Face Morphing Forgery Detection: Application of StirTrace for Impact - Simulation of Different Processing Steps. *Proc. International Workshop on Biometrics and Forensics* (IWBF2017). Chang-Tsun Li (Ed.), April 4th - 5th, 2017, Coventry, UK, University of Warwick, UK.

[7] R. Raghavendra, K. Raja, C. Busch. 2016. Detecting Morphed Facial Images. In *Proceedings of 8th IEEE International Conference on Biometrics: Theory, Applications and Systems* (BTAS-2016), September 6-9, Niagra Falls, USA.

[8] U. Scherhag, R. Raghavendra, K.B. Raja, M. Gomez-Barrero, C. Rathgeb, C. Busch. 2017. On the Vulnerability of Face Recognition Systems Towards Morphed Face Attacks. In *Proc. International Workshop on Biometrics and Forensics* (IWBF2017). Chang-Tsun Li (Ed.), April 4th - 5th, 2017, Coventry, UK, University of Warwick, UK.

[9] M. Gomez-Barrero, C. Rathgeb, U. Scherhag, C. Busch. 2017. Is Your Biometric System Robust to Morphing Attacks? In *Proc. International Workshop on Biometrics and Forensics* (IWBF2017). Chang-Tsun Li (Ed.), April 4th - 5th, 2017, Coventry, UK, University of Warwick, UK.

[10] REWIND Deliverable D3.1.2011. *State-of-the-art on multimedia footprint detection*. Technical Report of the REWIND Project (EU Grant Agreement No. 268478).

[11] W. Wei, L. Sun, D. Tang, Y. Zhao, H. Li. 2012. A Survey of Passive Image Forensics. In *Proc. Network Computing and Information Security: Second International Conference* (NCIS 2012), Shanghai, China, December 7-9, Springer Berlin Heidelberg, pp. 45-55.

[12] A. Oliveira, P. Ferrara, A. De Rosa, A. Piva, M. Barni, S. Goldenstein, Z. Dias, A. Rocha. 2016. Multiple Parenting Identification in Image Phylogeny. *IEEE Transactions on Information Forensics and Security*, Vol. 11, No. 2, Feb.2016.

[13] A. Wolf. 2016. *Portrait Quality (Reference Facial Images for MRTD)*. Version: 0.06 ICAO, Published by authority of the Secretary General.

[14] International Organization for Standardization (ISO). 2016. *ISO/IEC 30107-1:2016 - Information technology -- Biometric presentation attack detection*. ISO, 2016.

[15] A. E. Dirik and N. Memon. 2009. Image tamper detection based on demosaicing artifacts. In *Proceedings of the 2009 IEEE International Conference on Image Processing* (ICIP 2009), 2009.

[16] David G. Low. 1999. Object Recognition from Local Scale-Invariant Features. In *Proc. of the International Conference on Computer Vision*.

[17] H. Bay, T. Tuytelaars and L.V. Gool. 2006. SURF: Speeded Up Robust Features. In *Proc. 9th European Conference on Computer Vision*, Springer Verlag.

[18] E. Rublee, V. Rabaud, K Konolige and G. Bradski. 2011. ORB: an efficient alternative to SIFT or SURF. *IEEE International Conference on Computer Vision* (ICCV), (2011)

[19] E. Rosten and T. Drummond "Fusing Points and Lines for High Performance Tracking" (2005) IEEE International Conference on Computer Vision. 2: 1508–1511 DOI:10.1109/ICCV.2005.104

[20] E. Mair, G.Hager, D. Burschka, M. Suppa and G. Hirzinger. 2010. *Adaptive and Generic Corner Detection Based on the Accelerated Segment Test*. Online: http://www6.in.tum.de/Main/Publications/20c.pdf last access: 02/07/2017

[21] J. Canny. 1986. A Computational Approach To Edge Detection. *IEEE Trans. Pattern Analysis and Machine Intelligence*, 8(6): pp.679–698.

[22] N. Kanopoulos, N. Vasanthavada, R.L. Baker. 1988. Design of an image edge detection filter using the Sobel operator. *IEEE Journal of Solid-State Circuits* (Volume: 23, Issue: 2, Apr 1988) DOI: 10.1109/4.996

[23] P. Viola, M.J. Jones. 2004. Robust real-time face detection. *International journal of computer vision* 57 (2), pp.137-154.

[24] D. Ramos-Castro, J. Gonzalez-Rodriguez, C. Champod, J. Fierrez-Aguilar, J. Ortega-Garcia. 2005. Between-Source Modelling for Likelihood Ratio Computation in Forensic Biometric Recognition. In *Proc. Audio- and Video-Based Biometric Person Authentication* (AVBPA 2005), LNCS 3546, Springer, pp. 1080-1089.

The Square Root Law of Steganography:
Bringing Theory Closer to Practice

Andrew D. Ker

Department of Computer Science
University of Oxford
Oxford OX1 3QD, UK
adk@cs.ox.ac.uk

ABSTRACT

There are two interpretations of the term 'square root law of steganography'. As a *rule of thumb*, that the secure capacity of an imperfect stegosystem scales only with the square root of the cover size (not linearly as for perfect stegosystems), it acts as a robust guide in multiple steganographic domains. As a *mathematical theorem*, it is unfortunately limited to artificial models of covers that are a long way from real digital media objects: independent pixels or first-order stationary Markov chains. It is also limited to models of embedding where the changes are uniformly distributed and, for the most part, independent.

This paper brings the theoretical square root law closer to the practice of digital media steganography, by extending it to cases where the covers are Markov Random Fields, including inhomogeneous Markov chains and Ising models. New proof techniques are required. We also consider what a square root law should say about adaptive embedding, where the changes are not uniformly located, and state a conjecture.

ACM Reference format:
Andrew D. Ker. 2017. The Square Root Law of Steganography: Bringing Theory Closer to Practice. In *Proceedings of IH&MMSec '17, June 20–22, 2017, Philadelphia, PA, USA, , 13 pages.*
DOI: http://dx.doi.org/10.1145/3082031.3083235

1 INTRODUCTION

The phrase 'square root law of steganography' was first coined in [26], to mean that steganographic payloads should scale with the square root of the size of the cover unless truly perfect steganography is available. It was inspired by small-scale experimental evidence in [16], heuristic theoretical predictions from [17], and a first mathematical theorem in [18].

A square root law has significant consequences for the practice of steganography, since it implies that an imperfect steganographic channel has zero 'rate': the more payload

is sent, the more sparsely it must be spread. The covert channel never completely dries up, but transmission times grow quadratically with the total payload ([19] seems to be the only literature on how practically to live within a square root law). This is especially so since perfect steganography is confined to extremely low-bandwidth scenarios, and is not achieved in digital media [24].

The theoretical work underpinning the square root law [2, 11, 18, 20–23] applies to highly artificial models of steganography, where the covers are typically assumed to have independent and identically distributed elements, or which form a stationary Markov chain, and an embedding operation that applies independently and identically to each location. We will survey the literature more thoroughly in Sect. 2.

The first proper experimental validation of a square root law was performed in [26], which analyzed detection accuracy versus cover and payload size for then-leading steganography and steganalysis algorithms, in raw and JPEG images. Close adherence to a square root capacity law was observed, even though pixels in digital images are far from independent or 1st-order Markov. To our knowledge, this 2008 study has yet to be repeated for modern image steganography and steganalysis, or for adaptive steganography with a knowing attacker [6], but in the linguistic domain the same law *has* been exhibited recently for adaptive steganography [35]. On the square root law's robustness, the survey [24] said

> 'What is remarkable about the square root law is that, although both asymptotic and proved only for artificial sources, it is robust and manifests in real life. This is despite the fact that ... empirical sources do not match artificial models.'

Our aim is to widen considerably the scope of artificial models for which a square root law holds, bringing the theory closer to the practice of digital media steganography.

In Sect. 2 we survey and collect existing square root laws into a common notation. In Sect. 3 we propose a different information-theoretic approach to demonstrating square root laws, and prove a lemma. Section 4 contains our main results, a new square root law for a Markov Random Field (MRF) cover model: one half applies to very broad classes of MRFs, the other to a more restricted class, but wide enough (Sect. 5) to include both inhomogeneous Markov chains and Ising models. In Sect. 6 we discuss how a square root law should be modified for *adaptive embedding*, where the embedding changes are neither uniformly located, nor necessarily independent. We conjecture on the result that might be shown using an extension of our techniques. In Sect. 7 we draw conclusions and suggest further research.

2 SQUARE ROOT LAWS

The first publication to analyze asymptotic steganography capacity [18] set the format for square root laws. They concern covers of size n and a payload size, dependent on the cover size, $m(n)$. They make certain assumptions about the probability distributions of cover and stego objects. Under such assumptions, the laws give a *critical rate* for $m(n)$, which we will call $r(n)$[1]. Then

(i) if m is above the critical rate, $m(n)/r(n) \to \infty$, then *an asymptotically perfect detector exists*;

(ii) if m is below the critical rate, $m(n)/r(n) \to 0$, then *every detector is asymptotically random*.

We call (i) the *upper bound*, and (ii) the *lower bound*, on asymptotic payload size, and will make the asymptotic detection notions more precise in a moment.

Typically, if n is the number of embedding locations in the cover, and steganography is performed without *source coding* [10], the critical rate is $r = \sqrt{n}$, hence the name *square root law*. Source coding can increase this to $r = \sqrt{n} \log n$, but not beyond: we will consider this case in Sect. 6.

Let us fix some notation that can unify the square root laws we discuss. They concern a binary classification model of steganalysis: the detector has an observation X_n drawn from either a cover distribution $\mathcal{P}_n$, or a stego distribution $\mathcal{Q}_n^m$; they wish to determine which distribution it came from with low false positive (mistaking $\mathcal{P}_n$ for $\mathcal{Q}_n^m$) and false negative (vice versa) error probabilities. Here X_n is some n-dimensional object consisting of perhaps n pixels, transform coefficients, frames, or other type depending on the medium (but in this paper we will just call them 'pixels'). We have emphasised that the stego distribution depends on the payload size m.

A *detector* has to be parameterized by the size of the object it is considering: think of a sequence of sets $(A_1, A_2, \ldots)$ determining the positive classifications for each cover size; if observation $X_n \in A_n$ then X_n is believed to come from $\mathcal{Q}_n^m$ rather than $\mathcal{P}_n$. To say that *an asymptotically perfect detector exists* means that there is such a sequence with

$$\mathrm{P}_{X_n \sim \mathcal{P}_n}[X_n \in A_n] + \mathrm{P}_{X_n \sim \mathcal{Q}_n^m}[X_n \notin A_n] \to 0 \text{ as } n \to \infty, \quad (1)$$

which is of course equivalent to requiring that both the false positive and false negative rates tend to zero. We do not enforce a condition on *how fast* they must tend to zero, which will depend on how much $m(n)$ exceeds the critical rate $r(n)$. In square root laws, (1) cannot hold if the cover and stego distributions are not different: we emphasise that square root laws do not apply to *perfect steganography* where $\mathcal{P}_n$ and $\mathcal{Q}_n^m$ are identical. Therefore they must impose what we shall call a *no free bits* condition,[2] enforcing some difference

---

[1]This is not a *rate* in the signal processing sense, since it is almost never linear in n.

[2]The payload bits are not *free* because each modification induces a change to the distribution, and therefore incurs a distortion *cost*.

between $\mathcal{P}_n$ and $\mathcal{Q}_n^m$: this condition depends on the cover model being studied.

To say that *every detector is asymptotically random* means

$$\mathrm{P}_{X_n \sim \mathcal{P}_n}[X_n \in A_n] + \mathrm{P}_{X_n \sim \mathcal{Q}_n^m}[X_n \notin A_n] \to 1 \text{ as } n \to \infty, \quad (2)$$

i.e. the detector's advantage over random guessing tends to zero. Such a property cannot hold if there are regions with no uncertainty in the cover distribution, so square root laws must impose what we shall call a *no determinism* condition, the form of which depends on the cover model. It will ensure that every cover has a probability bounded away from zero.

2.1 Existing Square Root Laws

Let us survey the existing literature on square root laws, identifying the cover and embedding models along with the *no determinism* and *no free bits* conditions on them. Note that the asymptotic results have not always been stated exactly in the form of (1) and (2) but are equivalent, or can be adapted, to them.

The first publication [18] is an outlier. It concerns steganography in n independent objects and makes the strong assumption that the detector reduces each to a *one-dimensional* continuous observation; the effect of an embedding operation in one cover is to shift this observation, in proportion to the payload embedded (which enforces a *no free bits* condition). This is a simple abstraction of quantitative steganalysis [30], but not very realistic. To make proof in [18] work, the observations must be independent and the second derivative of their log density bounded below. The *no determinism* condition is that the support of these observations is infinite.

The simplest square root law of the type we study here, single objects with n pixels, is found in [20]. The cover model $\mathcal{P}_n$ consists of pixels which are independent and identically distributed discrete random variables with mass function $p(x)$. There are two common embedding models:

(a) replace a uniformly-chosen m out of n pixels, or

(b) independently with probability $\frac{m}{n}$ replace each pixel,

by random variables with mass function $q(x)$. (a) is a good model for simple uncoded embedding operations such as bit flipping; (b) is not a good model for a fixed payload, but it is rather easier to analyze because the stego pixels remain independent. The *no free bits* condition is that p and q differ. The *no determinism* condition is that $p(x)$ is nonzero for all x. Both cases (a) and (b) are proved in [20] (Thms. 2 and 1, respectively). The case (b) is extended to independent but not identically distributed pixels in [23, Thm. 2].

The proofs of these results depend critically on independence between the n elements in $\mathcal{P}_n$. This may be a reasonable model for batch steganography (the n elements are separate objects) with a fixed cover source, but it is absurd for pixels or transform coefficients in a digital image, or frames from audio or video. In [11] the cover distribution $\mathcal{P}_n$ is generalized to a stationary finite-valued Markov chain. It is required that its transition matrix contain no zeros, which functions as a conditional *no determinism* criterion. The embedding (termed 'mutually independent embedding') is of the type (b), above, and the *no free bits* condition is that the second order co-occurrence probabilities are not preserved by the embedding process [11, Assumption 3].

A different generalization can be made to account for *source coding* in the embedding process [13], which every modern stegosystem should employ [24]. Source coding has two effects on square root laws: it may cause embedding changes that are not independent, and the number of embedding changes is sublinear in the size of the payload. We will discuss the former in Sect. 6. For the latter, the critical rate is increased from $r(n) = \sqrt{n}$ to $r(n) = \sqrt{n} \log n$ (rate-distortion bounds show that it cannot be increased further). A square root law for source coding was proved in [21], for the independent pixel model. The *no free bits* and *no determinism* conditions are the same as in [20].

The above results all assume that the detector has perfect knowledge of both (a) the cover distribution $\mathcal{P}_n$, and (b) the embedding process and payload size m, which gives perfect knowledge of $\mathcal{Q}_n^m$. It is not difficult to generalize them to the case where m is unknown (although such proofs have not been published) but the case where $\mathcal{P}_n$ is imperfectly known has proved more challenging, in part because the information theoretic machinery does not deal well with compound hypotheses. In the case of an extremely simple i.i.d. Bernoulli cover model, where the Bernoulli parameter is learned empirically, a modified square root law is proved in [22]: here, the critical rate depends on the amount of training data available to the detector, but the square root order is maintained as long as the amount of training data is at least linear in the amount of testing data. There is investigation of a highly artificial nonstationary version in [23]. To our knowledge there has been no further progress on square root laws where the detector has imperfect knowledge. In this work we will confine our attention to the perfect knowledge case, but return to it for future study.

Finally, there is a square root law for steganography in continuous noisy channels, [2]. There is not space to re-state the result here, but we note that what seem major differences with the previous models (the signal is continuous; there is no pre-existing cover; both the receiver and the detector receive the sender's signal subject to different, independent, additive Gaussian noise) are not so great on closer examination. The noise functions as a cover, the *no free bits* condition is enforced by additivity of the signal, and the *no determinism* condition by nonzero noise amplitude. The proof of the upper bound is a close continuous analogue of the i.i.d. discrete case. For the lower bound, as well as a continuous analogue of the information theoretic arguments for the discrete case, it is also necessary to construct a codebook with enough robustness to defeat the noise.

We should briefly discuss some non-square root capacity results in the literature. These are linear capacity laws for perfect steganography [3, 5, 31, 34]. Such systems are closer to *cover generation* than the *cover modification* paradigm we consider. If the cover source is completely known the embedder will mimic it, or otherwise they learn about it empirically. These systems have the opposite of a *no free bits* condition:

either exactly or asymptotically, all payload bits are 'free', because stego objects match the cover distribution. However, we stress that systems are only perfect *for a particular cover model* (i.i.d. in the case of [3, 5, 34], k-order Markov in the case of [31]). If the true cover source deviates even slightly from the artificial model, this could be exploited (with exponentially vanishing error rates) by a knowledgeable detector. Perhaps this explains why (imperfect) cover modification is overwhelming dominant for digital media steganography, and square root laws are observed in practice.

We argue that the largest gap between theory of published square root laws and the practice of multimedia steganography is the cover model. The most complex so far analyzed is a first-order Markov source which, although having simple memory, is a poor model for images because of its one-dimensional nature. Although [11] claims that the result can be generalized to a Markov chain of overlapping patches, it is not clear that this is true: the *no determinism* condition bans zeros in the transition matrix, which would have to be present in a transition matrix of overlapping patches. In any case, it still would not model two-dimensional dependence as fully as, say, a Markov Random Field. At a stretch one might model a digital video as a one-dimensional chain of frames (a Markov version of the batch steganography model), but we know from video compression that inter-frame dependence is long-range and bidirectional.

The main focus of this work is to prove a square root law for a wide class of multidimensional covers, with almost arbitrary finite-range dependence between the elements. This includes inhomogeneous Markov chains and some $d \geq 2$-dimension Ising models. We will do so in Sect. 4.

Furthermore, we would wish to combine such a cover model with an embedding operation that permits source coding. At present, the results of [21] and [11] cannot easily be fused. Now a *no determinism* cover condition seems too strong: if parts of the cover are deterministic (too risky to change) they will simply be avoided by the embedder, which is possible if source coding is employed. We should only require that *enough* cover locations satisfy a (conditional) no determinism condition. This must be part of a square root law for *adaptive steganography*, whose form we discuss briefly in Sect. 6.

3 TOTAL VARIATION

Typically the upper bound of a square root law (recall: if m is above the critical rate then an asymptotically perfect detector exists) is proved by construction. A detector is proposed, and its error rates bounded using tail inequalities. Typically the lower bound (recall: if m is below the critical rate then every detector is asymptotically random) is proved by showing that $D_{\mathrm{KL}}(X \sim \mathcal{P}_n, X \sim \mathcal{Q}_n^m) \to 0$, where

$$D_{\mathrm{KL}}(X \sim \mathcal{P}, X \sim \mathcal{Q}) = \sum_{x \in \mathcal{X}} \mathrm{P}_{\mathcal{P}}[X = x] \log\left(\frac{\mathrm{P}_{\mathcal{P}}[X=x]}{\mathrm{P}_{\mathcal{Q}}[X=x]}\right)$$

is the Kullback-Leibler Divergence (KLD) from distribution $\mathcal{P}$ to $\mathcal{Q}$. The sum over $\mathcal{X}$ denotes all possible (nonzero probability) values of X; in digital media objects such distributions will be finite-valued, and in this paper we will consider the finite case. We expect that generalizations to infinite discrete and continuous probability measures are also possible.

KLD has many notations in the literature; we have included name of the random variable X in case the distributions $\mathcal{P}$ and $\mathcal{Q}$ define other random variables not available to the detector. Note that KLD is only well-defined if X has the same support under distributions $\mathcal{P}$ and $\mathcal{Q}$.

Proving that $D_{\mathrm{KL}}(X \sim \mathcal{P}_n, X \sim \mathcal{Q}_n^m) \to 0$ (known as *convergence in KLD*) is sufficient to show that every detector is asymptotically random, something known since Cachin's early work on the information theory of steganography [3]. Cachin defined a stegosystem to be 'ϵ-secure' if $D_{\mathrm{KL}}(X \sim \mathcal{P}_n, X \sim \mathcal{Q}_n^m) < \epsilon$, and bounded the performance of detectors via an information processing inequality. It is likely that theoreticians have focused on KLD because of Cachin's example. Furthermore, KLD has useful connections with *error exponents* in the case of batch imperfect steganography in stationary independent covers with a constant embedding rate, although the square root law tells us that such a rate would be ill-advised.

However, convergence in KLD is a strictly stronger condition than every detector being asymptotically random. For example, imagine 'cover' and 'stego' objects of n independent pixels, distributed according to

$$\mathrm{P}_{\mathcal{P}_n}[X_i = 1] = \frac{1}{n^2}, \quad \mathrm{P}_{\mathcal{Q}_n}[X_i = 1] = e^{-n^2}. \quad (3)$$

It is routine to show $D_{\mathrm{KL}}((X_1,\ldots,X_n) \sim \mathcal{P}_n, (X_1,\ldots,X_n) \sim \mathcal{Q}_n) \to \infty$ as $n \to \infty$, yet asymptotically with probability one every cover object is entirely zeros, and so is every stego object, so any 'detector' that tries to discriminate between the two cases is asymptotically random. It follows that 'ϵ-security', for ϵ small, is a sufficient but not necessary condition for steganographic security.

Furthermore, KLD is not easy to work with. There is the strong requirement that $\mathcal{P}_n$ and $\mathcal{Q}_n$ have exactly the same nonzero probability events, even if those probabilities tend to zero and are therefore negligible for detection. The logarithm in the definition makes analysis complicated (see e.g. [21]). And, while easy to bound for independent pixels (it is additive across independent components), KLD can be extremely awkward to bound for dependent components: the square root law for Markov chains [11] uses a highly technical lemma, proved in [7], that requires difficult analytic arguments. Perhaps this is why square root laws have not yet been extended to more realistic cover distributions.

In this work we use a different information theoretic quantity. The Total Variation (TV) between $\mathcal{P}$ and $\mathcal{Q}$, again distributions defining a random variable X over the set $\mathcal{X}$, is

$$D_{\mathrm{TV}}(X \sim \mathcal{P}, X \sim \mathcal{Q}) = \frac{1}{2}\sum_{x \in \mathcal{X}}\Big|\mathrm{P}_{X \sim \mathcal{P}}[X = x] - \mathrm{P}_{X \sim \mathcal{Q}}[X = x]\Big|.$$

It is not necessary for the zero probability values of X to be identical under $\mathcal{P}$ and $\mathcal{Q}$. Note that some omit the constant factor. Other authors have briefly used TV in square root laws, but only by immediate appeal to Pinsker's inequality

$$2D_{\mathrm{TV}}(X \sim \mathcal{P}, X \sim \mathcal{Q})^2 \le D_{\mathrm{KL}}(X \sim \mathcal{P}, X \sim \mathcal{Q}). \quad (4)$$

An equivalent formula for TV is given by

$$D_{\mathrm{TV}}(X \sim \mathcal{P}, X \sim \mathcal{Q}) = \sup_{A \subseteq \mathcal{X}}\Big|\mathrm{P}_{X \sim \mathcal{P}}[X \in A] - \mathrm{P}_{X \sim \mathcal{Q}}[X \in A]\Big|,$$

which gives a strong connection with detection:

LEMMA 3.1. *An asymptotically perfect detector based on X exists if and only if $D_{\mathrm{TV}}(X \sim \mathcal{P}_n, X \sim \mathcal{Q}_n^m) \to 1$. Every detector based on X is asymptotically random if and only if $D_{\mathrm{TV}}(X \sim \mathcal{P}_n, X \sim \mathcal{Q}_n^m) \to 0$.*

The proof is elementary, for example see [27, Thm. 13.1.1]. In example (3), $D_{\mathrm{TV}}((X_1,\ldots,X_n) \sim \mathcal{P}_n, (X_1,\ldots,X_n) \sim \mathcal{Q}_n) \to 0$, proving asymptotic undetectability for this example, and demonstrating how TV can give a more refined analysis than KLD.

Total variation can still be extremely difficult to compute, and indeed there are few closed formulae for total variation between standard distributions, but it can be easier to bound than KLD. It is not additive, but is subadditive across independent components. Unlike KLD, it satisfies the triangle inequality, and in a moment we will prove a useful result about side information and TV.

3.1 Side Information for the Detector

As with KL divergence, TV cannot be decreased by the presence of side information. Because TV is more forgiving of impossible events in $\mathcal{P}$ that are not impossible in $\mathcal{Q}$ (as long as their probability tends to zero), we can prove a lemma that will be used in our main result.

We need a conditional version of total variation, which does not seem a widely-used concept (it appears in [32]):

Definition 3.2. Let S be a random variable that has the same distribution under $\mathcal{P}$ and $\mathcal{Q}$. Then

$$D_{\mathrm{TV}}(X \sim \mathcal{P}, X \sim \mathcal{Q} \mid S = s) =$$
$$\frac{1}{2}\sum_{x \in \mathcal{X}}\Big|\mathrm{P}_{(X,S) \sim \mathcal{P}}[X = x \mid S = s] - \mathrm{P}_{(X,S) \sim \mathcal{Q}}[X = x \mid S = s]\Big|.$$

LEMMA 3.3. *Let $\mathcal{S}$ denote the possible values of S. If $\mathcal{S}$ is partitioned into $\mathcal{S}_0$ and $\mathcal{S}_1$ then*

$$D_{\mathrm{TV}}(X \sim \mathcal{P}, X \sim \mathcal{Q})$$
$$\le \mathrm{P}[S \in \mathcal{S}_0] + \max_{s \in \mathcal{S}_1} D_{\mathrm{TV}}(X \sim \mathcal{P}, X \sim \mathcal{Q} \mid S = s). \quad (5)$$

PROOF. Abbreviating $X = x$ as simply X,

$$D_{\mathrm{TV}}(X \sim \mathcal{P}, X \sim \mathcal{Q})$$
$$= \frac{1}{2}\sum_{x \in \mathcal{X}}\Big|\sum_{s \in \mathcal{S}}\mathrm{P}_{\mathcal{P}}[S]\,\mathrm{P}_{\mathcal{P}}[X \mid S] - \sum_{s \in \mathcal{S}}\mathrm{P}_{\mathcal{Q}}[S]\,\mathrm{P}_{\mathcal{Q}}[X \mid S]\Big|$$
$$\overset{(i)}{\le} \frac{1}{2}\sum_{s \in \mathcal{S}}\sum_{x \in \mathcal{X}}\mathrm{P}[S]\Big|\mathrm{P}_{\mathcal{P}}[X \mid S] - \mathrm{P}_{\mathcal{Q}}[X \mid S]\Big|$$
$$= \sum_{s \in \mathcal{S}}\mathrm{P}[S]\,D_{\mathrm{TV}}(X \sim \mathcal{P}, X \sim \mathcal{Q} \mid S)$$
$$\overset{(ii)}{\le} \sum_{s \in \mathcal{S}_0}\mathrm{P}[S] + \max_{s \in \mathcal{S}_1}D_{\mathrm{TV}}(X \sim \mathcal{P}, X \sim \mathcal{Q} \mid S)\sum_{s \in \mathcal{S}_1}\mathrm{P}[S]$$
$$\le \mathrm{P}[S \in \mathcal{S}_0] + \max_{s \in \mathcal{S}_1}D_{\mathrm{TV}}(X \sim \mathcal{P}, X \sim \mathcal{Q} \mid S).$$

Above, (i) uses $P_{\mathcal{P}}[S = s] = P_{\mathcal{Q}}[S = s]$ and the triangle inequality. (ii) uses $D_{\mathrm{TV}}(X \sim \mathcal{P}, X \sim \mathcal{Q} \mid S = s) \leq 1$. $\square$

We will think of S as a 'hint' for the detector. The set $\mathcal{S}_0$ are 'bad hints' that give too much information: we will ensure that the probability of a bad hint tends to zero. The hints in $\mathcal{S}_1$ are 'good hints' that give enough conditional information to the detector to make $D_{\mathrm{TV}}(X \sim \mathcal{P}, X \sim \mathcal{Q} \mid S = s)$ amenable to analysis, but little enough information so that it still tends to zero, for any $s \in \mathcal{S}_1$, below the critical rate.

We also state a simple result confirming that side information independent of the observed variables conveys nothing:

LEMMA 3.4. *If X is independent of S under both $\mathcal{P}$ and $\mathcal{Q}$, and S has the same distribution under $\mathcal{P}$ and $\mathcal{Q}$, then*

$$D_{\mathrm{TV}}\big((X, S) \sim \mathcal{P}, (X, S) \sim \mathcal{Q}\big) = D_{\mathrm{TV}}(X \sim \mathcal{P}, X \sim \mathcal{Q}). \quad (6)$$

4 A SQUARE ROOT LAW FOR DEPENDENT PIXELS

Our square root law applies to covers whose pixels form a Markov Random Field (MRF) [14] with bounded degree. With only the addition of a *no asymptotic determinism* condition, we will prove the lower bound in Subsect. 4.1. Further assumptions (ensuring exponential decay of covariance) will be needed, as well as a *no free bits* condition, to prove the upper bound in Subsect. 4.2.

We will need to identify individual pixels within an n-element cover, which we write $\boldsymbol{X} = (X_1, \dots, X_n)^3$. A bounded-degree MRF may be concisely described as follows: each pixel X_i is allowed to depend directly only on a *neighbourhood* $\boldsymbol{N_i}$, which is of bounded size. Any dependence with X_i outside the neighbourhood is indirectly via $\boldsymbol{N_i}$.

More precisely, there is a universal constant D (not depending on n) and for each i there exists N_i such that

$$N_i \subset \{1, \dots, n\}, \quad i \notin N_i, \quad |N_i| \leq D. \quad (\textbf{C1})$$

(We will label our assumptions, as above, in order to refer to them later.) We also require that neighbourhoods are symmetric in the sense that

$$i \in N_j \text{ if and only if } j \in N_i, \quad (\textbf{C2})$$

for all i and j.

We write $\boldsymbol{N_i} = (X_j \mid j \in N_i)$ and the non-neighbourhood as $\overline{\boldsymbol{N_i}} = (X_j \mid j \notin N_i, j \neq i)$. The local Markov property of MRFs is that, conditional on $\boldsymbol{N_i}$, X_i is independent of $\overline{\boldsymbol{N_i}}$. This is sometimes written

$$X_i \perp\!\!\!\perp \overline{\boldsymbol{N_i}} \mid \boldsymbol{N_i}. \quad (\textbf{C3})$$

An example of a two-dimensional model of this type is in Fig. 1, (an Ising model, of which more in Subsect. 5.2). The pixels are indexed (i, j) and the distribution of each depends on the values of its four immediate neighbours, so that there are both horizontal and vertical dependencies. Here $D = 4$ and $N_{(i,j)} = \{(i-1, j), (i+1, j), (i, j-1), (i, j+1)\}$. There will also be some boundary conditions, either periodic (pixels

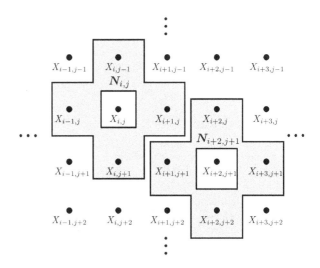

Figure 1: An example of a MRF cover model for which the square root law can hold. Each pixel X_{ij} is dependent on its immediate neighbours, and conditionally independent of the rest.

at the top/left and bottom/right are neighbours) or imposed via auxiliary (fixed) edge rows and columns.

For embedding, we use the model of [20]. It is case (a) from Subsec. 2.1, where exactly $m = m(n)$ *embedding locations* are selected; they are changed by some random procedure[4], identical at each location and independent of other changes and the locations used. Unused locations are unchanged. In a square root law for adaptive embedding it makes more sense to consider case (b) from Subsec. 2.1, which is the *mutually independent embedding* model of [11], for which see Sect. 6. Our model seems more natural for uncoded embedding such as LSB or Ternary Embedding, where the number of changes is always bounded by a multiple of the payload size.

Formally, let $L = \{L_1, \dots L_m\}$ be the embedding locations. We assume:

$$\{L_1, \dots L_m\} \text{ is drawn uniformly from } \{1, \dots, n\}. \quad (\textbf{E1})$$

Suppose that $\beta(x, y)$ is the probability that pixel value x is changed to y at each embedding location. Write $\boldsymbol{X}_{\setminus L}$ for the vector of pixels not in L. Then the stego distribution is given by

$$P_{\mathcal{Q}_n^m}[\boldsymbol{X_L} = \boldsymbol{y}, \boldsymbol{X}_{\setminus L} = \boldsymbol{z} \mid L] =$$
$$\sum_{x_1} \cdots \sum_{x_m} P_{\mathcal{P}_n}[\boldsymbol{X_L} = \boldsymbol{x}, X_{\setminus L} = \boldsymbol{z}] \prod_i \beta(x_i, y_i). \quad (\textbf{E2})$$

We need one further condition, ensuring that no pixel value is made impossible by the embedding process. There should exist $\delta > 0$ such that

$$\text{for all } y \text{ there exists } x \text{ with } \beta(x, y) \geq \delta. \quad (\textbf{E3})$$

---

[3]This is slightly different from the notation of Sect. 2, where X_n represented an entire cover of size n.

[4]The randomness comes from the embedding key and payload. It may be assumed that both are indistinguishable from uniform random, which is a good model for compressed or encrypted data and well-chosen keys.

Together, (**E1**) and (**E2**) describe how the stego distribution $\mathcal{Q}_n^m$ is derived from the cover distribution $\mathcal{P}_n$. Observe that the stego distribution will contain dependencies not present in the cover MRF, and in general need not be a MRF of bounded degree, because of the non-local property that there are never more than m changes[5].

4.1 Lower Bound

The lower bound can be proved without further conditions on the cover and embedding models, except for a no determinism condition. It requires that each cover pixel value X_i is possible, conditional on its neighbourhood: this prevents a certain stego pattern from occurring that could never occur in covers, leading to a perfect detector. In fact, such a condition is usually included in the definition of a MRF (all probabilities must be positive) but we need a more uniform bound since we consider covers of growing size, and potentially anisotropic (nonstationary).

Thus we assume a *no asymptotic determinism* condition, also banning the likelihood of any pixel from tending to zero as $n \to \infty$ (it parallels the requirement in [23]). There exists a universal $\epsilon > 0$ (not depending on n) such that

$$P(X_i = x_i \mid \boldsymbol{N_i} = \boldsymbol{n_i}) \geq \epsilon \quad \text{for all } i, x_i, \boldsymbol{n_i}. \quad \textbf{(NAD)}$$

THEOREM 4.1. *Assume* (**C1**), (**C2**), (**C3**), (**E1**), (**E2**), (**E3**), *and* (**NAD**). *If m is below the critical rate, $m(n)/\sqrt{n} \to 0$, then every detector is asymptotically random.*

PROOF. We will see that, with probability tending to one, no embedding change will lie in the neighbourhood of another. Conditional on their neighbourhoods, the pixels involved are independent. So if we give the detector side information about which pixels have been changed (which can only make their task easier) then we have reduced the problem to the lower bound of an independent pixel square root law.

However, we cannot give the detector the exact embedding locations, because this would effectively reduce n to m (part of the essence of a square root law is in the detector's uncertainty about where to look). Instead, we give them a *shortlist* of *possible* embedding locations, chosen so that conditional independence still holds, but of length $O(n)$ so that they still have plenty of confusion about the true embedding locations.

Of course, the embedding process does not really produce a shortlist of possible embedding locations, but we can create one by a method akin to those used in coupling arguments.

Identify a set of embedding locations $\{X_{l_1}, \ldots, X_{l_k}\}$ by their indices $L = \{l_1, \ldots, l_k\}$. Let $\mathcal{L}^k$ denote all possible sets of k embedding locations:

$$\mathcal{L}^k = \{L \subset \{1, \ldots, n\} \mid |L| = k\}.$$

[5]The results of this paper can be modified for the mutually independent embedding model, where each location is in L independently with probability m/n. A small addition is needed to the lower bound proof of Subsect. 4.1, to show that too many embedding locations has negligible probability. The upper bound proof in Subsect. 4.2 still applies, but it could be simplified since there are no long-range dependencies.

Where $i \in N_j$ we can say that the embedding locations i and j *interfere*, because their distributions are not conditionally independent. Let $\mathcal{L}_0^k$ be the sets of embedding locations where at least two interfere:

$$\mathcal{L}_0^k = \{L \in \mathcal{L}^k \mid i \in N_j \text{ for some } i, j \in L\},$$

and $\mathcal{L}_1^k = \mathcal{L}^k \setminus \mathcal{L}_0^k$. According to (**E1**), L is drawn uniformly from $\mathcal{L}^m$. If $L \in \mathcal{L}_0^m$, set $S = L$. Otherwise, set $s = \lceil n/2D \rceil$ and choose uniformly

$$S \in \{S \in \mathcal{L}_1^s \mid L \subseteq S\}.$$

By construction, this still chooses L uniformly $\mathcal{L}^m$, but the side information S, a shortlist of $s = O(n)$ non-interfering locations in which the true m locations can be found, can be generated *whether or not embedding takes place*. It will be used to bound the total variation between cover and stego objects. The cases where $L \in \mathcal{L}_0^m$ are special, since no non-interfering shortlist can contain L. The embedder may as well give up and confess guilt to the detector in such a case, because it has negligible probability:

$$
\begin{aligned}
1 - P[L \in \mathcal{L}_0^m] &\overset{(i)}{=} \prod_{i=2}^{m} 1 - \frac{1}{n}\Big|\bigcup_{j=1}^{i-1} N_{l_j} \cup \{l_j\}\Big| \\
&\overset{(ii)}{\geq} \prod_{i=2}^{m} 1 - \frac{(D+1)(i-1)}{n} \\
&\overset{(iii)}{\geq} \prod_{i=2}^{m} \exp\big(\tfrac{-2(D+1)(i-1)}{n}\big) \\
&\geq \exp\big(\tfrac{-(D+1)m^2}{n}\big)
\end{aligned}
$$

For (i), consider adding l_i to non-interfering set $\{l_1, \ldots, l_{i-1}\}$: its location is uniformly chosen, and we must avoid choosing from $l_1, \ldots, l_{i-1}$ or their neighbourhoods. By (**C2**) this also ensures that none of $l_1, \ldots, l_{i-1}$ lie in N_{l_i}. (ii) uses (**C1**). (iii) follows from $1 - x \geq \exp(-2x)$, at least for $x \leq \frac{1}{2}$: here $x \leq \frac{(D+1)m}{n}$, which certainly tends to zero if $m^2/n \to 0$. This establishes that, below the critical rate,

$$p_0 = \mathrm{P}[L \in \mathcal{L}_0^m] \to 0. \quad (7)$$

Next, fix any nonempty shortlist $S = \{l_1, \ldots, l_s\}$. Write $\boldsymbol{X_S} = (X_{l_1}, \ldots, X_{l_s})$ for the pixels on the shortlist, and $\boldsymbol{N} = \bigcup_{i=1}^{s} \boldsymbol{N_{l_i}}$ for their neighbourhoods. Write $\boldsymbol{R} = \boldsymbol{X} \setminus \boldsymbol{N} \setminus \boldsymbol{X_S}$ (the remaining pixels). This decomposition is illustrated in Fig. 2. We can ignore the locations $\boldsymbol{R}$, since

$$
\begin{aligned}
D_{\mathrm{TV}}(\boldsymbol{X} &\sim \mathcal{P}_n, \boldsymbol{X} \sim \mathcal{Q}_n^m \mid S, \boldsymbol{N}) \\
&= D_{\mathrm{TV}}(\boldsymbol{X_S} \sim \mathcal{P}_n, \boldsymbol{X_S} \sim \mathcal{Q}_n^m \mid \boldsymbol{N}), \quad (8)
\end{aligned}
$$

because the MRF property of the cover (**C3**) implies $\boldsymbol{X_S} \perp\!\!\!\perp \boldsymbol{R} \mid \boldsymbol{N}$, and using (6). Conditional on $\boldsymbol{N}$, we have reduced the problem to a cover of independent random variables, since the $X_{l_i} \perp\!\!\!\perp X_{l_j} \mid \boldsymbol{N}$. The stego object does not have the same property, because choosing *exactly* m of n locations (conditional on the shortlist, m of s) introduces weak dependency, but this problem has already been attacked in [20].

Fix $\boldsymbol{N}$, and write $\mathcal{P}_s$ for the conditional cover distribution of $\boldsymbol{X_S}$ given $\boldsymbol{N}$. This is the independent product of the mass functions for each shortlisted cover element $p_i(k) = \mathrm{P}[X_{l_i} =$

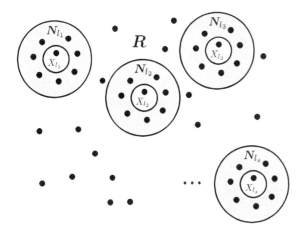

Figure 2: Decomposition of X into a non-interfering shortlist $(X_{l_1}, \ldots, X_{l_s})$, their neighbourhoods, and remaining pixels $\boldsymbol{R}$. Conditional on $\bigcup \boldsymbol{N}_{l_i}$, the X_{l_i} are independent of each other and $\boldsymbol{R}$. m of the s shortlisted locations are used for embedding.

$k \mid \boldsymbol{N}_{l_i}]$. Write $\mathcal{Q}_s^m$ for the conditional stego distribution of $\boldsymbol{X}_S$ given $\boldsymbol{N}$. By (**E2**),

$$\mathrm{P}_{\mathcal{Q}_s^m}[\boldsymbol{X}_S = (x_1 \ldots x_s)] = \frac{1}{\binom{s}{m}} \sum_{\substack{L \subseteq \{1,\ldots,s\}, \\ |L|=m}} \prod_{i \notin L} p_i(x_i) \prod_{i \in L} q_i(x_i)$$

where

$$q_i(y) = \sum_x \beta(x, y) p_i(x)$$

is the mass function of element l_i if the embedding operation is applied to it.

Applying Pinsker's inequality (4),

$$2 D_{\mathrm{TV}}(\boldsymbol{X}_S \sim \mathcal{P}_n, \boldsymbol{X}_S \sim \mathcal{Q}_n^m \mid \boldsymbol{N})^2 \\ \leq D_{\mathrm{KL}}(\boldsymbol{X}_S \sim \mathcal{P}_s, \boldsymbol{X}_S \sim \mathcal{Q}_s^m). \quad (9)$$

KL divergence between distributions of this form has been studied. In the proof of [20, Thm. 2(ii)], it is bounded above by Cm^2/s, for a constant C, subject to some conditions. We need to generalize the proof, however, because [20] does not permit the pixels to have different distribution. But the change is not difficult, and we spare the reader an almost identical proof. In [20] the distribution of $p(x)$ is required to have two properties. First, $p(x) > 0$ for all x. This must be modified to $p_i(x) > 0$ for all i and x, which follows from (**NAD**). Second, in the proof of the 'embedding probability lemma' in [20, Appendix A], the key line is

'there exists $c > 0$ such that, for all x, $p(x) \leq cq(x)$.'

In the non-identical distribution case, we require a positive constant c such that, for all i and x, $p_i(x) \leq cq_i(x)$. By (**E3**) and (**NAD**), $q_i(x) \geq \epsilon\delta$, so $c = 1/\epsilon\delta$ will do. Combining this bound with (8) and (9), we have

$$2 D_{\mathrm{TV}}(\boldsymbol{X} \sim \mathcal{P}_n, \boldsymbol{X} \sim \mathcal{Q}_n^m \mid S, \boldsymbol{N})^2 \leq Cm^2/s. \quad (10)$$

Furthermore, because c is independent of S and $\boldsymbol{N}$, so is C.

Putting this together we have shown, when $m/\sqrt{n} \to 0$,

$$D_{\mathrm{TV}}(\boldsymbol{X} \sim \mathcal{P}_n, \boldsymbol{X} \sim \mathcal{Q}_n^m)$$

$$\overset{(i)}{\leq} p_0 + \max_{S \in \mathcal{L}_1} D_{\mathrm{TV}}(\boldsymbol{X} \sim \mathcal{P}_n, \boldsymbol{X} \sim \mathcal{Q}_n^m \mid S)$$

$$\overset{(ii)}{\leq} p_0 + \max_{\boldsymbol{N} \in \mathcal{N}} \max_{S \in \mathcal{L}_1} D_{\mathrm{TV}}(\boldsymbol{X} \sim \mathcal{P}_n, \boldsymbol{X} \sim \mathcal{Q}_n^m \mid S, \boldsymbol{N})$$

$$\overset{(iii)}{\leq} p_0 + \sqrt{CDm^2/n}$$

$$\overset{(iv)}{\to} 0.$$

Here (i) uses (5) with $\mathcal{S}_0 = \mathcal{L}_0^m$, $\mathcal{S}_1 = \mathcal{L}_1^s$; (ii) uses (5) again with $S_0 = \emptyset$, and $\mathcal{N}$ all possible values of $\boldsymbol{N}$ given S; (iii) uses (10) and $s \geq n/2D$; and finally (iv) uses (7). Thanks to Lemma 3.1, we have proved that every detector is asymptotically random below the critical rate. $\square$

4.2 Upper Bound

The upper bound that we prove here is not as general, making further assumptions of the cover MRF: polynomial growth in neighbourhood size, and exponential decay of covariance.

Let us define a *distance* between locations to mean the distance in the neighbourhood graph of the MRF. That is, $d(i, j)$ is the smallest d with

$$l_0 = i, \ l_d = j, \ l_i \in N_{i-1} \text{ for } i = 1, \ldots, d.$$

We require a polynomial $p(x)$ with the property that, for all i and $d \geq 0$,

$$\big|\{j \mid d(i, j) \leq d\}\big| \leq p(d). \quad (\textbf{C4})$$

This bans tree-like topologies, for which d-neighbourhoods can be exponentially large.

Since we will now focus on distributions of pixels jointly with their neighbours, it will convenient to abbreviate

$$R_i = \{i\} \cup N_i, \quad \boldsymbol{R}_i = (X_i, \boldsymbol{N}_i).$$

Observe that $R_i \cap R_j \neq \emptyset$ if and only if $d(i, j) \leq 2$.

The other condition is that there exist positive constants c and C such that, for every set of indicators $I_1, \ldots, I_n$ on $\boldsymbol{R}_1, \ldots, \boldsymbol{R}_n$,

$$\big|\mathrm{Cov}(I_i, I_j)\big| \leq C \exp\big(-cd(i, j)\big). \quad (\textbf{C5})$$

Finally, there must be a *no free bits* condition, that the distribution of each $\boldsymbol{R}_i$ is altered by the embedding process. There should be a universal constant $\epsilon > 0$ such that

$$D_{\mathrm{TV}}(\boldsymbol{R}_i \sim \mathcal{P}_n, \boldsymbol{R}_i \sim \mathcal{Q}_n^m) \geq \epsilon \frac{m}{n} \text{ for all } i. \quad (\textbf{NFB})$$

Theorem 4.2. *Assume* (**C1**), (**C2**), (**C3**), (**C4**), (**C5**), (**E1**), (**E2**), *and* (**NFB**). *If m is above the critical rate, $m(n)/\sqrt{n} \to \infty$, an asymptotically perfect detector exists.*

Proof. By (**NFB**), for each i there is an indicator I_i with

$$\mathrm{P}_{I_i \sim \mathcal{Q}_m^n}[I_i = 1] - \mathrm{P}_{I_i \sim \mathcal{P}_n}[I_i = 1] \geq \epsilon \frac{m}{n}. \quad (11)$$

An asymptotically perfect detector will be constructed from $\sum_i^n I_i$, similarly to proofs of upper bounds in independent and Markov chain square root laws, counting occurrences of local events more likely in stego than cover. The mean of this sum differs by at least $O(m)$ between case of cover and stego, thanks to (**NFB**). In the absence of independence, the exponential decay of cover correlation (**C5**) prevents its variance from growing more than $O(n)$ in covers, and weak dependence of embedding locations will prove the same for stego objects. Standard arguments will then construct a detector, asymptotically perfect above the critical rate.

To avoid many subscripts, let us write I_i for the indicator in the cover distribution, and J_i for the same indicator in the stego distribution $\mathcal{Q}_n^m$. Henceforth the distributions can remain implicit. Summing (11) over all locations,

$$\mathrm{E}[\textstyle\sum_i J_i] - \mathrm{E}[\textstyle\sum_i I_i] \geq \epsilon m. \tag{12}$$

To bound $\mathrm{Var}[\sum_i I_i]$,

$$
\begin{aligned}
\sum_j \mathrm{Cov}[I_i, I_j] &\overset{(i)}{\leq} \sum_j C \exp(-cd(i,j)) \\
&\overset{(ii)}{\leq} \sum_{d=0}^{\infty} C \exp(-cd) \left| \{ j \mid d(i,j) \leq d \} \right| \\
&\overset{(iii)}{\leq} \sum_{d=0}^{\infty} C \exp(-cd) p(d) \\
&\overset{(iv)}{\leq} C_1,
\end{aligned}
$$

a constant independent of i. (i) is from (**C5**). (ii) enumerates the same terms (multiple times). (iii) is from (**C4**). (iv) is because the sum is convergent: the ratio of terms tends to $\exp(-c) < 1$, so d'Alembert's test applies. It follows that

$$\mathrm{Var}[\textstyle\sum_i I_i] = \sum_i \sum_j \mathrm{Cov}[I_i, I_j] \leq C_1 n. \tag{13}$$

We also need to bound the same variance in the stego case. Recall that the embedding process can introduce long-range (not exponentially diminishing) dependency, since exactly m locations are used. We now find a sufficient condition for such dependency to be negligible.

First, we can dispose of regions that overlap. Recall that this happens only when $d(i,j) \leq 2$. Then

$$
\begin{aligned}
\sum_i \sum_j \left| \mathrm{Cov}[J_i, J_j] \right| &= \sum_{d(i,j)\leq 2} \left| \mathrm{Cov}[J_i, J_j] \right| + \sum_{d(i,j)>2} \left| \mathrm{Cov}[J_i, J_j] \right| \\
&\leq np(2) + \sum_{d(i,j)>2} \left| \mathrm{Cov}[J_i, J_j] \right|. \tag{14}
\end{aligned}
$$

The first term is $O(n)$, so it remains to bound the cases where $R_i \cap R_j = \emptyset$.

Let E_i indicate the event that at least one pixel is changed in region R_i. Let $I_{i_1}, \ldots I_{i_K}$ be indicators for the possible cover regions that can change to the region indicated by I_i. Let $C_{i_1}, \ldots, C_{i_K}$ be indicators for the event that each of these changes happens, given that at least one change is made. Exactly one of $C_{i_1}, \ldots, C_{i_K}$ will be one, the rest zero, and they can take the same distribution regardless of whether E_i is zero or one. With these indicators,

$$J_i = I_i(1 - E_i) + E_i \sum_{k=1}^{K} C_{i_k} I_{i_k} = I_i + E_i H_i$$

where $H_i = \sum_{k=1}^{K} C_{i_k} I_{i_k} - I_i$. Since $E_i \perp\!\!\!\perp I_i, \{I_{i_k}\}, \{C_{i_k}\}$, $E_i \perp\!\!\!\perp H_i$. Therefore

$$
\begin{aligned}
&\left| \mathrm{Cov}[J_i, J_j] \right| \\
&= \left| \mathrm{Cov}[I_i + E_i H_i, I_j + E_j H_j] \right| \\
&\overset{(i)}{=} \left| \mathrm{Cov}[I_i, I_j] + \mathrm{E}[E_i]\mathrm{Cov}[H_i, I_j] + \mathrm{E}[E_j]\mathrm{Cov}[I_i, H_j] \right. \\
&\quad \left. + \mathrm{E}[E_i E_j]\mathrm{Cov}[H_i, H_j] + \mathrm{E}[H_i]\mathrm{E}[H_j]\mathrm{Cov}[E_i, E_j] \right| \\
&\overset{(ii)}{\leq} \left| \mathrm{Cov}[I_i, I_j] \right| + \left| \mathrm{Cov}[H_i, I_j] \right| + \left| \mathrm{Cov}[I_i, H_j] \right| \\
&\quad + \left| \mathrm{Cov}[H_i, H_j] \right| + \left| \mathrm{Cov}[E_i, E_j] \right|. \tag{15}
\end{aligned}
$$

(i) is a property of covariance[6] and (ii) is by the triangle inequality and because all the random variables have absolute value at most 1.

The first three terms of (15) are easily bounded by 1, 2, and 2 times $C \exp(-cd(i,j))$, respectively. For example

$$
\begin{aligned}
\left| \mathrm{Cov}[H_i, I_j] \right| &= \left| \sum_k \mathrm{E}[C_{i_k}]\mathrm{Cov}[I_{i_k}, I_j] - \mathrm{Cov}[I_i, I_j] \right| \\
&\leq 2C \exp(-cd(i,j)) \tag{16}
\end{aligned}
$$

by $\{C_{i_k}\} \perp\!\!\!\perp \{I_{i_k}\}, I_j$ (which comes from (**E2**)), (**C5**) and the triangle inequality. The fourth term is similar; we omit the boring calculation but note that we need to take a step

$$\mathrm{Cov}[C_{i_k} I_{i_k}, C_{j_{k'}} I_{j_{k'}}] = \mathrm{E}[C_{i_k}]\mathrm{E}[C_{j_{k'}}]\mathrm{Cov}[I_{i_k}, I_{j_{k'}}]$$

which requires $\{C_{i_k}\} \perp\!\!\!\perp \{C_{j_{k'}}\}$; this is only necessarily true because $R_i \cap R_j = \emptyset$ (otherwise the decision on what to change in region R_i will constrain the decision in R_j).

For the fifth term of (15) it is more convenient to consider F_i, the complement of E_i, i.e. the probability that no changes occur in R_i. Note that $\mathrm{Cov}[E_i, E_j] = \mathrm{Cov}[F_i, F_j]$.

$$
\begin{aligned}
\left| \mathrm{Cov}[F_i, F_j] \right| &= \left| \mathrm{P}[F_i](\mathrm{P}[F_j \mid F_i] - \mathrm{P}[F_j]) \right| \\
&\overset{(i)}{\leq} \mathrm{P}[F_j] - \mathrm{P}[F_j \mid F_i] \\
&\overset{(ii)}{=} \left(1 - \frac{m}{n}\right)\left(1 - \frac{m}{n-1}\right) \cdots \left(1 - \frac{m}{n-|R_j|+1}\right) \\
&\quad - \left(1 - \frac{m}{n-|R_i|}\right) \cdots \left(1 - \frac{m}{n-|R_i|-|R_j|+1}\right) \\
&\overset{(iii)}{\leq} C_3/n, \tag{17}
\end{aligned}
$$

for a constant C_3. (i) is because $P[F_i] \leq 1$, and $P[F_j] > P[F_j \mid F_i]$ since we assumed $R_i \cap R_j = \emptyset$, so avoiding the locations in R_i can only make it less likely to also avoid those in R_j. (ii) imagines that the m embedding locations are fixed while regions R_i and R_j are chosen uniformly at random, and counts forbidden choices. (iii) is routine, tedious, and mostly omitted: some calculation shows that $\left(1 - \frac{m}{n-k}\right) < \left(1 - \frac{m}{n-D-k}\right) + \alpha/n$, for some constant α independent of m, and this implies the required result.

Finally,

$$\mathrm{Var}[\textstyle\sum J_i] \overset{(i)}{\leq} C_2 n + \sum_{d(i,j)\geq 2} \left| \mathrm{Cov}[E_i, E_j] \right| \overset{(ii)}{\leq} (C_2 + C_3)n. \tag{18}$$

---

[6]If $X \perp\!\!\!\perp X'$ and $Y \perp\!\!\!\perp Y'$ then $\mathrm{Cov}[XX', YY'] = \mathrm{E}[XY]\mathrm{Cov}[X', Y'] + \mathrm{E}[X']\mathrm{E}[Y']\mathrm{Cov}[X, Y]$. If also $X' \perp\!\!\!\perp Y'$ then the first term vanishes.

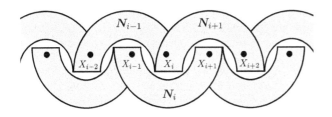

Figure 3: A Markov chain in the MRF cover model.

(i) combines (14), (15), inequalities of the form (16), and the same argument as (13). This step only depends on properties of the cover. (ii) is from (17), which bounds the effect of long-range dependencies in the embedding process.

Now we construct an asymptotically perfect detector using standard arguments. Define

$$I = \sum_i I_i, \quad \mu = \mathrm{E}_{\mathcal{P}_n}[I]$$

and give a positive detection if $I > \mu + \frac{1}{2}m\epsilon$. The sum of false positive and negative errors is

$$\mathrm{P}_{\mathcal{P}_n}[I > \mu + \tfrac{1}{2}m\epsilon] + \mathrm{P}_{\mathcal{Q}_n^m}[I \le \mu + \tfrac{1}{2}m\epsilon]$$

$$\overset{(i)}{\le} \frac{\mathrm{Var}_{\mathcal{P}_n}[I]}{(\tfrac{1}{2}m\epsilon)^2} + \frac{\mathrm{Var}_{\mathcal{Q}_n^m}[I]}{(\tfrac{1}{2}m\epsilon)^2}$$

$$\overset{(ii)}{\le} \frac{4(C_1 + C_2 + C_3)n}{m^2\epsilon^2} \to 0$$

above the critical rate. (i) is Chebyschev's inequality and (12), and (ii) uses (13) and (18). □

Note that $\sum_i \sum_j |\mathrm{Cov}[E_i, E_j]| = O(n)$ functions as the condition that long-range dependencies introduced by the embedding process must overall be weak.

5 EXAMPLES

We briefly discuss some cover models that meet the conditions for the generalized square root law. We assume the same embedding model, so that (**E1**), (**E2**), and (**E3**) hold.

5.1 Markov Chains

Let n pixels $(X_1, \dots, X_n)$, $X_i \in \{1, \dots, K\}$, be the realization of a Markov chain

$$\mathrm{P}[X_1 = i] = p_i, \quad \mathrm{P}[X_{k+1} = j \mid X_k = i] = p_{ij}.$$

The first state has distribution p_i and the transition matrix is $P = (p_{ij})$. This fits in the MRF cover model with $N_i = \{i-1, i+1\}$, as depicted in Fig. 3, with boundary cases $N_1 = \{2\}$ and $N_n = \{n-1\}$. Clearly $D = 2$, (**C1**) and (**C2**) hold. (**C3**) follows from the Markov property.

As long as

$$p_i > 0 \text{ and } p_{ij} > 0 \text{ for all } i \text{ and } j, \tag{19}$$

then the lower bound holds. (**NAD**) requires

$$\mathrm{P}[X_i = k \mid X_{i-1} = j, X_{i+1} = l] > \epsilon,$$

but this conditional probability is equal to

$$\frac{\mathrm{P}[X_i = k \mid X_{i-1} = j]\mathrm{P}[X_{i+1} = l \mid X_i = k]}{\mathrm{P}[X_{i+1} = l \mid X_{i-1} = j]}$$

which is bounded below by $(\min p_{ij})^2$.

For the upper bound, $d(i, j) = |i - j|$ and $p(x) = 2x + 1$ works for (**C4**). (**C5**) follows from the exponential forgetting (also known as exponential or geometric ergodicity) property of Markov chains [28, Thm. 4.9]: there are positive constants C and c such that, for all values x and y,

$$D_{\mathrm{TV}}(X_{i+k} \mid X_i = x, \ X_{i+k} \mid X_i = y) \le C \exp(-ck). \tag{20}$$

In the case of (19) this can be proved by a simple coupling argument [28, Ex. 5.1 & Thm. 5.2]. It is not difficult to transform (20) into (**C5**), but for lack of space we will omit the elementary proof.

Our no free bits condition (**NFB**) is equivalent to that in [11]: the second-order co-occurrence probabilities are not preserved by the embedding process. This might be difficult to establish in practice, but thanks to [8] it has a simple equivalent condition: there exist two pairs (x, y), (x', y'), such that one can possibly change to the other by embedding ($\beta(x, x')\beta(y, y') > 0$) and which are not given the same adjacent probability in covers:

$$\mathrm{P}[X_i = x, X_{i+1} = y] \ne \mathrm{P}[X_i = x', X_{i+1} = y']. \tag{21}$$

Thus we have verified all the conditions of Thms. 4.1 and 4.2.

We remark that this upper bound comes from essentially the same place as the proof in [11] – the exponential forgetting property of Markov chains – though our analysis of the stego variance is complicated by the long-range weak dependencies we allow in the embedding. Unlike [11], our lower bound does not use exponential forgetting; indeed it seems to be completely different from the technical uniform continuity proof used there, as well as more elementary.

Because we do not require even the existence of a stationary distribution, the square root law can now be generalized to *nonstationary* (inhomogeneous) Markov chains

$$\mathrm{P}[X_1 = i] = p_i, \quad \mathrm{P}[X_{k+1} = j \mid X_k = i] = p_{ij}^k,$$

with (19) strengthened to

$$\forall k, i, j. \ p_{ij}^k \ge \delta,$$

and (21) to

$$\forall k. \ \exists(x, y), (x', y'). \ \beta(x, x')\beta(y, y') > 0 \ \wedge$$
$$\mathrm{P}[X_k = x, X_{k+1} = y] - \mathrm{P}[X_k = x', X_{k+1} = y'] \ge \delta,$$

where δ is a positive constant not depending on n. The lower bound argument is exactly as above, and the upper bound follows because such a nonstationary chain is still exponentially forgetting, thanks to a small tweak to the coupling argument that proves (20).

5.2 Ising Models

Let $n = N^2$ pixels, $(X_{ij} \mid i, j \in \{1, \dots, N\})$, be the realization of a 2-dimensional Ising model [14, Ex. 2.1], depicted in Fig. 1. In such a random field the pixels are binary, and we follow convention and assign them values $X_{ij} = \pm 1$[7]. The probability distribution is given by

$$\mathrm{P}[\boldsymbol{X} = \boldsymbol{x}] \propto \exp\Big(\beta H \sum_{i,j} x_{ij} + \beta J \sum_{i,j} \sum_{(i',j') \in \mathcal{N}_{ij}} x_{ij} x_{i'j'}\Big) \quad (22)$$

where conventionally $\beta > 0$ is called the *inverse temperature*, $H \in \mathbb{R}$ the strength of an *external magnetic field*, and $J \in \mathbb{R}$ the *interaction strength* (we will impose some conditions on them in a moment). Higher positive values of βH bias the pixels more towards $+1$, and negative values towards -1; higher positive values of βJ bias neighbours to be equal more often, and negative values bias them to be unequal more often. The sum is over immediate neighbours in the grid, $N_{ij} = \{(i-1,j), (i,j-1), (i+1,j), (i,j+1)\}$. We will take the case of *toroidal* boundary conditions, where row (resp. column) 1 is considered adjacent to row (column) N.

This fits the MRF model: $D = 4$, and (**C1**,**C2**,**C3**) hold. The no asymptotic determinism condition (**NAD**) can be established by direct computation:

$$\mathrm{P}[X_{ij} = +1 \mid \boldsymbol{N_{ij}}] = \frac{1}{1 + e^{-2\beta H - 2\beta J(N^+ - N^-)}}$$

where N^+ (resp. N^-) is the number of $+1$ (-1) states in $\boldsymbol{N_{ij}}$; this conditional probability is bounded away from zero. We have established the lower bound of the square root law.

For the upper bound, $d((i,j),(i',j')) = |i-i'| + |j-j'|$ and the regular 2d grid gives $p(x) = 1 + 2x(x+1)$ for (**C4**). For (**C5**) we use some standard results from statistical physics: (22) satisfies *Dobrushin's uniqueness condition* at least for the cases $|H|$ sufficiently large (pixels biased away from uniform), or $H = 0$ and β sufficiently small (inter-pixel dependencies not too great) [4]. Random fields satisfying such a condition have many interesting properties, including [29] 'any finite volume covariance between two local functions f and g decays exponentially fast with the distance between their supports, with a rate that is uniform in … the choice of f and g', see also [14, Thm. 2.1.3]. This is (**C5**).

Without solving the model, we can show that the no free bits condition (**NFB**) holds for any sublinear payload. The only exception is if $H = 0$ *and* $J = 0$ (i.e. a completely uniform independent field). To see why, consider any region $\boldsymbol{R_{ij}} = (X_{ij}, \boldsymbol{N_{ij}})$. Take $\boldsymbol{x}$ to be the (or, if there is more than one, a) most likely cover configuration on $\boldsymbol{R_{ij}}$, and let $\boldsymbol{x}'$ be strictly less likely and differ from $\boldsymbol{x}$ in one location. Write $K = \mathrm{P}_{\mathcal{P}_n}[\boldsymbol{R_{ij}} = \boldsymbol{x}] - \mathrm{P}_{\mathcal{P}_n}[\boldsymbol{R_{ij}} = \boldsymbol{x}'] > 0$. Then compute

$$\mathrm{P}_{\mathcal{P}_n}[\boldsymbol{R_{ij}} = \boldsymbol{x}] - \mathrm{P}_{\mathcal{Q}_n^m}[\boldsymbol{R_{ij}} = \boldsymbol{x}]$$

$$\overset{(i)}{=} \mathrm{P}_{\mathcal{P}_n}[\boldsymbol{R_{ij}} = \boldsymbol{x}] - \sum_{\boldsymbol{y}} \mathrm{P}_{\mathcal{P}_n}[\boldsymbol{R_{ij}} = \boldsymbol{y}] \alpha(\boldsymbol{y}, \boldsymbol{x})$$

$$\overset{(ii)}{\geq} \alpha(\boldsymbol{x}', \boldsymbol{x}) K$$

$$\overset{(iii)}{=} \frac{m}{n} \frac{n-m}{n-1} \frac{n-m-1}{n-2} \frac{n-m-2}{n-3} \frac{n-m-3}{n-4} K.$$

(i) is by (**E2**), and where $\alpha(\boldsymbol{y}, \boldsymbol{x})$ is the probability that $\boldsymbol{y}$ is changed to $\boldsymbol{x}$ by the embedding process. (ii) is because $\sum_{\boldsymbol{y}} \alpha(\boldsymbol{y}, \boldsymbol{x}) = 1$ and using the fact that $\boldsymbol{x}$ was a most likely cover configuration. (iii) simply computes the probability

---

[7]Non-binary Gibbs fields would be a valuable generalization.

that $\boldsymbol{x}$ is changed in one location to $\boldsymbol{x}'$. As long as $m/n \leq c < 1$, we have shown (**NFB**).

This result can be extended to other Ising models:

- Give fixed boundary conditions instead of toroidal periodicity. Only (**NFB**) needs more work, because the neighbourhoods are no longer identically distributed, and we must ensure that $\mathrm{P}_{\mathcal{P}_n}[\boldsymbol{R_{ij}} = \boldsymbol{x}] - \mathrm{P}_{\mathcal{Q}_n^m}[\boldsymbol{R_{ij}} = \boldsymbol{x}]$ cannot approach zero. The result follows because Dobrushin's condition ensures that influence of the boundary decays exponentially fast (there is some detail here that lack of space precludes).
- The conditions on H, J, and β can be relaxed somewhat [33]. Note that Dobrushin's condition is sufficient, but not necessary, for (**C5**).
- We can consider dimensions higher than 2, or models where interactions occur at bounded distance rather than only between immediate neighbours. The only part of the argument that needs to change is verification of Dobrushin's condition, which holds at least for $H = 0$, $J > 0$, and β sufficiently small (this follows from [14, Ex. 2.1.3]).

6 TOWARDS AN ADVERSARIAL SQUARE ROOT LAW

Having extended the square root law to a wider class of cover models, we now consider the embedding model. Until now, square root laws have applied to 'dumb' embedding models, which apply some fixed random function to either m uniformly chosen locations (as here), or to each location independently with probability m/n. This is only a good model for steganography without source coding, which (particularly syndrome coding [13]) is now prevalent in well-constructed steganography, for both reducing the number of embedding changes and choosing less-detectable change options.

Rate distortion arguments [13] show that a payload of at most $O(c \log \frac{n}{c})$ can be embedded while making c changes in an n-element cover; the critical rate should therefore rise to $\sqrt{n} \log n$. But there are two complications before a square root law can be proved.

First, codes vary: the bound is only achieved in trivial circumstances, and some codes do not even approach it as $n \to \infty$; of those that do, some are computationally infeasible. A result that only applies to a particular code could become redundant if new codes are discovered. Second, using a code means that certain combinations of changes will not happen, thus introducing long-range dependencies into the embedding process: can we be sure that this is not exploited by the detector?

We propose to abstract away details of the code, and concentrate only on the probabilities of change. Let us say that $\boldsymbol{\pi}(n)$ is an *embedding process* if, for any fixed cover of size n, it describes a probability distribution on the stego object (see also [9]): we ignore the coding itself. We write $H(\boldsymbol{\pi}(n))$ for the conditional entropy of the stego object given the cover, which is an upper bound for the payload size. Since useful codes exist that convey payload within a multiple of this entropy [9], proving a square root law for embedding processes is sufficient to prove one for practical codes as well.

Codes that introduce long-range dependencies can be described by such a model. In practice we would not expect a good embedding process to introduce many strong dependencies, because this only reduces its capacity (entropy). Considering only capacity, embedding processes that induce *independent* changes are optimal: they maximize entropy. But the same is not necessarily true of security against a detector: it is reasonable to conjecture that optimal embedding noise might have similar covariances to the cover.

Note that a square root (here $\sqrt{n} \log n$) law cannot hold for *all* embedding processes, because there are some that are not asymptotically efficient (simple overwriting is an obvious example). It suffices for there to be *some* process that guarantees $o(\sqrt{n} \log n)$ asymptotically undetectable payload bits. On the other hand, we will require the upper bound to be inescapable by *any* embedding processes. Hence,

CONJECTURE 6.1. *Under similar assumptions to* (**C1**), (**C2**), (**C3**), (**C4**), (**C5**), *no free bits* (**NFB**) *and no determinism in covers* (**NAD**) *or stego objects* (**E3**),

(i) *if* $m(n)/\sqrt{n} \log n \to \infty$, *then for* every *embedding process* $\boldsymbol{\pi}(n)$ *with* $H(\boldsymbol{\pi}(n)) \geq m(n)$, *an asymptotically perfect detector exists;*

(ii) *if* $m(n)/\sqrt{n} \log n \to 0$, *then there exists embedding processes* $\boldsymbol{\pi}(n)$ *with* $H(\boldsymbol{\pi}(n)) = m(n)$ *and such that every detector is asymptotically random.*

Consider the detector's choice of detection statistic to be their *strategy*, and the embedder's choice of embedding process theirs. Add some payoff related to detectability and this is a game-theoretic formulation of steganography. The above result, which we call an *adversarial square root law*, proves that above the critical rate the detector has a winning strategy (regardless of the embedder's choice) and conversely below it. Unlike other game-theoretic analyses applicable to steganography [1, 15, 25], we are not locating an equilibrium, rather we prove something about its asymptotic behaviour[8].

What does this tell us of adaptive embedding, since it does not appear in the statement of the theorem? We will have shown that it cannot escape the $\sqrt{n} \log n$ capacity law: whether coding is used purely to improve embedding efficiency or whether it takes account of different embedding costs, as long as no costs are zero (which would violate *no free bits*) or infinite (violating *no determinism*) then the critical rate is the same. The costs can affect capacity up to constant multiples, but they do not affect the order of growth.

Part (ii) of Conjecture 6.1 should be the easier half, because we get to choose the embedding process. We cannot overwrite a fixed m locations, because this does not have enough entropy, but we can make use of the same trick as in [21]: break the cover into $o(\sqrt{n})$ blocks of size $\omega(\sqrt{n})$ and make exactly one change per block. This will have enough entropy for $o(\sqrt{n} \log n)$ payload bits, and we expect to be

able to adapt the 'shortlist' idea from Subsect. 4.1 to the structure in this embedding process. Such an embedding code is well below optimal, of course, but for the asymptotic result it is enough to be within a constant factor of optimal.

Part (i) will be the more difficult, as the embedding process might have long-range dependencies. Either they will have to be bounded by assumption, or it will be necessary to show that too many dependencies that are too strong will reduce the entropy of the embedding process too much.

An advantage of source coding is that so-called 'wet' locations (in the language of [12]), where a change is considered perfectly detectable, can be avoided. Paralleling this, we expect to weaken the no determinism assumption (**NAD**), so that not all locations need satisfy it. We would then replace the cover size n by the number of 'dry' locations that do satisfy (**NAD**).

7 CONCLUSIONS

When embedding is perfect – a process that does not change the probability distribution of covers – or if the embedding learns a cover model so that the embedding tends to perfect, there is typically a *linear law of steganographic capacity*. When embedding can introduce groups of pixels that are impossible in cover objects, there is typically a *constant capacity* that does not grow with the cover size. Once we exclude the first case (with a *no free bits* condition) and the second (with a *no determinism* condition), it takes few additional assumptions to prove a *square root law*.

We extended the square root law to inhomogeneous Markov chains and a variety of Ising models, but more generally for covers subject to two main conditions: direct dependence of finite range, and exponential decay of covariance. We may reasonably expect these properties to be true for the acquisition chain of most digital media (for example: CCD leakage, demosaicking, and resampling all cause only local dependencies), but might not hold when there are macroscopic dependencies caused by scene content (for example: consistency of light sources). However, it is difficult to imagine a detector able to exploit such dependencies.

We do not claim that the sufficient conditions, from which the results of this paper have been proved, are always necessary. Consider for example a cover model without exponential decay of covariance: do strong cover interactions make detection more difficult, or easier? One might expect the latter[9], in which case it should be possible to drop the assumption. But consider binary pixels drawn from a Pólya Process, a MRF with unbounded dependence: it can be shown that the lower bound holds anyway; covariance does not decay (at all, let alone exponentially) and the upper bound does *not* hold. Space precludes further discussion of this fascinating example. Space also precludes discussion of infinite-range Ising models, which in some cases can be analyzed with extensions of the methods used here. Another generalization would be

---

[8]In [1] the payoff itself is concerned with asymptotic behaviour: the exponential rate at which detection tends to perfect in the case of a constant-rate payload.

[9]Adaptive steganography typically employs the following heuristic: cover locations that can be well-predicted from others are bad choices for embedding.

to weaken the no free bits assumption to a conditional rather than joint distributional difference.

We have only considered cases where the cover and stego distributions $\mathcal{P}_n$ and $\mathcal{Q}_n^m$ are known to the detector. Of course, in absence of this knowledge the lower bound still applies. When can the critical rate be raised? How much knowledge is required to keep the upper bound? These are questions for further research. Note that the model where a detector that learns about the cover source [22] is problematic when the cover is nonstationary, unless what is learned in the past gives information about the future.

In this paper we have omitted a third clause included in some square root laws: if $m(n)/r(n) \to c$, embedding *on the* critical rate, we can sometimes calculate or bound the KLD between cover and stego objects, proving ϵ-security for some value $\epsilon(c)$ (e.g. [11, 21]); equivalently, compute the Fisher Information of the embedding. In view of the discussion of KLD and TV in Sect. 3 the focus should probably be on TV instead, but the proof methods of this paper – inequalities rather than exact asymptotics – could only give loose bounds.

Finally, we have made a conjecture about a square root law for adaptive embedding, which is of an adversarial nature. Given that adaptive embedding is now dominant in image and video steganography, a proof should bring the theory even closer to practice.

REFERENCES

[1] M. Barni and B. Tondi. 2013. The Source Identification Game: An Information-Theoretic Perspective. *IEEE Transactions on Information Forensics and Security* 8, 3 (2013), 450–463.

[2] B. A. Bash, D. Goeckel, and D. Towsley. 2012. Square Root Law for Communication with Low Probability of Detection on AWGN Channels. In *Proc. International Symposium on Information Theory.* IEEE, Piscataway, NJ, 448–452.

[3] C. Cachin. 2004. An Information-Theoretic Model for Steganography. *Information and Computation* 192, 1 (2004), 41–56.

[4] J.-R. Chazottes, P. Collet, and F. Redig. 2016. On Concentration Inequalities and their Applications for Gibbs Measures in Lattice Systems. (2016). arXiv:1610.06502 (submitted for publication).

[5] P. Comesaña and F. Pérez-González. 2007. On the Capacity of Stegosystems. In *Proc. 9th Workshop on Multimedia & Security (MM&Sec).* ACM, New York, NY, 15–24.

[6] T. Denemark, V. Sedighi, V.and Holub, R. Cogranne, and J. Fridrich. 2014. Selection-Channel-Aware Rich Model for Steganalysis of Digital Images. In *Proc. International Workshop on Information Forensics and Security (WIFS).* IEEE, Piscataway, NJ, 48–53.

[7] T. Filler. 2008. *Important Properties of Normalized KL-Divergence under HMC Model.* Technical Report. DDE Lab, SUNY Binghamton. http://dde.binghamton.edu/filler/kl-divergence-hmc.pdf Techncial Report.

[8] T. Filler and J. Fridrich. 2009. Complete Characterization of Perfectly Secure Stego-systems with Mutually Independent Embedding Operation. In *Proc. International Conference on Acoustics, Speech, and Signal Processing.* IEEE, Piscataway, NJ, 1429–1432.

[9] T. Filler and J. Fridrich. 2010. Gibbs Construction in Steganography. *IEEE Transactions on Information Forensics and Security* 5, 4 (2010), 705–720.

[10] T. Filler, J. Judas, and J. Fridrich. 2011. Minimizing Additive Distortion in Steganography using Syndrome-Trellis Codes. *IEEE Transactions on Information Forensics and Security* 6, 3 (2011), 920–935.

[11] T. Filler, A. D. Ker, and J. Fridrich. 2009. The Square Root Law of Steganographic Capacity for Markov Covers. In *Media Forensics and Security XI (Proc. SPIE),* Vol. 7254. SPIE, Article 08, 11 pages.

[12] J. Fridrich, M. Goljan, D. Soukal, and P. Lisoněk. 2005. Writing on Wet Paper. *IEEE Transactions on Signal Processing* 53, 10 (2005), 3923–3935.

[13] J. Fridrich and D. Soukal. 2006. Matrix Embedding for Large Payloads. *IEEE Transactions on Information Forensics and Security* 1, 3 (2006), 390–394.

[14] X. Guyon. 1995. *Random Fields on a Network: Modeling, Statistics, and Applications.* Springer-Verlag, New York. Translated by C. Ludena.

[15] B. Johnson, P. Schöttle, A. Laszka, J. Grossklags, and R. Böhme. 2015. *Adaptive Steganography and Steganalysis with Fixed-Size Embedding.* Springer, Berlin, Heidelberg, 69–91.

[16] A. D. Ker. 2004. Improved Detection of LSB Steganography in Grayscale Images. In *Proc. 6th Information Hiding Workshop (LNCS),* Vol. 3200. Springer, Berlin, Heidelberg, 97–115.

[17] A. D. Ker. 2006. Batch Steganography and Pooled Steganalysis. In *Proc. 8th Information Hiding Workshop (LNCS),* Vol. 4437. Springer, Berlin, Heidelberg, 265–281.

[18] A. D. Ker. 2007. A Capacity Result for Batch Steganography. *IEEE Signal Processing Letters* 14, 8 (2007), 525–528.

[19] A. D. Ker. 2009. Locally Square Distortion and Batch Steganographic Capacity. *International Journal of Digital Crime and Forensics* 1, 1 (2009), 29–44.

[20] A. D. Ker. 2009. The Square Root Law Requires a Linear Key. In *Proc. 11th Workshop on Multimedia and Security.* ACM, New York, NY, 85–92.

[21] A. D. Ker. 2010. The Square Root Law Does Not Require a Linear Key. In *Proc. 11th Workshop on Multimedia and Security.* ACM, New York, NY, 213–223.

[22] A. D. Ker. 2010. The Square Root Law in Stegosystems with Imperfect Information. In *Proc. Information Hiding, 12th International Conference (LNCS),* Vol. 6387. Springer, Berlin, Heidelberg, 145–160.

[23] A. D. Ker. 2011. A Curiosity Regarding Steganographic Capacity of Pathologically Nonstationary Sources. In *Media Watermarking, Security, and Forensics XIII (Proc. SPIE),* Vol. 7880. SPIE, Article 0E, 12 pages.

[24] A. D. Ker, P. Bas, R. Böhme, R. Cogranne, S. Craver, T. Filler, J. Fridrich, and T. Pevný. 2013. Moving Steganography and Steganalysis from the Laboratory into the Real World. In *Proc. 1st Workshop on Information Hiding and Multimedia Security.* ACM, New York, NY, 45–58.

[25] A. D. Ker, T. Pevný, and P. Bas. 2016. Rethinking Optimal Embedding. In *Proc. 4th Workshop on Information Hiding and Multimedia Security.* ACM, New York, NY, 93–102.

[26] A. D. Ker, T. Pevný, J. Kodovský, and J. Fridrich. 2008. The Square Root Law of Steganographic Capacity. In *Proc. 10th Workshop on Multimedia and Security.* ACM, New York, NY, 107–116.

[27] E. L. Lehmann and J. P. Romano. 2005. *Testing Statistical Hypotheses* (3rd ed.). Springer-Verlag, New York.

[28] D. A. Levin, Y. Peres, and E. L. Wilmer. 2009. *Markov Chains and Mixing Times.* American Mathematical Society, Providence, RI.

[29] F. Martinelli. 2000. An Elementary Approach to Finite Size Conditions for the Exponential Decay of Covariances in Lattice Spin Models. In *In: On Dobrushins Way. From Probability Theory to Statistical Physics.* Translations Series 2, Vol. 198. American Mathematical Society, Providence, RI, 169–181.

[30] T. Pevný, J. Fridrich, and A. D. Ker. 2012. From Blind to Quantitative Steganalysis. *IEEE Transactions on Information Forensics and Security* 7, 2 (2012), 445–454.

[31] B. Ryabko and D. Ryabko. 2011. Constructing Perfect Steganographic Systems. *Information and Computation* 209, 9 (2011), 1223–1230.

[32] D. Ryabko. 2011. On the Relation Between Realizable and Non-Realizable Cases of the Sequence Prediction Problem. *Journal of Machine Learning Research* 12 (2011), 2161–2180.

[33] R. H. Schonmann and S. B. Shlosman. 1995. Complete Analyticity for 2D Ising Completed. *Communications in Mathematical Physics* 170, 2 (1995), 453–482.

[34] Y. Wang and P. Moulin. 2008. Perfectly Secure Steganography: Capacity, Error Exponents, and Code Constructions. *IEEE Transactions on Information Theory* 55, 6 (2008), 2706–2722.

[35] A. Wilson and A. D. Ker. 2016. Avoiding Detection on Twitter: Embedding Strategies for Linguistic Steganography. In *Media Watermarking, Security, and Forensics 2016.* IS&T, Article 9, 9 pages.

Nonlinear Feature Normalization in Steganalysis

Mehdi Boroumand
Binghamton University
Department of ECE
Binghamton, NY 13902-6000
mboroum1@binghamton.edu

Jessica Fridrich
Binghamton University
Department of ECE
Binghamton, NY 13902-6000
fridrich@binghamton.edu

ABSTRACT

In this paper, we propose a method for normalization of rich feature sets to improve detection accuracy of simple classifiers in steganalysis. It consists of two steps: 1) replacing random subsets of empirical joint probability mass functions (co-occurrences) by their conditional probabilities and 2) applying a non-linear normalization to each element of the feature vector by forcing its marginal distribution over covers to be uniform. We call the first step random conditioning and the second step feature uniformization. When applied to maxSRMd2 features in combination with simple classifiers, we observe a gain in detection accuracy across all tested stego algorithms and payloads. For better insight, we investigate the gain for two image formats. The proposed normalization has a very low computational complexity and does not require any feedback from the stego class.

KEYWORDS

Steganography, steganalysis, machine learning, normalization, random conditioning, uniformization

ACM Reference format:
Mehdi Boroumand and Jessica Fridrich. 2017. Nonlinear Feature Normalization in Steganalysis. In *Proceedings of IH&MMSec '17, Philadelphia, PA, USA, June 20-22, 2017,* 10 pages.
https://doi.org/10.1145/3082031.3083239

1 INTRODUCTION

Currently, the most popular approach to steganalysis of digital images puts emphasis on the feature representation rather than machine learning. The so-called rich models consist of joint probability mass functions (co-occurrences) of neighboring noise residuals extracted using a large bank of both linear and non-linear filters (pixel predictors). Due to the high dimensionality of the features and the ensuing training complexity, researchers resorted to low-complexity machine learning paradigms, such as the ensemble classifier [17], its linear version [3], and regularized linear discriminants [4].

One possibility to improve the detection and better utilize the information contained in the feature vector without employing a

more complex machine learning tool is to transform or preprocess the feature vector prior to classification. In [2], the authors showed that a non-linear feature transformation may enable better separation of cover and stego features with a simple decision boundary as long as the feature is a collection of co-occurrences. The approach was linked to approximating implicit feature maps in kernelized support vector machines with an explicit transformation [22, 32].

In this paper, we propose a related but different and much more simple idea based on applying a non-linear normalization to the features. It consists of two steps: L_1 normalization of random subsets of features and forcing the marginal distribution of each feature across images to be uniform. The first step is equivalent to changing the descriptor from joint distributions to conditional distributions, which is why we call it in this paper random conditioning. The second step is executed by applying the empirical cumulative density function (cdf) to each feature bin and is thus essentially a non-linear bin-dependent coordinate transformation that maximizes the entropy of each feature bin across cover images.

It is rather interesting that the proposed feature normalization leads to slightly larger gains in detection accuracy than the previously proposed explicit approximations of positive definite kernels [2]. Curiously, combining these approaches does not lead to further gain. We report the gain on four steganographic schemes embedding in the spatial domain and a wide range of payloads on two image sources – uncompressed images of BOSSbase 1.01 and its quality 85 JPEG version (decompressed JPEGs).

Our work was inspired by normalization techniques applied in convolutional neural networks conceived of to mimic inhibition schemes observed in the biological brain. In the context of machine learning, this technique is known as contrast normalization or neighborhood (local) response normalization [16, 18, 21, 26].

In the next section, we explain random conditioning and search for its single scalar parameter, the size of the random subsets. Section 3 contains description and analysis of uniformization. The proposed non-linear feature normalization is tested in Section 4, where we also discuss and interpret the results. A summary of the paper appears in Section 5.

2 FROM JOINT TO CONDITIONAL

The very first higher-order steganalysis features introduced in mid 2000's were formed as empirical Markov transition probability matrices. This applies both to the original publications on steganalysis of JPEGs [28] and spatial domain images [33] as well to the follow up work [25] and the SPAM feature [23]. The move from conditional to joint statistics (co-occurrences) came with the introduction of the embedding algorithm HUGO [24], where large third-order joint distributions of pixel differences were approximately preserved by the design of the distortion function minimized in HUGO. Co-occurrences were then ported into the design of the spatial rich model [7] and its many variants [6, 8, 30, 31]. The authors of this article are not aware of any work aimed at reinvestigating the suitability of conditional probability distributions for steganalysis.

First, we briefly introduce the concept of a noise residual, its quantized form, and a joint probability distribution, the co-occurrence. For an $n_1 \times n_2$ grayscale image $x_{ij} \in \{0, \ldots, 255\}$, $1 \leq i \leq n_1$, $1 \leq j \leq n_2$, let r_{ij} be a noise residual obtained by subtracting from each pixel value x_{ij} its predicted value $\hat{x}_{ij}$, $r_{ij} = x_{ij} - \hat{x}_{ij}$. Before forming co-occurrences, the residual is quantized using a quantizer $Q : \mathbb{R} \rightarrow \mathcal{Q}$ with $2T + 1$ centroids $\mathcal{Q} = \{-T, -T + 1, \ldots, T\}$, $T \in \mathbb{N}$:

$$z_{ij} = Q_Q(r_{ij}/q) \in \mathcal{Q}, \text{ for each } i, j, \quad (1)$$

where $q > 0$ is a quantization step. Typically, for 8-bit grayscale images, $q \in \{1, 1.5, 2\}$ in the SRM [7]. To curb the dimensionality of co-occurrences built from z_{ij} and to keep them well populated, small values of the threshold are typically used, such as $T = 2$.

A four-dimensional co-occurrence along the horizontal direction is a four-dimensional array $\mathbf{C} \in \mathcal{Q}^4$ defined as

$$C_{d_1 d_2 d_3 d_4} = \frac{1}{n_1(n_2 - 3)} \sum_{i=1}^{n_1} \sum_{j=1}^{n_2-3} [r_{ij} = d_1 \ \& \ r_{i,j+1} = d_2$$
$$\& \ r_{i,j+2} = d_3 \ \& \ r_{i,j+3} = d_4], \quad (2)$$

where $d_m \in \mathcal{Q}$, $m = 1, 2, 3, 4$ and $[P]$ is the Iverson bracket equal to 0 when statement P is true and zero otherwise. Thus, the dimensionality of $\mathbf{C}$ is $|\mathcal{Q}|^4$. For compactness, we will use vector notation for the four-dimensional indices $\mathbf{d} = (d_1 d_2 d_3 d_4)$ belonging to $\mathcal{S} \triangleq \{(d_1, d_2, d_3, d_4)|d_m \in \mathcal{Q}\} = \mathcal{Q}^4$.

In this article, we will consider a more general approach to conditioning. Let and let $\mathcal{S}_1, \ldots, \mathcal{S}_k$ be k disjoint subsets of $\mathcal{S}$ whose union is $\mathcal{S} = \cup_{l=1}^{k} \mathcal{S}_l$. For convenience, we introduce an index mapping $J : \mathcal{Q}^4 \rightarrow \{1, \ldots, k\}$ that assigns to each $\mathbf{d} \in \mathcal{Q}^4$ the unique index $l \in \{1, \ldots, k\}$ such that $(d_1 d_2 d_3 d_4) \in \mathcal{S}_l$. We say that the four-dimensional array $\tilde{\mathbf{C}} \in \mathcal{Q}^4$ is obtained from $\mathbf{C}$ by conditioning on $\mathcal{S}_1, \ldots, \mathcal{S}_k$ when all elements of $\tilde{\mathbf{C}}$ are obtained from $\mathbf{C}$ by

$$\tilde{C}_{\mathbf{d}} = \Pr\{\mathbf{d}|\mathbf{d} \in \mathcal{S}_{J(\mathbf{d})}\}$$
$$= \frac{C_{\mathbf{d}}}{\sum_{\mathbf{e} \in \mathcal{S}_{J(\mathbf{d})}} C_{\mathbf{e}}}, \quad (3)$$

for all $\mathbf{d} \in \mathcal{Q}^4$. One can alternatively say that $\mathbf{C}$ has been L_1 normalized on $\mathcal{S}_1, \ldots, \mathcal{S}_k$.

Replacing the joint distribution $\mathbf{C}$ with the conditional one $\tilde{\mathbf{C}}$ increases the contrast of bins from each $\mathcal{S}_l$, $l = 1, \ldots, k$, equalizing the magnitude of the co-occurrence bins across the index sets. When the sets $\mathcal{S}_l$ are selected at random, we call this normalization *random conditioning*.

Conditioning bears strong similarity to normalization in neural networks [16, 18] applied across feature maps as implemented in, e.g., 'cuda convnets' with a local response normalization layer. The convnet documentation states that this type of normalization layer "encourages competition for big activities among nearby groups of neurons." The parallel between this layer and our conditioning becomes more clear when one considers individual co-occurrence bins as elements of feature maps that enter the normalization layer.

Table 1: Detection error of S-UNIWARD at 0.4 bpp on BOSS-base 1.01 with the non-symmetrized EDGE3x3 SRM sub-model of dimensionality 625 (the last row) and its four versions conditioned on index sets of cardinality 5 and 25.

$\mathcal{S}_l$	$|\mathcal{S}_l|$	P_E
$(d_1, d_2, d_3, .)$	5	0.2851 ± 0.0033
$(d_1, d_2, ., .)$	25	0.2829 ± 0.0041
Random 5	5	0.2854 ± 0.0032
Random 25	25	0.2752 ± 0.0018
Original	625	0.2875 ± 0.0028

To get a feeling for the effect of conditioning on steganalysis features, we start with a single SRM submodel 'EDGE3x3' (sometimes called KB submodel) on BOSSbase 1.01 [1] images with the steganographic algorithm S-UNIWARD [15] for payload 0.4 bits per pixel (bpp). We keep the feature in its non-symmetrized form, meaning its dimensionality is $5^4 = 625$ rather than 169 as in the SRM to allow for easier switching to conditional probabilities.

Table 1 shows the minimal total error probability (average of false-alarm and missed-detection rates P_{FA} and P_D) under equal priors

$$P_E = \min_{P_{FA}} \frac{1}{2}(P_{FA} + P_{MD}) \quad (4)$$

averaged over ten 50/50 splits of the database into training and testing sets obtained with the FLD-ensemble classifier [17] and the KB submodel conditioned on four different tessellations of all 5^4 co-occurrence indices $\mathcal{S}$. The statistical spread is the mean absolute deviation (MAD) across the ten database splits. The first two rows of the table correspond to the cases when the conditioning is performed on the first three indices $d_1 d_2 d_3$ and on the first two $d_1 d_2$, respectively. Formally, for the first row, $\mathcal{S}_{d_1 d_2 d_3} = \{(d_1, d_2, d_3, d_4)|d_4 \in \mathcal{Q}\}$, $\mathcal{Q} = \{-2, -1, 0, 1, 2\}$, and thus $|\mathcal{S}_{d_1 d_2 d_3}| = 5$ for all $d_1 d_2 d_3$ and $\mathcal{S}_{d_1 d_2} = \{(d_1, d_2, d_3, d_4)|d_3, d_4 \in \mathcal{Q}\}$ with $|\mathcal{S}_{d_1 d_2}| = 25$ for the second row. The third and fourth rows correspond to $\mathcal{S}_l$ being selected uniformly at random from $\mathcal{Q}^4$. The last row is for the original KB feature vector. The conclusion that can be made from this initial experiment is that, considering the statistical spread, the transition probability matrices offer about the same detection as the joint or random conditioning on groups of five bins. Conditioning on random groups of 25, however, leads to a statistically significant improvement. Selecting the index sets $\mathcal{S}_l$ randomly seems better than in a structured manner obtained when considering the residuals as a Markov chain, which hints at the importance of diversity for the index sets. To obtain more insight, as our next experiment we forced diversity on $\mathcal{S}_l$. For the experiment, we moved to the full maxSRMd2 feature vector on BOSSbase 1.01 images for HILL and WOW embedding algorithms at 0.4 bpp while keeping the FLD-ensemble as the classifier. To prevent potential problems when conditioning on bins that are always zero, we removed from the feature all bins that are guaranteed to be zero independently of the input image (see Section 4.1 in [2] for more detail regarding the zeros in rich models). After removing the zero bins, the maxSRMd2 feature vector has a dimensionality of $D = 32,016$.

Table 2: Detection error P_E as a function of the index sets size $s = |S_l|$ for HILL and WOW at 0.4 bpp with the maxSRMd2 feature when conditioning on index sets (5) with diversity forced in four different ways as explained in the text.

					HILL 0.4 bpp				
s	2	3	4	8	12	16	24	46	58
Mean	.2122±.0029	.2041±.0034	.2018±.0026	.2016±.0017	.2017±.0023	.2030±.0030	.2035±.0028	.2072±.0025	.2077±.0030
Var	.2123±.0020	.2055±.0037	.2011±.0030	.1999±.0017	.2007±.0032	.2029±.0026	.2036±.0033	.2062±.0039	.2062±.0031
σ/μ	.2067±.0018	.2035±.0029	.2021±.0029	.2008±.0024	.2003±.0013	.2033±.0027	.2029±.0024	.2061±.0029	.2077±.0019
Corr	.2106±.0025	.2043±.0025	.2027±.0026	.2018±.0040	.2013±.0021	.2016±.0029	.2030±.0031	.2060±.0021	.2056±.0027
					WOW 0.4 bpp				
Mean	.1346±.0013	.1285±.0025	.1270±.0026	.1321±.0032	.1337±.0022	.1356±.0034	.1389±.0033	.1446±.0028	.1469±.0034
Var	.1334±.0015	.1285±.0021	.1286±.0022	.1292±.0032	.1341±.0032	.1350±.0038	.1395±.0024	.1425±.0022	.1448±.0028
σ/μ	.1333±.0030	.1304±.0024	.1301±.0022	.1349±.0028	.1380±.0038	.1383±.0024	.1395±.0033	.1447±.0027	.1437±.0023
Corr	.1337±.0021	.1297±.0019	.1283±.0027	.1319±.0024	.1358±.0045	.1363±.0022	.1397±.0036	.1436±.0033	.1455±.0030

The diversity was forced on S_l by first ordering the features in the maxSRMd2 feature vector according to some scalar quantity and then selecting s equally spaced (interleaved) bins from the ordered feature vector. Given an integer s that divides the feature dimensionality D,

$$S_l = \{l + nD/s | n = 0, \ldots, s-1\}, l = 1, \ldots, D/s. \qquad (5)$$

For example, when $s = 8$ $S_1 = \{1, 4003, 8005, 12007, 16009, 20011, 24013, 28015\}$ and the last $S_{4002} = \{4002, 8004, 12006, 16008, 20010, 24012, 28014, 32016\}$.

We denote the ith feature (bin) in the maxSRMd2 feature vector of jth cover image as $f_i^{(j)}$, $i = 1, \ldots, D$, $j = 1, \ldots, N_{trn}$, where N_{trn} is the number of images in the training set. The following scalar quantities were investigated for ordering:

(1) Sample mean bin population across all training cover images $\mu_i = 1/N_{trn} \sum_{j=1}^{N_{trn}} f_i^{(j)}$.

(2) Sample variance of the bin $\sigma_i^2 = 1/(N_{trn}-1) \sum_{j=1}^{N_{trn}} (f_i^{(j)} - \mu_i)^2$.

(3) Relative statistical spread σ_i/μ_i.

(4) Sample correlation between bins,

$$\rho_{km} = \frac{1/N_{trn} \sum_{j=1}^{N_{trn}} (f_k^{(j)} - \mu_k)(f_m^{(j)} - \mu_m)}{\sigma_k \sigma_l}. \qquad (6)$$

To obtain the ordering, all D^2 values ρ_{kl}, $1 \leq k, l \leq D$ are ordered from the largest to the smallest: $\rho_{k_1 l_1} \geq \rho_{k_2 l_2} \geq \rho_{k_3 l_3} \geq \ldots$. Then, the ordering is obtained as $k_1, l_1, k_2, l_2, k_3, l_3, \ldots$, while skipping over indices already present in the sequence.

Table 2 shows the detection error P_E as a function of the index subset size s for HILL [20] and WOW [11] at 0.4 bpp with the maxSRMd2 feature set. All four orderings seem to produce similar results with a minimal detection error for $4 \leq s \leq 8$. A simple way to force diversity is to choose the index sets S_l randomly, all of cardinality $s = |S_l|$. Figure 1, shows the detection error $P_E(s)$ and its statistical spread over ten database splits as a function of s on four steganographic algorithms and payload 0.4 bpp. Lennard–Jones potential function [19] in the form $V(x) = ax^{12} + bx^6$ was used to obtain the fit. The detection error for the original maxSRMd2 feature vector is shown on the far right to highlight the gain due to random conditioning. We note that a qualitatively similar behavior was observed for payload 0.2 bpp.

To conclude the experiments in this section, we can say that random conditioning provides approximately the same detection gain as forcing diversity with index sets (5). We choose random conditioning for the rest of this paper because this feature normalization is independent of the properties of images across the source and does not need examples of cover or stego images to estimate any parameters.

Since random conditioning contains randomness, the detection error P_E will slightly vary even when all other experimental parameters are fixed. Figure 2 shows the histogram of the detection error averaged over ten splits of the database repeated for 50 different seeds used for random conditioning. The figure was obtained for HILL at relative payload 0.2 and 0.4 bpp (left and right). We wish to point out that the distribution appears symmetrical and unimodal. The difference in P_E between the best and worst detection is approximately 0.5%. We investigated whether it is possible to identify a good seed that would consistently give good results across embedding algorithms and payloads. We could not, however, identify any consistent fluctuations. Thus, to simplify the matters, we recommend that the randomness in random conditioning be simply fixed.

3 UNIFORMIZATION

Besides conditioning as described in the previous section, the second measure we propose in this paper is normalization across images. Because a typical linear normalization would have no effect when coupled with a linear classifier, we apply a non-linear procedure that ensures that the marginal distribution of each feature j has the maximal entropy. That is, we force it to be uniform on $[0, 1]$ across images (j), $f_i^{(j)} \sim U[0, 1]$ for each bin i.

In general, given n independent realizations $x_1, \ldots, x_n$ of a random variable X sorted from the smallest to the largest in a non-decreasing sequence, the empirical cumulative density function (c.d.f.) of X is

$$F(x) = \begin{cases} \frac{l-1}{n}, l = \arg\min_l x < x_l, & \text{when } x < x_n \\ 1 & \text{when } x \geq x_n. \end{cases} \qquad (7)$$

To force $f_i^{(j)} \sim U[0, 1]$ across images j for each bin i, we use the realizations $f_i^{(j)}$, $j = 1, \ldots, N_{trn}$, to estimate the empirical c.d.f. $F_i(x)$ using Eq. (7). Because this normalization is a property

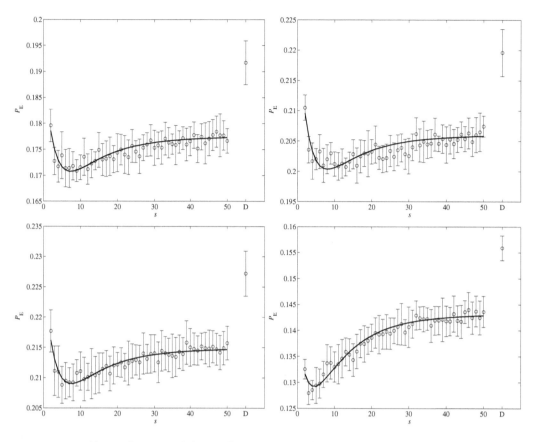

Figure 1: Detection error $P_E(s)$ as a function of the random set size $s = |S_l|$. The last datapoint corresponds to $s = D$, the full feature dimensionality (no conditioning). Left to right, top to bottom: S-UNIWARD, HILL, MiPOD, WOW, payload 0.4 bpp, BOSSbase 1.01, maxSRMd2.

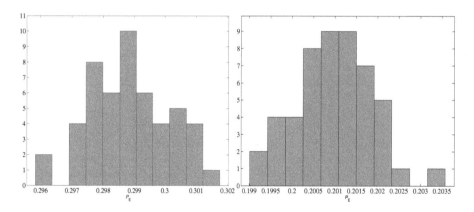

Figure 2: Histogram of the average detection error P_E across 50 seeds used for random conditioning with $s = 8$ for HILL on BOSSbase 1.01 using maxSRMd2. Left: payload 0.2 bpp, Right: payload 0.4 bpp.

Table 3: Detection error P_E for HILL and WOW at 0.4 bpp with the maxSRMd2 feature when applying the uniformization to all bins (row 2), combing uniformization on all bins with random conditioning (RC), and combining uniformization on selected bins coupled with random conditioning (rows 4–7).

	Normalization	HILL	WOW
1	Original	0.2196±0.0039	0.1559±0.0024
2	Uniform	0.2072±0.0031	0.1349±0.0025
3	RC only	0.2008±0.0030	0.1295±0.0025
4	32,016 + RC	0.1995±0.0028	0.1263±0.0025
5	20,000 + RC	0.1972±0.0027	0.1255±0.0022
6	15,000 + RC	0.1987±0.0029	0.1243±0.0025
7	10,000 + RC	0.1996±0.0030	0.1248±0.0032
8	5,000 + RC	0.1989±0.0031	0.1257±0.0022

of the source, it needs a training set of cover images from which the empirical c.d.f. is estimated.

To observe the effect of uniformization, we selected two embedding algorithms, HILL and WOW, and payload 0.4 bpp on BOSSbase. All results appear in Table 3, which we now comment upon. The first four rows show the detection error for the original maxSRMd2 feature vector after applying uniformization to all bins, applying only random conditioning (RC), and combining uniformization with random conditioning. The parameter s for RC was chosen $s = 4$ for WOW and $s = 8$ for HILL, respectively. Comparing the effect of RC with uniformization (row 3 and 2) to the original feature (row 1), one can conclude that while both measures boost the detection, the RC has a more beneficial effect. Also, an additional small gain is obtained when combining them (row 4).

The marginal distribution of the individual bins in the maxSRMd2 feature vector varies greatly. Figure 3 shows four examples of such distributions (left column) together with the impact of embedding on the bin (right column) in the form of graphs showing the bin population after embedding versus before embedding (stego vs. cover bin population). The diagonal line should help the reader infer the impact of embedding on the bin population. Notice the scale of the x axis, which informs us about the typical population of the bin across images. The embedding has a strong impact on the bin shown in the top graph, only a rather small impact on the next two bins, and virtually no impact on the fourth bin at the bottom of the figure. Generally speaking, we noticed that all bins whose marginal distribution is similar to what is shown in the first graph are affected by embedding the most. One can also say that the bins with marginal distribution similar to the first bin correspond to the most populated and most correlated bins from the feature vector. Based on extensive experiments, we determined that such bins benefit from being non-linearly normalized (uniformized) while it is beneficial to not apply such a normalization to the remaining bins.

Based on this finding, we adjusted the uniformization to be applied only to the first w bins when ordering them according to their correlation as explained in the previous section. Rows 4–8 contain the detection error when the maxSRMd2 feature is first randomly conditioned and then the first $w \in \{D, 20000, 15000, 10000, 5000\}$ bins uniformized with the remaining $D - w$ bins left untouched.

A further small gain seems to be obtained when applying the uniformization only to the first $w \approx D/2$ bins when sorting them based on correlation. This finding is consistent with what was observed for other embedding algorithms, payloads, and across sources.

In general, we found it rather difficult to optimize the non-linear coordinate normalization by trying to find alternative ways to selectively normalize. In fact, if the individual bins were independent, the log-likelihood ratio in its empirical form learned (estimated) from the training set would be an optimal "normalization" or, more properly, statistical test for steganalysis. However, in the presence of complex non-linear dependencies among individual bins, we were forced to resort to heuristics.

Even though the selective uniformization is unlikely to be close to an optimal way of normalizing the bins, it is beneficial as it lowers the detection error and decreases the computational complexity.

4 EXPERIMENTS

In this section, we experimentally evaluate the proposed feature normalization on four steganographic algorithms, five payloads, and two cover sources - BOSSbase 1.01 and BOSSbaseJ85. BOSSbaseJ85 (J as in JPEG, 85 is the JPEG quality factor) was formed from BOSSbase 1.01 images by JPEG compressing them with quality factor 85 and then decompressing to the spatial domain and representing the resulting image as an 8-bit grayscale. The low-pass character of JPEG compression makes the images less textured and much less noisy. The tested steganographic schemes include MiPOD [27], HILL [20], S-UNIWARD [15], and WOW [11].

Before we present the results of the detection, we provide a pseudo-code for the experimental routine to clarify the procedure that was applied to the features before classification.

Algorithm 1 Training a classifier with N_{trn} training images by normalizing with D-dimensional cover/stego features stored as matrices $\mathbf{f}^{(c)} \in \mathbb{R}^{N_{trn} \times D}$ and $\mathbf{f}^{(s)} \in \mathbb{R}^{N_{trn} \times D}$. The same random conditioning with permutation P is done to features from the test set. The uniformization learned on the training set (the permutation R and $F_{R(i)}$, $i = 1, \ldots, D/2$) is then also applied to all features from the testing set.

1: Set set size for RC
2: Generate random permutation P of indices $1, \ldots, D$
3: Apply random conditioning to each row of $\mathbf{f}$:
4: **for** $l = 1, \ldots, D/s$ **do**
5:      **for** $j = 1 : N_{trn}$ **do**
6:          $\mathbf{f}^{c/s}(j, P((l-1)s + 1 : ls)) \leftarrow \dfrac{\mathbf{f}^{c/s}(j, P((l-1)s+1:ls))}{\sum_{k=(l-1)s+1}^{ls} \mathbf{f}^{c/s}(j,k)}$
7:      **end for**
8: **end for**
9: Order all D cover features by correlation (Eq. (6)), denote order R (a permutation of $1, \ldots, D$)
10: **for** $i = 1, \ldots, D/2$ **do**
11:     Compute $F_{R(i)}$ (Eq. (7)) for N_{trn} samples $\mathbf{f}^c(:, R(i))$
12:     **for** $j = 1 : N_{trn}$ **do**
13:         Apply $F_{R(i)}$ to $\mathbf{f}^c(j, R(i))$ and $\mathbf{f}^s(j, R(i))$
14:     **end for**
15: **end for**

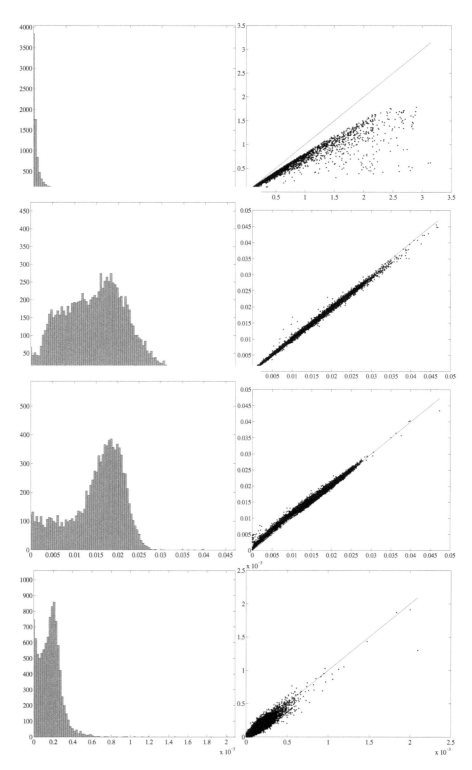

Figure 3: Examples of marginal (cover) distributions of four bins (left) from maxSRMd2 feature vector and the impact of embedding on the bin by plotting the cover bin population vs. stego bin population (right). The graphics was obtained across the entire BOSSbase database for HILL at 0.4 bpp. The bin indices are 16054, 24327, 19107, and 23974 in the maxSRMd2 feature after removing all zero bins.

Table 4: Detection error $\overline{P}_E$ for four steganographic schemes and five payloads in bpp on BOSSbase 1.01 with the FLD-ensemble trained with maxSRMd2 features.

S-UNI	Payload (bits per pixel)				
	0.1	0.2	0.3	0.4	0.5
maxSRMd2	0.3652±0.0008	0.2919±0.0023	0.2374±0.0023	0.1917±0.0042	0.1569±0.0035
Square root	0.3588±0.0025	0.2851±0.0034	0.2276±0.0021	0.1785±0.0033	0.1433±0.0026
exp-Hellinger	0.3608±0.0033	0.2803±0.0027	0.2181±0.0028	0.1720±0.0020	0.1348±0.0025
RC	0.3614±0.0030	0.2818±0.0026	0.2190±0.0028	0.1721±0.0034	0.1334±0.0030
RC+SU	0.3618±0.0020	0.2788±0.0014	0.2156±0.0023	0.1701±0.0035	0.1307±0.0032
HILL					
maxSRMd2	0.3742±0.0022	0.3105±0.0033	0.2580±0.0033	0.2196±0.0039	0.1815±0.0033
Square root	0.3669±0.0032	0.3007±0.0025	0.2512±0.0036	0.2116±0.0026	0.1736±0.0030
exp-Hellinger	0.3653±0.0024	0.2974±0.0028	0.2451±0.0024	0.2004±0.0019	0.1649±0.0031
RC	0.3661±0.0030	0.2998±0.0024	0.2453±0.0030	0.2031±0.0044	0.1655±0.0039
RC+SU	0.3655±0.0020	0.2980±0.0014	0.2408±0.0022	0.2008±0.0022	0.1627±0.0020
MiPOD					
maxSRMd2	0.3949±0.0031	0.3246±0.0034	0.2709±0.0027	0.2272±0.0037	0.1865±0.0029
Square root	0.3926±0.0047	0.3185±0.0022	0.2635±0.0027	0.2209±0.0036	0.1818±0.0022
exp-Hellinger	0.3911±0.0038	0.3148±0.0026	0.2568±0.0024	0.2104±0.0028	0.1720±0.0031
RC	0.3903±0.0037	0.3115±0.0027	0.2541±0.0021	0.2112±0.0044	0.1733±0.0032
RC+SU	0.3900±0.0029	0.3111±0.0032	0.2516±0.0046	0.2068±0.0030	0.1690±0.0033
WOW					
maxSRMd2	0.2984±0.0020	0.2331±0.0018	0.1907±0.0028	0.1559±0.0024	0.1279±0.0030
Square root	0.2854±0.0033	0.2140±0.0031	0.1702±0.0026	0.1375±0.0020	0.1118±0.0033
exp-Hellinger	0.2820±0.0024	0.2094±0.0025	0.1645±0.0031	0.1310±0.0028	0.1068±0.0032
RC	0.2826±0.0040	0.2113±0.0027	0.1633±0.0039	0.1301±0.0035	0.1055±0.0019
RC+SU	0.2801±0.0032	0.2051±0.0019	0.1588±0.0023	0.1257±0.0036	0.1017±0.0024

We note that the permutation P of indices $\{1, \ldots, D\}$ for random conditioning is generated and then fixed across all experiments. The feature order R by correlation (6) and the c.d.f.s $F_{R(i)}, i = 1, \ldots, D/2$, are learned from all N_{trn} cover features from the training set and then applied to the testing set. The size of the random subsets is set to four for WOW and eight for other embedding schemes. The results of experiments on BOSSbase 1.01 and BOSSbaseJ85 are reported in Tables 4 and 5, respectively. As above, random conditioning is abbreviated as RC and, when combined with selective uniformization, we abbreviate as RC+SU. The results are also contrasted with what can be achieved with preprocessing the features using explicit non-linear maps [2]. Note that in most cases random conditioning achieves the same performance as the transformation with the exponential Hellinger kernel. As explained in the previous section, due to the randomness in RC, the results for RC can be slightly better or worse depending upon which seed is used for the random permutation. In our experiments, we fixed our seed ('seed = 1' in Matlab's Mersenne twister generator) for all tested steganographic methods, payloads, and image sources.

While combining random conditioning with selective uniformization further improves the detection performance, the improvement due to random conditioning is much larger than that of selective uniformization. The detection accuracy can be enhanced by up to 2.5% using random conditioning and up to 0.6% additional improvement can be achieved using selective uniformization. The effect of selective uniformization is most pronounced for WOW.

Since BOSSbaseJ85 is less noisy than BOSSbase 1.01, it is easier to steganalyze thus the detection error rates are overall much lower. While a consistent gain is observed for random conditioning, selective uniformization generally does not help for this source.

Figure 4 shows a graphical representation of how the proposed normalization affects the detection performance of maxSRMd2 for all tested embedding methods at two payloads, 0.2 bpp and 0.4 bpp, for both image sources. Normalization generally helps more for larger payloads than for smaller payloads. As already mentioned above, selective uniformization does not bring any performance boost in BOSSbaseJ85. Its effect also fades at the lower payloads for BOSSbase.

Finally, we note that, similar to the previously proposed explicit non-linear mappings of features, random conditioning and selective uniformization do not improve performance of features formed by histograms of residuals, such as the projection spatial rich model [12] and JPEG-phase-aware features [5, 13, 14, 29] for detection of modern JPEG steganography [9, 10, 15]. This is likely due to the fact that the bins of such feature vectors are better populated with far smaller differences between the least and most populated

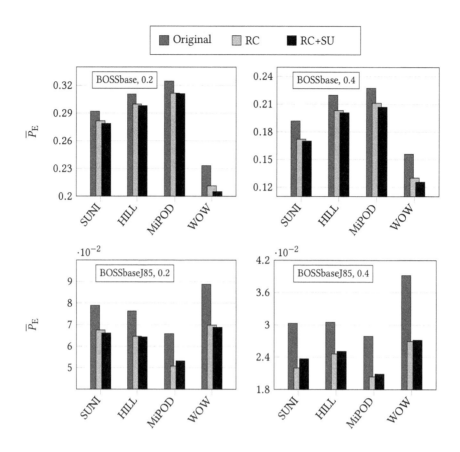

Figure 4: $\overline{P}_E$ **for four different embedding schemes and two image sources at 0.2 bpp and 0.4 bpp with the FLD-ensemble trained with maxSRMd2 feature set and its normalized versions.**

bins. With a more uniform distribution of the bins across images, the normalization methods proposed here are naturally less likely to be effective.

5 CONCLUSION

In this paper, we propose a low-complexity method for feature normalization of rich feature sets built as co-occurrences to improve the detection performance of simple classifiers. It adds only negligible computational overhead to feature computation and can be considered as a cheap pre-processing step before feeding the feature sets to a classifier.

We introduced two types of normalization: normalization on random subsets of the feature set called random conditioning and normalization of each bin across the database, uniformization. Random conditioning can be interpreted as switching from a joint distribution to a conditional distribution. It does not require any training data and can be applied to feature sets independently of the cover source, embedding algorithm, and payload. Since the inherent randomness associated with this process causes fluctuations in the final detection rate by approximately ±0.5% in terms of P_E, the authors encourage researchers employing this normalization method to specify the seed used for generating the random subsets in their papers.

Experimental results show a consistent performance improvement across all tested steganographic methods, payloads, and databases. Random conditioning is more effective than selective uniformization and is responsible for most of the gain we observed. In particular, in decompressed JPEGs, selective uniformization was observed as ineffective.

6 ACKNOWLEDGMENTS

The work on this paper was supported by Air Force Office of Scientific Research under the research grant number FA9950-12-1-0124. The U.S. Government is authorized to reproduce and distribute reprints for Governmental purposes notwithstanding any copyright notation there on. The views and conclusions contained herein are those of the authors and should not be interpreted as necessarily representing the official policies, either expressed or implied of AFOSR or the U.S. Government. The authors would like to thank anonymous reviewers for their insightful comments.

REFERENCES

[1] P. Bas, T. Filler, and T. Pevný. 2011. Break Our Steganographic System – the Ins and Outs of Organizing BOSS. In *Information Hiding, 13th International Conference* (Lecture Notes in Computer Science), T. Filler, T. Pevný, A. Ker, and S. Craver (Eds.), Vol. 6958. Prague, Czech Republic, 59–70.

Table 5: Detection error $\overline{P}_E$ for four steganographic schemes and five payloads in bpp on BOSSbaseJ85 with the FLD-ensemble trained with maxSRMd2 features.

S-UNI	Payload (bits per pixel)				
	0.1	0.2	0.3	0.4	0.5
maxSRMd2	0.1527±0.0019	0.0789±0.0016	0.0470±0.0018	0.0303±0.0013	0.0189±0.0011
Square root	0.1410±0.0016	0.0698±0.0018	0.0404±0.0012	0.0253±0.0015	0.0164±0.0012
exp-Hellinger	0.1404±0.0020	0.0691±0.0017	0.0402±0.0018	0.0241±0.0009	0.0147±0.0011
RC	0.1381±0.0018	0.0675±0.0021	0.0373±0.0006	0.0220±0.0014	0.0133±0.0009
RC+SU	0.1355±0.0024	0.0661±0.0020	0.0384±0.0016	0.0237±0.0015	0.0143±0.0007
HILL					
maxSRMd2	0.1404±0.0012	0.0763±0.0020	0.0474±0.0024	0.0305±0.0011	0.0213±0.0011
Square root	0.1311±0.0019	0.0697±0.0027	0.0407±0.0016	0.0271±0.0011	0.0188±0.0015
exp-Hellinger	0.1284±0.0014	0.0670±0.0023	0.0390±0.0020	0.0257±0.0013	0.0172±0.0009
RC	0.1235±0.0019	0.0646±0.0019	0.0378±0.0018	0.0246±0.0017	0.0158±0.0008
RC+SU	0.1241±0.0017	0.0643±0.0017	0.0383±0.0013	0.0251±0.0011	0.0159±0.0010
MiPOD					
maxSRMd2	0.1191±0.0016	0.0658±0.0023	0.0416±0.0023	0.0279±0.0016	0.0203±0.0008
Square root	0.1135±0.0024	0.0627±0.0021	0.0395±0.0021	0.0280±0.0020	0.0190±0.0007
exp-Hellinger	0.1083±0.0024	0.0555±0.0014	0.0344±0.0021	0.0228±0.0016	0.0161±0.0010
RC	0.1038±0.0020	0.0507±0.0030	0.0312±0.0016	0.0204±0.0013	0.0136±0.0008
RC+SU	0.1061±0.0026	0.0532±0.0025	0.0326±0.0007	0.0209±0.0008	0.0147±0.0008
WOW					
maxSRMd2	0.1599±0.0021	0.0887±0.0027	0.0582±0.0026	0.0392±0.0019	0.0262±0.0016
Square root	0.1452±0.0026	0.0783±0.0020	0.0499±0.0018	0.0325±0.0016	0.0223±0.0020
exp-Hellinger	0.1398±0.0012	0.0755±0.0025	0.0468±0.0014	0.0304±0.0012	0.0198±0.0012
RC	0.1383±0.0023	0.0698±0.0015	0.0438±0.0015	0.0270±0.0012	0.0172±0.0013
RC+SU	0.1332±0.0017	0.0688±0.0019	0.0427±0.0018	0.0272±0.0017	0.0179±0.0011

[2] M. Boroumand and J. Fridrich. 2016. Boosting Steganalysis with Explicit Feature Maps. In *4th ACM IH&MMSec. Workshop*, F. Perez-Gonzales, F. Cayre, and P. Bas (Eds.). Vigo, Spain.

[3] R. Cogranne and J. Fridrich. 2015. Modeling and Extending the Ensemble Classifier for Steganalysis of Digital Images Using Hypothesis Testing Theory. *IEEE Transactions on Information Forensics and Security* 10, 2 (December 2015), 2627–2642.

[4] R. Cogranne, V. Sedighi, T. Pevný, and J. Fridrich. 2015. Is Ensemble Classifier Needed for Steganalysis in High-Dimensional Feature Spaces?. In *IEEE International Workshop on Information Forensics and Security*. Rome, Italy.

[5] T. Denemark, M. Boroumand, and J. Fridrich. 2016. Steganalysis Features for Content-Adaptive JPEG Steganography. *IEEE Transactions on Information Forensics and Security* 11, 8 (Aug 2016), 1736–1746.

[6] T. Denemark, V. Sedighi, V. Holub, R. Cogranne, and J. Fridrich. 2014. Selection-Channel-Aware Rich Model for Steganalysis of Digital Images. In *IEEE International Workshop on Information Forensics and Security*. Atlanta, GA.

[7] J. Fridrich and J. Kodovský. 2011. Rich Models for Steganalysis of Digital Images. *IEEE Transactions on Information Forensics and Security* 7, 3 (June 2011), 868–882.

[8] M. Goljan, R. Cogranne, and J. Fridrich. 2014. Rich Model for Steganalysis of Color Images. In *Sixth IEEE International Workshop on Information Forensics and Security*. Atlanta, GA.

[9] L. Guo, J. Ni, and Y.-Q. Shi. 2012. An Efficient JPEG Steganographic Scheme Using Uniform Embedding. In *Fourth IEEE International Workshop on Information Forensics and Security*. Tenerife, Spain.

[10] L. Guo, J. Ni, and Y. Q. Shi. 2014. Uniform Embedding for Efficient JPEG Steganography. *IEEE Transactions on Information Forensics and Security* 9, 5 (2014).

[11] V. Holub and J. Fridrich. 2012. Designing Steganographic Distortion Using Directional Filters. In *Fourth IEEE International Workshop on Information Forensics and Security*. Tenerife, Spain.

[12] V. Holub and J. Fridrich. 2013. Random Projections of Residuals for Digital Image Steganalysis. *IEEE Transactions on Information Forensics and Security* 8, 12 (December 2013), 1996–2006.

[13] V. Holub and J. Fridrich. 2015. Low-Complexity Features for JPEG Steganalysis Using Undecimated DCT. *IEEE Transactions on Information Forensics and Security* 10, 2 (Feb 2015), 219–228.

[14] V. Holub and J. Fridrich. 2015. Phase-Aware Projection Model for Steganalysis of JPEG Images. In *Proceedings SPIE, Electronic Imaging, Media Watermarking, Security, and Forensics 2015*, A. Alattar and N. D. Memon (Eds.), Vol. 9409. San Francisco, CA.

[15] V. Holub, J. Fridrich, and T. Denemark. 2014. Universal Distortion Design for Steganography in an Arbitrary Domain. *EURASIP Journal on Information Security, Special Issue on Revised Selected Papers of the 1st ACM IH and MMS Workshop* 2014:1 (2014).

[16] K. Jarrett, K. Kavukcuoglu, M. Ranzato, and Y. LeCun. 2009. What is the best Multi-Stage Architecture for Object Recognition?. In *2009 IEEE 12th International Conference on Computer Vision*. Kyoto, Japan, 2146–2153.

[17] J. Kodovský, J. Fridrich, and V. Holub. 2012. Ensemble Classifiers for Steganalysis of Digital Media. *IEEE Transactions on Information Forensics and Security* 7, 2 (2012), 432–444.

[18] A. Krizhevsky, I. Sutskever, and G. E. Hinton. 2012. ImageNet Classification with Deep Convolutional Neural Networks. In *Proceedings of Neural Information Processing Systems (NIPS)*. Lake Tahoe, Nevada.

[19] J. E. Lennard-Jones. 1924. On the Determination of Molecular Fields. *Proc. R. Soc. Lond. A* 106, 738 (1924), 463–477.

[20] B. Li, M. Wang, and J. Huang. 2014. A new cost function for spatial image steganography. In *Proceedings IEEE, International Conference on Image Processing, ICIP*. Paris, France.

[21] S. Lyu and E. Simoncelli. 2008. Nonlinear image representation using divisive normalization. In *IEEE Conference on Computer Vision and Pattern Recognition (CVPR)*.

[22] F. Perronnin, J. Sanchez, and Yan Liu. 2010. Large-scale image categorization with explicit data embedding. In *Computer Vision and Pattern Recognition (CVPR), 2010 IEEE Conference on*. 2297–2304.

[23] T. Pevný, P. Bas, and J. Fridrich. 2010. Steganalysis by Subtractive Pixel Adjacency Matrix. *IEEE Transactions on Information Forensics and Security* 5, 2 (June 2010), 215–224.

[24] T. Pevný, T. Filler, and P. Bas. 2010. Using High-Dimensional Image Models to Perform Highly Undetectable Steganography. In *Information Hiding, 12th International Conference* (Lecture Notes in Computer Science), R. Böhme and R. Safavi-Naini (Eds.), Vol. 6387. Springer-Verlag, New York, Calgary, Canada, 161–177.

[25] T. Pevný and J. Fridrich. 2007. Merging Markov and DCT Features for Multi-Class JPEG Steganalysis. In *Proceedings SPIE, Electronic Imaging, Security, Steganography, and Watermarking of Multimedia Contents IX*, E. J. Delp and P. W. Wong (Eds.), Vol. 6505. San Jose, CA, 3 1–14.

[26] N. Pinto, D. D. Cox, and J. J. DiCarlo. 2008. Why is real-world visual object recognition hard? *PLOS Computational Biology* (January 25 2008).

[27] V. Sedighi, R. Cogranne, and J. Fridrich. 2016. Content-Adaptive Steganography by Minimizing Statistical Detectability. *IEEE Transactions on Information Forensics and Security* 11, 2 (2016), 221–234.

[28] Y. Q. Shi, C. Chen, and W. Chen. 2006. A Markov Process Based Approach to Effective Attacking JPEG Steganography. In *Information Hiding, 8th International Workshop* (Lecture Notes in Computer Science), J. L. Camenisch, C. S. Collberg, N. F. Johnson, and P. Sallee (Eds.), Vol. 4437. Springer-Verlag, New York, Alexandria, VA, 249–264.

[29] X. Song, F. Liu, C. Yang, X. Luo, and Y. Zhang. 2015. Steganalysis of Adaptive JPEG Steganography Using 2D Gabor Filters. In *3rd ACM IH&MMSec. Workshop*, P. Comesa na, J. Fridrich, and A. Alattar (Eds.). Portland, Oregon.

[30] W. Tang, H. Li, W. Luo, and J. Huang. 2014. Adaptive Steganalysis Against WOW Embedding Algorithm. In *2nd ACM IH&MMSec. Workshop*, A. Uhl, S. Katzenbeisser, R. Kwitt, and A. Piva (Eds.). Salzburg, Austria, 91–96.

[31] W. Tang, H. Li, W. Luo, and J. Huang. 2016. Adaptive Steganalysis Based on Embedding Probabilities of Pixels. *IEEE Transactions on Information Forensics and Security* 11, 4 (April 2016), 734–745.

[32] A. Vedaldi and A. Zisserman. 2012. Efficient Additive Kernels via Explicit Feature Maps. *Pattern Analysis and Machine Intelligence, IEEE Transactions on* 34, 3 (March 2012), 480–492.

[33] D. Zou, Y. Q. Shi, W. Su, and G. Xuan. 2006. Steganalysis based on Markov model of thresholded prediction-error image. In *Proceedings IEEE, International Conference on Multimedia and Expo*. Toronto, Canada, 1365–1368.

Improving GFR Steganalysis Features by Using Gabor Symmetry and Weighted Histograms

Chao Xia
[1]State Key Laboratory of
Information Security, Institute of
Information Engineering, Chinese
Academy of Sciences,
Beijing, China 100093
[2]School of Cyber Security,
University of Chinese Academy of
Sciences,
Beijing, China 100093
xiachao@iie.ac.cn

Qingxiao Guan*
[1]State Key Laboratory of
Information Security, Institute of
Information Engineering, Chinese
Academy of Sciences,
Beijing, China 100093
[2]School of Cyber Security,
University of Chinese Academy of
Sciences,
Beijing, China 100093
guanqingxiao@iie.ac.cn

Xianfeng Zhao
[1]State Key Laboratory of
Information Security, Institute of
Information Engineering, Chinese
Academy of Sciences,
Beijing, China 100093
[2]School of Cyber Security,
University of Chinese Academy of
Sciences,
Beijing, China 100093
zhaoxianfeng@iie.ac.cn

Zhoujun Xu
Beijing Information Technology
Institute,
Beijing, China 100094
pl_xzj@uestc.edu.cn

Yi Ma
Beijing Information Technology
Institute,
Beijing, China 100094
mayi_5501@126.com

ABSTRACT

The GFR (Gabor Filter Residual) features, built as histograms of quantized residuals obtained with 2D Gabor filters, can achieve competitive detection performance against adaptive JPEG steganography. In this paper, an improved version of the GFR is proposed. First, a novel histogram merging method is proposed according to the symmetries between different Gabor filters, thus making the features more compact and robust. Second, a new weighted histogram method is proposed by considering the position of the residual value in a quantization interval, making the features more sensitive to the slight changes in residual values. The experiments are given to demonstrate the effectiveness of our proposed methods.

KEYWORDS

Steganalysis, JPEG, adaptive steganography, Gabor filters, weighted histograms

ACM Reference format:
Chao Xia, Qingxiao Guan, Xianfeng Zhao, Zhoujun Xu, and Yi Ma. 2017. Improving GFR Steganalysis Features by Using Gabor Symmetry and Weighted Histograms. In *Proceedings of*

---

*Corresponding author

IH&MMSec '17, June 20–22, 2017, Philadelphia, PA, USA
© 2017 ACM. ACM ISBN 978-1-4503-5061-7/17/06. . . $15.00
DOI: http://dx.doi.org/10.1145/3082031.3083243

IH&MMSec '17, June 20–22, 2017, Philadelphia, PA, USA, ,
12 pages.
DOI: http://dx.doi.org/10.1145/3082031.3083243

1 INTRODUCTION

The purpose of steganography is to embed secret messages into cover objects without arousing a warder's suspicion. Steganalysis, the counterpart of steganography, aims to detect the presence of hidden data. Since JPEG is widely used in modern society, especially in the Internet communication, much attention has been attached to this ideal cover. With the advent of the STCs (Syndrome-Trellis Codes) coding technique [2], some adaptive JPEG steganographic methods have been designed in recent years, such as UED (Uniform Embedding Distortion) [3] and J-UNIWARD (JPEG Universal Wavelet Relative Distortion) [8]. These adaptive methods are difficult to detect because the embedding changes are localized in complex content which is hard to model.

To attack adaptive JPEG steganography well, the DCTR (Discrete Cosine Transform Residual) [6] opens up a new framework of JPEG phase-aware features. The DCTR, using the histograms of residuals obtained with 64 DCT kernels, not only has relatively low complexity but also provides good detection performance. In [7], the PHARM (Phase-Aware Projection Model), following this phase-aware framework, computes the histograms of multiple random projections of residuals obtained with linear pixel predictors. Random projections diversify the model in a similar manner as in the PSRM (Projection Spatial Rich Model) [4], improving the detection accuracy further. There are three important observations in the design of the DCTR and the PHARM. **First**, unlike the previous JPEG steganalysis feature sets (e.g., PEV [14], JRM [10]), both the DCTR and the PHARM are constructed in the spatial domain rather than the JPEG domain. Before obtaining noise residuals, JPEG images are decompressed to the spatial domain without rounding to integers. This is probably because the statistical characteristics captured in the spatial domain are more sensitive to adaptive JPEG embedding algorithms [5]. **Second**, phase-awareness is employed in these two feature sets. Instead of directly computing the histogram features from all values of the whole residual, both feature sets compute the histograms from 64 subsets of the residual, for the statistical properties of pixels in a decompressed JPEG image differ w.r.t. their positions within the 8×8 pixel grid. **Third**, symmetrization is useful for forming the final features. The symmetries are utilized to reduce the feature dimension and make them more robust. The GFR (Gabor Filter Residual) [15] is motivated by these three observations. The difference is that the GFR uses the histograms of residuals obtained using 2D Gabor filters. The 2D Gabor filters can describe image texture features from different scales and orientations. Thus, the GFR can achieve the state-of-the-art performance in most of the cases when steganalyzing adaptive JPEG steganography.

In this paper, we revisit the design of the GFR and attempt to further improve its performance. The main contributions can be concluded as follows. **First**, a new histogram merging method is proposed. In the GFR, the histograms computed from 64 subsets of one Gabor residual are merged with the method designed for the DCTR. But this strategy is not proper, for the symmetric properties of the Gabor filters differ from the DCT filters. Thus, we merge the histograms of one Gabor residual in a different way. Then, according to the symmetries between Gabor filters, histograms of different Gabor residuals are merged further to make the final features more compact and powerful. **Second**, a novel weighted histogram method is proposed. In the GFR, histograms are computed from quantized residuals. Although the quantization is meaningful for steganalysis, it may inevitably lose part of useful information. With the quantization, the histograms in the GFR can only reflect the changes that enable the residual values to shift from a quantization interval to another, while leaving out those small changes. To avoid this situation, we propose a novel way to compute the histograms using a weighted voting scheme without a rounding operation. This scheme takes into account the small disturbance of residual values within a quantization interval, thus making the histogram features more effective.

In this paper, we call the new feature set the GFR-GW (GFR-Gabor symmetric merging and Weighted histograms) which applies the proposed histogram merging method and our weighted histogram method. And the histogram features only using the proposed merging method are called the GFR-GSM (GFR-Gabor Symmetric Merging) features. The experimental results will be given to show the advantages of the proposed features in the detection of adaptive JPEG steganography. The rest of this paper is organized as follows. In Section 2, we describe the original GFR features briefly. In Section 3, we discuss the reason why the histograms of 64 subsets of one Gabor residual can not be merged with

the same method in the DCTR. In Section 4, based on the symmetries between Gabor filters, we propose our method to merge the histograms of the subsets of different Gabor residuals. In Section 5, our weighted voting scheme for histogram computation is introduced. In Section 6, the proposed features (the GFR-GSM and the GFR-GW) are compared with other JPEG steganalysis features by experiments. Conclusions and future work are given in Section 7.

2 ORIGINAL GFR FEATURES

The GFR features compute the histograms from the subsets of residuals obtained using 2D Gabor filters. The 2D Gabor filters help the GFR to capture the effect of the steganography in different scales and orientations. In this section, we briefly describe how to calculate the original GFR features to make this paper self-contained. We do not go into the details which can be seen in the original literature [15].

For the GFR, the calculation procedures are described as follows.

Step 1: A JPEG image is decompressed to the spatial domain without rounding the pixel values to the discrete set $\{0,1, \ldots, 255\}$, i.e., the gray values of pixels are preserved in the form of real numbers.

Step 2: The 2D Gabor filter bank is generated and the bank in [15] includes 2D Gabor filters with 2 phase offsets ($\phi = 0, \pi$), 4 scales ($\sigma = 0.5, 0.75, 1, 1.25$) and 32 orientations ($\theta = 0, \pi/32, \ldots, 31\pi/32$).

Step 3: The decompressed JPEG image is convolved with the 8×8 2D Gabor filter $\mathbf{G}^{\phi,\sigma,\theta}$ to get the corresponding residual image $\mathbf{U}^{\phi,\sigma,\theta}$.

Step 4: According to the JPEG phase (a,b) ($0 \le a, b \le 7$), the residual $\mathbf{U}^{\phi,\sigma,\theta}$ is divided into 64 subsets $\mathbf{U}_{a,b}^{\phi,\sigma,\theta}$ by interval 8 down-sampling.

Step 5: The histogram feature $\mathbf{h}_{a,b}^{\phi,\sigma,\theta}$ is computed from each subset $\mathbf{U}_{a,b}^{\phi,\sigma,\theta}$.

$$\mathbf{h}_{a,b}^{\phi,\sigma,\theta}(r) = \frac{1}{\left|\mathbf{U}_{a,b}^{\phi,\sigma,\theta}\right|} \sum_{u \in \mathbf{U}_{a,b}^{\phi,\sigma,\theta}} [Q_T(|u|/q) = r], \qquad (1)$$

where Q_T is a quantizer quantizing the residual samples to integer centroids $\{0, 1, \ldots, T\}$, q is the quantization step, and $[P]$ is the Iverson bracket equal to 1 when statement P is true and 0 when P is false.

Step 6: For residual $\mathbf{U}^{\phi,\sigma,\theta}$, all the 64 histograms $\mathbf{h}_{a,b}^{\phi,\sigma,\theta}$ are merged into 25 according to the same method in the DCTR [6]. Then these 25 histograms are concatenated to obtain the histogram feature $\mathbf{h}^{\phi,\sigma,\theta}$ of residual $\mathbf{U}^{\phi,\sigma,\theta}$.

Step 7: The histogram features $\mathbf{h}^{\phi,\sigma,\pi-\theta}$ and $\mathbf{h}^{\phi,\sigma,\theta}$ are merged together according to the symmetric orientations.

Step 8: All the merged histograms are concatenated to form the GFR features.

3 DIFFERENCE BETWEEN GABOR FILTERS AND DCT FILTERS

From the description of the GFR, it can be seen that there are two steps in merging histograms in the GFR. First, in

Step 6, the histograms of 64 subsets of one Gabor residual are merged together. Second, in **Step 7**, we merge the histograms of two residuals with symmetric directions. In this section, we discuss **Step 6**, where the 64 histograms $\mathbf{h}_{a,b}^{\phi,\sigma,\theta}$ are merged in the same manner as in the DCTR where the residuals are obtained using the DCT filters. In the DCTR, 64 histograms computed from 64 subsets of one DCT residual are merged into 25 according to the symmetries of the projection vectors of DCTR. However, the symmetric properties of the Gabor filters differ from the DCT filters, which leads to different kinds of the symmetries of the projection vectors of GFR. Hence, it is more reasonable to merge the histograms $\mathbf{h}_{a,b}^{\phi,\sigma,\theta}$ in a different way rather than in **Step 6** of the GFR.

In this section, we first introduce the symmetric properties of the DCT filters and the Gabor filters respectively and show the difference between them. After describing the merging method in the DCTR, we discuss how to merge the histograms of 64 subsets of one Gabor residual.

In this paper, the DCT filter is denoted as $\mathbf{B}^{i,j}$, where i, j indicate the spatial frequencies, and $0 \le i,j \le 7$. The Gabor filter is denoted as $\mathbf{G}^{\phi,\sigma,\theta}$, where θ is the orientation parameter, σ is the scale parameter and ϕ is the phase shift.

3.1 Symmetric Properties of DCT Filters and Gabor Filters

The symmetric properties of filters are related to the symmetries of the projection vectors. Therefore, we first introduce the symmetric properties of the DCT filters and the Gabor filters, respectively.

For the DCT filter $\mathbf{B}^{i,j}$ ($0 \le i,j \le 7$), it is symmetric or antisymmetric in either direction:

$$\mathbf{B}^{i,j} = \begin{cases} \text{flipud}(\mathbf{B}^{i,j}) & i \text{ is even} \\ -\text{flipud}(\mathbf{B}^{i,j}) & i \text{ is odd} \\ \text{fliplr}(\mathbf{B}^{i,j}) & j \text{ is even} \\ -\text{fliplr}(\mathbf{B}^{i,j}) & j \text{ is odd} \end{cases}, \quad (2)$$

where flipud($\cdot$) denotes the flipping operator that flips a matrix vertically and fliplr($\cdot$) denotes the operator that flips a matrix horizontally.

For the Gabor filter $\mathbf{G}^{\phi,\sigma,\theta}$, both in [15] and in this paper, the phase shift ϕ is set as 0 and $\pi/2$. Then, we have

$$\mathbf{G}^{\phi,\sigma,\pi+\theta} = -\mathbf{G}^{\phi,\sigma,\theta}, \ 0 \le \theta < \pi. \quad (3)$$

The absolute values of residual images generated by convolving with $\mathbf{G}^{\phi,\sigma,\theta}$ are the same as those with $\mathbf{G}^{\phi,\sigma,\pi+\theta}$. Thus, we only consider the condition of $0 \le \theta < \pi$ and select the same 32 orientations ($\theta = 0, \pi/32, \ldots, 31\pi/32$) as in the original GFR [15].

Now we examine the symmetric properties of the Gabor filters $\mathbf{G}^{\phi,\sigma,\theta}$ ($0 \le \theta < \pi$). When $\theta = \{0, \pi/2\}$, the Gabor filter $\mathbf{G}^{0,\sigma,\theta=\{0,\pi/2\}}$ is symmetric in both directions, and the Gabor filter $\mathbf{G}^{\pi/2,\sigma,\theta=\{0,\pi/2\}}$ is symmetric in one direction

and antisymmetric in the other direction:

$$\begin{aligned} \mathbf{G}^{0,\sigma,0} &= \text{flipud}\left(\mathbf{G}^{0,\sigma,0}\right) &= \text{fliplr}\left(\mathbf{G}^{0,\sigma,0}\right) \\ \mathbf{G}^{0,\sigma,\frac{\pi}{2}} &= \text{flipud}\left(\mathbf{G}^{0,\sigma,\frac{\pi}{2}}\right) &= \text{fliplr}\left(\mathbf{G}^{0,\sigma,\frac{\pi}{2}}\right) \\ \mathbf{G}^{\frac{\pi}{2},\sigma,0} &= \text{flipud}\left(\mathbf{G}^{\frac{\pi}{2},\sigma,0}\right) &= -\text{fliplr}\left(\mathbf{G}^{\frac{\pi}{2},\sigma,0}\right) \\ \mathbf{G}^{\frac{\pi}{2},\sigma,\frac{\pi}{2}} &= -\text{flipud}\left(\mathbf{G}^{\frac{\pi}{2},\sigma,\frac{\pi}{2}}\right) &= \text{fliplr}\left(\mathbf{G}^{\frac{\pi}{2},\sigma,\frac{\pi}{2}}\right) \end{aligned} . \quad (4)$$

However, when $\theta \ne \{0, \pi/2\}$, unlike DCT filters, $\mathbf{G}^{\phi,\sigma,\theta\ne\{0,\pi/2\}}$ is neither symmetric nor antisymmetric in any direction. But $\mathbf{G}^{\phi,\sigma,\theta\ne\{0,\pi/2\}}$ is centrosymmetric or anti-centrosymmetric. When $\phi = 0$, the Gabor filter $\mathbf{G}^{0,\sigma,\theta\ne\{0,\pi/2\}}$ is centrosymmetric, and when $\phi = \pi/2$, the Gabor filter $\mathbf{G}^{\pi/2,\sigma,\theta\ne\{0,\pi/2\}}$ is anti-centrosymmetric:

$$\forall \phi, \ \sigma, \ \theta \ne 0, \frac{\pi}{2}$$
$$\mathbf{G}^{\phi,\sigma,\theta} \ne \pm \text{flipud}\left(\mathbf{G}^{\phi,\sigma,\theta}\right), \ \mathbf{G}^{\phi,\sigma,\theta} \ne \pm \text{fliplr}\left(\mathbf{G}^{\phi,\sigma,\theta}\right),$$

$$\forall \sigma, \ \theta \ne 0, \frac{\pi}{2}$$
$$\mathbf{G}^{0,\sigma,\theta} = \text{rot180}\left(\mathbf{G}^{0,\sigma,\theta}\right), \ \mathbf{G}^{\frac{\pi}{2},\sigma,\theta} = -\text{rot180}\left(\mathbf{G}^{\frac{\pi}{2},\sigma,\theta}\right),$$
$$(5)$$

where rot180($\cdot$) is a rotation operator that rots the matrix by 180 degrees.

3.2 Merging Method in the DCTR

In order to realize the relationship between the symmetric properties of the filters and the method of merging histograms, we rephrase the merging method in the DCTR, which is also used in the original GFR. As shown in **Figure 1**, from the computing process of a residual image (DCT residual or Gabor residual), we find that the modification of one DCT coefficient (D_{ij} in the DCT block D in **Figure 1(a)**) will affect the values of all 8×8 pixels in the corresponding block in the spatial domain (pixels in the 8×8 pixel block D' in **Figure 1(b)**) because of the JPEG decompression. Then the values of 15×15 residual samples (the shaded region in **Figure 1(c)**) will be changed by convolving with an 8×8 filter (DCT filter or Gabor filter). Specifically, due to changing one DCT coefficient, a 15×15 neighborhood of values in the DCT residual will be modified by

$$\mathbf{R}^{(i,j)(k,l)} = \mathbf{B}^{i,j} \otimes \mathbf{B}^{k,l}, \quad (6)$$

where the modified DCT coefficient is in mode (k,l), $\mathbf{B}^{i,j}$ denotes the DCT filter used to convolve the decompressed JPEG image, and $\otimes$ denotes the full cross-correlation.

According to the symmetric properties of the DCT filters (2), we can see that when indexing $\mathbf{R}^{(i,j)(k,l)} \in \mathbb{R}^{15 \times 15}$ with indices in $\{ -7, -6, \ldots, -1, 0, 1, \ldots, 6, 7\}$, $\mathbf{R}^{(i,j)(k,l)}$ satisfies

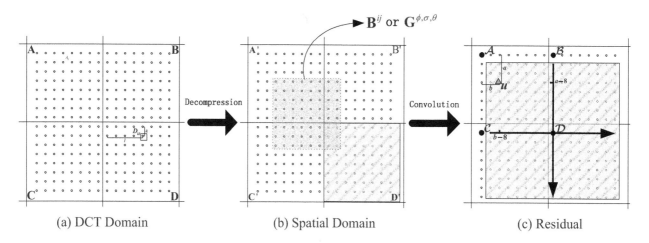

Figure 1: The computing process of a residual image (DCT residual or Gabor residual). Left: Dots indicate the DCT coefficients, and A, B, C, D are four neighboring DCT blocks. Middle: Dots indicate the pixels in the decompressed JPEG image, and A', B', C', D' are the corresponding pixel blocks. Right: Dots indicate the residual samples in the DCT residual or Gabor residual, and the element u is generated by convolving 64 pixels in the dotted line block with $\mathbf{B}^{i,j}$ or $\mathbf{G}^{\phi,\sigma,\theta}$. The change of the DCT coefficient D_{kl} will affect all 8×8 pixels in block D'. And a 15×15 neighborhood of values in the residual image (in the shaded region) will be modified. The position of the residual sample $\mathcal{D}$ is at the center of the shaded region and the coordinate of the position of u (the triangle) in the shaded region is $(a-8, b-8)$.

the following symmetry

$$
R_{a,b}^{(i,j)(k,l)} = \begin{cases} R_{-a,b}^{(i,j)(k,l)} & (i+k) \text{ is even} \\ -R_{-a,b}^{(i,j)(k,l)} & (i+k) \text{ is odd} \\ R_{a,-b}^{(i,j)(k,l)} & (j+l) \text{ is even} \\ -R_{a,-b}^{(i,j)(k,l)} & (j+l) \text{ is odd} \end{cases} . \quad (7)
$$

From the symmetry of $\mathbf{R}^{(i,j)(k,l)}$ (7), we can see that $\left| \mathbf{R}^{(i,j)(k,l)} \right|$ is symmetric about both axes

$$
\begin{aligned} \left| R_{a,b}^{(i,j)(k,l)} \right| &= \left| R_{-a,b}^{(i,j)(k,l)} \right| \\ \left| R_{a,b}^{(i,j)(k,l)} \right| &= \left| R_{a,-b}^{(i,j)(k,l)} \right| \end{aligned} . \quad (8)
$$

We now show how to compute a particular value u in the DCT residual (the location of u is marked by a triangle in **Figure 1(c)**). In **Figure 1(c)**, four residual samples $\mathcal{A}$, $\mathcal{B}$, $\mathcal{C}$, $\mathcal{D}$ (black circles in **Figure 1(c)**) are computed by positioning the DCT filter $\mathbf{B}^{i,j}$ within one pixel block (e.g., $\mathcal{D}$ is generated by only convolving 8×8 pixels in D' with $\mathbf{B}^{i,j}$). After decompression and convolution, the effect of the DCT coefficient D_{kl} on the DCT residual can be expressed as $Q_{kl}D_{kl}\mathbf{R}^{(i,j)(k,l)}$. The location of $\mathcal{D}$ is at the center of $Q_{kl}D_{kl}\mathbf{R}^{(i,j)(k,l)}$ and the relative position of u w.r.t $\mathcal{D}$ is $(a-8, b-8)$. Similarly, the relative locations of u w.r.t. the other three centers $\mathcal{A}$, $\mathcal{B}$, $\mathcal{C}$ are (a,b), $(a,b-8)$ and $(a-8,b)$,

respectively. The value u can be calculated as follows:

$$
\begin{aligned} u = \sum_{k=0}^{7} \sum_{l=0}^{7} Q_{kl} \Big[&A_{kl}R_{a,b}^{(i,j)(k,l)} + B_{kl}R_{a,b-8}^{(i,j)(k,l)} \\ &+ C_{kl}R_{a-8,b}^{(i,j)(k,l)} + D_{kl}R_{a-8,b-8}^{(i,j)(k,l)} \Big], \end{aligned} \quad (9)
$$

where A_{kl}, B_{kl}, C_{kl}, D_{kl} are the DCT coefficients of the corresponding four neighboring DCT blocks (A, B, C, D), and Q_{kl} is the quantization step of the (k,l)th DCT mode.

The value u can also be denoted as a projection of 256 dequantized DCT coefficients from the four adjacent DCT blocks with a projection vector of DCTR $\mathbf{P}_{a,b}^{i,j}$

$$
u = \begin{pmatrix} Q_{00}A_{00} \\ \vdots \\ Q_{00}B_{00} \\ \vdots \\ Q_{00}C_{00} \\ \vdots \\ Q_{00}D_{00} \\ \vdots \\ Q_{77}D_{77} \end{pmatrix}^{T} \cdot \underbrace{\begin{pmatrix} R_{a,b}^{(i,j)(0,0)} \\ \vdots \\ R_{a,b-8}^{(i,j)(0,0)} \\ \vdots \\ R_{a-8,b}^{(i,j)(0,0)} \\ \vdots \\ R_{a-8,b-8}^{(i,j)(0,0)} \\ \vdots \\ R_{a-8,b-8}^{(i,j)(7,7)} \end{pmatrix}}_{\mathbf{P}_{a,b}^{i,j}} . \quad (10)
$$

From the symmetry of $\left| \mathbf{R}^{(i,j)(k,l)} \right|$ (8) and the definition of the projection vector (10), we can see that the absolute values of the projection vector $\left| \mathbf{P}^{i,j} \right|$ follow the symmetry

$$\left| \mathbf{P}^{i,j}_{a,b} \right| = \left| \mathbf{P}^{i,j}_{a,-b} \right| = \left| \mathbf{P}^{i,j}_{-a,b} \right| = \left| \mathbf{P}^{i,j}_{-a,-b} \right|. \tag{11}$$

Because the size of the DCT block is 8×8, the projection vectors of DCTR satisfy the following symmetry as described in [6]

$$\left| \mathbf{P}^{i,j}_{a,b} \right| = \left| \mathbf{P}^{i,j}_{a,b-8} \right| = \left| \mathbf{P}^{i,j}_{a-8,b} \right| = \left| \mathbf{P}^{i,j}_{a-8,b-8} \right|. \tag{12}$$

Combining (11) and (12), we have the symmetry that is used in the merging method in the DCTR

$$\left| \mathbf{P}^{i,j}_{a,b} \right| = \left| \mathbf{P}^{i,j}_{a,8-b} \right| = \left| \mathbf{P}^{i,j}_{8-a,b} \right| = \left| \mathbf{P}^{i,j}_{8-a,8-b} \right|. \tag{13}$$

According to (13), hence, we can merge the histograms of the subsets corresponding to the positions (a, b), $(8 - a, b)$, $(a, 8 - b)$, $(8 - a, 8 - b)$ in a DCT residual.

3.3 Merging Histograms of one Gabor Residual

However, the symmetric properties of the Gabor filters are different from the DCT filters, which causes the projection vectors of GFR to satisfy another kind of symmetry. Thus, the histograms $\mathbf{h}^{\phi,\sigma,\theta}_{a,b}$ of 64 subsets of one Gabor residual can be merged in a different way.

When one DCT coefficient is modified, a 15×15 neighborhood of values in the Gabor residual will be modified by

$$\mathbf{R}^{(\phi,\sigma,\theta)(k,l)} = \mathbf{G}^{\phi,\sigma,\theta} \otimes \mathbf{B}^{k,l}, \tag{14}$$

where the modified DCT coefficient is in mode (k, l), $\mathbf{G}^{\phi,\sigma,\theta}$ denotes the Gabor filter used to convolve the decompressed JPEG image, and $\otimes$ denotes the full cross-correlation.

According to the symmetric properties of the Gabor filters (4) and (5) described in Section 3.1, we find that the symmetric properties of $\left| \mathbf{R}^{(\phi,\sigma,\theta)(k,l)} \right|$ depend on the value of the parameter θ. When $\theta = \{0, \pi/2\}$, $\left| \mathbf{R}^{(\phi,\sigma,\theta)(k,l)} \right|$ satisfies the same symmetry as $\left| \mathbf{R}^{(i,j)(k,l)} \right|$ in the DCTR. That is,

$$\left| R^{(\phi,\sigma,\theta)(k,l)}_{a,b} \right| = \left| R^{(\phi,\sigma,\theta)(k,l)}_{-a,b} \right| = \left| R^{(\phi,\sigma,\theta)(k,l)}_{a,-b} \right| = \left| R^{(\phi,\sigma,\theta)(k,l)}_{-a,-b} \right|. \tag{15}$$

However, when $\theta \neq \{0, \pi/2\}$, $\left| \mathbf{R}^{(\phi,\sigma,\theta)(k,l)} \right|$ only satisfies the centrosymmetry

$$\begin{aligned}
\left| R^{(\phi,\sigma,\theta)(k,l)}_{a,b} \right| &= \left| R^{(\phi,\sigma,\theta)(k,l)}_{-a,-b} \right| \\
&\neq \left| R^{(\phi,\sigma,\theta)(k,l)}_{-a,b} \right|. \\
&\neq \left| R^{(\phi,\sigma,\theta)(k,l)}_{a,-b} \right|
\end{aligned} \tag{16}$$

For the GFR, a particular value u in the Gabor residual $\mathbf{U}^{\phi,\sigma,\theta}$ can be computed as follows:

$$\begin{aligned}
u = \sum_{k=0}^{7} \sum_{l=0}^{7} Q_{kl} &\left[A_{kl} R^{(\phi,\sigma,\theta)(k,l)}_{a,b} + B_{kl} R^{(\phi,\sigma,\theta)(k,l)}_{a,b-8} \right. \\
&\left. + C_{kl} R^{(\phi,\sigma,\theta)(k,l)}_{a-8,b} + D_{kl} R^{(\phi,\sigma,\theta)(k,l)}_{a-8,b-8} \right].
\end{aligned} \tag{17}$$

That is,

$$u = \begin{pmatrix} Q_{00}A_{00} \\ \vdots \\ Q_{00}B_{00} \\ \vdots \\ Q_{00}C_{00} \\ \vdots \\ Q_{00}D_{00} \\ \vdots \\ Q_{77}D_{77} \end{pmatrix}^T \cdot \underbrace{\begin{pmatrix} R^{(\phi,\sigma,\theta)(0,0)}_{a,b} \\ \vdots \\ R^{(\phi,\sigma,\theta)(0,0)}_{a,b-8} \\ \vdots \\ R^{(\phi,\sigma,\theta)(0,0)}_{a-8,b} \\ \vdots \\ R^{(\phi,\sigma,\theta)(0,0)}_{a-8,b-8} \\ \vdots \\ R^{(\phi,\sigma,\theta)(7,7)}_{a-8,b-8} \end{pmatrix}}_{\mathbf{P}^{\phi,\sigma,\theta}_{a,b}}, \tag{18}$$

where $\mathbf{P}^{\phi,\sigma,\theta}_{a,b}$ is a projection vector of GFR.

From the symmetry of $\left| \mathbf{R}^{(\phi,\sigma,\theta)(k,l)} \right|$ (15), (16) and the definition of the projection vector of GFR (18), it can be seen that $\left| \mathbf{P}^{\phi,\sigma,\theta} \right|$ follows the symmetry:

$\forall \phi, \sigma, \theta \in \{0, \pi/2\}$

$$\left| \mathbf{P}^{\phi,\sigma,\theta}_{a,b} \right| = \left| \mathbf{P}^{\phi,\sigma,\theta}_{-a,b} \right| = \left| \mathbf{P}^{\phi,\sigma,\theta}_{a,-b} \right| = \left| \mathbf{P}^{\phi,\sigma,\theta}_{-a,-b} \right|; \tag{19}$$

$\forall \phi, \sigma, \theta \neq 0, \pi/2$

$$\begin{aligned}
\left| \mathbf{P}^{\phi,\sigma,\theta}_{a,b} \right| &= \left| \mathbf{P}^{\phi,\sigma,\theta}_{-a,-b} \right| \\
&\neq \left| \mathbf{P}^{\phi,\sigma,\theta}_{-a,b} \right|. \\
&\neq \left| \mathbf{P}^{\phi,\sigma,\theta}_{a,-b} \right|
\end{aligned} \tag{20}$$

The projection vectors of GFR also satisfy the following symmetry

$$\left| \mathbf{P}^{\phi,\sigma,\theta}_{a,b} \right| = \left| \mathbf{P}^{\phi,\sigma,\theta}_{a,b-8} \right| = \left| \mathbf{P}^{\phi,\sigma,\theta}_{a-8,b} \right| = \left| \mathbf{P}^{\phi,\sigma,\theta}_{a-8,b-8} \right|. \tag{21}$$

From (19) and (21), we find that when $\theta = \{0, \pi/2\}$, the projection vectors of GFR $\left| \mathbf{P}^{\phi,\sigma,\theta} \right|$ satisfy the same symmetry as $\left| \mathbf{P}^{i,j} \right|$ in the DCTR,

$$\left| \mathbf{P}^{\phi,\sigma,\theta}_{a,b} \right| = \left| \mathbf{P}^{\phi,\sigma,\theta}_{a,8-b} \right| = \left| \mathbf{P}^{\phi,\sigma,\theta}_{8-a,b} \right| = \left| \mathbf{P}^{\phi,\sigma,\theta}_{8-a,8-b} \right|. \tag{22}$$

Hence, for the residual $\mathbf{U}^{\phi,\sigma,\theta=\{0,\pi/2\}}$ generated with the Gabor filter whose orientation parameter $\theta = 0, \pi/2$, the histograms of 64 subsets of $\mathbf{U}^{\phi,\sigma,\theta=\{0,\pi/2\}}$ can be merged in the same way as in the DCTR. We can merge together the histograms of the subsets corresponding to the positions (a, b), $(8-a, b)$, $(a, 8-b)$, $(8-a, 8-b)$ in $\mathbf{U}^{\phi,\sigma,\theta=\{0,\pi/2\}}$, and 64 histograms can be merged into 25.

However, from (20) and (21), we find that when $\theta \neq \{0, \pi/2\}$, the projection vectors of GFR $\left|\mathbf{P}^{\phi,\sigma,\theta}\right|$ satisfy a different kind of symmetry than $\left|\mathbf{P}^{i,j}\right|$ in the DCTR,

$$
\begin{aligned}
\left|\mathbf{P}_{a,b}^{\phi,\sigma,\theta}\right| &= \left|\mathbf{P}_{8-a,8-b}^{\phi,\sigma,\theta}\right| \\
\left|\mathbf{P}_{a,b}^{\phi,\sigma,\theta}\right| &\neq \left|\mathbf{P}_{8-a,b}^{\phi,\sigma,\theta}\right| \quad . \\
\left|\mathbf{P}_{a,b}^{\phi,\sigma,\theta}\right| &\neq \left|\mathbf{P}_{a,8-b}^{\phi,\sigma,\theta}\right|
\end{aligned}
\tag{23}
$$

Thus, the histograms of 64 subsets of $\mathbf{U}^{\phi,\sigma,\theta \neq \{0,\pi/2\}}$ can not be merged in the same way as in the DCTR. However, we can merge the histograms of the subsets corresponding to the positions (a,b), $(8-a, 8-b)$ in $\mathbf{U}^{\phi,\sigma,\theta \neq \{0,\pi/2\}}$, and 64 histograms can be merged into 34.

4 PROPOSED HISTOGRAM MERGING METHOD

In order to further reduce the dimension, we introduce our histogram merging method in this section, taking into consideration the symmetries between Garbor filters. As shown in **Figure 2**, after merging the 64 histograms $\mathbf{h}_{a,b}^{\phi,\sigma,\theta}$ of one Gabor residual (in the dashed boxes in **Figure 2**), we further merge the histograms of different Gabor residuals in two steps.

Step 1: According to the symmetry between Gabor filters $\mathbf{G}^{\phi,\sigma,\theta}$ and $\mathbf{G}^{\phi,\sigma,\pi-\theta}$ (see **Figure 3(a)** and **3(b)**), we can merge together the histograms of the subsets of residual images $\mathbf{U}^{\phi,\sigma,\theta}$ and $\mathbf{U}^{\phi,\sigma,\pi-\theta}$. Specifically, we merge the histograms $\mathbf{h}_{a,b}^{\phi,\sigma,\theta}$, $\mathbf{h}_{8-a,8-b}^{\phi,\sigma,\theta}$ (corresponding to the (a,b)th and $(8-a,8-b)$th subsets of $\mathbf{U}^{\phi,\sigma,\theta}$) and the histograms $\mathbf{h}_{8-a,b}^{\phi,\sigma,\pi-\theta}$, $\mathbf{h}_{a,8-b}^{\phi,\sigma,\pi-\theta}$ (corresponding to the $(8-a,b)$th and $(a,8-b)$th subsets of $\mathbf{U}^{\phi,\sigma,\pi-\theta}$).

The merging method in **Step 1** is different from the method used in the DCTR and the original GFR (**Step 6** in Section 2). As shown in **Figure 4**, in the original GFR, the histograms $\mathbf{h}_{a,b}^{\phi,\sigma,\theta}$, $\mathbf{h}_{8-a,8-b}^{\phi,\sigma,\theta}$, $\mathbf{h}_{8-a,b}^{\phi,\sigma,\theta}$ and $\mathbf{h}_{a,8-b}^{\phi,\sigma,\theta}$ are from one Gabor residual. However, in **Step 1**, we merge the histograms $\mathbf{h}_{a,b}^{\phi,\sigma,\theta}$, $\mathbf{h}_{8-a,8-b}^{\phi,\sigma,\theta}$ and $\mathbf{h}_{8-a,b}^{\phi,\sigma,\pi-\theta}$, $\mathbf{h}_{a,8-b}^{\phi,\sigma,\pi-\theta}$ that are from two Gabor residuals $\mathbf{U}^{\phi,\sigma,\theta}$ and $\mathbf{U}^{\phi,\sigma,\pi-\theta}$. In **Figure 4**, there is an interesting finding that when computing the subsets whose histograms will be merged according to our method in **Step 1**, the 8×8 window of the Gabor filter $\mathbf{G}^{\phi,\sigma,\theta}$ is symmetric with the window of $\mathbf{G}^{\phi,\sigma,\pi-\theta}$ about the boundaries of the 8×8 pixel blocks (i.e., the blue windows are symmetric with the red windows about the boundaries).

Step 2: Due to the transposition relation between $\mathbf{G}^{\phi,\sigma,\theta}$ and $\mathbf{G}^{\phi,\sigma,\pi/2-\theta}$ (see **Figure 3(a)** and **3(c)**), we merge together the histograms of the (a,b)th subset of residual $\mathbf{U}^{\phi,\sigma,\theta}$ and the (b,a)th subset of $\mathbf{U}^{\phi,\sigma,\pi/2-\theta}$.

The merging method in **Step 2** is based on the argument that a decompressed JPEG image still somehow preserves the symmetric properties. Although it is known that the symmetries of a natures image are broken by the quantization in JPEG compression due to the rounding operation and the non-symmetric quantization table, we argue that this situation is not serious and it is still reasonable to merge

$$
\begin{bmatrix}
-0.0027 & 0.0305 & -0.1208 & 0.1609 & -0.0691 & 0.0078 & 0.0001 & 0.0000 \\
-0.0023 & 0.0399 & -0.2286 & 0.4432 & -0.2965 & 0.0671 & -0.0050 & 0.0001 \\
0.0002 & 0.0152 & -0.1816 & 0.5527 & -0.5391 & 0.1767 & -0.0200 & 0.0008 \\
0.0022 & -0.0232 & 0.0434 & 0.1660 & -0.3946 & 0.2098 & -0.0349 & 0.0019 \\
0.0019 & -0.0349 & 0.2098 & -0.3946 & 0.1660 & 0.0434 & -0.0232 & 0.0022 \\
0.0008 & -0.0200 & 0.1767 & -0.5391 & 0.5527 & -0.1816 & 0.0152 & 0.0002 \\
0.0001 & -0.0050 & 0.0671 & -0.2965 & 0.4432 & -0.2286 & 0.0399 & -0.0023 \\
0.0000 & 0.0001 & 0.0078 & -0.0691 & 0.1609 & -0.1208 & 0.0305 & -0.0027
\end{bmatrix}
$$

(a) Gabor filter $\left(\phi=0, \sigma=1, \theta=\dfrac{\pi}{16}\right)$

$$
\begin{bmatrix}
0.0000 & 0.0001 & 0.0078 & -0.0691 & 0.1609 & -0.1208 & 0.0305 & -0.0027 \\
0.0001 & -0.0050 & 0.0671 & -0.2965 & 0.4432 & -0.2286 & 0.0399 & -0.0023 \\
0.0008 & -0.0200 & 0.1767 & -0.5391 & 0.5527 & -0.1816 & 0.0152 & 0.0002 \\
0.0019 & -0.0349 & 0.2098 & -0.3946 & 0.1660 & 0.0434 & -0.0232 & 0.0022 \\
0.0022 & -0.0232 & 0.0434 & 0.1660 & -0.3946 & 0.2098 & -0.0349 & 0.0019 \\
0.0002 & 0.0152 & -0.1816 & 0.5527 & -0.5391 & 0.1767 & -0.0200 & 0.0008 \\
-0.0023 & 0.0399 & -0.2286 & 0.4432 & -0.2965 & 0.0671 & -0.0050 & 0.0001 \\
-0.0027 & 0.0305 & -0.1208 & 0.1609 & -0.0691 & 0.0078 & 0.0001 & 0.0000
\end{bmatrix}
$$

(b) Gabor filter $\left(\phi=0, \sigma=1, \theta=\dfrac{15\pi}{16}\right)$

$$
\begin{bmatrix}
-0.0027 & -0.0023 & 0.0002 & 0.0022 & 0.0019 & 0.0008 & 0.0001 & 0.0000 \\
0.0305 & 0.0399 & 0.0152 & -0.0232 & -0.0349 & -0.0200 & -0.0050 & 0.0001 \\
-0.1208 & -0.2286 & -0.1816 & 0.0434 & 0.2098 & 0.1767 & 0.0671 & 0.0078 \\
0.1609 & 0.4432 & 0.5527 & 0.1660 & -0.3946 & -0.5391 & -0.2965 & -0.0691 \\
-0.0691 & -0.2965 & -0.5391 & -0.3946 & 0.1660 & 0.5527 & 0.4432 & 0.1609 \\
0.0078 & 0.0671 & 0.1767 & 0.2098 & 0.0434 & -0.1816 & -0.2286 & -0.1208 \\
0.0001 & -0.0050 & -0.0200 & -0.0349 & -0.0232 & 0.0152 & 0.0399 & 0.0305 \\
0.0000 & 0.0001 & 0.0008 & 0.0019 & 0.0022 & 0.0002 & -0.0023 & -0.0027
\end{bmatrix}
$$

(c) Gabor filter $\left(\phi=0, \sigma=1, \theta=\dfrac{7\pi}{16}\right)$

Figure 3: Examples of three 2D Gabor filters with different orientations: (a) $\mathbf{G}^{0,1,\pi/16}$, (b) $\mathbf{G}^{0,1,15\pi/16}$, and (c) $\mathbf{G}^{0,1,7\pi/16}$.

the statistical characteristics according to the spatial diagonal symmetry. First, for a standard JPEG quantization table (see **Figure 5**), the elements for low-frequency DCT coefficients are symmetric w.r.t. the 8×8 block main diagonal, especially for high quality factors. Second, since most high-frequency DCT coefficients are zeros, they mitigate the impact of non-symmetric elements in the quantization table because actually they produce the same zero value in the dequantization. From **Figure 6**, we find that when computing the subsets whose histograms will be merged according to the method in **Step 2**, the 8×8 window of the Gabor filter $\mathbf{G}^{\phi,\sigma,\theta}$ is symmetric with the window of $\mathbf{G}^{\phi,\sigma,\pi/2-\theta}$ about the main diagonal (i.e., the blue window is symmetric with the red window about the main diagonal).

In the following, we will demonstrate the reasons for merging histograms in the above two steps and show the details.

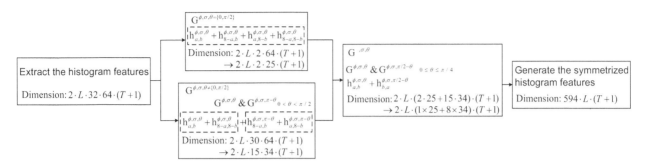

Figure 2: The flow of the proposed merging method. The parameter L denotes the number of scales of the Gabor filters, the parameter T means the threshold on residual values, the number of phases of the Gabor filters is 2, the number of orientations of the Gabor filters is 32 and the number of JPEG phases is 64.

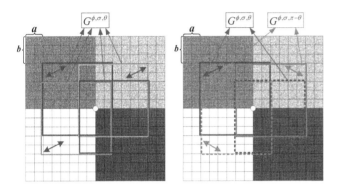

Figure 4: Left: The merging method (Step 6 in Section 2) in the original GFR. (The blue windows denote the Gabor filter $\mathbf{G}^{\phi,\sigma,\theta}$. When $\mathbf{G}^{\phi,\sigma,\theta}$ is located at these four positions, four subsets $\mathbf{U}_{a,b}^{\phi,\sigma,\theta}$, $\mathbf{U}_{a,8-b}^{\phi,\sigma,\theta}$, $\mathbf{U}_{8-a,b}^{\phi,\sigma,\theta}$, $\mathbf{U}_{8-a,8-b}^{\phi,\sigma,\theta}$ are computed. The histograms of these four subsets can be merged with the merging method in Step 6 in Section 2.) Right: The merging method in Step 1 (Section 4) based on the symmetry between $\mathbf{G}^{\phi,\sigma,\theta}$ and $\mathbf{G}^{\phi,\sigma,\pi-\theta}$. (The blue windows denote the Gabor filter $\mathbf{G}^{\phi,\sigma,\theta}$, and the red ones denote $\mathbf{G}^{\phi,\sigma,\pi-\theta}$. When $\mathbf{G}^{\phi,\sigma,\theta}$ and $\mathbf{G}^{\phi,\sigma,\pi-\theta}$ are located at these positions, four subsets $\mathbf{U}_{a,b}^{\phi,\sigma,\theta}$, $\mathbf{U}_{8-a,8-b}^{\phi,\sigma,\theta}$, $\mathbf{U}_{a,8-b}^{\phi,\sigma,\pi-\theta}$, $\mathbf{U}_{8-a,b}^{\phi,\sigma,\pi-\theta}$ are computed. The histograms of these four subsets can be merged with the merging method in Step 1 in Section 4.)

$$
\begin{bmatrix}
2 & 1 & 1 & 2 & 2 & 4 & 5 & 6 \\
1 & 1 & 1 & 2 & 3 & 6 & 6 & 6 \\
1 & 1 & 2 & 2 & 4 & 6 & 7 & 6 \\
1 & 2 & 2 & 3 & 5 & 9 & 8 & 6 \\
2 & 2 & 4 & 6 & 7 & 11 & 10 & 8 \\
2 & 4 & 6 & 6 & 8 & 10 & 11 & 9 \\
5 & 6 & 8 & 9 & 10 & 12 & 12 & 10 \\
7 & 9 & 10 & 10 & 11 & 10 & 10 & 10
\end{bmatrix}
$$

Figure 5: The standard JPEG quantization table of quality factor 95.

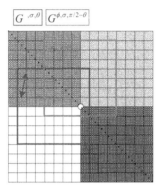

Figure 6: The merging method in Step 2 (Section 4) based on the symmetry between $\mathbf{G}^{\phi,\sigma,\theta}$ and $\mathbf{G}^{\phi,\sigma,\pi/2-\theta}$. (The blue window denotes the Gabor filter $\mathbf{G}^{\phi,\sigma,\theta}$, and the red one denotes $\mathbf{G}^{\phi,\sigma,\pi/2-\theta}$. When $\mathbf{G}^{\phi,\sigma,\theta}$ and $\mathbf{G}^{\phi,\sigma,\pi/2-\theta}$ are located at these positions, two subsets $\mathbf{U}_{a,b}^{\phi,\sigma,\theta}$, $\mathbf{U}_{b,a}^{\phi,\sigma,\pi/2-\theta}$ are computed. The histograms of these two subsets can be merged with the merging method in Step 2 in Section 4.)

4.1 Analysis of Merging Method in Step 1

We find the fact that there exit symmetries between $\mathbf{G}^{\phi,\sigma,\theta}$ and $\mathbf{G}^{\phi,\sigma,\pi-\theta}$ $(0 \leq \theta < \pi, \theta \neq \{0, \pi/2\})$:

$$
\begin{aligned}
\mathbf{G}^{\phi=0,\sigma,\theta} &= \text{fliplr}(\mathbf{G}^{\phi=0,\sigma,\pi-\theta}) = \text{flipud}(\mathbf{G}^{\phi=0,\sigma,\pi-\theta}) \\
\mathbf{G}^{\phi=\frac{\pi}{2},\sigma,\theta} &= \text{fliplr}(\mathbf{G}^{\phi=\frac{\pi}{2},\sigma,\pi-\theta}) = -\text{flipud}(\mathbf{G}^{\phi=\frac{\pi}{2},\sigma,\pi-\theta})
\end{aligned}
\tag{24}
$$

Thus, from (2) and (24), we can find the symmetry between $\left|\mathbf{R}^{(\phi,\sigma,\theta)(k,l)}\right|$ and $\left|\mathbf{R}^{(\phi,\sigma,\pi-\theta)(k,l)}\right|$:

$$
\begin{aligned}
\left|R_{a,b}^{(\phi,\sigma,\theta)(k,l)}\right| &= \left|R_{-a,b}^{(\phi,\sigma,\pi-\theta)(k,l)}\right| \\
\left|R_{a,b}^{(\phi,\sigma,\theta)(k,l)}\right| &= \left|R_{a,-b}^{(\phi,\sigma,\pi-\theta)(k,l)}\right|
\end{aligned}
\tag{25}
$$

According to the definition of projection vector $\mathbf{P}_{a,b}^{(\phi,\sigma,\theta)(k,l)}$ (18), we can see the following symmetry by (25),

$$\left|\mathbf{P}_{a,b}^{(\phi,\sigma,\theta)(k,l)}\right| = \left|\mathbf{P}_{-a,b}^{(\phi,\sigma,\pi-\theta)(k,l)}\right|$$
$$\left|\mathbf{P}_{a,b}^{(\phi,\sigma,\theta)(k,l)}\right| = \left|\mathbf{P}_{a,-b}^{(\phi,\sigma,\pi-\theta)(k,l)}\right| \qquad (26)$$

From (26) and (21), we have

$$\left|\mathbf{P}_{a,b}^{(\phi,\sigma,\theta)(k,l)}\right| = \left|\mathbf{P}_{a-8,b}^{(\phi,\sigma,\theta)(k,l)}\right| = \left|\mathbf{P}_{8-a,b}^{(\phi,\sigma,\pi-\theta)(k,l)}\right|$$
$$\left|\mathbf{P}_{a,b}^{(\phi,\sigma,\theta)(k,l)}\right| = \left|\mathbf{P}_{a,b-8}^{(\phi,\sigma,\theta)(k,l)}\right| = \left|\mathbf{P}_{a,8-b}^{(\phi,\sigma,\pi-\theta)(k,l)}\right| \qquad (27)$$

Combining the symmetry (27) with the symmetry $\left|\mathbf{P}_{a,b}^{(\phi,\sigma,\theta)(k,l)}\right| = \left|\mathbf{P}_{8-a,8-b}^{(\phi,\sigma,\theta)(k,l)}\right|$ (23) , we have

$$\left|\mathbf{P}_{a,b}^{(\phi,\sigma,\theta)(k,l)}\right| = \left|\mathbf{P}_{8-a,8-b}^{(\phi,\sigma,\theta)(k,l)}\right|$$
$$= \left|\mathbf{P}_{a,8-b}^{(\phi,\sigma,\pi-\theta)(k,l)}\right|. \qquad (28)$$
$$= \left|\mathbf{P}_{8-a,b}^{(\phi,\sigma,\pi-\theta)(k,l)}\right|$$

According to the above symmetry (28), the subsets of residual $\mathbf{U}^{\phi,\sigma,\theta}$ obtained with $\mathbf{G}^{\phi,\sigma,\theta}$ and the subsets of residual $\mathbf{U}^{\phi,\sigma,\pi-\theta}$ obtained with $\mathbf{G}^{\phi,\sigma,\pi-\theta}$ can be considered together. As shown in **Figure 4**, thus, we can merge the histograms of the subsets corresponding to the positions (a,b), $(8-a,8-b)$ in $\mathbf{U}^{\phi,\sigma,\theta}$ and the subsets corresponding to $(8-a,b)$, $(a,8-b)$ in $\mathbf{U}^{\phi,\sigma,\pi-\theta}$. That is,

$$\mathbf{h}_{a,b}^{\phi,\sigma,\theta} \leftarrow \mathbf{h}_{a,b}^{\phi,\sigma,\theta} + \mathbf{h}_{8-a,8-b}^{\phi,\sigma,\theta} + \mathbf{h}_{8-a,b}^{\phi,\sigma,\pi-\theta} + \mathbf{h}_{a,8-b}^{\phi,\sigma,\pi-\theta}, 0 < \theta < \pi/2 \qquad (29)$$

Note that these indices, (a,b), $(8-a,8-b)$, $(8-a,b)$ and $(a,8-b)$, should stay within $\{0,1,\ldots,7\} \times \{0,1,\ldots,7\}$. When $(8-a)$ or $(8-b)$ is $8 \notin \{0,1,\ldots,7\}$, we can take mod8 of these indices $(\bmod(8,8) = 0)$.

For the condition of $\theta \neq \{0,\pi/2\}$, there are 30 orientations, L scales and 2 phase shifts, so the number of the Gabor filters is $2 \cdot L \cdot 30$. Without the merging method, the total dimension of the histograms is $2 \cdot L \cdot 30 \cdot 64 \cdot (T+1)$, where T is the histogram threshold. From **Figure 7**, it can be seen that according to the symmetry between $\mathbf{G}^{\phi,\sigma,\theta}$ and $\mathbf{G}^{\phi,\sigma,\pi-\theta}$, the dimensions can be reduced to $2 \cdot L \cdot 15 \cdot 34 \cdot (T+1)$ by merging together the histograms of the subsets labeled with the same number (regardless of the color and the underline).

4.2 Analysis of Merging Method in Step 2

For $\mathbf{G}^{\phi,\sigma,\theta} (0 \leq \theta \leq \pi/2)$, we find that

$$\mathbf{G}^{\phi,\sigma,\theta} = \left(\mathbf{G}^{\phi,\sigma,\pi/2-\theta}\right)^T, \qquad (30)$$

where $(\cdot)^T$ indicates the transpose operation. Thus, according to the symmetry between $\mathbf{G}^{\phi,\sigma,\theta}$ and $\mathbf{G}^{\phi,\sigma,\pi/2-\theta}$, the residuals $\mathbf{U}^{\phi,\sigma,\theta}$ and $\mathbf{U}^{\phi,\sigma,\pi/2-\theta}$, which are obtained using the filter $\mathbf{G}^{\phi,\sigma,\theta}$ and its transposed version $\mathbf{G}^{\phi,\sigma,\pi/2-\theta}$, can be considered together. We can merge together the histograms of the residuals $\mathbf{U}^{\phi,\sigma,\theta}$ and $\mathbf{U}^{\phi,\sigma,\pi/2-\theta}$ to further decrease the feature dimension and endow them more robustness. This idea has been adopted in the PSRM which is

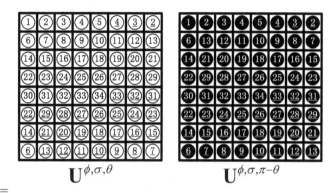

Figure 7: The subsets of $\mathbf{U}^{\phi,\sigma,\theta}$ and $\mathbf{U}^{\phi,\sigma,\pi-\theta}$ (a circle denotes a subset ($\mathbf{U}_{a,b}^{\phi,\sigma,\theta}$ or $\mathbf{U}_{a,b}^{\phi,\sigma,\pi-\theta}$), where (a,b) is the circle's location in the 8×8 grid).

one of the most effective steganalysis features in the spatial domain. As shown in **Figure 6**, we can merge the histogram $\mathbf{h}_{a,b}^{\phi,\sigma,\theta}$ and $\mathbf{h}_{b,a}^{\phi,\sigma,\pi/2-\theta}$,

$$\mathbf{h}_{a,b}^{\phi,\sigma,\theta} \leftarrow \mathbf{h}_{a,b}^{\phi,\sigma,\theta} + \mathbf{h}_{b,a}^{\phi,\sigma,\pi/2-\theta}, \ 0 \leq \theta \leq \pi/4 \qquad (31)$$

where $\mathbf{h}_{a,b}^{\phi,\sigma,\theta}$ is the histogram of the (a,b)th subset of residual $\mathbf{U}_{a,b}^{\phi,\sigma,\theta}$, and $\mathbf{h}_{b,a}^{\phi,\sigma,\pi/2-\theta}$ is the histogram of the (b,a)th subset of $\mathbf{U}_{b,a}^{\phi,\sigma,\pi/2-\theta}$. Note that the indices of these two subsets, $\mathbf{U}_{a,b}^{\phi,\sigma,\theta}$ and $\mathbf{U}_{b,a}^{\phi,\sigma,\pi/2-\theta}$, are transposed to avoid mixing up different statistical characteristics. This is because when the filter is transposed, the phase-aware statistics of the filtered image are transposed accordingly.

According to the symmetry between $\mathbf{G}^{\phi,\sigma,\theta}$ and $\mathbf{G}^{\phi,\sigma,\pi/2-\theta}$, the dimensions can be decreased furthermore. For the condition of $\theta \neq \{0,\pi/2\}$, the feature vector of $2 \cdot L \cdot 15 \cdot 34 \cdot (T+1)$ dimensions can be reduced to $2 \cdot L \cdot 8 \cdot 34 \cdot (T+1)$. For the condition of $\theta = \{0,\pi/2\}$, the $2 \cdot L \cdot 2 \cdot 25 \cdot (T+1)$ dimensions can be reduced to $2 \cdot L \cdot 1 \cdot 25 \cdot (T+1)$.

To sum up, with our proposed merging method in Section 4, the dimension of the improved GFR features (GFR-GSM) is $594 \cdot L \cdot (T+1)$[1]. If the number of scales $L = 4$ and the histogram threshold $T = 4$ are the same as in the original GFR [15], the dimensions are reduced to 11880. From the experiments in Section 6, when compared with the 17000-dimensional GFR, the 11880-dimensional GFR-GSM$_4$ (the subscript 4 denotes the number of scales $L = 4$) can achieve better detection performance with smaller dimensions.

5 PROPOSED WEIGHTED HISTOGRAM METHOD

No matter in the GFR or in the DCTR, all the absolute values of residuals are quantized to the integer values before computing the phase-aware histograms. Specifically, in the GFR, the residual $|\mathbf{U}^{\phi,\sigma,\theta}| = |u_{kl}^{\phi,\sigma,\theta}|$ is divided by the quantization step q and quantized with a quantizer Q_T with $T+1$ centroids $Q = \{0,1,\ldots T\}$,

---

[1] $2 \cdot L \cdot 8 \cdot 34 \cdot (T+1) + 2 \cdot L \cdot 1 \cdot 25 \cdot (T+1) = 594 \cdot L \cdot (T+1)$

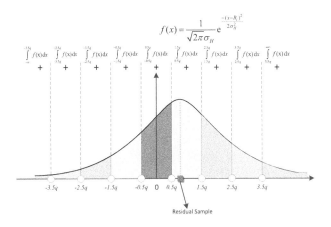

Figure 8: Our weighted voting scheme for histogram computation.

$$Q_T(|u_{kl}^{\phi,\sigma,\theta}|/q) = \text{trunc}_T\left(\text{round}\left(|u_{kl}^{\phi,\sigma,\theta}|/q\right)\right), \quad (32)$$

where round($\cdot$) denotes the rounding operation, and trunc$_T(\cdot)$ denotes the truncation with the threshold T. The values of residuals are mapped to the integers (Q) through the above quantization. Although the quantization can curb the dimensionality of the feature space, it inevitably leads to loss of useful information. With the quantization, the residual samples, which are quantized to the same centroid, are always located in different positions within the same interval. This means the slight changes in residual samples caused by embedding may be left out, which may affect the detection accuracy.

In this section, we associate a residual sample with a Gaussian function and use the integrals over all quantization intervals as the weights that will be accumulated into the corresponding histogram bins. This method refers to the soft voting scheme that has been used in other fields of machine learning [12]. This histogram method can also be applied to other histogram features, such as the PSRM, the PHARM and the DCTR.

Each residual sample is associated with a Gaussian function centered at u_{kl}, **Gauss**(u_{kl}, σ_H^2), where u_{kl} is the value of the residual sample and σ_H is an important parameter that needs to be adjusted carefully. In our method, there are $2T+1$ centroids $\{-Tq, \ldots, -q, 0, q, \ldots, Tq\}$. The interval I_i w.r.t. the centroid i can be expressed as:

$$I_i = \begin{cases} (-\infty, & (-T+1/2)q] & i = -T, \\ ((i-1/2)q, & (i+1/2)q] & i = \{-T+1, \ldots, -1\}, \\ (-1/2q, & 1/2q) & i = 0, \\ [(i-1/2)q, & (i+1/2)q) & i = \{1, \ldots, T-1\}, \\ [(T+1/2)q, & \infty) & i = T. \end{cases} \quad (33)$$

As shown in **Figure 8**, P_i is the integral of **Gauss** over the interval I_i, and it can be computed as:

$$P_i = \begin{cases} \int_{-\infty}^{(-T+1/2)q} \frac{1}{\sqrt{2\pi}\sigma_H} \exp\left(-(x-u_{kl})^2/\sigma_H^2\right) dx \\ \quad i = -T, \\ \int_{(i-1/2)q}^{(i+1/2)q} \frac{1}{\sqrt{2\pi}\sigma_H} \exp\left(-(x-u_{kl})^2/\sigma_H^2\right) dx \\ \quad i = \{-T+1, \ldots, T-1\}, \\ \int_{(T+1/2)q}^{\infty} \frac{1}{\sqrt{2\pi}\sigma_H} \exp\left(-(x-u_{kl})^2/\sigma_H^2\right) dx \\ \quad i = T. \end{cases} \quad (34)$$

In the original GFR, if $|u_{kl}|$ falls into the quantization interval I_i, we add a 1 to the histogram bin b_i. In our method, however, the weights P_i are accumulated into the corresponding histogram bins b_i. For $T = 2$, we add P_{-2} to the histogram bin b_{-2} corresponding to the interval $I_{-2} = (-\infty, -1.5q)$, while adding P_{-1}, P_0, P_1, P_2 to the histogram bins b_{-1}, b_0, b_1, b_2, respectively. After computing the weights of all intervals, P_i is merged with P_{-i} due to the sign-symmetry

$$P_i = \begin{cases} P_i + P_{-i} & i = \{1, 2, \ldots, T\}, \\ P_0 & i = 0. \end{cases} \quad (35)$$

Consequently, the final weighted histogram consists of $T+1$ bins (b_i, $i = 0, 1, \ldots, T$). The complete weighted histogram **h**$_{\text{WEIGHT}}$ is computed by summing the contributions of all the samples in the residual image

$$\mathbf{h}_{\text{WEIGHT}}(i) = \sum_{k,l} \int_{I_i \bigcup I_{-i}} \frac{1}{\sqrt{2\pi}\sigma_H} \exp\left(-(x-u_{kl})^2/\sigma_H^2\right) dx, \quad (36)$$

where $i \in \{0, 1, \ldots, T\}$.

There are two main differences between our histogram method and the conventional histogram method in the GFR. First, in our method, the contribution of a residual sample to a bin is a real value rather than a constant value 1 in the conventional method. Second, in our method, a residual sample contributes to all bins rather than only one bin in the conventional method.

Our histogram method takes into consideration the positions of residual values in the quantization interval, thus reflecting the slight shift in the interval. We take **Figure 9** as an example. We can see that residual sample 1 and residual sample 2 with different values are in the same interval, even with the same distance to the centroid. The conventional histogram method in the GFR can not differentiate them. However, the integral values obtained from the Gaussian function of residual sample 1 are different from residual sample 2. These integral values, as the weights, are accumulated into the histogram, so these two residual samples have different influence on the weighted histogram in our method.

6 EXPERIMENTS

This section is organized as follows. In section 6.1, the parameters are discussed for better detection performance. In section 6.2, experimental results show the advantages of the proposed steganalysis features. In the experiments, 10000 512×512 grayscale images from BOSSbase are converted

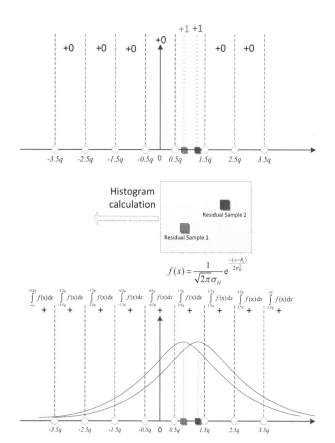

Figure 9: The difference between the weighted histogram and the conventional histogram.

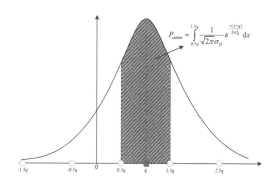

Figure 10: The Gaussian function is centered at the centroid of a quantization interval and the integral over this quantization interval is P_{center}.

Table 1: The effect of the parameter P_{center} (decided by σ_H) on detection accuracy for $\sigma = 1$ and quality factor 75 ($q = 6$).

σ_H	1.8182	2.0833	2.3438	2.6087	2.8846
P_{center}	0.9	0.85	0.8	0.75	0.7
$\overline{P}_{\text{E}}$	0.3160	0.3151	0.3149	**0.3134**	0.3142

into JPEG images with quality factors 75 and 95 as cover images. The advanced adaptive steganographic schemes UED-JC and J-UNIWARD are used to generate stego images with different embedding rates.

The detection accuracy is quantified using the minimal total error probability under equal priors $P_{\text{E}} = \min_{P_{\text{FA}}} \frac{1}{2}(P_{\text{FA}} + P_{\text{MD}})$, where P_{FA} and P_{MD} are the false-alarm and missed-detection probabilities. The FLD ensemble classifier [11] is used in the training and testing stages. The $\overline{P}_{\text{E}}$ is averaged over ten random 5000/5000 database splits.

6.1 Parameter Setting

6.1.1 Number of Scales of 2D Gabor Filter. In this paper, the parameters of 2D Gabor filters ϕ and θ are the same as in the original GFR. If the scale parameter σ of 2D Gabor filters is the same as in the original GFR ($\sigma = 0.5, 0.75, 1, 1.25$), there are 4 scales and the total dimension of the proposed GFR-GSM$_4$ (or GFR-GW$_4$) is 11880. Since our histogram merging method in Section 4 reduces the dimensions dramatically, we can increase the number of scales by adding $\sigma = 1.5, 1.75$ to improve the accuracy. This gives our final steganalysis feature set GFR-GW$_6$ the dimension of 17820,

which is close to the dimension of the original GFR. The setting of the quantization step q is related to the value of the scale parameter σ. For the scale parameter in this paper $\sigma = 0.5, 0.75, 1, 1.25, 1.5, 1.75$, by referring to the literature [15], q is set as $q = 2, 4, 6, 8, 10, 12$, respectively when the quality factor is 75, and $q = 0.5, 1, 1.5, 2, 2.5, 3$, respectively when the quality factor is 95.

6.1.2 Parameter σ_H in Weighted Histogram Method. To better determine the value of the parameter σ_H, we first introduce a new parameter P_{center}. As shown in **Figure 10**, when the Gaussian function is centered at the centroid of a quantization interval I_i, the integral over the interval I_i is called P_{center}, $0 < P_{\text{center}} < 1$. The value of P_{center} depends on the parameter σ_H and the quantization step q. In **Table 1** and **Table 2**, the effects of the parameter P_{center} on detection accuracy are shown for J-UNIWARD with 0.2 bpnzac payload for quality factors 75 and 95. From **Table 1** and **Table 2**, it can be seen that for the scale parameter $\sigma = 1$ and quality factors 75 and 95, the best detection accuracy is achieved when P_{center} is equal to 0.75. For each experiment, since the scale σ and the quality factor are fixed, the quantization step q is fixed and P_{center} is only decided by σ_H. Thus, we maintain that in the case of various scales σ and quality factors, σ_H is always set to make P_{center} equal to 0.75 for better performance.

6.2 Experimental Results

Numerous experiments are conducted to demonstrate the effectiveness of the proposed methods. **Table 3** demonstrates

Table 3: Difference between GFR and our proposed features.

features	number of scales of 2D Gabor filter	dimension	using new histogram merging method described in Section 4	using our weighted histogram method described in Section 5
GFR	4	17000	×	×
GFR-GSM$_4$	4	11880	√	×
GFR-GW$_4$	4	11880	√	√
GFR-GW$_6$	6	17820	√	√

Table 2: The effect of the parameter P_{center} (decided by σ_H) on detection accuracy for $\sigma = 1$ and quality factor 95 ($q = 1.5$).

σ_H	0.4545	0.5208	0.5859	0.6522	0.7212
P_{center}	0.9	0.85	0.8	0.75	0.7
$\overline{P}_{\text{E}}$	0.4307	0.4307	0.4305	**0.4297**	0.4311

the characteristics of our three proposed feature sets and shows the difference between the GFR and our feature sets.

From **Table 4**, compared to the 17000-dimensional GFR, the GFR-GSM$_4$ with 11880 dimensions, which exploits the proposed histogram merging method, has better detection performance for different steganographic algorithms and embedding rates. This demonstrates that our merging method not only reduces more dimensions but also improves the detection accuracy. Next, the GFR-GW$_4$ using our weighted histogram method achieves better detection accuracy than the GFR-GSM$_4$ because the weighted histograms are more sensitive to the small changes than the conventional histograms. In addition, the detection accuracy of the GFR-GW$_6$ is higher than the GFR-GW$_4$. This is because the extraction of features from more scales can enhance the diversity and effectiveness of the features. In contrast to 17000-dimensional GFR, the 17820-dimensional GFR-GW$_6$ significantly improves the detection performance regardless of quality factors, embedding algorithms and embedding rates. The maximum performance improvement of the GFR-GW$_6$ over the original GFR is close to 2.5% for the UED-JC for quality factor 75 with an embedding rate of 0.1 bpnzac.

7 CONCLUSION

In this paper, we modify the original GFR features for better detection performance. There are two main contributions in this paper. First, according to the symmetries between different Gabor filters, we merge the histograms in a special way, thus compactifying the features furthermore while improving the detection accuracy. Second, our weighted histogram method is more sensitive to the small changes in residuals, simply placing a Gaussian on each of the residual samples and using the integrals over quantizing intervals. With these two improvements, the proposed GFR-GW$_6$ with similar dimensions is more powerful than the original GFR.

The future work will focus on the following several aspects. First, we can merge the DCTR features according to the transposition relation between different DCT kernels to reduce the dimensions furthermore. Second, in our weighted histogram method, the integral values of the Gaussian function are computed via the MATLAB command 'normcdf', which is expensive in computation time. So we can first save the table of integrals in the memory and then use the method of table look-up to make our histogram method more practically efficient. Third, when computing the histograms using a weighted voting scheme, the weight can be calculated with other strategies. Fourth, some parameters in our methods, such as σ_H, are tuned thanks to preliminary experiments done on BOSSbase, which may lead to a kind of overfitting on the BOSSbase. So we will further validate the effectiveness of the parameters on other image bases. Fifth, as a universal feature set, the GFR-GW$_6$ can also be modified to be a selection-channel-aware version with the method in [1] to detect adaptive steganography more accurately. Sixth, like the GPU-version of steganalysis features (e.g., GPU-PSRM [9], GPU-SRM and GPU-DCTR [16]), our proposed features can also be implemented on the GPU device to make them more efficient. Although the Gabor filters is not separable, it can be decomposed using the SVD method to accelerate the filtering [13]. So it is not very difficult to implement our features on a GPU.

ACKNOWLEDGMENTS

This work was supported by the NSFC under U1536105 and U1636102, and National Key Technology R&D Program under 2014BAH41B01, 2016YFB0801003 and 2016QY15Z2500.

REFERENCES

[1] T. Denemark, M. Boroumand, and J. Fridrich. 2016. Steganalysis features for content-adaptive JPEG steganography. *IEEE Transactions on Information Forensics and Security* 11, 8 (August 2016), 1736–1746.
[2] T. Filler, J. Judas, and J. Fridrich. 2011. Minimizing additive distortion in steganography using syndrome-trellis codes. *IEEE Transactions on Information Forensics and Security* 6, 3 (September 2011), 920–935.
[3] L. Guo, J. Ni, and Y. Q. Shi. 2014. Uniform embedding for efficient JPEG steganography. *IEEE Transactions on Information Forensics and Security* 9, 5 (May 2014), 814–825.
[4] V. Holub and J. Fridrich. 2013. Random projections of residuals for digital image steganalysis. *IEEE Transactions on Information Forensics and Security* 8, 12 (December 2013), 1996–2006.
[5] V. Holub and J. Fridrich. 2014. Challenging the doctrines of JPEG steganography. *Proc. SPIE* 9028 (2014), 902802–902802-8.

Table 4: Detection error $\overline{P}_E$ for UED-JC and J-UNIWARD for quality factors 75 and 95 when steganalyzed with PHARM, GFR, and our three feature sets.

J-UNI, QF 75	0.05 bpnzac	0.1 bpnzac	0.2 bpnzac	0.3 bpnzac	0.4 bpnzac
12600D PHARM	0.4741±0.0023	0.4294±0.0034	0.3164±0.0042	0.2099±0.0036	0.1271±0.0024
17000D GFR	0.4638±0.0028	0.4089±0.0016	0.2866±0.0025	0.1786±0.0033	0.1028±0.0028
11880D GFR-GSM$_4$	0.4623±0.0031	0.4058±0.0027	0.2824±0.0032	0.1743±0.0025	0.0990±0.0023
11880D GFR-GW$_4$	0.4586±0.0023	0.3994±0.0028	0.2722±0.0040	0.1651±0.0024	0.0908±0.0029
17820D GFR-GW$_6$	0.4575±0.0024	0.3975±0.0026	0.2685±0.0040	0.1628±0.0038	0.0895±0.0023

UED-JC, QF 75	0.05 bpnzac	0.1 bpnzac	0.2 bpnzac	0.3 bpnzac	0.4 bpnzac
12600D PHARM	0.4217±0.0017	0.3295±0.0034	0.1694±0.0030	0.0798±0.0029	0.0346±0.0022
17000D GFR	0.4090±0.0041	0.3124±0.0038	0.1547±0.0035	0.0707±0.0022	0.0304±0.0019
11880D GFR-GSM$_4$	0.4070±0.0040	0.3071±0.0032	0.1487±0.0023	0.0660±0.0021	0.0271±0.0015
11880D GFR-GW$_4$	0.3962±0.0022	0.2943±0.0030	0.1369±0.0037	0.0611±0.0025	0.0248±0.0014
17820D GFR-GW$_6$	0.3920±0.0035	0.2870±0.0032	0.1336±0.0037	0.0585±0.0025	0.0231±0.0012

J-UNI, QF 95	0.05 bpnzac	0.1 bpnzac	0.2 bpnzac	0.3 bpnzac	0.4 bpnzac
12600D PHARM	0.4945±0.0022	0.4821±0.0023	0.4378±0.0035	0.3803±0.0038	0.3090±0.0033
17000D GFR	0.4932±0.0023	0.4751±0.0020	0.4232±0.0042	0.3506±0.0038	0.2703±0.0056
11880D GFR-GSM$_4$	0.4910±0.0025	0.4738±0.0020	0.4202±0.0034	0.3477±0.0045	0.2661±0.0032
11880D GFR-GW$_4$	0.4899±0.0019	0.4715±0.0034	0.4157±0.0025	0.3421±0.0037	0.2611±0.0042
17820D GFR-GW$_6$	0.4897±0.0020	0.4709±0.0017	0.4153±0.0026	0.3417±0.0025	0.2583±0.0034

UED-JC, QF 95	0.05 bpnzac	0.1 bpnzac	0.2 bpnzac	0.3 bpnzac	0.4 bpnzac
12600D PHARM	0.4799±0.0018	0.4482±0.0035	0.3698±0.0038	0.2789±0.0034	0.1966±0.0020
17000D GFR	0.4695±0.0028	0.4325±0.0028	0.3420±0.0037	0.2486±0.0030	0.1647±0.0031
11880D GFR-GSM$_4$	0.4682±0.0018	0.4297±0.0029	0.3380±0.0025	0.2413±0.0040	0.1602±0.0024
11880D GFR-GW$_4$	0.4663±0.0021	0.4258±0.0036	0.3299±0.0050	0.2345±0.0038	0.1551±0.0036
17820D GFR-GW$_6$	0.4654±0.0020	0.4243±0.0031	0.3257±0.0039	0.2334±0.0029	0.1521±0.0033

[6] V. Holub and J. Fridrich. 2015. Low-complexity features for JPEG steganalysis using undecimated DCT. *IEEE Transactions on Information Forensics and Security* 10, 2 (February 2015), 219–228.

[7] V. Holub and J. Fridrich. 2015. Phase-aware projection model for steganalysis of JPEG images. *Proc. SPIE* 9409 (2015), 94090T–94090T–11.

[8] V. Holub, J. Fridrich, and T. Denemark. 2014. Universal distortion function for steganography in an arbitrary domain. *EURASIP Journal on Information Security* 2014, 1 (2014), 1–13.

[9] A. D. Ker. 2014. Implementing the projected spatial rich features on a GPU. *Proc. SPIE* 9028 (2014), 90280K–90280K–10.

[10] J. Kodovský and J. Fridrich. 2012. Steganalysis of JPEG images using rich models. *Proc. SPIE* 8303 (2012), 83030A–83030A–13.

[11] J. Kodovský, J. Fridrich, and V. Holub. 2012. Ensemble classifiers for steganalysis of digital media. *IEEE Transactions on Information Forensics and Security* 7, 2 (April 2012), 432–444.

[12] H. B. Mitchell and P. A. Schaefer. 2001. A soft K-nearest neighbor voting scheme. *International Journal of Intelligent Systems* 16, 4 (2001), 459–468.

[13] W. M. Pang, K. S. Choi, and J. Qin. 2016. Fast Gabor texture feature extraction with separable filters using GPU. *Journal of Real-Time Image Processing* 12, 1 (June 2016), 5–13.

[14] T. Pevný and J. Fridrich. 2007. Merging Markov and DCT features for multi-class JPEG steganalysis. *Proc. SPIE* 6505 (2007), 650503–650503–13.

[15] X. Song, F. Liu, C. Yang, X. Luo, and Y. Zhang. 2015. Steganalysis of adaptive JPEG steganography using 2D Gabor filters. In *Proceedings of the 3rd ACM Workshop on Information Hiding and Multimedia Security (IH&MMSec'15)*. ACM, New York, NY, USA, 15–23.

[16] C. Xia, Q. Guan, X. Zhao, and C. Zhao. 2016. Highly accurate real-time image steganalysis based on GPU. *Journal of Real-Time Image Processing* (2016), 1–14.

Deep Convolutional Neural Network to Detect J-UNIWARD

Guanshuo Xu
independent researcher
228 Stewart Ave.
Kearny, NJ 07032, USA
guanshuo.xu@gmail.com

ABSTRACT

This paper presents an empirical study on applying convolutional neural networks (CNNs) to detecting J-UNIWARD — one of the most secure JPEG steganographic method. Experiments guiding the architectural design of the CNNs have been conducted on the JPEG compressed BOSSBase containing 10,000 covers of size 512×512. Results have verified that both the pooling method and the depth of the CNNs are critical for performance. Results have also proved that a 20-layer CNN, in general, outperforms the most sophisticated feature-based methods, but its advantage gradually diminishes on hard-to-detect cases. To show that the performance generalizes to large-scale databases and to different cover sizes, one experiment has been conducted on the CLS-LOC dataset of ImageNet containing more than one million covers cropped to unified size of 256×256. The proposed 20-layer CNN has cut the error achieved by a CNN recently proposed for large-scale JPEG steganalysis by 35%. Source code is available via GitHub: https://github.com/GuanshuoXu/deep_cnn_jpeg_steganalysis

CCS CONCEPTS

• **Computing methodologies → Machine learning**

KEYWORDS

Steganalysis, forensics, convolutional neural networks, deep learning, residual net

1 INTRODUCTION

Current published works on applying convolutional neural networks (CNNs) to image steganalysis mainly focus on detecting steganography embedding in the original spatial domain [1–6]. Studies on applying CNNs for JPEG steganalysis have not been extensively carried out even though JPEG steganography could be more conveniently used in practice. Recently, Zeng et al. [7] for large-scale JPEG steganalysis

IH&MMSec '17, June 20-22, 2017, Philadelphia, PA, USA
© 2017 Association for Computing Machinery.
ACM ISBN 978-1-4503-5061-7/17/06...$15.00
http://dx.doi.org/10.1145/3082031.3083236

designed a hybrid CNN optimized upon various quantized DCT subbands of decompressed input images. It is worth noting that only three convolutional layers exist in their proposed CNN, and average pooling which frequently appear in spatial domain steganalysis [2,4] has also been employed. Experiments have been performed on subsets of the whole ImageNet Database with more than 14 million images. Results demonstrate that their CNN outperform traditional feature-based methods in detecting JPEG steganography provided that the number of training data is huge. However, as will be shown in this study, both the shallow architecture and the average pooling layers are too conservative to fully bring the strength of deep learning into play.

Spatial domain Steganography, as its name indicates, makes changes directly to the pixel values in the original spatial domain. Because of the variation in the locations and values of the changes made on image pixels during information embedding, the CNNs, extremely powerful in mining local patterns, run the risk of memorizing the embedding patterns which would eventually harm the generalization of the trained models. Hence, CNNs are forced to be shallow (5–6 layers [2,4]) for spatial domain steganalysis, and, average pooling, rarely used in computer vision, has also found its value because averaging neighboring elements reduced the risk of memorizing exact embedding locations. In contrast, JPEG steganography makes embedding changes to the quantized DCT coefficients. When transformed back to the spatial domain, the changes made on the DCT coefficients spread to all the pixels in their 8x8 blocks, exposing JPEG steganography more to the fire of deep CNNs compared with its counterpart in the spatial domain.

This paper presents the latest results using CNN to detect the most secure JPEG steganography method — the JPEG version of the universal distortion function (J-UNIWARD) [15]. It has been discovered that the designed all-convolutional 20-layer CNN, equipped with batch normalization and shortcut connections for efficient gradient back-propagation, has generally better performance compared with the most sophisticated feature-based methods, when tested on the BOSSBase compressed with JPEG quality factors of 75 and 95, and embedded by J-UNIWARD using Gibbs simulator with rates of 0.1, 0.2, 0.3, and 0.4 bpnzAC. To show that the performance of the designed CNN generalizes to large-scale databases and to different image sizes, one experiment has been conducted on the CLS-LOC dataset of ImageNet, which contains more than one million covers cropped to 256×256, and recompressed with QF75, then embedded with rate of 0.4 bpnzAC. The proposed 20-layer CNN has cut the error achieved by a CNN recently proposed for large-scale JPEG steganalysis [7] by 35%.

The architecture of the 20-layer CNN will be introduced in Section 2. All the experiments will be presented in Section 3. Section 4 summarizes this paper.

2 THE PROPOSED CNN ACHITECTURE

The entire architecture of our proposed CNN is included in Fig. 1. Only the forward pass appears in the figure, as should be enough for understanding the ideas.

Similar to what has been done in the traditional feature-based steganalysis methods [8,9,11], the input in the JPEG format are first transformed to the spatial domain (without the last rounding step), then go through a set of filter banks. In the proposed CNN, undecimated DCT of size 4×4 are selected to project every single input to 16 different frequency bands. The DCT kernels are fixed and not optimized during training. During the initial stage of this study, DCT sizes of 2×2, 3×3, 4×4, 5×5, and 8×8 have been tested; the best results are obtained with size 4×4. Also have been tested are removing the DC subband or the highest frequency subbands, but no obvious improvement have been observed. Other types of filter banks, e.g., the Garbor filters [9], have not been studied yet and should belong to future research. Same as in [7–9,11], in this work, only the magnitudes of the subbands are used, and they are further truncated with a slightly tuned global threshold value of 8. Quantization as another essential ingredient in the traditional feature extraction procedure has been abandoned to prevent unnecessary information loss; after all, the CNNs do not explicitly assemble histograms for statistical modeling. Zeng et al. [7] propose to learn a sub-CNN on each of the quantized versions of the subbands, it can be argued that such a design could potentially over-complicate the problem, because the CNN should be able to learn something similar to quantization with better information preserving and gradient-decent friendly operations such as linear scaling and non-linear activations. Nevertheless, truncation to limit the range of input data seems still necessary; it has been observed that without truncation the CNNs experienced slow convergence.

Following these pre-processing steps is the core part of the CNN comprising 20 convolutional layers and a global average pooling layer. This part of the CNN is responsible for learning optimized function to transform each of the pre-processed input into a 384-D feature vector for classification. All the convolutional layers are followed by Batch-Normalization (BN) to reduce internal covariant shift [17] and the most widely used Rectified Linear Unit (ReLU) [21] as the non-linear activation function. The convolution kernels have a unified size of 3×3 along spatial dimensions. The width of the CNN is mainly constrained by the GPU memory; we managed to fit this CNN in a single GPU with 12GB memory. It is essential for the CNNs to reduce the spatial resolutions by pooling while going deeper, though attention should be paid that operations with strides skips modes in the 8x8 JPEG blocks, which would cause more information loss in JPEG steganalysis. Let the CNNs take into considerations of the non-stationarity of the input, similar to the mode-wise statistical modeling done in traditional feature-based steganalysis [8,9], could be a valuable future work. In our CNN, pooling is achieved by convolutional layers with stride 2, after which the spatial sizes of data are cut by half and the number of channels doubles. Empirical study carried out in Section 3.1 compares convolution with average and max pooling and suggests a clear advantage for convolution with stride over average and max pooling for JPEG steganalysis; after all, convolutional layers at least introduce more learnable parameters and therefore increase the depth of CNN. Our deep CNN contrasts the shallow CNN [7] containing only three convolutional layers. The importance of depth will be further verified in Section 3.1.

A 20-layer CNN, even though already equipped with BN and ReLU, still more or less suffers from the gradient vanishing problem causing inefficient training, as will be shown in Section 3.1. To overcome this issue, the structure of shortcut connections inspired by [16–20] is brought into play. All the shortcut connections added in the CNN are concisely illustrated in Fig. 1 (Left) as curved arrows. The solid curved arrows denote direct shortcut connections allowing the convolutional layers in the middle to learn only residuals [19,20]; the dashed curved arrows denote transformed shortcut connections elaborated in Figure 1 (Right) because the element-wise addition requires input data of exactly same sizes. With shortcut connections, the depth following the shortest path is only 5, whereas the longest path has 20 layers, achieving both the strength of modeling and efficient training.

The linear classification module following the global pooling layer is simply composed of a fully-connected layer (no more hidden layers and no non-linear activations) and a softmax layer to transform the feature vectors to posterior probabilities for each class. Final class labels are determined by choosing the class corresponding to the larger posteriors.

3 EXPERIMENTS

The primary database used in this study is the BOSSbase v1.01 [12] containing 10,000 uncompressed images, initially taken by seven cameras in the RAW format, and transformed to 8-bit grayscale images, then cropped to obtain the size of 512×512. To generate covers for JPEG steganography, the images were compressed with QF75 and QF95 as representatives for low and high quality using Matlab's imwrite function. The corresponding stegos were generated through data embedding into the compressed images. Hence, for each classification problem, the dataset contains 10,000 cover–stegos pairs. J-UNIWARD served as the only steganographic method in this study. According to the steganalysis results presented in [8,9,11], J-UNIWARD should be the most secure algorithm embedding in the JPEG domain. Embedding rates of 0.1, 0.2, 0.3, and 0.4 bpnzAC were selected for experiments.

All of the experiments using the CNN reported in this study were performed on a modified version of the Caffe toolbox [14]. Mini-batch stochastic gradient descent was used to solve all the CNNs in experiments. The momentum was fixed to 0.9. The learning rate was initialized to 0.001, and scheduled to decrease

10% every 5000 training iterations. Parameters in the convolution kernels were randomly initialized from zero-mean Gaussian distribution with standard deviation of 0.01; bias learnings were disabled in convolutional layers and fulfilled in the BN layers. Parameters in the last fully-connected layers were initialized using Xavier initialization. Weight decay was only enabled in the final fully-connected layer. A mini-batch of 32 images comprising 16 cover–stego pairs was the input for each training iteration. Each input pair during training were randomly horizontally mirrored and rotated by a multiple of 90 degrees in a synchronized manner for cover-stego to guarantee that the CNN always learns the difference caused by data embedding. The training set was randomly shuffled for each epoch of training. After every multiple of 5000 iterations, the parameters in the CNN were saved.

Table 1: Classification Errors with QF75

	Embedding rates (bpnzAC)			
	0.1	0.2	0.3	0.4
Proposed (Fig1)	0.3283	0.1947	0.1124	0.0641
Proposed (finetune)	0.3469	0.2086	0.1141	0.0641
SCA-GFR [11]	0.3598	0.2316	0.1409	0.0807

Table 2. Classification Errors with QF95

	Embedding rates (bpnzAC)			
	0.1	0.2	0.3	0.4
Proposed (Fig1)	0.5000	0.3974	0.3106	0.2364
Proposed (finetune)	0.4554	0.3852	0.3067	0.2364
SCA-GFR [11]	0.4629	0.3998	0.3303	0.2620

3.1 Deeper is Better

Results in Section 3.1 are obtained with narrower CNNs (2/3 of the width in Fig. 1), on the BOSSBase with embedding rate of 0.4bpnzAC, and QF75 and QF95. We used half of the data for training and the other half for validation. We ran all the experiments 150,000 iterations to ensure the CNNs have enough time to converge.

The first experiment aim to choose the best pooling method from three common options: convolution, average pooling, and max pooling, all with stride 2. Architectures of the CNNs used for comparisons are illustrated in Fig. 2. Please refer to the description under Fig. 1 if there is any confusion with the elements in the figure. Results shown in Fig. 3 demonstrate that pooling with convolution has significantly lower validation errors. Note that pooling with convolution makes the CNN deeper (11 layers versus 6 layers).

Inspired from this, it would be natural to add more layers to further enhance the performance. In this paper we add up to 20 layers. Not surprisingly, adding more layers causing trouble in training; this can be observed in Fig. 4 showing abnormally higher training errors achieved by a more complex 20-layer CNN, and there is no question that the validation performance also suffer. Fortunately, adding shortcut connections (same as displayed in Fig. 1) solves the problem. This can be clearly observed in Fig. 5.

3.2 Results on the BOSSbase

Table 1 and Table 2 show the final ensemble results on the BOSSBase using the CNN in Fig. 1. We stopped the training of CNNs after 90000 iterations (288 epochs). Final testing results for each CNN were obtained by averaging the probability output of the test data from the CNNs models saved on their 80000, 85000 and 90000 training iterations; we ensembled four CNNs for each train-test split. The performance of the proposed CNN shown in the first rows of Table 1 and Table 2 clearly outperforms the best feature-based method without even using the information of the selection-channel, but we can also observe that in harder scenarios, e.g., at the rate of 0.2 bpnzAC with QF95, the CNN has almost no advantage. In extreme cases, i.e., 0.1 bpnzAC with QF95, after running for 40,000 iterations the CNNs failed to reduce the training error and we just stopped and put the number 0.5 which means random guess. Instead of training from scratch for all the embedding rates, we also provide our finetuning results by initializing the CNNs with parameters optimized by the tasks of higher embedding rates, which is similar to what have been done in [3]. Better results are observed for QF95, but in the cases of QF75, funetuning failed to improve the performance.

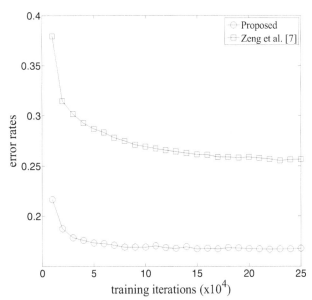

Figure 6: Comparison of validation errors versus training iterations between the proposed CNN and the CNN in [7] at 0.4bpnzAC embedding rate.

3.3 Results on The CLS-LOC dataset

The CLS-LOC dataset after being cropped to 256×256, and recompressed with QF75 has 1,152,197 covers in the training set, 48,627 covers in the validation set, and 97,296 covers in the testing set. We only tested rate of 0.4 bpnzAC due to constraints on computation facilities. Results are given in Fig. 6, the testing errors obtained by the saved models with best validation results are 0.256 for the CNN in [7] and 0.168 for the proposed CNN. This is a significant performance improvement as the proposed has cut the error by about 35%.

4 CONCLUSION

In this paper, a 20-layer CNN has been proposed and tested on both the BOSSBase with cover size of 512×512 and the CLS-LOC dataset with processed cover size of 256×256. It has been demonstrated that deep CNN can beat feature-based methods except in very difficult cases, and is therefore a promising research direction for further performance improvement.

Future works to further move this research ahead includes the following:

1. Replace 4×4 DCT with more effective filter banks or something equivalent.
2. Bring the information caused by pooling (subsampling) back by making the CNN phase-ware.
3. Making the CNN even deeper ...
4. Test the proposed CNN on other JPEG steganographic algorithms.

REFERENCES

[1] Shunquan Tan and Bin Li. 2014. Stacked convolutional auto-encoders for steganalysis of digital images. *Signal and Information Processing Association Annual Summit and Conference (APSIPA), Asia-Pacific* (Dec. 2014). DOI: http://dx.doi.org/10.1109/APSIPA.2014.7041565
[2] Yinlong Qian, Jing Dong, Wei Wang and Tieniu Tan. 2015. Deep learning for steganalysis via convolutional neural networks. In *Proceeding of SPIE 9409, Media Watermarking, Security, and Forensics 2015, 94090J (March, 2015).* DOI: http://dx.doi.org/10.1117/12.2083479
[3] Yinlong Qian, Jing Dong, Wei Wang and Tieniu Tan. 2016. Learning and transferring representations for image steganalysis using convolutional neural network, *2016 IEEE International Conference on Image Processing (ICIP Sep. 2016),* 2752–2756. DOI: http://dx.doi.org/10.1109/ICIP.2016.7532860
[4] Guanshuo Xu, Han-Zhou Wu and Yun-Qing Shi. 2016. Structural design of convolutional neural networks for steganalysis. *IEEE Signal Processing Letters (Volume 23, Issue 5, May 2016),* 708-712. DOI: http://dx.doi.org/10.1109/LSP.2016.2548421
[5] Guanshuo Xu, Han-Zhou Wu and Yun-Qing Shi. 2016. Ensemble of CNNs for steganalysis: An empirical study. In *Proceeding of 4th ACM Workshop on Information Hiding and Multimedia Security* (IH&MMSec '16). 103–107. DOI: http://dx.doi.org/10.1145/2909827.2930798
[6] Vahid Sedighi and Jessica Fridrich. 2017. Histogram Layer, Moving Convolutional Neural Networks Towards Feature Based Steganalysis. In *Proceeding of IS&T Electronic Imaging 2017 (Media Watermarking, Security, and Forensics),* San Francisco, CA, Jan, 2017.
[7] Jishen Zeng, Shunquan Tan, Bin Li and Jiwu Huang. 2017. Large-scale JPEG image steganalysis using hybrid deep-learning framework. arXiv: 1611.03233v2, Jan. 2017.
[8] Vojtěch Holub and Jessica Fridrich. 2015. Low-Complexity Features for JPEG Steganalysis Using Undecimated DCT. *IEEE Transactions on Information Forensics and Security (Volume 10, Issue 2, Feb. 2015),* 219-228. DOI: http://dx.doi.org/10.1109/TIFS.2014.2364918
[9] Xiaofeng Song, Fenlin Liu, Chunfang Yang, Xiangyang Luo and Yi Zhang. 2016. Steganalysis of Adaptive JPEG Steganography Using 2D Gabor Filters. In *Proceeding of 3th ACM Workshop on Information Hiding and Multimedia Security* (IH&MMSec '15). 15–23. DOI: http://dx.doi.org/10.1145/2756601.2756608
[10] Jan Kodovský and Jessica Fridrich. 2012. Ensemble classifiers for steganalysis of digital media. *IEEE Transactions on Information Forensics and Security (Volume 7, Issue 2, April 2012),* 432-444. DOI: http://dx.doi.org/10.1109/TIFS.2011.2175919
[11] Tomáš D. Denemark, Mehdi Boroumand and Jessica Fridrich. 2016. Steganalysis features for content-adaptive JPEG steganography. *IEEE Transactions on Information Forensics and Security (Volume 11, Issue 8, Aug. 2016),* 1736-1746. DOI: http://dx.doi.org/10.1109/TIFS.2016.2555281
[12] Patrick Bas, Tomáš Filler and Tomáš Pevný. 2011. Break our steganographic system – the ins and outs of organizing BOSS. In *Proceeding of 13th International Conference (IH 2011), Prague, Czech Republic (May, 2011).* 59–70.
[13] Olga Russakovsky, Jia Deng, Hao Su, Jonathan Krause, Sanjeev Satheesh, Sean Ma, Zhiheng Huang, Andrej Karpathy, Aditya Khosla, Michael Bernstein, Alexander C. Berg and Li Fei-Fei. 2014. ImageNet Large Scale Visual Recognition Challenge. arXiv:1409.0575
[14] Yangqing Jia, Evan Shelhamer, Jeff Donahue, Sergey Karayev, Jonathan Long, Ross Girshick, Sergio Guadarrama and Trevor Darrell. 2014. Caffe: Convolutional architecture for fast feature embedding. In *Proceeding of ACM Int. Conf. Multimedia 2014,* 675–678.
[15] Vojtech Holub, Jessica Fridrich and Tomáš Denemark. 2014. Universal distortion function for steganography in an arbitrary domain. *EURASIP Journal on Information Security, (Volume 2014, No.1, Dec. 2014),* 1–13. DOI: http://dx.doi.org/10.1186/ 1687-417X-2014-1
[16] Christian Szegedy, Wei Liu, Yangqing Jia, Pierre Sermanet, Scott Reed, Dragomir Anguelov, Dumitru Erhan, Vincent Vanhoucke and Andrew Rabinovich. 2015. Going deeper with convolutions. *2015 IEEE Conference on Computer Vision and Pattern Recognition (CVPR).* DOI: http://dx.doi.org/10.1109/CVPR.2015.7298594
[17] Sergey Ioffe and Christian Szegedy. 2015. Batch normalization: accelerating deep network training by reducing internal covariate shift. In *Proceeding of Int. Conf. Mach. Learn. (ICML 2015),* 448–456.
[18] Christian Szegedy, Vincent Vanhoucke, Sergey Ioffe, Jonathon Shlens and Zbigniew Wojna. 2016. Rethinking the inception architecture for computer vision. *2016 IEEE Conference on Computer Vision and Pattern Recognition (CVPR),* DOI: http://dx.doi.org/10.1109/CVPR.2016.308
[19] Kaiming He, Xiangyu Zhang, Shaoqing Ren and Jian Sun. 2016. Deep residual learning for image recognition. *2016 IEEE Conference on Computer Vision and Pattern Recognition (CVPR),* DOI: http://dx.doi.org/10.1109/CVPR.2016.90
[20] Kaiming He, Xiangyu Zhang, Shaoqing Ren and Jian Sun. 2016. Identity mappings in deep residual networks. In *Proceeding of European Conference on Computer Vision (Oct. 2016).* 630-645.
[21] Vinod Nair and Geoffrey E. Hinton. 2010. Rectified linear units improve restricted boltzmann machines. In *Proceeding of the 27th International Conference on Machine Learning* (ICML-10), 807-814.

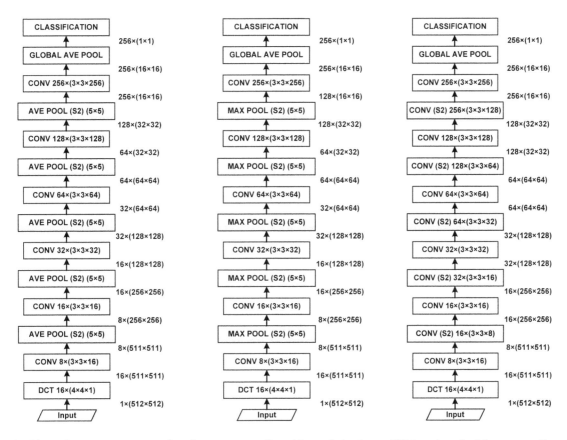

Figure 2: (Left) A 6-layer CNN equipped with average pooling. (Center) A 6-layer CNN equipped with max pooling. (Right) An 11-layer all convolutional CNN

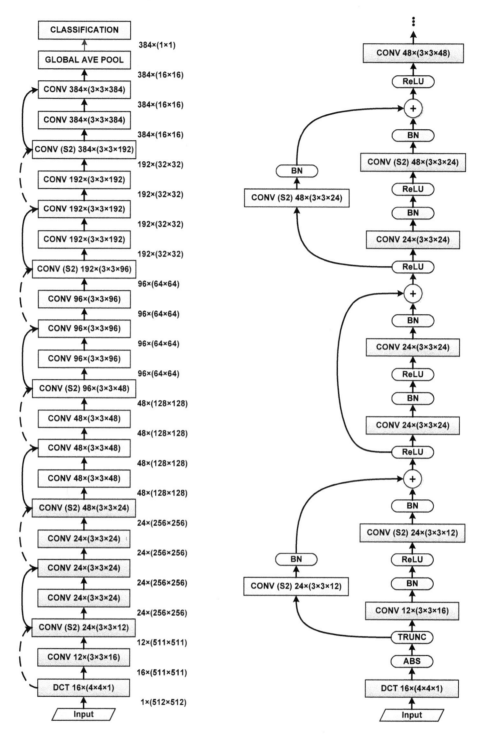

Figure 1: (Left) The proposed CNN architecture in the concise form. Data sizes following (number of channels) × (height × width) are displayed on the right side. CONV denotes convolutional layers, with kernel sizes following (number of kernels) × (height × width × number of channels). Spatial subsampling is fulfilled by convolution with stride equals 2 (S2). Solid curved arrows denote direct shortcut connections; dashed curved arrows denote transformed shortcut connections. Padding is applied wherever is necessary. (Right) A complete elaboration of the marked portion in the left figure. The *plus* signs indicate element-wise additions.

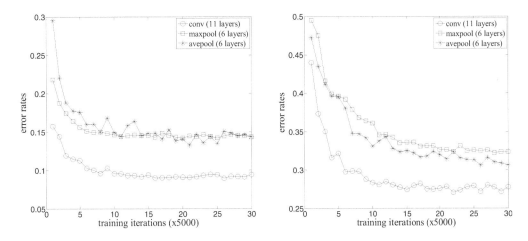

Figure 3: Comparison of validation errors versus training iterations between three types of pooling (convolution, max, and average) at 0.4bpnzAC embedding rate for (Left) QF75 and (Right) QF95.

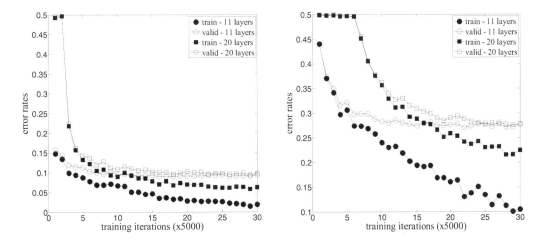

Figure 4: Comparison of training and validation errors versus training iterations between a 11-layer CNN and a 20-layer CNN without shortcut connections at 0.4bpnzAC embedding rate for (Left) QF75 and (Right) QF95.

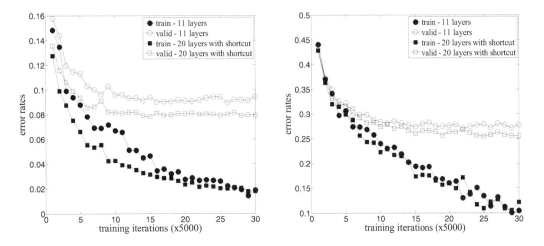

Figure 5: Comparison of training and validation errors versus training iterations between a 11-layer CNN and a 20-layer CNN with shortcut connections at 0.4bpnzAC embedding rate for (Left) QF75 and (Right) QF95.

JPEG-Phase-Aware Convolutional Neural Network for Steganalysis of JPEG Images

Mo Chen, Vahid Sedighi, Mehdi Boroumand, and Jessica Fridrich

Binghamton University

Department of ECE

Binghamton, NY 13902

mochen8@gmail.com,{vsedigh1,mboroum1,fridrich}@binghamton.edu

ABSTRACT

Detection of modern JPEG steganographic algorithms has traditionally relied on features aware of the JPEG phase. In this paper, we port JPEG-phase awareness into the architecture of a convolutional neural network to boost the detection accuracy of such detectors. Another innovative concept introduced into the detector is the "catalyst kernel" that, together with traditional high-pass filters used to pre-process images allows the network to learn kernels more relevant for detection of stego signal introduced by JPEG steganography. Experiments with J-UNIWARD and UED-JC embedding algorithms are used to demonstrate the merit of the proposed design.

KEYWORDS

Steganography, steganalysis, convolutional neural network, JPEG, phase aware, catalyst kernel

ACM Reference format:

Mo Chen, Vahid Sedighi, Mehdi Boroumand, and Jessica Fridrich. 2017. JPEG-Phase-Aware Convolutional Neural Network for Steganalysis of JPEG Images. In *Proceedings of IH&MMSec'17, Philadelphia, PA, USA, Jun 20-22, 2017*, 10 pages.
https://doi.org/http://dx.doi.org/10.1145/3082031.3083248

1 INTRODUCTION

Steganography in its modern form is a private, covert communication method in which the sender hides the message inside an innocuous looking cover object using an algorithm driven by a secret shared with the recipient. The communication channel is observed by an adversary or warden who tries to establish whether the communicating parties use steganography. While covers can have many different forms, the most popular and also practical choices for the steganographers are digital media files. Among them, the JPEG format is by far the most prevalent image format in current use due to its efficiency to compress images with a small loss of perceptual quality.

The first steganographic algorithms designed for the JPEG format were Jsteg [26] and OutGuess [17], followed by the F5 [28], Steghide [11], and Model-Based Steganography [20]. Because Jsteg and OutGuess predictably modify the histogram of DCT coefficients, the early attacks were based on first-order statistics of Discrete Cosine Transform (DCT) coefficients [32]. Later, significantly more accurate detectors were constructed as likelihood ratio tests with the aid of better models of cover DCT coefficients [24, 25]. The best detectors for F5 and its improved version nsF5 [7] as well as for Model-Based Steganography and Steghide are currently constructed as classifiers trained on features formed from quantized DCT coefficients, the JPEG Rich Model (JRM) [15]. Modern schemes, such as J-UNIWARD [14] and variants of UED [9, 10] are currently best detected using the so-called JPEG-phase-aware features formed from residuals extracted in the spatial domain split by their JPEG phase. Examples of such features include DCTR [12], GFR [22], PHARM [13], and their selection-channel-aware versions [5]. The key concept in their design is the notion of JPEG phase, which is the location of the residual with respect to the JPEG 8×8 grid. By splitting the statistics collected from the residuals by their phase more accurate detectors can be built.

Recently, novel detector architectures implemented within the paradigm of Convolutional Neural Networks (CNN) have been proposed for steganalysis of spatial-domain steganography [18, 23, 29, 30]. In this paper, we adapt CNN-based detectors for detection of modern JPEG-domain steganography by porting the concept of JPEG-phase-awareness into the network architecture. To this end, we implement a new phase-split layer and study two ways for incorporating phase awareness within the network architecture. Additionally, we augment the KV kernel traditionally used to prefilter images for CNN detectors by a second fixed kernel that works as a "catalyst" and allows the network to learn kernels that are more suitable for detecting stego noise introduced by JPEG-domain embedding schemes. After initial experiments with the number of layers, kernels, the network depth and height, and forming ensembles of networks by bagging on the training set, we arrived at a design capable of improving upon the state-of-the-art selection-channel-aware Gabor Filter Residuals (GFR) [5].

In the next section, we briefly introduce what we call JPEG phase. In Section 3, we describe two possible network architectures capable of working with phase-aware feature maps, the PNet and the VNet, and explain our design choices. Section 4 contains the results of all experiments on two steganographic algorithms, J-UNIWARD and UED-JC across a range of payloads and two JPEG quality factors. The performance is reported for both PNets and VNets in their individual forms as well as ensembles over bagged training sets.

Additionally, we study the impact of both cover and stego source mismatch on the detectors' accuracy. The paper is concluded in Section 5 where we also outline our future effort.

2 JPEG PHASE

In this section, we briefly review the concept of JPEG phase as used in steganalysis. WLOG, we will assume that the image is grayscale with $n_1 \times n_2$ pixels with n_1, n_2 multiples of 8. In a decompressed JPEG, the statistical properties of the stego signal are not spatially invariant within each 8×8 block because they depend on the position of the pixel and its neighborhood within the JPEG 8×8 pixel grid. It thus makes sense to collect statistics of pixels separately for each phase (i, j), $0 \le i, j \le 7$, which is defined as a sublattice of pixels with indices

$$\mathcal{L}_{ij} = \{(i + 8k, j + 8l) | 0 \le k < n_1/8, 0 \le l < n_2/8\}. \quad (1)$$

The computation of JPEG-phase-aware features starts with computing noise residuals by convolving the decompressed (non-rounded) JPEG image $\mathbf{x} \in \mathbb{R}^{n_1 \times n_2}$ with kernels $\mathbf{g} \in \mathbb{R}^{k_1 \times k_2}$ from some filter bank $\mathcal{B}$, $\mathbf{z}(\mathbf{x}, \mathbf{g}) = \mathbf{x} \star \mathbf{g}$. For example, in GFR [22] the bank $\mathcal{B}$ is formed by discretized 2D Gabor bases

$$g_{\lambda, \theta, \phi}(x, y) = e^{-(x'^2 + \gamma^2 y'^2)/2\sigma^2} \cos\left(2\pi \frac{x'}{\lambda} + \phi\right), \quad (2)$$

where $x' = x\cos\theta + y\sin\theta$, $y' = -x\sin\theta + y\cos\theta$, $\sigma = 0.56\lambda$, $\gamma = 0.5$. Next, $\mathbf{z}$ is quantized, $\mathbf{r} = Q_Q(\mathbf{z}/q)$, where $q > 0$ is a fixed quantization step and $Q = \{-T, \ldots, -1, 0, 1, 2, \ldots, T\}$ a set of $2T + 1$ bin centroids with a truncation threshold T. Each residual is used to compute 64 histograms for each JPEG phase $0 \le i, j \le 7$, $0 \le m \le T$:

$$h_m^{(i,j)}(\mathbf{x}, \mathbf{g}, Q) = \sum_{(a,b) \in \mathcal{L}_{ij}} [|r_{ab}(\mathbf{x}, \mathbf{g}, Q)| = m], \quad (3)$$

where $[P]$ is the Iverson bracket equal to 1 when the statement P is true and 0 otherwise. All $T + 1$ values, $h_0^{(i,j)}, \ldots, h_T^{(i,j)}$ from each histogram are concatenated into a vector of $64 \times (T + 1)$ values and these vectors are then concatenated for all kernels $\mathbf{g} \in \mathcal{B}$. The resulting feature vector with $64 \times (T + 1) \times |\mathcal{B}|$ elements is finally symmetrized based on the symmetries of natural images and kernels $\mathbf{g}$. Depending on the filter bank, different versions of JPEG-phase-aware features can be obtained [12, 13, 22].

In [5], the authors showed how the knowledge of the selection channel (the embedding change probabilities) can be incorporated into phase-aware features in a manner that can be considered as a generalization of the principle used in the maxSRM feature vector [4] used for steganalysis in the spatial domain. The detectors proposed here will be evaluated against this selection-channel-aware version of GFR features abbreviated as SCA-GFR.

3 THE PROPOSED PHASE-AWARE CNN

In this section, we describe the overall architecture of the proposed JPEG-phase-aware CNN. All key design components are explained and justified through experiments.

Recently, Xu et al. [29, 30] introduced a five-layer CNN for spatial-domain steganalysis with competitive performance. Each layer in this network processes the feature maps outputted by the previous layer in four steps: convolution, batch normalization, non-linear

activation, and pooling. This CNN structure design contains a few key elements that are important to CNN-based steganalysis. In the first convolutional layer, an absolute value activation (ABS) layer is used to facilitate and improve statistical modeling in the subsequent layers. The TanH activation is employed at the early stages to limit the range of data values and prevent the deeper layers from modeling statistically insignificant large values, while the batch normalization (BN) is applied before each non-linear activation to normalize the weak stego noise and improve the net convergence. The spatial size of convolutional kernels in deeper layers is 1×1 to limit the receptive filter size and reduce the support region of modeling. From now on, we refer to this architecture as XuNet.

In our investigation, we started with the XuNet and modified it to allow the network to process information for each JPEG phase separately, together with several other important modifications. We view the first two layers of XuNet (not counting the fixed kernel) as "feature extractors" (non-linear residuals), which are then in layers 3–5 combined and compacted into a low-dimensional feature vector used for detection.

To incorporate phase awareness into this architecture, we need to disable pooling in the first two layers because it would mix different phases. The phase-split layer is applied to feature maps outputted by the second layer by subsampling each feature map on 64 sublattices (1). The network than continues the computation on 64 eight-times smaller feature maps.

We investigated two possibilities for the network architecture behind the phase-split layer. In what we termed a 'PNet' (Fig. 1 left), after the phase split we let each JPEG phase go through its own independent channel. This is similar in spirit to how JPEG-phase-aware features are formed. Forcing the split, however, increases the number of channels from 16 to 1024 (by factor of 64) and the net becomes wider towards the last layers. This increases memory requirements and also slows down training and testing due to increased computational complexity.

As an alternative, we allowed the net itself to merge or split the channels, which resulted in an alternative architecture depicted in Fig. 1 right, the VNet. This version allows channel merging and is more compact and faster to train. It also allows the model to take advantage of the correlation between different phases in layers 3–5.

In a VNet, instead of being grouped the outputs of the PhaseSplit module, 64 $16 \times (64 \times 64)$ feature maps, are concatenated into 1024 $\times$ (64×64) feature maps and fully convolved in the convolutional layer in Group 3. This channel reduction speeds up training and testing. Both versions of the CNN are shown in Fig. 1 in their final forms, which will now be justified on experiments.

To determine the network architecture, we used a greedy approach in which we incrementally modified one layer of the CNN while keeping everything else fixed and tested it on a fixed experimental setup described next. We describe the details of this process for the PNet only due to space limitations.

3.1 Standard developer setup

This setup involves attacking J-UNIWARD [14] at payload 0.4 bpnzac (bits per non-zero AC DCT coefficient) on BOSSbase 1.01 [1] compressed with JPEG quality factor 75. This source was split

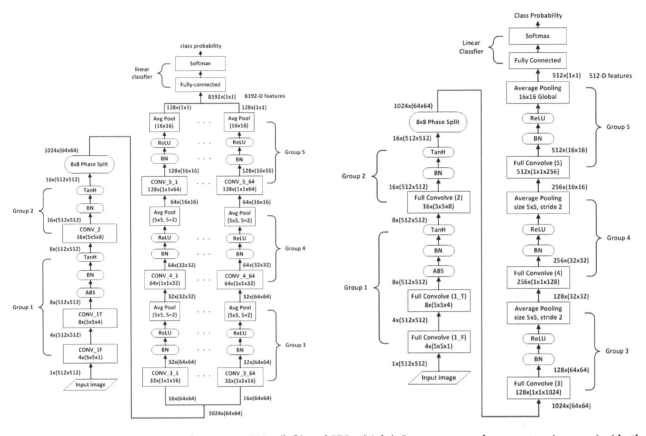

Figure 1: Two phase-aware CNN architectures: PNet (left) and VNet (right). Layer types and parameter sizes are inside the boxes. Data sizes are displayed on the sides. The dimensions of convolution kernels follow the format: (number of kernels) × (height × width × number of input feature maps) and the dimensions of data: (number of feature maps) × (height × width). Padding by 2 is applied in all convolutional layers and pooling layers except for the last pooling layer.

into a training and testing set by randomly selecting the images in a 60/40 ratio. The detection performance was measured with the total classification error probability under equal priors $P_{\mathrm{E}} = \min_{P_{\mathrm{FA}}} \frac{1}{2}(P_{\mathrm{FA}} + P_{\mathrm{MD}})$, where P_{FA} and P_{MD} are the false-alarm and missed-detection probabilities. Sometimes in this paper, we will present the error $P_{\mathrm{E}} \in [0, 1]$ in percentage units, which is $P_{\mathrm{E}} \times 100$. To assess the robustness of the detector, we also report the testing error on BOWS2 [2] to see the impact of testing on a different source than the source on which the detector was trained.

3.2 Overall architecture

The PNet depicted in Fig. 1 left consists of a convolutional module that transforms an input image into a "feature vector" of dimensionality 8192, and a linear classification module consisting of a fully-connected layer and a softmax layer outputting the probabilities for each class (cover vs. stego).

Similar to XuNet, the convolutional module has five groups of layers marked as 'Group 1' to 'Group 5' in Fig. 1. The CNN is also equipped with the TanH non-linear activation in Groups 1 and 2, and the Rectified Linear Unit (ReLU) in Groups 3–5. In Group 1, an absolute value activation (ABS) layer is used to force the statistical modeling to take into account the sign symmetry of noise residuals.

Additionally, Batch Normalization (BN) is performed right before each non-linear activation layer to normalize each feature map to zero-mean and unit-variance, and thus help the gradient descend back-propagation algorithm avoid being trapped in local minima. The network employs TanH instead of ReLU in Groups 1 and 2 to limit the range of data values and prevent the deeper layers from modeling large values, as they are sparse and not statistically significant. In Groups 3–5, the size of the convolutional kernels is limited to 1 × 1 to model patterns of correlations in small local regions.

The main differences between PNet (VNet) and XuNet can be summarized as follows:

(1) Group 1 consists of two concatenated convolutional layers (1F) and (1T). The 1F layer consists of four 5 × 5 high pass kernels whose parameters are fixed during training. The layer 1T contains eight 5 × 5 kernels whose parameters are learned during training. The fixed kernels increase the SNR between the cover image and the stego signal. They also act as regularizers to narrow down the feasible feature space and thus help facilitate the convergence of the network.

(2) There is no pooling in Groups 1 and 2 because it would lead to phase loss and mixing.

(3) We insert a PhaseSplit module between Groups 2 and 3, that splits Group 2's outputs $16 \times (512 \times 512)$ by their JPEG phase into 64 groups of $16 \times (64 \times 64)$. In other words, each 512×512 feature map will be split into 64 64×64 maps, one map per JPEG phase.

(4) The last three layers are similar to XuNet but each of the 64 JPEG feature groups consisting of $16 \times (64 \times 64)$ feature maps are first convolved with $32 \times (1 \times 1)$ kernels to get $32 \times (32 \times 32)$ feature maps with ReLU and average pooling by 2. In the next layer, convolution with $64 \times (1 \times 1)$ kernels leads to $64 \times (16 \times 16)$ feature maps with ReLU and average pooling by 2. And, in the last convolutional layer, convolutions with $128 \times (1 \times 1)$ kernels are applied to obtain a $128 \times (1 \times 1)$ feature map with ReLU and average pooling by 16. In a PNet, each phase group is processed independently, which means that in the end there are 64×128 outputs fully connected to the "classifier" part of the network.

Note that the 64 parallel channels do not need to be implemented as a directed acyclic graph. They can be implemented by chaining layers by using the convolutional filter group options supported by most CNN packages. To be more specific, the convolutional module computes the convolution of the input map **x** with a bank of D" multi-dimensional filters **f** to get the output **y**. Here, $\mathbf{x} \in \mathbb{R}^{H \times W \times D}$, $\mathbf{f} \in \mathbb{R}^{D'' \times (H' \times W' \times D)}$, $\mathbf{y} \in \mathbb{R}^{(H'' \times W'' \times D'')}$, where the data **x** and **y** have a spatial structure (height×width×number of feature maps), and the filter **f** has the structure output feature map×(height×width×number of input feature maps). The filter group option is the flexibility to group input feature maps **x** and apply different subsets of filters to each group. To use this feature, one specifies as input a bank of D" filters $\mathbf{f} \in \mathbb{R}^{D'' \times (H' \times W' \times D')}$ such that D' divides the number of input dimensions D. These are treated as $g = D/D'$ filter groups; the first group is applied to dimensions $d = 1, \ldots, D'$ of the input **x**; the second group is applied to dimensions $d = D' + 1, \ldots, 2D'$ of the input **x**, and so on.

3.3 PhaseSplit module

The JPEG phase-split module is illustrated in Fig. 2. Each feature map **x** is subsampled on 64 sublattices $\mathcal{L}_{ij}$ (1) obtaining thus 64 feature submaps (for each sublattice $\mathcal{L}_{ij}$) from each feature map **x**.

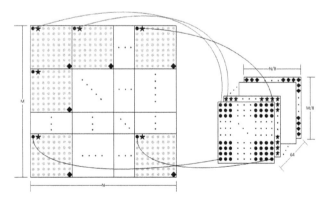

Figure 2: PhaseSplit module.

3.4 Refined batch normalization

Batch normalization is an important design element for training the proposed CNNs. Its allows us to use a larger learning rate and thus speed up the learning, making the training process less dependent on proper initialization. It also improves the detection accuracy.

The standard way to learn the BN's per-channel mean and standard deviation is via moving average during training. However, our architecture has too many BN parameters. For example, the PNet has $8 + 16 + 2048 + 4096 + 8192 = 14,360$ pairs of mean and standard deviation. Small errors propagate to the end and diminish the performance. This "moment drift" is especially undesirable in steganalysis because the stego signal is very week. The consequence of this are large fluctuations in the validation error during training. To alleviate this problem, we refined the BN moment learning in the following manner:

(1) Train the network as usual, without paying attention to the BN moment learning rate.

(2) Every 8–10 epochs, freeze all net parameters and put the net into the evaluation mode. Feed it with 2000/ 3000 mini-batches from the randomized training set and calculate and record the BN moments (mean and standard deviation) for all these mini-batches.

(3) Set the BN moments to the median values across the computed moments, validate, and test.

To further improve the accuracy, the batch size used in this refinement step can be chosen to be a very large number compared with the one used during training since there is no need for backward propagation of the gradients during this step.

3.5 Fixed linear filters

The four 5×5 high pass kernels in the convolutional layer 1F are shown in Fig. 3. The first filter, F_{KV}, is 'SQUARE5x5' from the Spatial Rich Model (SRM) [6], also used in one of the first CNN steganalysis detectors [18] and in XuNet. Due to its sign-changing symmetric checkerboard pattern, this filter suppresses correlated components (image content) while largely preserving the high-frequency stego signal. The second filter F_P is a point high-pass filter chosen to complement F_{KV}. It acts like a catalyst (activator in chemical reactions) and allows the network to learn the kernels in the second layer that are better at extracting the stego noise introduced by JPEG steganography as will be seen below. The F_H and F_V are two second-order horizontal and vertical Gabor filters (2), with $\varphi = \pi/2, \sigma = 1, \theta = 0$ and $\theta = \pi/2$, respectively. These two filters are added because F_{KV} and F_P are not directional.

Fig. 4 shows the effect of different combinations of fixed kernels on the detection error for our standard developer setup (Sec. 3.1). With only the F_{KV} kernel, the detection error rate saturates at about 18–19%. However, after adding the catalyst high-pass filter F_P, the detection error rate quickly drops to 8.6%. With the addition of F_H and F_V, the error rate further decreases to 7.9%.

Leveraging the fact that convolution is associative and distributive, the combined action of the convolutional layers 1F and 1T is equivalent to convolutions with eight 9×9 kernels. The equivalent kernels of the CNN trained with only F_{KV} and with both F_{KV} and F_P are illustrated in Fig. 5, which sheds light on the role of the point filter F_P. With only F_{KV}, the trained 9×9 kernels in Group 1 still

$$F_{\mathrm{KV}} = \begin{bmatrix} -.0833 & +.1667 & -.1667 & +.1667 & -.0833 \\ +.1667 & -.5000 & +.6667 & -.5000 & +.1667 \\ -.1667 & +.6667 & -1.0000 & +.6667 & -.1667 \\ +.1667 & -.5000 & +.6667 & -.5000 & +.1667 \\ -.0833 & +.1667 & -.1667 & +.1667 & -.0833 \end{bmatrix}$$

(a) KV filter.

$$F_{\mathrm{P}} = \begin{bmatrix} 0 & 0 & +.0199 & 0 & 0 \\ 0 & +.0897 & +.1395 & +.0897 & 0 \\ -.0199 & +.1395 & -1.0000 & +.1395 & +.0199 \\ 0 & +.0897 & +.1395 & +.0897 & 0 \\ 0 & 0 & +.0199 & 0 & 0 \end{bmatrix}$$

(b) Point high-pass filter.

$$F_{\mathrm{H}} = \begin{bmatrix} +.0562 & -.1354 & 0 & +.1354 & -.0562 \\ +.0818 & -.1970 & 0 & +.1970 & -.0818 \\ +.0926 & -.2233 & 0 & +.2233 & -.0926 \\ +.0818 & -.1970 & 0 & +.1970 & -.0818 \\ +.0562 & -.1354 & 0 & +.1354 & -.0562 \end{bmatrix}$$

(c) Horizontal 2D Gabor filter.

$$F_{\mathrm{V}} = \begin{bmatrix} -.0562 & -.0818 & -.0926 & -.0818 & -.0562 \\ +.1354 & +.1970 & +.2233 & +.1970 & +.1354 \\ 0 & 0 & 0 & 0 & 0 \\ -.1354 & -.1970 & -.2233 & -.1970 & -.1354 \\ +.0562 & +.0818 & +.0926 & +.0818 & +.0562 \end{bmatrix}$$

(d) Vertical 2D Gabor filter.

Figure 3: Four fixed 5×5 kernels used in the first convolutional layer (1F).

adhere to the checkerboard pattern similar to F_{KV} (c.f. a similar observation made in [21]). However, with the introduction of F_{P}, they exhibit a correlated structure more suitable for detection of stego signal spanned by discrete cosines. To put this another way, while the F_{KV} filter works well for detection of high-frequency stego signals introduced by typical spatial-domain embedding schemes, the impact of embedding in the JPEG domain examined in the spatial domain is very different because the difference between cover and stego images is due to changes to quantized DCT coefficients. And because most DCT coefficients that are modified are in the low to medium frequency band, the nature of the stego signal is different. High-pass filters, such as F_{KV}, suppress together with the content also the stego signal. In fact, this is most likely why Gabor filters work better for steganalysis of JPEG files than SRM high-pass filters.

As our last note in this section and to complete the investigation of the most appropriate structure of the 1F layer, we tested whether another improvement can be obtained by including a larger set of Gabor kernels in this layer. Specifically, we formed the 1F layer with eight 8×8 filters obtained from Eq. (2) with parameters $\sigma = 1$, $\varphi = [0, \pi/2]$, and $\theta = [0, \pi/4, \pi/2, 3\pi/4]$. In our standard developer setup, a PNet with these fixed filters, however, lagged 2% behind the PNet with the above mentioned four fixed kernels.

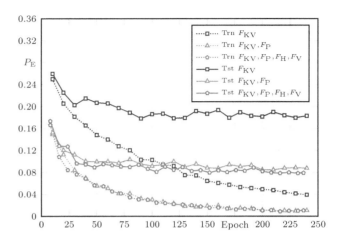

Figure 4: Detection error with different filter combinations under standard developer setup.

Table 1: Detection error (in %) of three PNet configurations under standard developer setup.

	$C_{1\mathrm{F}}4 \times C_{1\mathrm{T}}8 \times C_2 16$	$C_{1\mathrm{F}}4 \times C_{1\mathrm{T}}12 \times C_2 16$	$C_{1\mathrm{F}}4 \times C_{1\mathrm{T}}12 \times C_2 24$
BOSSbase (8,000)	7.91±0.03	8.10±0.10	8.08±0.11
BOWS2 (20,000)	9.15±0.09	8.91±0.07	9.09±0.18

3.6 Configuration before phase split

Fixing the parameters of the fixed filter (1F) and the portion of the net after the PhaseSplit module, we investigate if further performance gain is possible by deepening the architecture, inserting more convolutional layers, and by widening the net. We abbreviate the net architecture in the first two groups by the number of convolutional feature maps. For example, the configuration in Fig. 1 left is named $C_{1\mathrm{F}}4 \times C_{1\mathrm{T}}8 \times C_2 16$. The following alternatives were studied:

(1) Increased number of kernels (1T) in Group 1 from $8 \times (5 \times 5)$ to $12 \times (5 \times 5)$, abbreviated as $C_{1\mathrm{F}}4 \times C_{1\mathrm{T}}12 \times C_2 16$.

(2) Increased the number of kernels (1T) in Group 1 from $8 \times (5 \times 5)$ to $12 \times (5 \times 5)$ and the number of kernels in Group 2 from $16 \times (5 \times 5)$ to $24 \times (5 \times 5)$, abbreviated $C_{1\mathrm{F}}4 \times C_{1\mathrm{T}}12 \times C_2 24$.

The impact of these modifications on the PNet was evaluated on the standard developer setup (Sec. 3.1) with the results shown in Table 1. In summary, we did not observe any statistically significant gain by enlarging the configuration of the PNet.

3.7 PNet vs. VNet

In this section, we compare the performance of PNet and VNet from Fig. 1. For a fair comparison, both detectors were trained with identical training and testing settings with the standard developer setup. The training and testing detection errors are shown in Fig. 6 and in Table 3. The ensembles of five nets were obtained by randomly splitting the training set into five disjoint subsets, training on four of them and using the fifth for validation as described in [29]. In

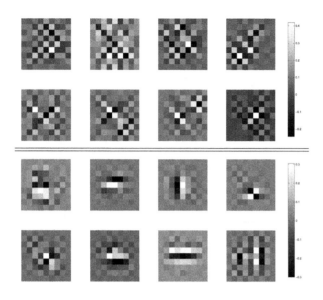

Table 3: Detection error (in %) of PNet and VNet and their bagging ensembles under standard developer setup.

	Individual PNets	Ensemble PNets	Individual VNets	Ensemble VNets
BOSSbase	7.60±0.24	6.56±0.10	8.70±0.28	7.05%±0.09
BOWS2	9.01±0.24	7.66±0.08	10.11±0.41	8.07%±0.10

amount. In contrast, the cover source mismatch in the spatial domain had a bigger negative impact on XuNet [30]. This is most likely due to the fact that JPEG compression has a tendency to equalize differences between sources.

4 EXPERIMENTS

In this section, we report the detection accuracy of the proposed JPEG-phase-aware CNNs and interpret the results.

4.1 Dataset and software platforms

Two JPEG-domain content-adaptive steganographic algorithms were tested: J-UNIWARD and UED-JC with a range of embedding rates. The results are contrasted with what can be achieved using conventional feature-based steganalysis with SCA-GFR features [5] with the FLD-ensemble [16]. All experiments using the CNNs were performed with a modified MatConvNet toolbox [27]. All tests are done using GTX 1080 and Titian X GPU cards.

As in the standard developer setup, we used BOSSbase 1.01 for training all detectors. The testing was done on the unused part of BOSSbase and in some experiments on BOWS2 to see the robustness of the detectors to cover source mismatch.

4.2 Training, validation, and testing

For each experiment reported in Table 4, BOSSbase was randomly split into 75/25 ratio. To build the ensembles, the training set was furthermore randomly split into five equally sizes folds, using four of them for training and the fifth fold for validation (bagging). Thus, each CNN detector was trained on 6,000 cover-stego pairs and validated on 1,500 pairs.

The testing is carried out on the remaining 2,500 cover-stego pairs from BOSSbase images and also on the entire BOWS2 database. The detection error and the statistical spread of each individual network is computed as the mean and standard deviation of error rates from the last five evaluation steps of each network during training using refined batch normalization (Section 3.4). The corresponding values for ensemble networks are computed over error rates from the last five steps of five different splits of the training set (a total of 25 values).

4.3 Hyper-parameters

Mini-batch stochastic gradient descent was used to train all CNNs. The momentum was fixed to 0.9, the learning rate for all parameters was initialized to 0.001 and scheduled to decrease 25% every 20 epochs ($20 \times 300 = 6,000$ iterations), up to 240 epochs. A mini-batch

Figure 5: Convolutions of F_{KV} with the kernels from the second convolutional layer (1T) equivalent to eight 9×9 kernels of the convolutional module in Group 1. Top: Kernels learned with only F_{KV}. Bottom: learned with both F_{KV} and F_P.

contrast to [29], in our ensemble we applied the majority voting rule on the decisions returned by the individual five nets.

The individually trained PNet is 1.1% better than the VNet when tested on both BOSSbase (5,000 images) and BOWS2 (20,000 images). The ensemble of five PNets improves upon the individual PNet by 1.04%, from 7.60% to 6.56%. On the other hand, since VNets are more over-trained (see Fig. 6), the ensemble of five VNets produces a larger boost (1.65%), decreasing the detection error of the ensemble of VNets from 8.70% to 7.05%. Therefore, the ensemble of five PNets is only 0.49% better than VNets. Similarly, when testing on BOWS2, the average testing detection error for PNets and VNets are 9.01% and 10.11%, respectively. The ensemble of five PNets is 7.66%, while the ensemble of VNets is 8.07%.

In summary, PNet gives a slightly better performance than VNet but is also more computationally demanding and takes longer to train (about two times longer). Table 2 contrasts the complexity of the two explored architectures. In the end, the specific demands of the application should determine which detector type is more suitable.

The experiments in this section also indicate that the cover source mismatch between BOSSbase and BOWS2 does not degrade the performance of either net architecture by any significant

Table 2: Net structure complexity of PNet and VNet under standard developer setup. The speed is evaluated on two GTX 1080 GPU cards using MatConvNet and batch size 40.

	Data Memory	Parameters Memory	Train Speed	Test Speed
PNet	11 GB	7.7e+05	25.4 images/sec	100.4 images/sec
VNet	4 GB	3.0e+05	57.1 images/sec	218.1 images/sec

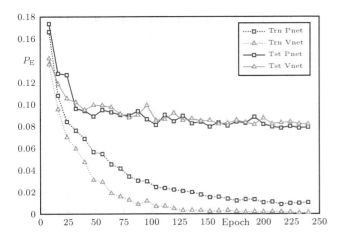

Figure 6: Detection error of PNets and VNets as a function of training epochs under standard developer setup.

Table 4: Detection error comparison between individual (Ind.) and ensemble of (Ens.) PNet(s) and VNet(s) with SCA-GFR features on J-UNIWARD and UED-JC.

(a) Detection error (in %) for J-UNIWARD

QF	Detector	0.1	0.2	0.3	0.4	0.5
	SCA GFR	35.54±0.54	22.47±0.38	13.44±0.28	7.53±0.21	4.15±0.13
	Ind. PNet	37.26±0.31	23.50±0.34	13.80±0.41	7.60±0.24	4.13±0.27
75	Ens. PNets	35.75±0.25	21.26±0.32	12.28±0.13	6.56±0.10	3.36±0.05
	Ind. VNet	37.59±0.45	24.57±0.54	15.05±0.41	8.70±0.28	4.74±0.24
	Ens. VNets	36.15±0.16	22.40±0.17	13.32±0.08	7.05±0.09	3.74±0.14
	SCA GFR	46.03±0.35	40.07±0.48	32.92±0.31	25.54±0.63	19.35±0.54
	Ind. PNet	46.76±0.22	41.52±0.50	34.74±0.84	28.01±1.14	20.42±1.15
95	Ens. PNets	45.89±0.29	39.89±0.17	31.91±0.11	25.36±0.23	17.49±0.15
	Ind. VNet	47.43±0.51	43.65±1.49	34.76±0.41	28.02±0.40	21.31±0.25
	Ens. VNets	47.07±0.22	42.73±0.58	33.28±0.12	25.93±0.21	19.67±0.15

(b) Detection error (in %) for UED-JC

QF	Detector	0.1	0.2	0.3	0.4	0.5
	SCA GFR	22.54±0.67	11.56±0.32	6.35±0.20	3.46±0.14	1.74±0.19
	Ind. PNet	20.11±0.38	9.55±0.21	4.56±0.23	2.81±0.17	1.48±0.17
75	Ens. PNets	17.77±0.31	8.52±0.11	3.90±0.05	2.34±0.43	1.33±0.02
	Ind. VNet	21.62±0.44	10.07±0.46	5.48±0.10	3.07±0.15	1.63±0.18
	Ens. VNets	18.97±0.16	8.04±0.12	4.07±0.04	2.32±0.03	1.20±0.02
	SCA GFR	39.20±0.51	30.48±0.62	22.55±0.61	15.92±0.48	10.52±0.45
	Ind. PNet	39.27±0.53	29.93±0.59	21.36±1.10	15.00±0.91	9.51±1.04
95	Ens. PNets	37.18±0.36	27.21±0.37	18.46±0.39	12.27±0.34	7.31±0.13
	Ind. VNet	42.00±1.11	31.52±1.41	22.39±0.62	15.75±0.51	9.98±0.45
	Ens. VNets	40.63±0.13	28.55±0.19	19.46±0.23	13.18±0.13	7.95±0.04

of 40 images (20 cover/stego pairs) was input for each iteration.[1] The training database is also randomly shuffled at the beginning of each epoch to help batch normalization and give the CNN detector a better ability to generalize. The parameters of convolution kernels were initialized from a zero-mean Gaussian distribution with standard deviation 0.01. As in XuNet [30], the bias learning in all convolutional layers, except for the last fully connected layer whose bias learning rate is set to be twice of the learning rate, were fixed to zero to make the feature maps sign symmetric. The parameters in the last fully-connected (FC) layers were initialized using Xavier initialization [8]. The weight decay (L2 regularization) was not enabled, except for the FC layer, which was set to 0.01.

For BN layers, the learning rate is the same as the global learning rate of the network with all scale and shift parameters initialized with 1 and 0, respectively. As explained in Sec. 3.4, the per-channel mean and standard deviation in BN were implemented using the moment refinement performed every 8 (or 4) epochs during training, which gives the net 2000 random mini-batches of size 48 from the training set to compute the refined moments.

4.4 Curriculum learning for steganalyzing different payloads

Due to the PhaseSplit module and the catalyst filter kernel, both PNets and VNets converge relatively quickly even for small payloads, such as 0.1 bpnzac, and high JPEG quality. The training can be further sped up by adopting the transfer learning strategy [19, 31] widely used in CNNs. In particular, for each steganographic scheme and JPEG quality factor, we first train a CNN on a training set embedded with 0.4 bpnzac payload (from randomly initialized weights). To train a detector for the other payloads (0.1−0.3, and 0.5), we initialized with the model trained on 0.4 bpnzac and then fine-tuned

this model on the same training set embedded with the corresponding payload. Curriculum learning enables us to decrease the number of training epochs by a factor of two.

Our experiments consistently show that the use of a pre-trained CNN outperforms, or in the worse case, performs as well as a CNN trained from randomly initialized weights. In addition, it is also possible to train CNNs with the pre-trained CNNs of other steganographic schemes, for example, to train UED-JC CNN detector, we can use a CNN pre-trained on J-UNIWARD.

4.5 Analysis

Below, we summarize lessons learned and the main results of our experiments.

- Batch normalization with proper moment refinement plays an important role in training JPEG-phase-aware CNNs because it normalizes each individual phase at different stages. Because the training batches are small, the moments computed over training and testing sets exhibit large fluctuations, makes it unclear when the network converged. The refined BN smooths the training and validation performance curves, helps find better convergence points, and also improves the model accuracy by 3−7% over models trained using moving average.

- While the individual phase-aware nets are slightly inferior to the SCA GFR for J-UNIWARD, an ensemble of five individually trained nets improves upon SCA GFR by 1%.

---

[1] As shown in Table 2, the memory requirement for PNet with batch size 40 is more than 11 GB, whichexceeds the GPU memory of any single common GPU card. This problem is solved by employing two GPUs for training. More specifically, the data (40 images) are further divided in two sub-batches of 20 images and distributed among two GPUs with some communication overhead.

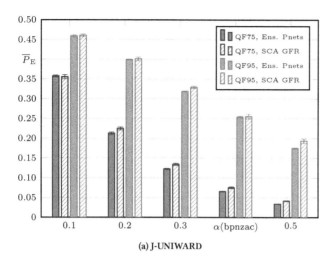

(a) J-UNIWARD

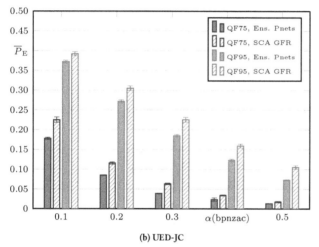

(b) UED-JC

Figure 7: Performance comparison between the ensemble of five PNets and SCA GFR for two embedding schemes.

- For UED-JC, the proposed CNN detectors clearly outperform conventional steganalysis. In general, each trained individual net is better than the SCA GFR with the FLD-ensemble. The ensemble of five PNets (or VNets) brings further improvement.

4.6 On the net transfer ability

In this section, we study the ability of the detector trained on one embedding algorithm to detect a different embedding algorithm to see how well it transfers to a different stego source. In particular, we trained a PNet on examples of cover and stego images embedded with J-UNIWARD and then tested it on UED-JC stego images, all stego images at 0.4 bpnzac (see Table 5). Although the test error rate 3.79% is higher when compared to the detector trained for UED-JC (2.3–2.4%), the detection accuracy drop is rather small. On the other hand, a PNet trained on UED-JC stego images performs rather poorly on J-UNIWARD images; the error rate is around

Table 5: Detection error (in %) to evaluate the transfer ability of three detectors when training on J-UNIWARD images and testing on UED-JC images and vice versa. Standard developer setup.

Detector	TRN Images	J-UNI TST Images	UED TST Images
SCA GFR	J-UNI	7.53±0.21	6.07±0.21
Ind. PNet	J-UNI	7.60±0.24	4.66±0.28
Ens. PNets	J-UNI	6.56±0.10	3.79±0.10
SCA GFR	UED	12.19±0.70	3.46±0.14
Ind. PNet	UED	27.50±1.51	2.81±0.17
Ens. PNets	UED	27.25±0.40	2.34±0.43

27.50%. This indicates that UED-JC introduces artifacts that the PNet discovers and that J-UNIWARD avoids. We hypothesize that a portion of the weights in the model trained on UED-JC become noticeably larger than the rest as the network focuses on a portion of the "features" that are strongly related to the artifacts created by UED embedding. The network thus basically "overtrains to UED" and does not generalize well to J-UNIWARD. This could likely be alleviated by introducing dropout.

For comparison, in the table we also report the performance of an FLD-ensemble trained on SCA GFR features. While this detector does not generalize as well as the PNet to UED test images when trained on J-UNIWARD, the loss observed when training on UED and testing on J-UNIWARD images is much smaller (12.19% vs. 27.50 for the PNet).

5 CONCLUSION AND FUTURE WORK

Convolutional neural networks (CNNs) only recently e-merged in the field of steganalysis as a competitive alternative to the "classical" approach based on training a classifier on features extracted from examples of cover and stego images. Since the moment they were introduced by Qian et al. in 2015 [18], they were touted as "fully automatic" tools in the sense of not requiring hand crafted features. The authors of this article feel that we are still rather far away from this ultimate goal of fully automatizing the process of developing steganalysis detectors. Human insight currently remains an indispensable element in designing network architectures and insight painstakingly gathered from classical approach to steganalysis is still extremely valuable. This paper only seems to confirm this thesis.

Inspired by the success of features aware of the JPEG phase, we introduce phase awareness into the architecture of a CNN to see whether current state-of-the-art steganalysis tools for detection of modern JPEG steganography can be improved. To this end, we started with a structural CNN design proposed by Xu et al. [29, 30] for spatial domain steganalysis and adjusted it for steganalysis in the JPEG domain in two different ways. The result are two network architectures, the PNet and VNet. While PNet gives slightly better results than VNet, the latter is faster to train and test and enjoys smaller memory requirements. We leave the choice of the detector in practice to the specifics required by the application.

While our investigation focused on phase awareness, along the way we discovered another interesting phenomenon, which we termed "catalytic kernel." Stego signal is a high-frequency noise modulated by content. Thus, to force the network to pay attention to this signal (and to converge), images need to be pre-filtered to incease the SNR between the signal of interest (the weak stego noise) and the noise – the image content. Fixed high-pass filters are usually used for this job in current network designs. While sign-changing high-pass filters, such as the ubiquitous "KV filter" work well for steganalysis of spatial-domain steganography, the stego signal introduced in the spatial domain by modifying quantized DCT coefficients is no longer high frequency in nature. After all, it is spanned by quantized discrete cosines and thus "inhabits" medium and low spatial frequencies as well. Pre-filtering images with filters, such as the KV, thus inevitably and undesirably suppresses the stego signal as well. To help the network find more suitable filters, we supply in the fixed layer another "point filter" that seems to play the role of a catalyst (regularizer) that allows the filters in the first convolutional layer to accept shapes more suitable for detecting stego noise caused by JPEG steganography. Just augmenting the KV filter with this point catalytic filter brought the detection performance of our networks from mediocre to highly competitive. We hypothesize that a similar effect may be achieved with the constrained convolutional layer recently proposed by Bayar et al. [3]. A more detailed investigation of this is postponed to our future effort.

In summary, we showed that JPEG phase awareness can be built into CNN architectures and that it indeed improves detection accuracy over classical steganalysis. The observed gain was significantly larger for UED-JC than for J-UNI-WARD. We also investigated the ability of the trained networks to generalize to previously unseen cover and stego sources.

All code used to produce the results in this paper, including the network configuration files, the PhaseSplit Layer, and the refined Batch Normalization layer is available from http://dde.binghamton.edu/download/ for download.

ACKNOWLEDGMENTS

The work on this paper was supported by Air Force Office of Scientific Research under the research grant number FA9950-12-1-0124. The U.S. Government is authorized to reproduce and distribute reprints for Governmental purposes notwithstanding any copyright notation there on. The views and conclusions contained herein are those of the authors and should not be interpreted as necessarily representing the official policies, either expressed or implied of AFOSR or the U.S. Government. The authors would like to thank anonymous reviewers for their insightful comments.

REFERENCES

[1] P. Bas, T. Filler, and T. Pevný. 2011. Break Our Steganographic System – the Ins and Outs of Organizing BOSS. In *Information Hiding, 13th International Conference* (Lecture Notes in Computer Science), T. Filler, T. Pevný, A. Ker, and S. Craver (Eds.), Vol. 6958. Springer Berlin Heidelberg, Prague, Czech Republic, 59–70.

[2] P. Bas and T. Furon. 2007. BOWS-2. http://bows2.ec-lille.fr. (July 2007).

[3] B. Belhassen and M. C. Stamm. 2016. A Deep Learning Approach to Universal Image Manipulation Detection Using a New Convolutional Layer. In *The 4th ACM Workshop on Information Hiding and Multimedia Security (IH&MMSec '16)*, F. Perez-Gonzales, F. Cayre, and P. Bas (Eds.). Vigo, Spain, 5–10.

[4] T. Denemark, V. Sedighi, V. Holub, R. Cogranne, and J. Fridrich. 2014. Selection-Channel-Aware Rich Model for Steganalysis of Digital Images. In *IEEE International Workshop on Information Forensics and Security*. Atlanta, GA.

[5] T. D. Denemark, M. Boroumand, and J. Fridrich. 2016. Steganalysis Features for Content-Adaptive JPEG Steganography. *IEEE Transactions on Information Forensics and Security* 11, 8 (August 2016), 1736–1746. https://doi.org/10.1109/TIFS.2016.2555281

[6] J. Fridrich and J. Kodovský. 2011. Rich Models for Steganalysis of Digital Images. *IEEE Transactions on Information Forensics and Security* 7, 3 (June 2011), 868–882.

[7] J. Fridrich, T. Pevný, and J. Kodovský. 2007. Statistically Undetectable JPEG Steganography: Dead Ends, Challenges, and Opportunities. In *Proceedings of the 9th ACM Multimedia & Security Workshop*, J. Dittmann and J. Fridrich (Eds.). Dallas, TX, 3–14.

[8] Xavier Glorot and Yoshua Bengio. 2010. Understanding the difficulty of training deep feedforward neural networks. In *Proceedings of the Thirteenth International Conference on Artificial Intelligence and Statistics (AISTATS '10)*. Sardinia, Italy, 249–256.

[9] L. Guo, J. Ni, and Y.-Q. Shi. 2012. An Efficient JPEG Steganographic Scheme Using Uniform Embedding. In *Fourth IEEE International Workshop on Information Forensics and Security*. Tenerife, Spain.

[10] L. Guo, J. Ni, and Y. Q. Shi. 2014. Uniform Embedding for Efficient JPEG Steganography. *IEEE Transactions on Information Forensics and Security* 9, 5 (May 2014), 814–825. https://doi.org/10.1109/TIFS.2014.2312817

[11] S. Hetzl and P. Mutzel. 2005. A Graph-Theoretic Approach to Steganography. In *Communications and Multimedia Security, 9th IFIP TC-6 TC-11 International Conference, CMS 2005* (Lecture Notes in Computer Science), J. Dittmann, S. Katzenbeisser, and A. Uhl (Eds.), Vol. 3677. Salzburg, Austria, 119–128.

[12] V. Holub and J. Fridrich. 2015. Low-Complexity Features for JPEG Steganalysis Using Undecimated DCT. *IEEE Transactions on Information Forensics and Security* 10, 2 (February 2015), 219–228.

[13] V. Holub and J. Fridrich. 2015. Phase-Aware Projection Model for Steganalysis of JPEG Images. In *Proceedings SPIE, Electronic Imaging, Media Watermarking, Security, and Forensics 2015*, A. Alattar and N. D. Memon (Eds.), Vol. 9409. San Francisco, CA, 0T 1–11.

[14] V. Holub, J. Fridrich, and T. Denemark. 2014. Universal Distortion Design for Steganography in an Arbitrary Domain. *EURASIP Journal on Information Security, Special Issue on Revised Selected Papers of the 1st ACM IH and MMS Workshop* 2014:1 (2014).

[15] J. Kodovský and J. Fridrich. 2012. Steganalysis of JPEG Images Using Rich Models. In *Proceedings SPIE, Electronic Imaging, Media Watermarking, Security, and Forensics 2012*, A. Alattar, N. D. Memon, and E. J. Delp (Eds.), Vol. 8303. San Francisco, CA, 0A 1–13.

[16] J. Kodovský, J. Fridrich, and V. Holub. 2012. Ensemble Classifiers for Steganalysis of Digital Media. *IEEE Transactions on Information Forensics and Security* 7, 2 (2012), 432–444.

[17] N. Provos. 2001. Defending Against Statistical Steganalysis. In *10th USENIX Security Symposium*. Washington, DC, 323–335.

[18] Y. Qian, J. Dong, W. Wang, and T. Tan. 2015. Deep learning for steganalysis via convolutional neural networks. In *Proceedings SPIE, Electronic Imaging, Media Watermarking, Security, and Forensics 2015*, A. Alattar and N. D. Memon (Eds.), Vol. 9409. San Francisco, CA, 0J 1–10.

[19] Y. Qian, J. Dong, W. Wang, and T. Tan. 2016. Learning and transferring representations for image steganalysis using convolutional neural network. In *IEEE International Conference on Image Processing (ICIP)*. Phoenix, AZ, 2752–2756.

[20] P. Sallee. 2005. Model-Based Methods for Steganography and Steganalysis. *International Journal of Image Graphics* 5, 1 (2005), 167–190.

[21] V. Sedighi and J. Fridrich. 2017. Histogram Layer, Moving Convolutional Neural Networks Towards Feature-based Steganalysis. In *Proceedings IS&T, Electronic Imaging, Media Watermarking, Security, and Forensics 2017*, A. Alattar and N. D. Memon (Eds.). Burlingame, CA.

[22] X. Song, F. Liu, C. Yang, X. Luo, and Y. Zhang. 2015. Steganalysis of Adaptive JPEG Steganography Using 2D Gabor Filters. In *The 3rd ACM Workshop on Information Hiding and Multimedia Security (IH&MMSec '15)*, A. Alattar, J. Fridrich, N. Smith, and P. Comesana Alfaro (Eds.). Portland, OR.

[23] S. Tan and B. Li. 2014. Stacked convolutional auto-encoders for steganalysis of digital images. In *Signal and Information Processing Association Annual Summit and Conference (APSIPA), 2014 Asia-Pacific*. 1–4. https://doi.org/10.1109/APSIPA.2014.7041565

[24] T. Thai, R. Cogranne, and F. Retraint. 2014. Statistical Model of Quantized DCT Coefficients: Application in the Steganalysis of Jsteg Algorithm. *IEEE Transactions on Image Processing* 23, 5 (May 2014), 1–14.

[25] T. H. Thai, R. Cogranne, and F. Retraint. 2014. Optimal Detection of OutGuess using an Accurate Model of DCT Coefficients. In *Sixth IEEE International Workshop on Information Forensics and Security*. Atlanta, GA.

[26] D. Upham. Steganographic algorithm JSteg. Software available at http://zooid.org/ paul/crypto/jsteg.

[27] A. Vedaldi and K. Lenc. 2014. MatConvNet - Convolutional Neural Networks for MATLAB. *CoRR* abs/1412.4564 (2014). http://arxiv.org/abs/1412.4564

[28] A. Westfeld. 2001. High Capacity Despite Better Steganalysis (F5 – A Steganographic Algorithm). In *Information Hiding, 4th International Workshop* (Lecture

Notes in Computer Science), I. S. Moskowitz (Ed.), Vol. 2137. Springer-Verlag, New York, Pittsburgh, PA, 289–302.

[29] G. Xu, H.-Z. Wu, and Y. Q. Shi. 2016. Ensemble of CNNs for Steganalysis: An Empirical Study. In *The 4th ACM Workshop on Information Hiding and Multimedia Security (IH&MMSec '16)*, F. Perez-Gonzales, F. Cayre, and P. Bas (Eds.). Vigo, Spain, 5–10.

[30] G. Xu, H. Z. Wu, and Y. Q. Shi. 2016. Structural Design of Convolutional Neural Networks for Steganalysis. *IEEE Signal Processing Letters* 23, 5 (May 2016),

708–712. https://doi.org/10.1109/LSP.2016.2548421

[31] J. Yosinski, J. Clune, Y. Bengio, and H. Lipson. 2014. How Transferable Are Features in Deep Neural Networks?. In *Proceedings of the 27th International Conference on Neural Information Processing Systems (NIPS'14)*. Cambridge, MA, 3320–3328.

[32] T. Zhang and X. Ping. 2003. A Fast and Effective Steganalytic Technique Against Jsteg-like Algorithms. In *Proceedings of the ACM Symposium on Applied Computing*. Melbourne, FL, 307–311.

Audio Steganalysis With Convolutional Neural Network

Bolin Chen
Sun Yat-sen University
School of Data and Computer
Science
Guangzhou, China
chenbl8@mail2.sysu.edu.cn

Weiqi Luo*
Sun Yat-sen University
School of Data and Computer
Science
Guangzhou, China
luoweiqi@mail.sysu.edu.cn

Haodong Li
Sun Yat-sen University
School of Data and Computer
Science
Guangzhou, China
lihaod@mail2.sysu.edu.cn

ABSTRACT

In recent years, deep learning has achieved breakthrough results in various areas, such as computer vision, audio recognition, and natural language processing. However, just several related works have been investigated for digital multimedia forensics and steganalysis. In this paper, we design a novel CNN (convolutional neural networks) to detect audio steganography in the time domain. Unlike most existing CNN based methods which try to capture media contents, we carefully design the network layers to suppress audio content and adaptively capture the minor modifications introduced by ± 1 LSB based steganography. Besides, we use a mix of convolutional layer and max pooling to perform subsampling to achieve good abstraction and prevent over-fitting. In our experiments, we compared our network with six similar network architectures and two traditional methods using handcrafted features. Extensive experimental results evaluated on 40,000 speech audio clips have shown the effectiveness of the proposed convolutional network.

CCS CONCEPTS

•**Security and privacy** →*Authentication;* •**Computing methodologies** →*Learning latent representations;*

KEYWORDS

Audio Steganalysis, Deep Learning, Convolutional Neural Network

ACM Reference format:
Bolin Chen, Weiqi Luo, and Haodong Li. 2017. Audio Steganalysis With Convolutional Neural Network. In *Proceedings of IH&MMSec '17, June 20–22, 2017, Philadelphia, PA, USA, ,* 6 pages.
DOI: http://dx.doi.org/10.1145/3082031.3083234

---

*Corresponding author.

---

1 INTRODUCTION

Steganography is the art of hiding secret messages into digital covers such as images, audio and video. On the contrary, steganalysis aims to expose the hidden secret messages with steganography. In the past decade, many steganalytic methods have been reported. However, most existing steganalytic methods are mainly dependent on the handcrafted features, which means that these methods have to carefully analyze the hiding property of the targeted steganography and design the special features for steganalysis. In this paper, we focus on audio steganalysis with deep learning, which is a popular machine learning technique based on learning representations of data.

Up to now, many statistical features have been investigated for audio steganalysis. For instance, in [8], the authors tried to build a linear basis to captures certain statistical properties of audio signal. In [10], the authors introduced the Mel-frequency based feature for audio steganalysis. In [13], the authors analyzed the statistics of the high-frequency spectrum and the Mel-cepstrum coefficients of the second-order derivative, and then in [14], they employed the Mel-cepstrum coefficients and Markov transition features from the second-order derivative of the audio signal. Besides, there are some effective features to detect audio steganography in the frequency domain, such as AMR based steganalysis [18] and MP3 based steganalysis [17]. The above methods are based on handcrafted features, and the performances with existing features are still far from satisfactory for the audio steganalysis in the time domain.

Unlike traditional methods, deep learning can effectively replace handcrafted features via feature learning and hierarchical feature extraction. Recently, various deep learning architectures such as Deep Belief Network (DBN)[4], Stacked Auto Encoder (SAE) [5], Convolutional Neural Network (CNN) [11] and Recurrent Neural Network (RNN) [6] have been proposed, and achieve state-of-the-art results in many areas, such as computer vision, audio recognition, and natural language processing. However, just several deep learning based methods have been proposed for digital forensics and steganalysis such as [1, 2, 15, 16, 19, 25].

In this paper, we proposed a new Convolutional Neural Network (CNN) to detect ± 1 LSB audio steganography in the time domain. Although this audio steganography in the time domain is a little bit old, to our best knowledge, the detection accuracy with existing steganalytic methods is still far from satisfactory until now. Since the modification introduced by the ± 1 LSB steganography is minor, the original

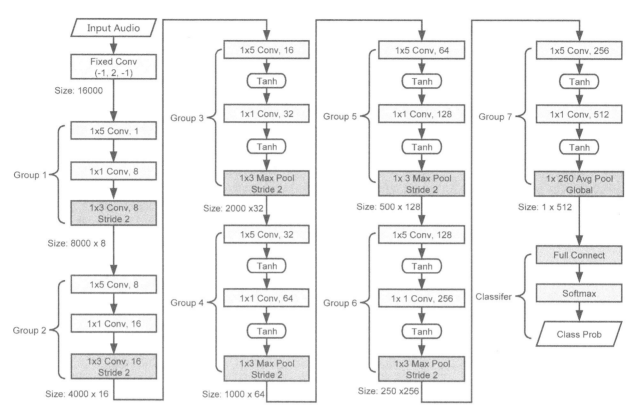

Figure 1: The proposed CNN Architecture. The parameters inside the boxes represent kernel size, layer type, and the number of channels, respectively. For example, "1×1 conv, 8" means a convolutional layer with 1x1 kernel size and 8 channels. The size of output data is showed following the subsampling layers (i.e., the purple boxes).

contents would be well preserved after data hiding. Thus, those typical network architectures that try to capture media contents would not be suitable for this steganalysis problem. In the proposed network, we first obtain the residual of an audio clip with a fixed convolutional layer. Then, seven groups of layers are applied for transforming the input data into a 512-D feature. Finally, a fully connected layer and a softmax layer are served as a classifier to output the class probabilities. In order to reduce the danger of overfitting and enhance the robustness of the proposed model, we have introduced several modifications into the groups of layers. For example, using 1×1 convolutional layers to reduce the number of parameters, performing different types of subsampling in different groups, omitting the activation function in the first two groups. The extensive results show that the proposed network outperforms its variants, and achieve significant improvement compared to the conventional steganalytic methods based on handcrafted features.

The rest of this paper is organized as follows. Section 2 describes the details of the proposed CNN architecture. Section 3 shows the experimental results. Finally, the concluding remarks and future works are given in Section 4.

2 THE PROPOSED CNN ARCHITECTURE

In this section, the overall architecture of the proposed CNN is first introduced, and then detailed analyses on different components of the proposed architecture are presented in the subsequent subsections.

2.1 Overall Architecture

The architecture of the proposed CNN is illustrated in Fig. 1. A convolutional layer with a fixed kernel $(-1, 2, -1)$ is placed at the beginning of the network, and then seven groups of layers (i.e., Group 1 to Group 7) are stacked one after another. Each group consecutively consists of a 1×5 convolutional layer, a 1×1 convolutional layer, and a subsampling layer. Among them, the 1×5 convolutional layer changes neither the number of channel nor the spatial size of the input data, while the 1×1 convolutional layer doubles the channel and the subsampling layer reduces the spatial size of the input data by half. Having been processed by the layer groups, the original data with size 16000 (see the experimental setups in Section 3.1) is finally transformed to a 512-D feature. This feature is then fed into a fully connected layer and a

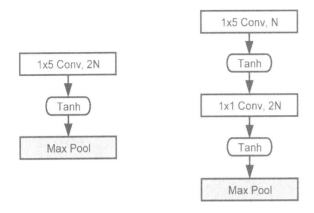

Figure 2: (a): a classical building block. (b): a building block with 1x1 convolutional layer.

softmax layer. This two layer perform like a classifier, producing the final output as the two class probabilities (i.e. cover or stego).

2.2 Fixed Convolutional Layer

CNN is a prevailing framework used in many tasks on image and audio classification. CNN has achieved great success because it is capable to learn discriminative features that represent the underlying properties of the original image/audio contents. However, steganalysis is different from the tasks in conventional image and audio classifications. In steganalysis, the key to perform a successful classification is capturing the artifacts introduced by steganography rather than modeling the media contents. Since the signal introduced by steganography is much weaker than the image/audio contents, applying CNN directly to the image/audio data may suffer from the negative impact of the contents, and thus leading to a poor local minima of the trained model. To solve this problem, some previous works such as [16, 25] on image steganalysis usually first applied a high-pass filtering to the input image, and then fed the filtered image (image residual) into a CNN architecture. In this paper, we try to attenuate the impact of audio contents in a similar manner, and use a convolutional layer with a kernel (-1, 2, -1) as it did in [14] to transform the input audio data into residuals. The kernel acts as a one dimensional high-pass filtering that suppresses the content of input data, thus it can prevent the model from learning the content features and make it more effective and robust. Unlike the common layer in CNN whose parameters are trainable, the parameters of this layer is fixed and thus we call it fixed convolutional layer.

2.3 1×1 Convolutional Layers

Typically, a building block of CNN consecutively consists of a convolutional layer, an activation function, and a subsampling layer, as shown in Fig. 2(a). Here we use a convolutional layer with size 1×5, the Tanh activation function and max pooling. To preserve enough feature information after subsampling, the convolutional layer right before the

subsampling needs to increase the number of channels (usually doubles the channel). As a result, this layer tends to introduce a lot of parameters especially when the kernel size is large. Take Fig. 2(a) as an example, supposing the input channel of the 1×5 convolutional layer is N and the output channel is $2N$, the number of introduced parameters (including the weights and biases) is:

$$1 \times 5 \times N \times 2N + 2N = 10N^2 + 2N.$$

When $N = 100$, the number of parameters is up to 100200. As introducing too many parameters would lead to the danger of overfitting, we need an approach for reducing the parameters. To this end, we adopt the 1×1 convolutional layer into the classical CNN building block, which is also used in some famous CNN architectures such as GoogLeNet [23] and ResNet [3] for controlling the number of parameters. Specifically, we add the 1×1 convolutional layer to increase the number of channels, while keeping the number of output channels of the 1×5 convolutional layer the same as its input channels, as shown in Fig. 2(b). In this way, the total number of parameters is given as follows:

$$1 \times 5 \times N \times N + N + 1 \times 1 \times N \times 2N + 2N = 7N^2 + 3N.$$

We can see that the number of parameters decreases by $3N^2 - N$. When $N = 100$, the decrement of parameters is 29900, about 30% of the parameters used in a classical CNN block. Due to the reduction of parameters, including the 1×1 convolutional layers can prevent overfitting to some extent, and thus can improve the detection performance.

2.4 Subsampling Layers

In order to reduce the spatial size of previous feature map and extract robust invariant feature, it is very common to insert a subsampling layer right after one or more convolutional layers in CNN. Subsampling is usually performed by pooling layer such as max pooling or average pooling, and max pooling is the most popular choice. Recently, some research, such as [21], prefer performing subsampling by convolutional layers with stride larger than 1. Such a subsampling approach can outperform max pooling or average pooling in certain tasks. In the proposed network, we found that a convolutional layer with stride 2 is more suitable for extracting features in lower layers compared with max pooling. Therefore, a convolutional layer with stride 2 is used for subsampling in the first two groups, while max pooling is chosen in the deeper groups. In the last group, we adopt a type of average pooling called global average pooling [12], which uses a kernel size equal to the size of the feature map and thus sums up the whole feature map learned by previous layers. The average pooling is with size 1×250 and stride 250.

2.5 Activation Function

In the proposed network, we choose Tanh as the activation function instead of the more popular Relu [20]. The reason is that the saturation region of the Tanh limit the range of data value, and thus it can enhance the performance and robustness of our model (refer to Section 3.2, compared with

Table 1: Network Indices and Descriptions

Index	Network Description
#1	The proposed CNN
#2	Remove the fixed convolutional layer
#3	Replace the activation function "Tanh" with "Relu"
#4	Remove the fixed convolutional layer & retain the activation functions in Group 1 & 2
#5	All groups use convolutional layers to perform subsampling
#6	All groups use max pooling to perform subsampling
#7	The first two groups use max pooling while the others use convolutional layers to perform subsampling

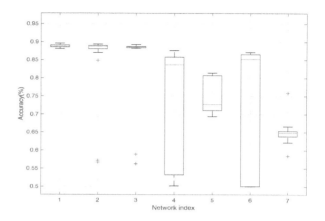

Figure 3: Box plots of the accuracies obtained by different networks.

Table 2: The average validation accuracy and the variance for each network

Index	Average	Variance
#1	**0.8885**	<0.0001
#2	0.8640	0.0063
#3	0.8551	0.0090
#4	0.7465	0.0226
#5	0.7512	0.0021
#6	0.6941	0.0327
#7	0.6472	0.0007

network #3). Besides, we discover that removing the activation function in the first two groups can slightly improve performance. Similar operation is found in some existing forensic works, such as [1].

3 EXPERIMENTAL RESULTS

3.1 Experimental Setups

In our experiments, we randomly select uncompressed speech clips from the public data set [7], and cut then into 40,000 small clips. The duration of each audio clip is 1s and the sampling rate is 16kHz. We use the ±1 LSB matching to obtain stego clips with an embedding rate of 0.50 bps (bit per sample). Totally, we obtain 40,000 cover-stego pairs. Half of the pairs are used for training, and the rest are used for testing. In the training stage, 4,000 pairs are set aside for validation, and the rest 16,000 pairs are used to train the network. To obtain convincing results, all the experiments are repeated 30 times by randomly splitting the training and testing data. In the following, we report the average results over 30 experiments for all the networks and two other conventional methods.

Instead of using the popular stochastic gradient descent (SGD), we use Adam algorithm[9] to train our model, which can make the model converge faster and perform better. The learning rate is fixed at 0.0001. We train the networks with 50,000 iterations, and in each iteration a mini-batch of 64 audio clips (32 cover/stego pairs) is used as input. At the beginning of the training, the trainable weights are initialized by random numbers generated from zero-mean truncated Gaussian distribution with standard deviation of 0.1, the trainable bias are initialized to zero. Please note that L2 regularization and Dropout [22] are not included because of little performance improvement based on our extensive experiments.

3.2 Comparison with Different Variants

In this experiment, we try to show the effectiveness of the proposed CNN by comparing it with its several variants. As listed in Table 1, six variant networks are used in the experiment, indexing from #2 to #7, whose components are slightly different from the proposed network #1. All the networks are trained for 30 times with the parameters described above. Since the accuracies of a certain network will fluctuate during training, and different networks may reach their highest accuracies after different iterations, it is unreliable to compare different networks using the accuracies after the same iteration. Therefore, during each time of training, the accuracy of validation set is checked every 1000 iterations and the highest validation accuracy is recorded as the accuracy for a network. In Fig. 3, we show the box plot of 30 accuracies for each network. After 30 times of training, we obtain the average accuracy and the variance of accuracies for each network, as show in Table 2.

From Fig. 3 and Table 2, we can observe that network #1 achieves the highest average accuracy of 88.85% and has a very stable performance over different times of training. Although network #2 and #3 achieve average accuracies between 85% and 87%, they sometimes fall into poor local minima and result in low accuracies. The average accuracies of the network #4, #5, #6 and #7 are between 64% and 76%,

Table 3: Accuracy Comparison

Approach	Accuracy
Proposed CNN	**0.8830**
Method #1 [14]	0.6313
Method #2 [13]	0.5449

which are much lower than that of the proposed network. Moreover, we can observe from Fig. 3 that the accuracies of network #4, #5 and #6 spread out in wide ranges, indicating that these networks are not stable enough.

To further evaluate the networks with relatively good performance (i.e., network #1, #2 and #3), we draw the curves of their training and validation accuracies during the training stage in Fig. 4. It is observed that the training accuracies of all these networks steadily increased with more iterations, while the validation accuracies of network #1 and #3 almost did not increase after about 10,000 iterations, meaning that network #1 and #3 both converged in this case and more iterations could not improve their validation accuracies. Network #2, which did not converge even after 50,000 iterations, can eventually converge after more iterations based on our experiment, although its final accuracy is still lower than that of network #1. Besides, we have additionally tested some other variants. For example, removing the 1×1 convolutional layers, keeping the activation function in early groups. The experimental results show that they always obtain lower accuracies compared with network #1, although the degradation of performance is not significant in some cases. As a result, the proposed network (#1) converges relatively fast and achieves the best validation accuracy, so it is the most effective network compared to other variants.

3.3 Comparison with Previous Methods

In this experiment, we compare the performance of proposed network with two typical steganalytic approaches (i.e. Method#1 [14], Method#2 [13], which employ conventional hand-crafted features and classification techniques. The classification accuracies on the testing data for different methods are given in Table 3. We can see that the proposed network achieves the classification accuracy of 88.3%, which is very close to the validation accuracy, meaning that the network does not suffer from overfitting. Compared with the conventional audio steganalytic methods Method#1 [14], Method #2 [13], the proposed method increases the testing accuracy by about 25% and 34%, respectively. Such a promising result indicates that the proposed network is very effective for audio steganalysis.

4 CONCLUSION

In this paper, we propose a CNN based method for digital audio steganalysis, and show that compared with the conventional steganalytic methods with handcrafted features, a well-designed CNN architecture can significantly improve the detection performances for audio stegangraphy in the time

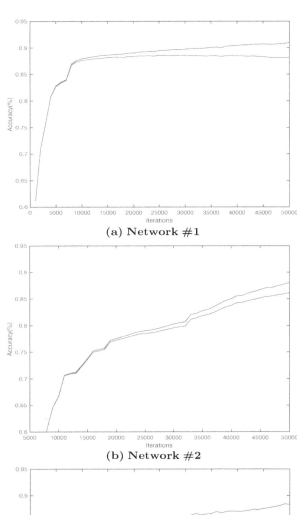

(a) Network #1

(b) Network #2

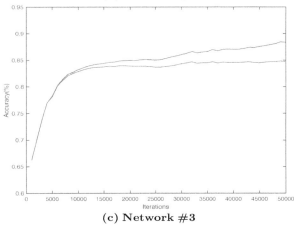

(c) Network #3

Figure 4: Accuracy curves of network #1, #2 and #3. Blue lines denote the training accuracy and orange lines denote the validation accuracy.

domain. We expect that some modern CNN architectures, such as ensembles of CNN [24], can be adopted for further improving the steganalytic performance.

In future, we will extend the proposed the CNN to detect other steganography in the frequency domain, such as MP3 and AMR, and detect various audio manipulations, such as scaling, compression, and electronic disguised voices.

ACKNOWLEDGMENTS

This work is supported in part by the NSFC (61672551), the Fok Ying-Tong Education Foundation (142003), and the Special plan of Guangdong Province (2015TQ01X365).

REFERENCES

[1] Belhassen Bayar and Matthew C Stamm. 2016. A Deep Learning Approach to Universal Image Manipulation Detection Using a New Convolutional Layer. In *ACM Workshop on Information Hiding and Multimedia Security*. ACM, 5–10.

[2] Jiansheng Chen, Xiangui Kang, Ye Liu, and Z. Jane Wang. 2015. Median Filtering Forensics Based on Convolutional Neural Networks. *IEEE Signal Processing Letters* 22, 11 (Nov 2015), 1849–1853.

[3] Kaiming He, Xiangyu Zhang, Shaoqing Ren, and Jian Sun. 2016. Deep residual learning for image recognition. In *IEEE Conference on Computer Vision and Pattern Recognition*. 770–778.

[4] Geoffrey E Hinton, Simon Osindero, and Yee-Whye Teh. 2006. A fast learning algorithm for deep belief nets. *Neural computation* 18, 7 (2006), 1527–1554.

[5] Geoffrey E Hinton and Ruslan R Salakhutdinov. 2006. Reducing the dimensionality of data with neural networks. *Science* 313, 5786 (2006), 504–507.

[6] Sepp Hochreiter and Jürgen Schmidhuber. 1997. Long short-term memory. *Neural computation* 9, 8 (1997), 1735–1780.

[7] Doug Paul John Garofolo, David Graff and David Pallett. 2013. Wall Street Journal Speech Database. https://catalog.ldc.upenn.edu/LDC93S6A

[8] Micah K. Johnson, Siwei Lyu, and Hany Farid. 2005. Steganalysis of recorded speech. *Proc. SPIE* 5681 (2005), 664–672.

[9] Diederik Kingma and Jimmy Ba. 2014. Adam: A method for stochastic optimization. *arXiv preprint arXiv:1412.6980* (2014).

[10] Christian Kraetzer and Jana Dittmann. 2007. Mel-cepstrum-based steganalysis for VoIP steganography. *Proc. SPIE* 6505 (2007), 650505–650505–12. DOI: http://dx.doi.org/10.1117/12.704040

[11] Yann LeCun, Léon Bottou, Yoshua Bengio, and Patrick Haffner. 1998. Gradient-based learning applied to document recognition. *Proc. IEEE* 86, 11 (1998), 2278–2324.

[12] Min Lin, Qiang Chen, and Shuicheng Yan. 2013. Network in network. *arXiv preprint arXiv:1312.4400* (2013).

[13] Qingzhong Liu, A.H. Sung, and Mengyu Qiao. 2009. Temporal Derivative-Based Spectrum and Mel-Cepstrum Audio Steganalysis. *IEEE Transactions on Information Forensics and Security* 4, 3 (Sept 2009), 359–368.

[14] Qingzhong Liu, Andrew H. Sung, and Mengyu Qiao. 2011. Derivative-based Audio Steganalysis. *ACM Transactions on Multimedia Computing Communications and Applications* 7, 3, Article 18 (Sept. 2011), 19 pages.

[15] Da Luo, Rui Yang, Bin Li, and Jiwu Huang. 2017. Detection of Double Compressed AMR Audio Using Stacked Autoencoder. *IEEE Transactions on Information Forensics and Security* 12, 2 (2017), 432–444.

[16] Yinlong Qian, Jing Dong, Wei Wang, and Tieniu Tan. 2015. Deep learning for steganalysis via convolutional neural networks. *Proc. SPIE* 9409 (2015), 94090J–94090J–10.

[17] Mengyu Qiao, Andrew H. Sung, and Qingzhong Liu. 2013. MP3 audio steganalysis. *Information Sciences* 231 (2013), 123 – 134.

[18] Yanzhen Ren, Tingting Cai, Ming Tang, and Lina Wang. 2015. AMR Steganalysis Based on the Probability of Same Pulse Position. *IEEE Transactions on Information Forensics and Security* 10, 9 (Sept 2015), 1801–1811.

[19] Daniel Seichter, Luca Cuccovillo, and Patrick Aichroth. 2016. AAC encoding detection and bitrate estimation using a convolutional neural network. In *IEEE International Conference on Acoustics, Speech and Signal Processing*. 2069–2073.

[20] Karen Simonyan and Andrew Zisserman. 2014. Very deep convolutional networks for large-scale image recognition. *arXiv preprint arXiv:1409.1556* (2014).

[21] Jost Tobias Springenberg, Alexey Dosovitskiy, Thomas Brox, and Martin Riedmiller. 2014. Striving for simplicity: The all convolutional net. *arXiv preprint arXiv:1412.6806* (2014).

[22] Nitish Srivastava, Geoffrey E Hinton, Alex Krizhevsky, Ilya Sutskever, and Ruslan Salakhutdinov. 2014. Dropout: a simple way to prevent neural networks from overfitting. *Journal of Machine Learning Research* 15, 1 (2014), 1929–1958.

[23] Christian Szegedy, Wei Liu, Yangqing Jia, Pierre Sermanet, Scott Reed, Dragomir Anguelov, Dumitru Erhan, Vincent Vanhoucke, and Andrew Rabinovich. 2015. Going deeper with convolutions. In *IEEE Conference on Computer Vision and Pattern Recognition*. 1–9.

[24] Guanshuo Xu, Han-Zhou Wu, and Yun Q Shi. 2016. Ensemble of CNNs for steganalysis: an empirical study. In *ACM Workshop on Information Hiding and Multimedia Security*. ACM, 103–107.

[25] Guanshuo Xu, Han-Zhou Wu, and Yun-Qing Shi. 2016. Structural Design of Convolutional Neural Networks for Steganalysis. *IEEE Signal Processing Letters* 23, 5 (2016), 708–712.

Using Stylometry to Attribute Programmers and Writers: IH&MMSec'17 Keynote-Invited Talk Abstract

Rachel Greenstadt
Drexel University
Philadelphia, Pennsylvania
rachel.a.greenstadt@drexel.edu

ABSTRACT

In this talk, I will discuss my lab's work in the emerging field of adversarial stylometry and machine learning. Machine learning algorithms are increasingly being used in security and privacy domains, in areas that go beyond intrusion or spam detection. For example, in digital forensics, questions often arise about the authors of documents: their identity, demographic background, and whether they can be linked to other documents. The field of stylometry uses linguistic features and machine learning techniques to answer these questions. We have applied stylometry to difficult domains such as underground hacker forums, open source projects (code), and tweets. I will discuss our Doppelgnger Finder algorithm, which enables us to group Sybil accounts on underground forums and detect blogs from Twitter feeds and reddit comments. In addition, I will discuss our work attributing unknown source code and binaries.

KEYWORDS

stylometry; attribution; machine learning; privacy

BIOGRAPHY

Rachel Greenstadt is an Associate Professor of Computer Science at Drexel University, where she research the privacy and security properties of intelligent systems and the economics of electronic privacy and information security. Her work is at "layer 8" of the networkfi!?analyzing the content. She is a member of the DARPA Computer Science Study Group and she runs the Privacy, Security, and Automation Laboratory (PSAL) which is a vibrant group of researchers. The privacy research community has recognized her scholarship with the PET Award for Outstanding Research in Privacy Enhancing Technologies, the NSF CAREER Award, and the Andreas Pfitzmann Best Student Paper Award. She currently is co-editor-in-chief of Proceedings on Privacy Enhancing Technologies (PoPETs) and co-program chair of the Privacy Enhancing Technologies Symposium (PETS).

Towards Imperceptible
Natural Language Watermarking for German

Oren Halvani*

Martin Steinebach

Lukas Graner

Fraunhofer Institute for Secure Information Technology SIT
Rheinstrasse 75, 64295 Darmstadt, Germany
FirstName.LastName@SIT.Fraunhofer.de

ABSTRACT

Watermarking natural language is still a challenge in the domain of digital watermarking. Here, only the textual information must be used as a cover. No format changes or modified illustrations are accepted. Still, natural language watermarking (NLW) has some important applications, especially in leakage tracking, where a small set of individually marked copies of a confidently text is distributed. Properties of watermarking schemes such as imperceptibility, blindness or adaptability to non-English languages are of importance here. In order to address these three simultaneously, we present a blind NLW scheme, consisting of four independent embedding methods, which operate on the phonetical, morphological, lexical and syntactical layer of German texts. An evaluation based on 1,645 assessments provided by 131 test persons reveals promising results.

KEYWORDS

Natural language watermarking; linguistic transformations; imperceptibility; automated paraphrasing.

1 INTRODUCTION

Digital watermarking today has a history of more than 20 years of research. Regarding multimedia data there are many mature solutions available for industrial applications. However, for other data types results are more sparse. Natural language is a good example here: while the need for embedding information into text is well known and reaches back to the beginnings of steganography, methods which automatically hide a message into written natural language without significant quality loss are rare. We want to stress that the cover is wording of the text and not its graphical representation or its formatting. The latter is a strategy often applied in *document watermarking* by e. g., modulating line spaces [7], word spaces [1], character spaces [15] or character encoding [11]. When it comes to mark textual information, various technical

---

*Corresponding author.

IH&MMSec '17, June 20–22, 2017, Philadelphia, PA, USA
© 2017 ACM. 978-1-4503-5061-7/17/06...$15.00
DOI: http://dx.doi.org/10.1145/3082031.3084682

terms have been coined such as *natural language watermarking*, *text watermarking*, or *linguistic steganography*.

In this paper, we will stick to the term *Natural Language Watermarking* (NLW), introduced by Topkara et al. [12], which led to numerous extensions and improvements. This term is appropriate, as NLW relies on natural language processing concepts for watermark embedding. According to the authors, NLW "*aims to embed information in text documents by manipulating the semantic and/or syntactic structure of sentences.*" [12]. However, we extend this statement slightly such that NLW aims to embed information in texts also by phonetical, morphological and lexical manipulations.

When comparing NLW to common media watermarking algorithms, the question of how the written text is modified is similar to the question in which domain (spacial or spectral) the information is embedded and which *perceptual assumption* is made. Models for estimating the impact of a change caused by the watermarking algorithm to the cover like human visual models for image watermarking are not available in linguistics. Instead, several sets of rules exist for a language, which can be applied as a linguistic model, setting the range of acceptable changes during embedding. Still, these rules are rather technical and following a rule may not always end up with a marked cover, which is perceived as of similar quality as the original. Evaluation by human readers is therefore necessary to verify the transparency of a NLW scheme.

One possible application for our approach is leakage tracking. Here, classified documents are distributed with an individual mark for each recipient or "soft DRM" for ebooks. Both fall in the category of *transaction watermarking*, where watermarking produces machine-distinguishable copies from one cover.

Transparency is vital in such an application. Neither meaning of the text nor the perceived quality of the written language must be reduced. Robustness to conversion between text formats is usually not a challenge for NLW, as the formatting does not influence the wording of the text. The only risk are errors, caused by OCR if a print/scan operation is executed. Robustness against copy/paste of text section is not addressed in this paper; we assume that complete texts are available for watermark retrieval. Re-synchronization after copy/paste attacks is an issue for further work. This type of robustness could be achieved by adding sync sequences into the watermarking message stream, but as the current payload of our approach is limited, this overhead cannot be accepted. The payload of our approach is discussed in the evaluation section; it is sufficient to individualize ebooks and longer reports.

To summarize: our NLW algorithm has its focus on transparency, but also provides a certain amount of robustness and security as will be discussed in Section 3. While it could be used for steganography, it is best suited for small batch transaction watermarking, e. g., for leakage tracking of confidential documents. Individualization of otherwise indistinguishable copies of a work is a common watermarking challenge our NLW scheme is able to meet.

Past and present research work in NLW focuses mainly on English, while research for German is almost non-existent. In contrast to English, German is a morphologically rich language that allows the construction of (very) long compound words. Additionally, word order and constituent structure in German are highly flexible, i. e. constituents in the middle field can be reordered in a number of variations. Depending on the sentence, constituents in the middle field can be even swapped with the pre-field constituent. These and other linguistic properties make German a promising candidate to apply NLW on different levels of linguistic layers.

We present a NLW scheme comprising four embedding methods that operate on the phonetical, morphological, lexical and syntactical layers of German text. Our scheme offers a number of benefits. First, it is blind and, thus, enables to detect and extract watermarks in absence of the non-watermarked text. Second, a part of our embedding methods preserve the identical structure and meaning of the original text. This results in a serious challenge to identify performed modifications, even for linguistic experts. Third, the methods can be adapted to other languages (i. e. English) and are, therefore, not bound to German.

2   RELATED WORK

In this section we mention three NLW and two linguistic steganography approaches, related to our NLW scheme.

Vybornova and Macq proposed an interesting NLW approach [13], based on the discourse-semantic phenomenon *presupposition*. Presupposition can be thought of implicit information, which is assumed by the speaker to be already known to the addressee. For the purpose of NLW they studied the behavior of seven presupposition triggers, such as possessives, interrogative words or factive predicative constructions. The authors define distinct rules to identify presupposition for each appropriate trigger and constructed transformation rules that enable the embedding of a watermark-bit b in a given sentence. Vybornova and Macq treat a text as a sequence of N ordered sentences. In order to embed a watermark $\mathcal{W} = (b_1, b_2, \ldots)$ they group all sentences into subsets $S_1, S_2, \ldots$, where each S_i comprise k sentences. The secret key of their embedding algorithm represents the choice of the particular arrangement of k sentences among N. For each S_i they mark $b = 1$ by forcing the amount of presuppositions p in S_i to be even. In contrast, they mark $b = 0$ by forcing p in the group to be odd. As a payload the authors mention $\frac{N}{k}$.

Another NLW approach that also operates on the sentence level was introduced by Meral et al. [8]. First, the authors split a given text into N sentences in order to transform each sentence into its syntactic tree representation, including hierarchies and functional dependencies. Given the prerequisite $N > \ell$, where ℓ denotes the number of watermarking bits, their NLW scheme executes morphosyntactic manipulations on the syntax tree representation of alterable sentences. Manipulations (e. g., adverb displacement, conjunct order change and verbs replacement) are performed under

control of WordNet and a dictionary of the syntax tree to avoid semantic drops. In order to measure imperceptibility and acceptability of manipulations, Meral et al. used edit-hit counts based on human judgments and report a payload of 0.81 bit per sentence.

Kim et al. proposed a NLW approach for Korean [5], based on morphological and syntactical analysis. Based on the fact that Korean is an agglutinative language and thus, has a high number of morphemes per word, the morphological division can hide information, by splitting words with two content morphemes into two new words. Syntactic displacement, the second technique, determines adverbial constituents and moves them inside the sentence without resulting in semantic distortions. Regarding their approach, the authors mention a payload of 0.86 bit per sentence.

Chang and Clark [2] proposed a linguistic steganography method, based on word permutations. The authors used the approach of Zhang et al. [16] as a word ordering realization system. After collecting cover sentences, they create corresponding bag-of-words representations that serve as an input for the word ordering realization system. However, since not all generated permutations are valid in terms of grammar/meaning, the authors proposed a MaxEnt classifier to determine the *naturalness* of the permutations. An evaluation regarding the classifier based on human judgements revealed 93.3% precision with 15.6% recall. Note that one of our embedding methods (Subsection 3.4) is also utilizes word ordering. However, instead of generating naive permutations, our method orders specific words according to a strict grammar rule.

Another noteworthy linguistic steganography approach was proposed by Wilson et al. [14]. Their system modifies Twitter tweets at the time of writing and can hide up to 4 bits of payload per tweet. First, a Twitter user U generates a cover tweet C. Next, the system generates several stego tweets from C and selects only those, that convey the desired payload. Afterwards, the selected stego tweets are ranked according to a given a distortion measure. Finally, U chooses the best stego tweet from the ranked list [14]. Compared to our proposed method there are a number of distinctions. First, our method is fully automated and, thus, does not depend on a *human-in-the-loop*. Second, our method focuses on German, for which it is not clear if the underlying linguistic resources are also available. Third, our method does require a user-specific language model that can be very error-prone, as it depends on the amount and quality of data as well as suitable features.

3   PROPOSED NLW SCHEME

In this section we present our NLW scheme, where first, we frame the picture of the whole system, followed by an introduction and algorithmic description of the underlying four embedding methods.

For embedding, our NLW system requires a natural language text $\mathcal{T}$ acting as a cover medium, a secret key $\mathcal{K}$ and a watermark $\mathcal{W} = (b_1, b_2, \ldots, b_n)$, which represents a sequence of n bits. In its current state, our scheme utilizes four embedding methods $\mathcal{A}_1, \ldots, \mathcal{A}_4$ that are able to seek positions in $\mathcal{T}$, which can be replaced by an alternative wording. Each A_i is an implementation of a set of specified linguistic rules that generates a deterministic result. For each found position, a pair (σ, σ') is provided, where σ denotes a wording found in $\mathcal{T}$ and σ' an alternative wording, based on the set of rules defined in $\mathcal{A}_i$. All results provided by $\mathcal{A}_1, \ldots, \mathcal{A}_4$ form a set $\mathcal{P}$, comprising potential marking positions that enable a blind NLW scheme: we simply apply a cryptographic hash (e.g. MD5) on σ and σ' and apply a rule similar to patchwork watermarking: if MD5(σ) > MD5(σ') then the binary value of the watermarking position is 0, else 1. For security reasons the hashes are salted by $\mathcal{K}$. As always both wordings are provided by $\mathcal{A}_i$ during embedding and detection, embedding is done by matching the binary value and b_i by selecting one of the two possible wordings based on the rule above. Detection is done by comparing the hashes of the wording found in $\mathcal{T}'$ and its alternative. The detector, therefore, only requires $\mathcal{T}'$ and $\mathcal{K}$.

Another role of $\mathcal{K}$ is selecting the actual marking positions from $\mathcal{P}$. Depending on the length of $\mathcal{W}$ and the number of potential positions, only a subset is used for embedding. The pseudo-random selection process is initiated with $\mathcal{K}$. Therefore, without knowledge of $\mathcal{K}$, an attacker is not able to determine the actual marking positions without $\mathcal{T}$. As $\mathcal{A}_1, \ldots, \mathcal{A}_4$ are supposed to be known, he could only randomly modify potential marking positions. If $\mathcal{P}$ is large, random changes can result into a quality loss stronger than the selective embedding process as the attacker modifies the text more aggressively than the embedder.

All four embedding methods require texts with annotations regarding sentences, tokens, lemmas, coarse-/fine-grained POS-tags as well as named-entities. In order to generate annotations, we developed a light-weight annotation framework that works similar to *UIMA*[1]. The framework requires the following components: *Morphy-Lexicon*[2] (lemmatization), *RFTagger*[3] (fine-grained POS-tagging) and *Stanford CoreNLP*[4] (tokenization, sentence splitting, coarse-grained POS-tagging and named-entity recognition[5]).

The following sub-sections describe our methods. For each method we provide examples, written in German (with English translations), where each example denotes a pair of the original text $\mathcal{T}$ and its watermarked form $\mathcal{T}'$. Here, the highlighted wording in $\mathcal{T}$ and $\mathcal{T}'$ represent respectively σ and σ'.

3.1 Contraction Splitting

In German many cases exist, where a preposition followed by an article can be merged into a shortened word that has the same meaning. The linguistic definition of this word formation process is called contraction and is the core idea behind the *Contraction Splitting* method (CoSp). By restoring internal characters, CoSp paraphrases contractions in the following manner:

$$\mathcal{T} = \text{``Er befindet sich \textbf{vorm} Haus.''}$$

$$\mathcal{T}' = \text{``Er befindet sich \textbf{vor dem} Haus.''}$$

("He is **in front of** the house.")

Algorithm: Since contractions cannot be splitted naively, we must make sure which cases are most likely possible. To achieve this, we extracted 3,614 sentences from all the training corpora (mentioned in the *Experiments* chapter), which were then labeled manually

---

[1] The Unstructured Information Management Architecture (UIMA) framework represents an open, scalable and extensible platform for building analytic applications, especially in the field of natural language processing.
[2] Available under http://bit.do/MorphyLexicon
[3] Available under http://bit.do/RFTagger
[4] Available under http://stanfordnlp.github.io/CoreNLP
[5] We use the pre-trained German model offered by [3].

	Articles			
	dem	**das**	**der**	**den**
an	am	ans		
auf		aufs		
bei	beim			
durch		durchs		
für		fürs		
hinter	hinterm	hinters		hintern
in	im	ins		
über	überm	übers		übern
um		ums		
unter	unterm	unters		untern
von	vom			
vor	vorm	vors		
zu	zum		zur	

Prepositions (row axis label)

Table 1: All existing preposition-article pairs and corresponding contractions in the German language.

according to the two possibilities *acceptable/unacceptable*. Next, we divided all labeled sentences into two subsets C_{train} (used for training) and C_{test} (used for testing). We trained a MaxEnt[6] classifier on C_{train}, where we used character 2-, 3-, and 4-grams as well as fine-grained POS-tags[7] of the three consecutive words right next to the found contraction, as features. The generated classification model was then applied on C_{test}. Based on the obtained results, we selected a subset of 10 contractions (highlighted in Table 1), which performed with $\geq$ 80% accuracy during training. Given the model, the classifier judges for each appropriate contraction found in $\mathcal{T}$, if it can be splitted into a preposition followed by an article, according to the mappings shown in Table 1.

3.2 Compound Decomposition

Optional rules[8] defined by the *Institute of German Language* allow a segmentation of compound words $\alpha\beta$ if:

(1) α is an adjective and β a participial adjective.
(2) α is an uninflected adjective that reinforces/weakens the second adjective β.
(3) α represents the negation word *"nicht"* ("not") and β an adjective.
(4) α is a primary adjective and β a verb, such that $\alpha\beta$ represents the result of a verbal process, i. e. *"kleinschneiden"* → *"klein schneiden"* ("cut into small pieces").
(5) α represents a verb and β the verb *"bleiben"* ("remain") or *"lassen"* ("let").
(6) α and β are both color adjectives, i. e. *"blaurot"* → *"blau-rot"* (*"blue-red"*).

Regarding rules (1-5) decomposition is performed by a space and regarding rule (6) by a hyphen. The *Compound Decomposition* method

---

[6] Available under http://nlp.stanford.edu/software/classifier.shtml
[7] These are features that encode information about gender, case, person, degree, etc.
[8] Listed in §36, (2) under [4].

(CoDe) makes use of these rules to paraphrase compounds e. g.,

$$\mathcal{T} = \text{“Bitte die Taschen } \textbf{\textit{leermachen}}!\text{”}$$

$$\mathcal{T}' = \text{“Bitte die Taschen } \textbf{\textit{leer machen}}!\text{”}$$

("Please **empty** the bags!")

Algorithm: The prerequisites of this algorithm are a whitelist[9] $\mathcal{L}_{val}$ containing valid decompositions for known compounds, two blacklists $\mathcal{L}_\alpha$ and $\mathcal{L}_\beta$ that include unsuitable prefixes for α and suffixes for β as well as a word-splitter[10]. Given these prerequisites, we extract all adjectives and verbs, denoted by w, from $\mathcal{T}$ with a lowercased initial and a length of more than 6 characters. Next, we check the presence of w in $\mathcal{L}_{val}$. When, in the trivial case, a known decomposition $w = \alpha\beta$ exists in $\mathcal{L}_{val}$, w is accepted as a valid candidate. If, on the other hand, $w \notin \mathcal{L}_{val}$ holds, a number of restrictions are taken into account to ensure (at least to some extent) that w has a grammatically valid decomposition.

First, we lemmatize each $w \notin \mathcal{L}_{val}$ in order to remove bound morphemes that can lead to wrong separations. For example, the word-splitter we use separates the adjective $w = kostenlose$ (free) into $kosten$ (costs) and $lose$ (lottery tickets), which is wrong, since $kosten$ is a free and $lose$ a bound morpheme of w. Resulting lemmas $\ell_1, \ell_2, \ldots$ are then passed to the word-splitter to check if a decomposition $\ell = \alpha\beta$ exists, such that $\alpha \in \mathcal{L}_\alpha$ or $\beta \in \mathcal{L}_\beta$ holds. If one of both conditions is true we reject w, otherwise we proceed by checking if w contains an interfix[11], which connects α and β. This is done by comparing the length of w to the length of α concatenated with β. If the lengths are unequal, or the word-splitter could not decompose w into α and β, we reject w. Else, we check the existence of α in $\mathcal{L}_\alpha$ and β in $\mathcal{L}_\beta$ entirely or (due, to possible inflections) partially. If α or β exists in the blacklists we reject w, otherwise we apply POS-tagging on the sentence that surrounds w, where we first replace w by $\alpha\beta$. From here, we match $\alpha\beta$ against the rules 1-6, where each successful match is accepted as a valid candidate.

3.3 Phoneme-invariant spelling substitution

According to a grammar rule[12] in German, a number of words containing specific characters can be substituted by words with phonetically equivalent characters. The *Phoneme-invariant spelling substitution* method (PhoS) utilizes this rule to apply slight modifications for individual cases e. g.,

$$\mathcal{T} = \text{“Orthogra}\underline{\textbf{ph}}\text{ie ist ein essen}\underline{\textbf{z}}\text{ieller}\ldots\text{”}$$

$$\mathcal{T}' = \text{“Orthogra}\underline{\textbf{f}}\text{ie ist ein essen}\underline{\textbf{t}}\text{ieller}\ldots\text{”}$$

("Orthogra**ph**y is an essen**t**ial...")

Algorithm: As a first step, we extract all words except those that belong to the POS tag FM (foreign word) or are a part of named-entity phrases. Remaining candidates are then matched against the following including characters $\{gh, ph, rh, th, zial, ziell\}$. Then, we define a list $\mathcal{L}_\gamma = \{\gamma_1, \gamma_2, \ldots\}$, where each γ denotes a matched candidate. As a next step we replace each γ with its phonetically

equivalent representation δ, where we use the following mappings:

$$\{gh \rightarrow g, ph \rightarrow f, rh \rightarrow r, th \rightarrow t, zial \rightarrow tial, ziell \rightarrow tiell\}$$

Each δ is then added to the new list $\mathcal{L}_\delta$. Next, we define an acceptance criterion to judge if $\gamma \in \mathcal{L}_\gamma$ and its corresponding representation $\delta \in \mathcal{L}_\delta$ (e. g., $\gamma = Telefon$, $\delta = Telephon$) are interchangeable. For this, we use the *Google N-Gram Corpus*[13] [9], in order to lookup if γ and δ exist. If this is the case, we compare their absolute frequencies[14] f_γ and f_δ against each other. Finally, we ensure that f_γ and f_δ are relatively evenly distributed to achieve a more suitable substitution. For this, we compute $max(f_\gamma, f_\delta)/min(f_\gamma, f_\delta) \leq \theta$, where θ denotes a threshold that we set to 1.2 (empirically obtained on the same training set, used in Section 3.1). Provided that θ is not exceeded, δ is accepted as a valid candidate.

3.4 Coordinated Adjective Reordering

A grammar rule[15] in German states that if two adjectives are not coordinated, they must not be separated by a comma. As an implication of this rule one can say that two adjectives must be coordinated in an presence of a separating comma. The *Coordinated Adjective Reordering* method (CoRe) uses this implication to paraphrase two adjectives through reordering as for instance:

$$\mathcal{T} = \text{“In der } \textbf{\textit{linken, oberen}} \text{ Ecke}\ldots\text{”}$$

$$\mathcal{T}' = \text{“In der } \textbf{\textit{oberen, linken}} \text{ Ecke}\ldots\text{”}$$

("In the **top left** corner...")

Algorithm: First, we extract a window of five tokens from $\mathcal{T}$ that begins with an arbitrary word except adjectives or adverbs (1), followed by two consecutive adjectives (separated through a comma) and ends with either a noun or a named entity. Note that (1) is required since adverbs describe adjectives and hence, reordering could cause semantic distortion, as for instance:

$$\mathcal{T} = \text{“Der } \underline{h\ddot{a}ufig} \textbf{ \textit{kranke, alte}} \text{ Mann}\ldots\text{”}$$

("The _frequently_ **ill, old** man...")

Therefore, we reject such candidates. In the next step, we reorder both adjectives and apply POS-tagging on the affected sentence to ensure all POS-tags remain equal, since word reordering can lead to wrongly classified POS-tags, due to the sensitivity of the involved POS-tagger. If the POS-tags remain equal we accept the candidate.

4 EXPERIMENTS

This section describes which corpora were used, how the evaluation was performed and the observations we have made.

4.1 Used corpora

In our experiments we used several corpora[16] for training, evaluation and performance measurement of all four embedding methods.

---

[9] Gathered from http://www.canoo.net
[10] Available under https://github.com/danielnaber/jwordsplitter
[11] These are: $\{-e-, -en-, -ens-, -er-, -es-, -n-, -s-\}$
[12] The rule is listed in [4] under §32, (2).

[13] We only use the 1-grams (for all letters) from the German dataset (Version 20120701).
[14] The match_count column in *Google's N-Gram Corpus* denotes the absolute frequency of a n-gram.
[15] The rule is listed in [4] under §71.
[16] Accessible under http://bit.ly/2lCrJar

$\mathcal{T}$ classified as $\mathcal{T}'$					$\mathcal{T}'$ correctly identified			
Very annoying	Annoying	Slightly annoying	Perceptible (not annoying)	Imperceptible	Perceptible (not annoying)	Slightly annoying	Annoying	Very annoying
-4	-3	-2	-1	0	1	2	3	4

Table 2: The rating scheme used in our human-based evaluation.

Corpus	Usage
deu_wikipedia_2010_100k	evaluation
deu_web_2002_100k	training
deu_news_2001_100k	training
deu_news_2002_120k	training
deu_news_2003_100k	training
deu_news_2006_120k	training
deu_news_2007_100k	training
deu_news_2015_100k	training
deu_wikipedia_2014_100k	training

Table 3: Corpora, used for training and evaluation.

Corpus	Sentences	|CoSp|	|CoDe|	|PhoS|	|CoRe|	Σ	Payload
C_{Faz}	43,449	1,174	170	279	308	1,296	0,03
C_{Gut}	206,362	7,765	733	902	3,802	12,469	0,06

Table 4: Payload statistics.

4.1.1 Training and evaluation corpora. In total, we used nine corpora, where eight served for training and one for the human-based evaluation. All corpora (listed in Table 3) form a part of the well-known *Leipzig Corpora Collection* [10]. The purpose of the training corpora was to extract linguistic patterns that helped us to optimize our methods. Given the evaluation corpus and our four embedding methods, we generated 1,000 sentence pairs ($\mathcal{T}_i, \mathcal{T}_i'$), where $\mathcal{T}_i$ and $\mathcal{T}_i'$ denote the original sentence and its watermarked form, respectively. All sentence pairs were equally distributed (250 sentence pairs per method) and comprise 80–220 characters.

4.1.2 Performance measurement corpora. In order to measure the payload of our NLW scheme we made use of two corpora. The first corpus C_{Faz} represents a concatenation of 600 articles, crawled from the German news portal *FAZ*. The second corpus C_{Gut} represents a concatenation of 100 ebooks, downloaded from *Project Gutenberg*[17]. We applied our NLW scheme on both corpora, which led to the statistics given in Table 4. Note each $|\cdot|$ denotes the amount of embeddable watermarking-bits regarding each embedding method. As can be observed, the payload (bit per sentence) of our scheme is low in comparison to the existing approaches discussed in Section 2. The most important reason for this is the fact that the involved rules in our scheme are fairly restrictive, which results in fewer but more promising embedding candidates. As a consequence, it should be highlighted that our scheme is appropriate for longer texts (e. g., ebooks).

4.2 Human-based evaluation

In order to measure the quality of a NLW scheme, which can cause semantic and stylistic distortion, we believe that a human-based evaluation is mandatory. Therefore, we asked 145 test persons to

participate in our web-based evaluation. All persons provided metadata about themselves including their language skills. 14 persons indicated to speak German to some extent, but in fact, were not German native speakers. As we focus on meaningful judgments rather than a bigger number of test persons, we decided to discard their entries from the database. Hence, our evaluation is based only on 131 test persons, who indicated to be German native speakers. The task of the test persons was to rate a set of sentence pairs, for which the order ($\mathcal{T}_i, \mathcal{T}_i'$) or ($\mathcal{T}_i', \mathcal{T}_i$) was not known to the test person beforehand. Inspired by the renowned Likert scale [6], we defined a rating scheme, shown in Table 2.

4.2.1 Results and observations. In total, we received 1,645 ratings for an overall of 978 sentence pairs (22 sentence pairs were not rated at all). From the 978 sentence pairs, 667 were rated twice (by different test persons), while the remaining 311 sentence pairs were reviewed once. In 134 out of 667 cases (the twice rated sentence pairs), unanimous decisions were provided by the test persons. As can be seen below, the majority of the unanimous decisions fall into the *imperceptible* rating category:

	−4	−3	−2	−1	**0**	1	2	3	4
Accordances	1	2	19	16	**42**	23	14	8	9

An exploration of the review-database revealed that CoRe received 20, PhoS 13, CoSp 6 and CoDe 3 unanimous decisions. We can infer from this that both CoRe and PhoS fulfill the property of imperceptibility, which is somewhat contradictory to the statement of Wilson et al. that "*even slight changes to a sentence often produce clearly incorrect results*" [14], as this is the case for CoRe and PhoS. If we consider the results shown in Table 5 one can see that all methods received 22.19% of *imperceptible* ratings. However, from the same table it can be easily observed that, again, both methods PhoS and CoRe primary constitute this percentage.

Furthermore, Figure 1 (which is the corresponding plot of Table 5) reveals that the CoSp method leads to the most misclassifications by the test persons. This can be interpreted in such a way that sentences paraphrased by CoSp seem to be more acceptable than the original sentences. In contrast, we can infer from Figure 1 that CoDe seems not to be mature enough, as its modifications were identified by the majority of the test persons.

We measured for all reviews per method, how many seconds a user needed to decide, which of both sentences represented the watermarked version. Due to the presence of outliers in the data we decided to compute the median instead of the average. The median regarding the CoSp, CoDe and PhoS reviews was the same (17 seconds), while for CoRe it was 20 seconds. Even though the difference is not significantly high, it could indicate a better imperceptibility regarding modifications performed by CoRe.

---

[17] Accessible under https://gutenberg.org/browse/languages/de

	-4	-3	-2	-1	0	1	2	3	4	Σ
CoSp	10	38	93	57	66	75	38	14	5	396
CoDe	9	11	44	44	51	51	88	59	48	405
PhoS	10	14	56	84	120	61	41	23	15	424
CoRe	3	12	40	57	128	65	70	35	10	420
Σ	32	75	233	242	365	252	237	131	78	1,645
%	1.95	4.56	14.16	14.71	22.19	15.32	14.41	7.96	4.74	

Table 5: Evaluation results.

5 CONCLUSIONS AND FUTURE WORK

We presented a blind NLW scheme, based on four embedding methods that operate on different linguistic layers. Despite of the fact that we considered German as the target language, our approach can be adopted to other languages, as the underlying linguistic rule sets not apply only for German. Some of our methods preserve the identical sentence structure (including word classes) as well as the meaning of the original text. Therefore, modifications are difficult to notice, as shown in the experiments. An evaluation based on 1,645 assessments provided by 131 test persons revealed several interesting observations regarding our system. According to the majority of the provided ratings, PhoS and CoRe meet the requirement of imperceptibility. Furthermore, we noticed that CoSp has led to the most misclassifications by the test persons, which can understand as a stylistic improvement of the paraphrased sentences, as they tend to be more acceptable than the original sentences.

However, our study has also a number of clear limitations. Due to the low payload, our scheme is unsuitable for short texts at this stage. Since this is a *Work-in-Progress* paper, one major issue for future work is to find a strategy to increase the payload. Besides quantity, the quality of CoSp and CoDe can also be improved if we could use NLP tools, which are able to detect stressed words in sentences. This, however, needs further investigation as to our best knowledge such tools do not exist (at least for German) at this time. Moreover, our methods would yield more suitable candidates if we used morphological parsers instead of naive word-splitters. During implementation, we encounter several technical challenges such as missing/incompatible libraries, missing model-files or reliable parsing results. When morphological parsers for German become sufficiently mature, we will address this subject in future work. Another issue is that we considered for the evaluation only pairs of original/paraphrased test sentences. A more sophisticated evaluation would take longer surrounding contexts into account, in order to enable the test persons a fine-grained control regarding their decisions. Last but not least, we mention again that robustness

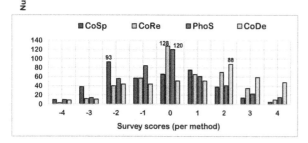

Figure 1: Reviews according to embedding methods.

was fairly little addressed in this paper and, thus, is also subject for future work.

6 ACKNOWLEDGEMENTS

This work was funded by the Hessian Ministry of the Interior and Sports (HMdIS) within the "Round Table Cybersecurity@Hessen". We would like to thank the reviewers for their suggestions and comments and the human judges for taking part in our evaluation.

REFERENCES

[1] Reem A. Alotaibi and Lamiaa A. Elrefaei. 2017. Improved Capacity Arabic Text Watermarking Methods based on Open Word Space. *Journal of King Saud University - Computer and Information Sciences* (2017), –. http://www.sciencedirect.com/science/article/pii/S1319157817300010

[2] Ching-Yun Chang and Stephen Clark. 2012. The Secret's in the Word Order: Text-to-Text Generation for Linguistic Steganography. In *COLING 2012, 24th International Conference on Computational Linguistics, Proceedings of the Conference: Technical Papers, 8-15 December 2012, Mumbai, India*, Martin Kay and Christian Boitet (Eds.). Indian Institute of Technology Bombay, 511–528. http://aclweb.org/anthology/C/C12/C12-1032.pdf

[3] Manaal Faruqui and Sebastian Padó. 2010. Training and Evaluating a German Named Entity Recognizer with Semantic Generalization. In *Proceedings of KONVENS 2010*. Saarbrücken, Germany.

[4] IDS. 2010. Institut für Deutsche Sprache (IDS): Regeln und Wörterverzeichnis. Entsprechend den Empfehlungen des Rats für deutsche Rechtschreibung. Überarbeitete Fassung des amtlichen Regelwerks 2004 mit den Nachträgen aus dem Bericht 2010. (2010). http://rechtschreibrat.ids-mannheim.de/download/regeln2006.pdf

[5] Mi-Young Kim, Randy Goebel, and Osmar R. Zaiane. 2010. Natural Language Watermarking Based on Syntactic Displacement and Morphological Division. *2012 IEEE 36th Annual Computer Software and Applications Conference Workshops* 00 (2010), 164–169.

[6] R. Likert. 1932. A Technique for the Measurement of Attitudes. *Archives of Psychology* 22, 140 (1932), 1–55.

[7] N. F. Maxemchuk and S. H. Low. 1997. Marking Text Documents. In *Proceedings of Int'l Conference on Image Processing*, Vol. 3. Santa Barbara, CA, 13. http://netlab.caltech.edu/publications/Image97.pdf

[8] Hasan Mesut Meral, Bülent Sankur, A. Sumru Özsoy, Tunga Güngör, and Emre Sevinç. 2009. Natural Language Watermarking via Morphosyntactic Alterations. *Comput. Speech Lang.* 23, 1 (Jan. 2009), 107–125.

[9] Jean-Baptiste Michel, Yuan Kui Shen, Aviva Presser Aiden, Adrian Veres, Matthew K. Gray, The Google Books Team, Joseph P. Pickett, Dale Holberg, Dan Clancy, Peter Norvig, Jon Orwant, Steven Pinker, Martin A. Nowak, and Erez Lieberman Aiden. 2010. Quantitative Analysis of Culture Using Millions of Digitized Books. *Science* (2010). http://www.sciencemag.org/content/331/6014/176.full

[10] U. Quasthoff, M. Richter, and C. Biemann. 2006. Corpus Portal for Search in Monolingual Corpora. In *Proceedings of the fifth international conference on Language Resources and Evaluation, LREC*. Genoa, 1799–1802.

[11] Stefano Giovanni Rizzo, Flavio Bertini, and Danilo Montesi. 2016. Content-preserving Text Watermarking Through Unicode Homoglyph Substitution. In *Proceedings of the 20th International Database Engineering & Applications Symposium (IDEAS '16)*. ACM, New York, NY, USA, 97–104.

[12] Mercan Topkara, Cuneyt M. Taskiran, and Edward J. Delp. 2005. Natural Language Watermarking. In *Proceedings of the SPIE International Conference on Security, Steganography, and Watermarking of Multimedia Contents*, Edward J. Delp and Ping W. Wong (Eds.), Vol. 5681. http://www.cs.purdue.edu/homes/mkarahan/ei05_5681_45.pdf

[13] Olga Vybornova and Benoît Macq. 2007. Natural Language Watermarking and Robust Hashing Based on Presuppositional Analysis. In *Proceedings of the IEEE International Conference on Information Reuse and Integration, IRI 2007, 13-15 August 2007, Las Vegas, Nevada, USA*. IEEE Systems, Man, and Cybernetics Society, 177–182.

[14] Alex Wilson, Phil Blunsom, and Andrew D. Ker. 2014. Linguistic Steganography on Twitter: Hierarchical Language Modeling with Manual Interaction. (2014). DOI: http://dx.doi.org/10.1117/12.2039213

[15] Khashayar Yaghmaie and Reza Davarzani. 2009. Farsi Text Watermarking Based on Character Coding. *2009 International Conference on Signal Processing Systems (ICSPS)* 00 (2009), 152–156.

[16] Yue Zhang, Graeme Blackwood, and Stephen Clark. 2012. Syntax-based Word Ordering Incorporating a Large-scale Language Model. In *Proceedings of the 13th Conference of the European Chapter of the Association for Computational Linguistics (EACL '12)*. Association for Computational Linguistics, Stroudsburg, PA, USA, 736–746. http://dl.acm.org/citation.cfm?id=2380816.2380906

Text Steganography with High Embedding Rate: Using Recurrent Neural Networks to Generate Chinese Classic Poetry

Yubo Luo
Department of Electronic Engineering
Tsinghua University
Tsinghua National Laboratory for
Information Science and Technology
Beijing, China 100086
luoyb14@mails.tsinghua.edu.cn

Yongfeng Huang
Department of Electronic Engineering
Tsinghua University
Tsinghua National Laboratory for
Information Science and Technology
Beijing, China 100086
yfhuang@tsinghua.edu.cn

ABSTRACT

We propose a novel text steganography method using RNN Encoder-Decoder structure to generate quatrains, one genre of Chinese poetry. Compared to other text-generation based steganography methods which have either very low embedding rate or flaws in the naturalness of generated texts, our method has higher embedding rate and better text quality. In this paper, we use the LSTM Encoder-Decoder model to generate the first line of a quatrain with a keyword and then generate the following lines one by one. RNN has proved effective in generating poetry, but when applied to steganograpy, poetry quality decreases sharply, because of the redundancy we create to hide information. To overcome this problem, we propose a template-constrained generation method and develop a word-choosing approach using inner-word mutual information. Through a series of experiments, it is proven that our approach outperforms other poetry steganography methods in both embedding rate and poetry quality.

KEYWORDS

text steganography; poetry generation; recurrent neural networks

ACM Reference format:
Yubo Luo and Yongfeng Huang. 2017. Text Steganography with High Embedding Rate: Using Recurrent Neural Networks to Generate Chinese Classic Poetry. In *Proceedings of IH&MMSec '17, June 20–22, 2017, Philadelphia, PA, USA, , 6 pages.*
DOI: http://dx.doi.org/10.1145/3082031.3083240

1 INTRODUCTION

Steganography approaches hide the existence of secret information and are usually classified by the type of multimedia carries that they are based on. As text is the most commonly used media carrier, text steganography is of great value. Generally, text steganography is mainly divided into two categories: format-based methods and content-based ones.

Format-based approaches hide secret information by making changes to the format features of text cover. Early works are based

ACM acknowledges that this contribution was authored or co-authored by an employee, contractor or affiliate of a national government. As such, the Government retains a nonexclusive, royalty-free right to publish or reproduce this article, or to allow others to do so, for Government purposes only.
IH&MMSec '17, June 20–22, 2017, Philadelphia, PA, USA
© 2017 ACM. 978-1-4503-5061-7/17/06...$15.00
DOI: http://dx.doi.org/10.1145/3082031.3083240

on embedding space characters in text [9], altering the space between words [8] or lines [1], etc. Content-based methods are usually based on lexical, syntactic or semantic manipulations. Most early approaches modify the semantic contents of existing texts to hide information, such as using synonym replacement strategy [10], changing the structures of sentences [5], etc. Then, many text-generation-based steganography methods were proposed, such as generating a random sequence [16] or considering context-free grammars [3].

With regard to poetry-based steganography, An information hiding algorithm based on poetry generation was proposed in the literature [18], and Liu et al. [11] proposed a segment-based method. But, they both choose words randomly during the generation process, totally ignoring word collocation and the relationship between lines. Thus, the generated poems lack central ideas and have high possibility of attracting suspicions. Luo et al. [12] proposed an approach based on Markov model. It produces better Ci-poetry but its embedding rate is quite low.

More recently, deep learning methods have emerged as an effective discipline, which considers the poetry generation as a machine translation problem and thus an encoder-decoder model can be used to generate poetry. Zhang and Lapata [19] compressed all previous information into a vector to guide the generation. Wang et al. [13, 14] and Yi et al. [17] use bidirectional recurrent neural network (RNN) with attention mechanism to help capture long time dependency between poetry lines. Wang et al. [15] proposed a planning-based method to ensure the coherence of generated poems.

However, if quatrain generation based on neural networks is applied to steganography directly, the quality of generated poems will decrease sharply, because we have to create redundancy by arranging several candidates for each char-position. This will cause a situation where characters from certain positions which should be regarded as a word cannot be treated as a word. For example, the first two characters of a quatrain line should always be treated as a word. If we happen to choose two characters which never appear within one word, this will definitely jeopardize the quality of generated quatrains.

To handle this issue, we propose a template-constrained generation method. As we know, all quatrains have fix rhythmic pattern, so we can segment all quatrain positions into two-char or three-char prosodic blocks according to rhythmic pattern, then we can obtain a template to guide the generation process. In each block, characters should be regarded as a word rather than separate characters. In order to make sure that randomly selected characters within one block can be treated as a word, we use inner-word mutual information to help us choose candidate characters. In this way, we can ensure that the chosen characters in one block can be treated as a natural word.

The contribution of this paper is two-fold. First, we introduce neural-based poetry generation to steganography, which has much higher embedding rate than previous poetry-based steganography methods. Second, we propose a template-constrained generation method and a word-choosing approach using inner-word mutual information, to alleviate the quality decline caused by information hiding.

2 BACKGROUND

In this section, we first give a brief overview of neural-based poetry generation framework, and then describe how we implement encoder-decoder models to build the poem generator.

2.1 Encoder-Decoder model

Classical Chinese quatrains have strong semantic relevance between adjacent lines. The four-line structure often follows the "beginning, continuation, transition, summary" process [7]. RNN encoder-decoder is well capable of learning the dependency between quatrain lines.

As shown in Figure 1, the entire framework is an attention-based model. Attention mechanism allows a model to automatically find the most relevant parts in the input sequence, then to generate the target sentence [2]. The encoder model first converts the input sequence into hidden states which contain the semantic meaning of each character of the input. Then the decoder model takes hidden states as input to accomplish the generation of target sequence. The task of attention mechanism is to help the decoder find most relevant input by taking into account the decoder's current state and the encoder's hidden states. Thus, the generated target sequence can well focus on specific relevant characters.

The simple RNN model has a severe problem, hard to remember the long time dependency [14]. It is not suitable to deal with quatrains which have four lines. To overcome this issue, we adopt bidirectional Long Short Term Memory (LSTM) model for the encoder and another LSTM for the decoder [13–15, 17]. In this way, the encoder-decoder model can well capture long distance patterns.

2.2 Poem generator

We use attention-based encoder-decoder model to build two modules (word-to-line and line-to-line) to generate a complete poem. A word-to-line module takes a word as input and then ouput a line, but a line-to-line module produces a line according to one line or multi-lines. Yi et al. [17] proposed a three-block system to generate a whole quatrain that was reported to work well in learning the rhyme automatically. However, the structure seems too complicated (four separate models in total). Wang et al. [15] only uses one model for both keyword input and line input, which will not work well when the input is a short word, as most training pairs are line-to-line pairs. Thus, we adopt two separate models, one for word-to-line and the other for line-to-line.

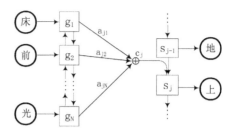

Figure 1: Encoder-Decoder model.

When generating a poem, we first use the word-to-line module to generate the first line of the poem according to the keyword that a user inputs. Next, the line-to-line module takes the first line as input to generate the seconde line, and then to generate the third and forth line according to all previously generated lines.

2.2.1 Line-to-line Module. We first introduce the line-to-line module. We assume that we have already obtained the first line l_1. Then, we will input l_1 to generate the second line l_2. The inputs for generating l_3 and l_4 are $l_1 l_2$ and $l_1 l_2 l_3$, respectively.

Let $X = (x_1, x_2, \ldots, x_N)$ be the input line. At time i, the hidden state for encoder is computed as Eq.(1)-Eq.(2):

$$h_i = f_{LSTM}(h_{i-1}, x_i), \tag{1}$$

$$g_i = [h_i; h'_i], \tag{2}$$

where h and h' are the forward and backward hidden states in the encoder, x is the input, and g represents the combined hidden state for the encoder.

As mentioned in Section 2.1, we use an attention-based bidirectional encoder-decoder model to build the line-to-line module. After the hidden state g of the encoder is calculated, it merges with the attention vector a_{ij} into context vector c_j. It is a_{ij} that helps the decoder to find the most relevant parts from the input. The context vector c_j is calculated by:

$$c_j = \sum_{i=1}^{N} \alpha_{ij} g_i, \tag{3}$$

where a_{ij} is the 'attention', that at j_{th} generation step the decoder has, to the i_{th} character of the input. The attention vector α_{ij} is computed by:

$$\alpha_{ij} = \frac{exp(e_{ij})}{\sum_{k=1}^{N} exp(e_{jk})}, \tag{4}$$

$$e_{ij} = v_a^\top tanh(W_a \cdot s_{j-1} + U_a \cdot g_i), \tag{5}$$

where s_{j-1} is the hidden state of decoder at the $(j-1)_{th}$ generation step; v_a, W_a and U_a are matrices that will be optimized in the training process [6, 14].

Finally, at the j_{th} generation step, the output y_j and hidden vector s_j are formulated by:

$$s_j = f(s_{j-1}, y_{j-1}, c_j), \tag{6}$$

$$y_j = p(y_{j-1}, s_j, c_j), \tag{7}$$

where, f(·) and p(·) are update functions determined by the model structre [14]. The output vector y_j is what we mainly work on to hide secret information, and we will discuss it detailly in next section.

2.2.2 Word-to-line Module. Basically, the encoder-decoder models for line-to-line and word-to-line are the same. During the training process, the input sequence, no matter it is a word or a line, will be converted into the same vector space. Because current generation systems are all based on characters, keywords are much shorter than lines. Besides, the majority of training data are line-to-line pairs, if we only use one model to deal with both keyword input and line input, it will not work well when the input is a short word [17].

Thus, we train word-to-line pairs in a separate word-to-line module. Of course, if we start the training of word-to-line module from scratch, it will not capture enough semantic relations, duo to the lack of word-to-line pairs. In practice, we start the training of word-to-line module from a pre-trained line-to-line module.

3 STEGANOGRAPHY SCHEME

The steganography part begins when the poem generator produces Y, the vector set of a poem line. Let us denote the line as $Y = (y_1, y_2, \ldots, y_N)$, where N is the character number this line contains. Each vector y_i contains the information about the probability of each character in the vocabulary being the generated one for a certain char-position. Thus, we can hide information by selecting several candidates for each char-position, coding them, and finally choosing one candidate according to the secret message.

3.1 Framework of poetry steganography

There are three steps in poetry steganography, as shown in Figure 2. The first step is to set parameters that regulate poetry generation. The second step is to use the poem generator discussed in section 2.2 to generate poetry lines, and we hide information in step 3, by coding candidates and choosing one character based on secret message.

Different from Ci-poetry which has many tonal patterns, 5-char and 7-char quatrains both only have four common used patterns [7], from which we randomly choose one pattern for generation. *Info* is the secret message that we want to hide in the stego-quatrain. In practice, *Info* will be converted into bit stream to guide character selection. *Key* is the keyword we need to input into the word-to-line model to generate the first line. *Size* is the size of candidate pool, in other words, the maximum number of candidates we can select for coding. Obviously, *Size* is the determinating factor of the embedding rate. The larger *Size* is, the higher the embedding rate will be.

In step 2, poem generator produces a poem line Y which contains N vectors. N is the number of characters contained in one line. y_i contains the information about the probability of each character in the vocabulary being the next generated one. For example, for $y_i = (p_1, p_2, \ldots, p_{|V|})$, where $|V|$ is the vocabulary size, p_j means the probability of the j_{th} character in the vocabulary being next generated one.

Step 3 is the most critical part of our steganography system. For each y_i, we first filter out all characters that do not meet the

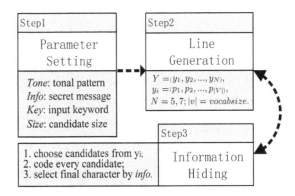

Figure 2: The framework of steganography system.

tone regulation, then select the most probable top-*Size* candidates and finally code these candidates by assigning each one a code (e.g. Huffman code). Next, the character whose code matches the beginning bits of *info* will be the final chosen character. In this way, the matched beginning bits of *info* are hidden in this character.

3.2 Improved char-choosing method

However, there is a severe problem during char-choosing process. If we choose characters for each char-position separately, the generated line is very likely nonsense, especially when *Size* is large. Because, the larger *Size* is, the more likely characters in certain positions can not be treated as a word. Next, we will discuss how to solve this problem.

3.2.1 Templated-constrained generation. When people read a 5-char quatrain line, they will automatically segment the line into the form of cc/ccc, and $cc/cc/ccc$ for a 7-char quatrain line. In fact, Yu et al. [18] and Wang et al. [11] built their poetry steganography system based on this segmentation method.

Thus, it is crucial that these small blocks (cc or ccc) should be meaningful when treated as a word. Actually, this is similar to the word collocaiton in English language where collocation are words that like to hang out together. In Chinese, some characters often locate together in the same block, while some do not. Thus, we should try to avoid characters who do not like to hang out together being generated in the same block.

Usually, neural-based poetry generation chooses the character with the highest probability [13, 14] at each char-position, or uses beam search algorithm to help choose characters [15, 17]. But, if we directly choose the candidates from the most probable top-n characters for each char-position, most generated blocks (cc and ccc) are nonsense when treated as a word. As a result, the quality of generated quatrains will decrease greatly.

To solve this problem, we propose a template-constrained generation approach. For the first char-position of a block, we prepare candidates directly from the most probable top-n characters, then code candidates and finally choose one character based on *info*. We denote the chosen character for this position as c_{pre}. Then, when we come to the second or third char-position of a block (cc/ccc), we no longer choose candidates only based on their probabilities.

Instead, we reorder y_i by taking into account the relationship between c_{pre} and the potential candidates in y_i. Next, we will introduce how to reorder y_i by using inner-word mutual information.

3.2.2 Inner-word mutual information. Mutual information has been widely used in natural language processing [4, 12]. Luo et al. [12] used mutual information to roughly evaluate the quality of generated poetry, and Church and Hanks [4] used mutual information to estimate word association norms from corpora. Thus, we use mutual information between c_{pre} and characters in y_i to reorder y_i. The higher the mutual information between c_{pre} and a certain character is, the upper position that character will be reordered to.

The problem we need to solve is to make blocks (cc and ccc) more like normal words. So, we use mutual information calculated within a word to help reorder potential candidates, which we call inner-word mutual information, and it is calculated by:

$$I(x, y) = log \frac{p(x, y)}{p(x)p(y)}, \qquad (8)$$

where we estimate $p(x)$ and $p(y)$ by counting how many times x and y appear in corpus, and normalizing by N, the size of the corpus. Similarly, $p(x, y)$ is estimated by the number of times that x is followed by y in the cc^1 block, and normalizing by N [4].

In this way, the proposed inner-word mutual information can ensure that generated characters in one block are more look like natural words. Now, we can enjoy the high embedding rate achieved by neural-based methods, but without worrying about the severe decline in the quality of generated poems.

3.3 Steganography example

In this section, we give a simple example to show how information is hidden during the process of poetry generation.

First, we need to determine the parameters mentioned in Figure 2. We take a 5-char quatrain line as the example. The initial parameters are set as follows:

- *Tone*: PPPZZ,PZZPP.ZZPPZ,PPZZP [2];
- *Info*: 0110110001...(converted from 'love');
- *Key*: 春风 (the word input in the word-to-line module);
- *Size*: 4 (the size of candidate pool).

At the beginning, we segment *PPPZZ* into *PP/PZZ* which will be used as the template to regulate the char-choosing process. Then, the keyword 春风 is input into the word-to-line module to generate the first line which is denoted as $Y_1 = (y_1, y_2, y_3, y_4, y_5)$. For the first char-position y_1, the tone is P, so we filter out all characters of y_i whose tone is not P and select the most probable top-4 characters as candidates. Huffman coding algorithm is then applied to assign each candidate a code (see Table 1, col 1). As the beginning bits of *Info* are 01, 青 is chosen for this char-position.

For the second char-position y_2, we first filter out characters whose tone is not P, and then we reorder y_2 by calculating the inner-word mutual information between 青 and characters in y_2. In practice, we will not do the calculation between 青 and all characters in y_2, because this may cause us to choose these characters

Table 1: Details of char-choosing in steganography

Candidates									
Char1		Char2		Char3		Char4		Char5	
萧	00	葭	00	鸣	00	雨	00	绿	00
青	01	帆	01	迷	01	雪	01	碧	01
一	10	风	10	生	10	草	10	动	10
归	11	鸣	11	烟	11	沙	11	细	11

who are irrelevant to the input keyword but only has a high mutual information with 青. To avoid this problem, we actually only do the calculation for the most probable top-M characters, where M is slightly larger[3] than *Size*. After y_2 is reordered, we again use Huffman coding algorithm to assign each candidate a code (see Table 1, col 2) and finally choose 风 according to *Info* whose beginning bits now are 10.

For the third char-position y_3, as it is the beginning char-position of a new block in the template (cc/ccc), its char-choosing process is exactly the same as y_1. Similarly, y_4 and y_5 follow the same procedure as y_2. Based on *Info*, the final generated stego-line is 青风烟雨碧.

Next, we input the generated line l_1 into the line-to-line module to obtain Y_2. We follow the same procedure as Y_1 to get the second generated line l_2. Then, $l_1 l_2$ is input into the line-to-line module to obtain Y_3, based on which the third line l_3 is generated. Finally, $l_1 l_2 l_3$ is responsible for the generation of the last line l_4.

In fact, we can also hide information during the keyword-choosing process, the same way as char-choosing part. If we suppose that there are m keywords in the keyword list, we can hide extra $log_2 m$ bits of information during the keyword-choosing process.

When the receiver obtains the stego-quatrain, he only needs the trained neural models and the keyword list that the sender uses, to extract the secret information, by following the same char-choosing procedure. The only difference between information hiding and extraction is that the sender chooses characters according to *Info* while the reciever obtains *Info* according to characters.

As shown in Figure 2, there are 4 initial parameters which need to be determined to start the generation process, including *Tone*, *Info*, *Key* and *Size*. For the receiver, *Tone* can be directly told by the received quatrain. *Info* is what the receiver wants to obtain. We suppose that the keyword list has m keywords and *Size* has n possible values, which means that there are $m \cdot n$ combinations in total. If the keyword and the value of *Size* that the receiver uses are not the same as the sender's setting, either the extraction process can not be finished, or the extracted message is nonsense. In other words, only the right combination can extract the right message. Thus, the receiver only needs to try out all combinations to extract the hidding information.

If the receiver can not afford too much time complexity, it is recommended to use a small keyword list and set *Size* to a fixed value. In short, m and n are flexible to be adjusted based on the user's own circumstance.

---

[1]The block of ccc could be segmented into the form of c/cc or cc/c. We count two characters' co-occurrence only when they appear together in cc.
[2]There are two types of tone, P and Z, which are 平 and 仄, respectively.

---

[3]Empirically, M is set to 1.5 or 2 times of *Size*. M is a pre-determined parameter by both the sender and receiver, so it is fixed during all stego-communications.

4 EXPERIMENTS

4.1 Dataset

There are many classical Chinese poetry corpora on the Internet, but quatrains written in different periods have different styles. So, we only collected quatrains from Tang dynasty. The corpus we used contains 74,474 quatrains in total, and we randomly selected 2,000 quatrains as validation set, and the rest as training set.

For the word-to-line module, we selected the top-1000 most frequently used words as our keyword list, and for each word, we selected 150 lines that contain this word to build word-to-line pairs [17]. For the line-to-line module, we extracted 3 line-to-line pairs from each quatrain. For example, from a quatrain $L=(l_1, l_2, l_3, l_4)$, we can get three pairs, $<l_1, l_2>, <l_1 l_2, l_3>$ and $<l_1 l_2 l_3, l_4>$ [15].

4.2 Training and decoding

During the training, we selected the top-8000 frequent characters as our vocabulary which is shared by both input and target sides. We built our model based on Keras. The word embedding layer has 512 units, and both the encoder and decoder contain 512 hidden units. The model was trained with Adagrad algorithm, where the minibatch size was set to 128. We selected the final model according to the loss on the validation set [14, 15]. For the line-to-line module, we trained 5-char and 7-char quatrains on one model, but for the word-to-line module, we trained 5-char and 7-char quatrains on two separate models.

In the decoding, we are supposed to input the generated line into the line-to-line model. However, due to the process of information hiding, we may select a character who has low probability. For example, when *Size* is 32, the final chosen character might be the one whose probability only ranks 32_{th}. These low ranking characters actually, to some extent, have deviated from the top ranking character in the meaning. The larger *Size* is, the more likely the final chosen character will deviate from the input keyword in its meaning. In practice, we do not input the original generated line into line-to-line module to avoid the deviation. Instead, for each line l_i, we forge a line l'_i whose characters are all selected from the top-1 candidate. The forged line l'_i will be input into line-to-line module rather than l_i. In this way, the whole quatrain is more likely to reveal the meaning of the input keyword.

5 EVALUATIONS

To evaluate a steganography system based on text generation, there are two important factors: one is the naturalness of generated text; the other is the embedding rate. Next, we evaluate our proposed method by comparison between different poetry steganography algorithms in these two factors.

5.1 Human evaluation

To accurately evaluate the quality of machine generated poetry is a notorious problem. Most researchers rely on human evaluation, in which experts are invited to evaluate generated poems with regard to their fluency, poeticness, meaning, etc. [14, 15, 17, 19]. However, our system is steganography-oriented, and our goal is to generate poems that will not attract suspicions from the third party. Thus,

we use the the famous Turing Test to evaluate our model, which is also adopted by [13, 15].

We designed a questionnaire which contains quatrains from four sources. The subject was asked to judge whether these poems were created by machine or written by a poet. According to how many machine-generated poems are identified as human created, we can evaluate the naturalness of poems generated by a specific steganography method.

We chose two poetry steganography methods and human created poems as baselines. All methods based on machine generation utilized the same corpus and parameter setting[4]. We selected eight poems from each source, containing four 5-char quatrains and four 7-char quatrains. So, each questionnaire includes 32 poems.

- Segment-based method [11]
- Markov-based method [12]
- Poet created poems
- Our method

To make the evaluation results more convincing. Subjects are all master or PhD students who are well educated. Moreover, we cleaned [5] returned questionnaires and obtained 20 valid samples out of 33 returned ones. The results are shown in Table 2.

Table 2: Human evaluation

	Identified as H	Identified as M
Segment-based	21.3%	78.7%
Markov-based	33.8%	66.2%
Our method	34.3%	65.7%
Poet	63.1%	36.9%

H: human-created, M: machine-generated

We can clearly see that, our method weakly passed the Turing test whose criterion is to fool people in no less than 30% of asked questions.

5.2 Embedding rate

Embedding rate is highly related to how much information we can hide in a stego-text. Previous methods have either very low embedding rate or flaws in the quality of generated texts. For example, the Markov-based method [12] can produce poems comparable to us in poem quality, but it has low embedding rate. As for the segment-based method [11] which has high embedding rate, its poem quality is far behind us.

The high embedding rate of our approach stems form that it is char-based generation, in which we can hide information at each char-position. Actually, apart from the generation process of the poem body, information can also be hidden when we choose the initial keyword from the keyword list. The keyword list we used in the experiment contains 1,000 words, so the embedding rate can be calculated by:

---

[4]The size of candidate pool for Markov-based and our neural-based method were both set to 32.
[5]Questionnaires that were finished in less than 2 minutes or more than 30 minutes were excluded. We also did not take into consideration the ones whose accuracy is below 50%.

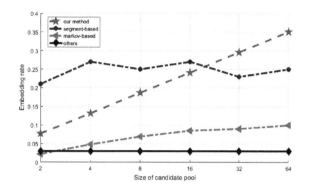

Figure 3: The comparison of embedding rate between different methods.

$$ER = \frac{4N \times log_2 Size + log_2 1000}{4(N+1) \times 16}, \qquad (9)$$

where *ER* is the embedding rate, *Size* is the size of candidate pool, *N* is the number of characters contained in one poem line. The comparison of embedding rate between different methods is shown in Figure 3. Obviously, our method outperforms other approaches and the embedding rate can reach about 35.0% (when *Size*=64, N=7).

5.3 Generation example

Finally, in Table 3, we show a 5-char quatrain generated by neural-based steganography. According to its poetic meaning, we name it as 'Returning Night', which is 归夜 in Chinese.

Table 3: A 5-char quatrain generated by neural-based steganography

归夜	Returning Night
风窗烟树中	Out the window stood the tree in mist
柔静雨光斑	Soft and quiet is the shining rain
夜里吹生下	Playing the flute in the night
归人乱浪宽	Traveling back from wide waves

6 CONCLUSION

In this paper we have presented a method that uses neural-based poetry generation to hide information. Attention-based neural model is the state-of-the-art approach in poetry generation. Even though it can produce poems that are coherent and semantically consistent, directly applying it to steganography does not work well. Thus, we propose a template-constrained generation method and use inner-word mutual information to alleviate the quality decline caused by steganography. Experimental results show that our method yields stego-poems with high quality, comparable to the state-of-the-art poetry steganography, but has a much higher embedding rate. In the future, we would like to continually improve the quality of generated poems, and explore poetry steganography using other genres, e.g. English sonnets or even normal-style texts.

7 ACKNOWLEDGEMENT

We thank all reviewers for their constructive reviews. Many thanks to Yixuan Wang for the translation of poem exapmle. This work is supported by the National Natural Science Foundation of China (Grant Nos. U1536207, U1536115 and U1536113).

REFERENCES

[1] A.M. Alattar and O.M. Alattar. 2004. Watermarking electronic text documents containing justified paragraphs and irregular line spacing. *Electronic Imaging 2004. International Society for Optics and Photonics* (2004), 685–695.

[2] D. Bahdanau, K. Cho, and Y. Bengio. 2014. Neural machine translation by jointly learning to align and translate. *arXiv preprint arXiv:1409.0473* (2014).

[3] M. Chapman and G. Davida. 1997. Hiding the hidden: A software system for concealing ciphertext as innocuous text. *International Conference on Information and Communications Security. Springer Berlin Heidelberg* (1997), 335–345.

[4] K.W. Church and P. Hanks. 1990. Word association norms, mutual information, and lexicography. *Computational linguistics* 6, 1 (1990), 22–29.

[5] J. Cong, D. Zhang, and M. Pan. 2010. Chinese Text Information Hiding Based on Paraphrasing Technology. *Information Science and Management Engineering (ISME), 2010 International Conference of. IEEE* (2010), 39–42.

[6] S. Ghosh, O. Vinyals, B. Strope, S. Roy, T. Dean, and L. Heck. 2016. Contextual LSTM (CLSTM) models for Large scale NLP tasks. *arXiv preprint arXiv:1602.06291* (2016).

[7] J. He, M. Zhou, and L. Jiang. 2012. Generating Chinese Classical Poems with Statistical Machine Translation Models. *AAAI* (2012).

[8] Y.W. Kim, K.A. Moon, and I.S. Oh. 2003. A Text Watermarking Algorithm based on Word Classification and Inter-word Space Statistics. *ICDAR* (2003), 775–779.

[9] I.S. Lee and W.H. Tsai. 2008. Secret communication through web pages using special space codes in HTML files. *International Journal of Applied Science and Engineering* 6, 2 (2008), 141–149.

[10] Y.L. Liu, X.M. Sun, G. Gan, and W. Hong. 2007. An efficient linguistic steganography for Chinese text. *IEEE International Conference on Multimedia and Expo* (2007), 2094–2097.

[11] Y.C. Liu, J. Wang, Z.B. Wang, Q.F. Qu, and S. Yu. 2016. A technique of high embedding rate text steganography based on whole poetry of song dynasty. *International Conference on Cloud Computing and Security* (2016), 178–189.

[12] Y.B. Luo, Y.F. Huang, F.F. Li, and C.C. Chang. 2016. Text Steganography Based on Ci-poetry Generation Using Markov Chain Model. *KSII Transactions on Internet and Information Systems* 10, 9 (2016), 4568–4584.

[13] Q.X. Wang, T.Y. Luo, and D. Wang. 2016. Can Machine Generate Traditional Chinese Poetry? A Feigenbaum Test. *Advances in Brain Inspired Cognitive Systems: 8th International Conference, BICS 2016* (2016), 34–46.

[14] Q.X. Wang, T.Y. Luo, and D. Wang. 2016. Chinese song iambics generation with neural attention-based model. *arXiv preprint arXiv:1604.06274* (2016).

[15] Z. Wang, W. He, H. Wu, H.Y. Wu, W. Li, H.F. Wang, and E.H. Chen. 2016. Chinese poetry generation with planning based neural network. *arXiv preprint arXiv:1610.09889* (2016).

[16] P. Wayner. 1992. Mimic functionsWayner P. *Cryptologia* 16, 3 (1992), 193–214.

[17] X. Yi, R. Li, and M. Sun. 2016. Generating chinese classical poems with rnn encoder-decoder. *arXiv preprint arXiv:1604.01537* (2016).

[18] Z.S. Yu and L.S. Huang. 2009. High Embedding Ratio Text Steganography by Ci-poetry of the Song Dynasty. *Journal of Chinese Information Processing* 23, 4 (2009), 55–62.

[19] X. Zhang and M. Lapata. 2014. Chinese Poetry Generation with Recurrent Neural Networks. *EMNLP* (2014), 670–680.

Audio Reversible Watermarking Scheme in the intDCT Domain with Modified Prediction Error Expansion

Alejandra Menendez-Ortiz*
Claudia Feregrino-Uribe
m.menendez@inaoep.mx
cferegrino@inaoep.mx
INAOE
Luis Enrique Erro #1
Sta. Ma. Tonantzintla, Puebla 72840, Mexico

Jose Juan Garcia-Hernandez
jjuan@tamps.cinvestav.mx
CINVESTAV
Parque Cientifico y Tecnologico TECNOTAM - Km. 5.5
carretera Cd. Victoria-Solo La Marina
Cd. Victoria, Tamaulipas 87130, Mexico

ABSTRACT

Reversible watermarking schemes (RWS) allow the restoration of the original signals after the watermarks are extracted. Most RWS for audio signals use time-domain for information hiding, although their transparency is hard to maintain for high embedding capacities. Some audio RWS use the frequency domain to improve transparency; however, their embedding capacity is lower than that of time-domain schemes. In this manuscript a RWS for audio signals is proposed, it differs from other schemes that work with the int-DCT domain in the use of auditory masking properties, which are exploited to improve transparency, and the increase on embedding capacity is explored through a modified prediction error expansion (PEE). The payload capacity is 27.5 kbps with a degradation over -2 ODG, which are adequate results for practical audio applications. A generalized multi-bit expansion is proposed and experimental results suggest that higher expansion factors improve transparency.

CCS CONCEPTS

•**Information systems** →*Multimedia information systems;*

KEYWORDS

Audio watermarking, auditory masking, multi-bit expansion, reversible watermarking

ACM Reference format:
Alejandra Menendez-Ortiz, Claudia Feregrino-Uribe, and Jose Juan Garcia-Hernandez. 2017. Audio Reversible Watermarking Scheme in the int-DCT Domain with Modified Prediction Error Expansion. In *Proceedings of IH&MMSec '17, Philadelphia, PA, USA, June 20–22, 2017,* 6 pages.
DOI: http://dx.doi.org/10.1145/3082031.3083246

1 INTRODUCTION

In application scenarios, such as in the military and medical fields, treatment of voice disorders or in systems for aviation warning

---

*Corresponding author.

IH&MMSec '17, June 20-22, 2017, Philadelphia, PA, USA
© 2017 ACM. ISBN 978-1-4503-5061-7/17/06...$15.00.
DOI: http://dx.doi.org/10.1145/3082031.3083246

[1, 2, 24], it is essential that the audio signals do not suffer any loss of data, therefore the need of RWS. The objective difference grade (ODG), recommended by ITU-R B.S.1387 [26], is a metric used to measure the degradation of audio signals, and an acceptable value for the applications previously mentioned is -2 ODG.

RWS were first proposed for images, and recent schemes aim to improve the trade-off between transparency and embedding capacity. Thodi and Rodriguez [27] presented the original PEE for images in spatial domain where the idea of embedding in the prediction errors is introduced. Ou et. al [22] present a PEE scheme in spatial domain that exploits the correlation of prediction errors to construct a 2D histogram where watermark insertion takes place.

RWS for audio signals have been less explored than for images. Most RWS for audio deal with signals in the time domain, such as [28] that uses amplitude expansion (AE), Bradley and Alattar [3], Nishimura [19, 20], and Huo et. al [15] present adaptations of PEE. Garcia-Hernandez [7] adapts an interpolation error expansion strategy to audio, where interpolated values are calculated from previous and consecutive samples to obtain the interpolation errors, a histogram from the latter is constructed and the watermark is inserted in the errors within an embedding region.

There are RWS for audio in the frequency domain, and all use the intDCT. Huang et. al [13] propose a scheme that uses AE, and underflow and overflow problems are addressed in a post-processing stage that optimizes embedding, however it does not totally solve these problems. Chen et al. [5] improve the work in [13] with the introduction of two embedding strategies, namely difference expansion and PEE. Instead of embedding directly in the amplitudes, they insert in the differences and prediction errors, respectively. However, these schemes have problems when underflow and overflow occur, specially if the payload capacity is to be increased. Huang et. al [14] improve their previous work by adaptively selecting the coefficients by estimating the errors that would be produce, then the errors with a lower distortion are selected for embedding; a sorting table is constructed to control which coefficients carry watermark data. The three schemes are designed for integrity verification, therefore the bit-rate capacity tested is lower than RWS for audio in time domain.

In this work, a RWS for audio signals is proposed. It reduces perceptual impact by exploiting the auditory masking properties of the signals, and increases the embedding capacity through a modification of PEE. This scheme improves the idea presented by Menendez-Ortiz et. al [18] by using the psychoacoustic characteristics of audio signals, where a masking threshold is obtained to select the frequencies that better mask the distortions. In addition, the proposed scheme uses a modification to PEE that increases the expansion of the prediction errors in order to insert more information in each coefficient. The combined use of psychoacoustic characteristics and a modified PEE allows the increase in embedding capacity while maintaining adequate transparency for practical applications.

The rest of the document is organized in the following way. Section 2 describes the proposed RWS for audio signals. Section 3 presents the results obtained with the proposed scheme. Section 4 gives a discussion on these results; and finally, Section 5 outlines the conclusions and future work.

2 PROPOSED AUDIO REVERSIBLE WATERMARKING SCHEME

The proposed RWS is divided in two processes, namely encoding and decoding, as depicted in Figure 1. This strategy assumes that the signals received by the decoding process did not suffer any modification. The particular steps in each process are explained below.

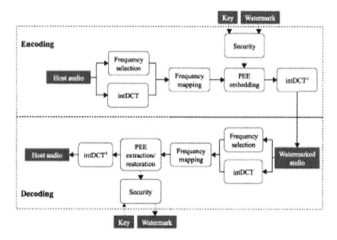

Figure 1: Block diagram of the proposed scheme.

2.1 intDCT transform

The intDCT is an approximation of the DCT-IV, which is calculated using the fast intMDCT algorithm proposed by [12]. This strategy divides the transform matrix in five sub-matrices, the multiplication by each of the five matrices is done through a lifting stage with a rounding operation, which produces integer results.

2.2 Frequency selection and masking threshold

The underlying strategy in our proposed scheme is to select frequency components from the audio signals that are less noticeable for human listeners, because of the imperceptibility of these frequencies it is expected that modifications to them remain unnoticed. Auditory masking, depicted in Figure 2, occurs when one faint but audible sound (Masked sounds S_1, and S_2) is made inaudible in the presence of a louder audible sound (Masker S_0) [17].

To determine which frequencies are masked by a predominant frequency, the masking threshold has to be obtained. The predominant frequency 'masks' other frequencies near it, therefore, insertion of a watermark can be done in the masked frequencies without audible differences. The masking threshold is calculated from the Fourier spectra and all the frequencies that fall under it are candidates for embedding. There are various audio coding strategies, most of them based on filter banks to separate audio components and reduce its representation [25]; however the most common audio encoding method is MPEG, for which all standards use the masking threshold to maintain quantization noise [9], for this reason the masking threshold is used to select frequencies for embedding.

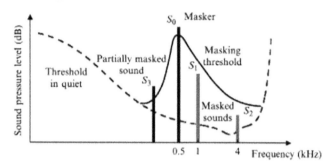

Figure 2: Masking threshold in auditory masking [17].

2.3 Frequency mapping

RWS require an integer representation of the samples so that no information is lost because of rounding errors. The most common frequency transforms map real-valued samples to complex-valued coefficients (for FFT), and to real-valued coefficients (for DCT). Any transformation that maps a time-domain integer signal to a frequency-domain integer representation could be used. In the literature there are several integer FFT strategies, such as [4, 21]; these strategies could be used for data hiding and the frequency mapping step could be avoided. However, in this scheme the use of the intDCT transform is preferred. To the best of our knowledge, RWS for audio that use a frequency-domain representation use the intDCT transform; to be in accordance the intDCT domain is also adopted in our scheme. Therefore, there is the need to map or to determine a correspondence between Fourier and intDCT frequencies.

The FFT spectrum of an N-point signal has $N/2$ frequency components, each corresponding to basis functions that linearly increase in frequency. The intDCT of the same signal yields N transform coefficients that correspond to cosine basis functions that also linearly increase in frequency, but with periods that increase in $1/2$ steps [23]. This means that, if the frequency f_i is at the i-th coefficient in the FFT spectrum, then f_i corresponds to the $2i$-th coefficient in the intDCT domain.

Suppose a watermark of length K is to be embedded into an audio signal. The masking threshold is calculated, and K FFT frequencies are selected as candidate ones, these candidate frequencies are at indexes $\{i_1, i_2, \cdots, i_K\}$, and the corresponding intDCT frequencies are at indexes $\{2i_1, 2i_2, \cdots, 2i_K\}$. For natural audio signals, it is expected that the highest frequencies fall under the masking threshold.

2.4 Security

After the FFT frequencies have been mapped to the intDCT domain, the next step is to insert the watermark into the selected coefficients. However, to ensure the security of the scheme, the watermark should be ciphered prior embedding based on a secret key. The security step of the proposed schemes uses an Advanced Encryption Standard (AES) algorithm, and a key of 256 bits is recommended. After the extraction of the embedded watermark, which is a cyphered version of the data, it must be de-cyphered with the same key as the one used during encoding, and this security step uses an AES algorithm.

2.5 Encoding

PEE was originally proposed for images [27]. The general idea of this strategy is that watermark bits can be embedded in the least significant bit (LSB) of the error calculated between an original sample and its predicted value. To avoid loss of data, instead of the direct substitution of the LSB used by classical watermarking schemes, PEE expands the error and then inserts the corresponding bit in the LSB.

2.5.1 PEE with multi-bit (MB) expansion. An audio signal $\mathbf{x}[n]$, $\{n = 1, 2, \cdots, N\}$ is received, and divided into non overlapping windows of size L_r, the intDCT transform of each window is obtained. The watermark to be embedded is denoted as $\mathbf{w}[k]$, where $k = \{1, 2, \cdots, K\}$, and K is its size. It is assumed that coefficients at odd indexes are more similar to other coefficients at odd indexes, and coefficients at even indexes are more similar to other coefficients at even indexes, as highlighted in [5]. The prediction value of the ith coefficient, denoted by $\hat{X}[i]$ is calculated as:

$$\hat{X}[i] = \lfloor (\mathbf{X}[i - 2] + \mathbf{X}[i - 4])/2 \rfloor, \tag{1}$$

and the prediction-error, denoted as p, is given by:

$$p = \mathbf{X}[i] - \hat{X}[i], \tag{2}$$

where i are the indexes of mapped intDCT frequencies. In the classical PEE strategy, only one bit per sample is inserted; however, the proposed algorithm uses multi-bit expansion, where multiple bits can be inserted in one sample. The proposed modification inserts two bits per frequency, and the prediction-error p is expanded as follows:

$$p_w = 4 \times p + (2 \times \mathbf{w}[k]) + \mathbf{w}[k + 1]. \tag{3}$$

The watermarked intDCT coefficients are obtained by:

$$\mathbf{Y}[i] = \hat{X}[i] + p_w. \tag{4}$$

The watermarked signal in its time domain representation is obtained by applying the inverse intDCT transform to Y.

This can be generalized for the insertion of l bits per frequency, the prediction-error is expanded by an 'expansion factor' ($e_f = 2^l$) in the following way:

$$p_w = e_f \times p + (\lfloor e_f/2 \rfloor \times \mathbf{w}[k]) + $$
$$(\lfloor e_f/4 \rfloor \times \mathbf{w}[k + 1]) + \cdots + \mathbf{w}[k + l - 1]) \tag{5}$$

2.5.2 Multilevel (ML) embedding. Multi-embedding, also known as multilevel embedding [6] was first explored for audio signals in [7]. The idea of this strategy is to apply the embedding algorithm in multiple levels, chaining the outputs of one level as the inputs of the next level. Suppose a host signal $\mathbf{x}$ is processed by the first level embedding, producing signal $\mathbf{y}$; then this signal is processed by a second level embedding, producing signal $\mathbf{y}'$, and so on.

2.6 Decoding

A watermarked signal $\mathbf{y}[n]$ is received and divided in windows in the same way as in the encoding process, the intDCT transform of each window is calculated, and the decoding process is applied to these transform coefficients. The frequencies for extraction are determined using the same masking threshold criteria as in the encoding.

2.6.1 Multi-bit extraction. The prediction value $\hat{Y}[i]$ is calculated as:

$$\hat{Y}[i] = \lfloor (\mathbf{Y}[i - 2] + \mathbf{Y}[i - 4])/2 \rfloor, \tag{6}$$

and the expanded prediction-error is given by:

$$p_w = \mathbf{Y}[i] - \hat{Y}[i], \tag{7}$$

where i represents the indexes of the frequencies in the intDCT domain. The original prediction-error p is obtained by:

$$p = \lfloor p_w/4 \rfloor, \tag{8}$$

and the watermark word, w_o, that contains 2 bits is extracted as:

$$w_o = p_w - 4 \times p, \qquad \mathbf{w}[k] = \mathrm{mod}(w_o, 2), \tag{9}$$
$$\mathbf{w}[k + 1] = \mathrm{mod}(\lfloor w_o/2 \rfloor, 2).$$

The original intDCT coefficients are restored by:

$$\mathbf{X}[i] = \hat{Y}[i] + p. \tag{10}$$

The original sample values in the time domain are obtained by applying the inverse intDCT transform to the restored intDCT coefficients.

The generalized extraction of l bits, with $e_f = 2^l$, is done in the following way:

$$p = \lfloor p_w/e_f \rfloor, \tag{11}$$

and the watermark word is extracted as:

$$w_o = p_w - e_f \times p, \tag{12}$$
$$\mathbf{w}[k] = \mathrm{mod}(w_o, 2),$$
$$\mathbf{w}[k + 1] = \mathrm{mod}(\lfloor w_o/2 \rfloor, 2),$$
$$\vdots$$
$$\mathbf{w}[k + l - 1] = \mathrm{mod}(\lfloor w_o/2^l \rfloor, 2).$$

2.6.2 Multilevel extraction. Multilevel extraction applies the original extraction process of PEE in multiple levels, in inverse order as the multilevel embedding. It is assumed that the decoder processes the signal the same number of levels as in the encoding process. Suppose a watermarked signal $\mathbf{y}'$ is received, a first level extraction is applied, producing signal $\mathbf{y}$; a second level extraction is applied to obtain the original signal $\mathbf{x}$. In the extraction process, the same number of levels used in embedding has to be used to obtain the correct results.

3 EXPERIMENTAL RESULTS

To test the proposed audio RWS, experiments with 3 databases were performed, namely the Music Audio Benchmark (MAB) of the University of Dortmund [11], the Ballroom (Ball) dataset [10], and a dataset compiled by our research group (Ours). The test audio signals from all the datasets have CD quality, quantized at 16 bits with a sampling frequency of 44.1 kHz, and each dataset has audio signals of various musical genres. The duration of the audio signals in each dataset is 10, 30, and 20 seconds, respectively. The MAB dataset has 1886 songs, the Ball dataset has 698 songs, and the dataset by our research group is a dataset with 50 songs constructed for fast testing.

The proposed scheme using PEE with multi-bit expansion inserting two bits per frequency was tested for the mentioned datasets. The payload inserted was 27,520 bps (bits per second), the ODG values were measured between host and watermarked signals. It is worth to mention that the free basic implementation of the PEAQ algorithm [16] is used to obtain the ODG results, therefore they are not exactly $\in [0, -4]$. Table 1 presents the median (med), interquartile range (IQR), minimum, and maximum ODG values. As it can be seen, all the median ODG values meet the transparency constrain of -2, which demonstrates that for the tested payload, the proposed scheme can be used in practical applications. Figure 3

Table 1: Embedding* ODG results for the tested datasets.

DS	Genre	ODG			
		Med	IQR	Min	Max
Ball	ChaChaCha	−1.0	0.6	−2.1	−0.4
	Jive	−1.0	0.6	−1.9	−0.5
	Quickstep	−0.9	0.4	−1.7	0.0
	Rumba	−0.9	0.3	−1.9	−0.4
	Tango	−0.9	0.9	−2.2	−0.4
	Waltz	−0.9	1.1	−2.2	−0.3
MAB	Alternative	−0.6	0.3	−1.7	0.1
	Blues	−0.5	0.4	−1.2	0.1
	Electronic	−0.7	0.5	−2.1	0.0
	Folk	−0.6	0.4	−1.4	0.1
	Funk	−0.6	0.3	−1.2	0.1
	Jazz	−0.6	0.4	−2.8	0.0
	Pop	−0.6	0.3	−1.3	0.1
	Rock	−0.6	0.4	−1.8	0.2
Ours	Jazz	−0.8	0.3	−1.3	−0.5
	Orchestra	−1.1	0.4	−2.1	−0.7
	Pop	−0.9	0.2	−1.2	−0.7
	Rock	−0.9	0.2	−1.1	−0.7
	Vocal	−0.8	0.2	−1.4	−0.6

*Embedded bitrate = 27.52 kbps

presents the distribution of the quality from the same watermarked audio signals measured with the peak signal to noise ratio (PSNR). From Figure 3, it can be observed that the median PSNR values for all genres is above 35 dB, which is an acceptable value for audio quality. With these metrics, the ODG results obtained from the proposed RWS are corroborated, which indicates that for the inserted payload of 27.5 kbps the signal degradation is acceptable for practical applications.

3.1 Multilevel (ML) vs. Multi-bit (MB)

Multi-bit (MB) embedding was compared to the multilevel (ML) embedding to determine which strategy produces better results in terms of transparency. Multi-bit was tested embedding two bits

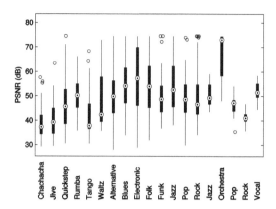

Figure 3: Distribution of PSNR values for watermarked signals.

per frequency, and multilevel was tested using two levels. Table 2 presents the median (Med), interquartile range (IQR), minimum, and maximum values measured with the PSNR, and ODG metrics. All the audio signals in the five genres from the dataset 'Ours' were watermarked embedding various payloads, and the results are reported in the table. For all the tested payloads the multi-bit strategy produces better PSNR results, highlighted in bold. The ODG results that are better in MB than in ML are also marked in bold.

Table 2: PSNR, and ODG results for multilevel (ML) and multi-bit (MB)*.

Bitrate (kbps)	Stgy.	PSNR				ODG			
		Med	IQR	Min	Max	Med	IQR	Min	Max
17.2	ML	54.8	11.7	39.4	78.5	0.1	0.1	−1.8	0.1
17.2	MB	**55.6**	11.7	40.3	78.4	0.1	0.1	−1.9	0.1
27.5	ML	47.7	11.2	34.6	75.7	−1.0	0.2	−2.1	−0.6
27.5	MB	**48.5**	11.2	35.4	74.5	**−0.9**	0.3	−2.1	−0.5
37.8	ML	42.4	12.0	29.5	72.5	−2.3	0.4	−2.9	−1.6
37.8	MB	**43.2**	12.0	30.3	70.2	−2.3	0.6	−3.1	−1.6
48.2	ML	35.4	10.6	25.6	68.4	−3.1	0.6	−3.6	−2.0
48.2	MB	**36.2**	10.5	26.4	65.7	**−3.0**	0.7	−3.8	−1.9

*Results obtained from all the genres in dataset 'Ours'.

3.2 Effect of expansion factor

To explore the embedding capacities of the generalized multi-bit PEE scheme proposed, various expansion factors were tested. All the audio signals from the five genres in the dataset 'Ours' were watermarked using the generalized scheme (eq. 5). A certain number of frequencies (NF) were selected, depending on the bitrate to be embedded, the prediction-errors for these were expanded by an expansion factor (e_f). Table 3 presents the median (Med), interquartile range (IQR), minimum, and maximum ODG values obtained for different e_f. The highest embedding capacity that meets the transparency is 68.8 kbps, marked in the red row. From this table, it can be observed that for a given payload (27.5 kbps) a better median ODG result is obtained by modifying less frequencies (20) and using a higher e_f (16), than modifying more frequencies (80) with a lower e_f (4). A similar behavior can be observed with the PSNR, which is better when modifying fewer frequencies than modifying more frequencies. This suggests that higher e_f can be used to improve the transparency given a fixed bitrate.

Table 3: ODG results for different e_f in various intDCT frequencies*.

NF	e_f	Bitrate (kbps)	ODG				PSNR			
			Med	IQR	Min	Max	Med	IQR	Min	Max
20	2	3.4	0.2	0.1	−1.7	0.2	77.4	11.6	58.8	90.5
20	4	6.9	0.2	0.1	−1.7	0.2	67.9	12.0	49.2	83.8
20	8	13.8	0.1	0.1	−1.8	0.2	60.6	12.0	41.9	76.8
20	16	27.5	0.1	0.1	−1.8	0.2	53.9	12.0	35.3	70.3
50	2	8.6	0.1	0.1	−1.8	0.2	65.2	11.7	49.8	86.8
50	4	17.2	0.1	0.1	−1.8	0.1	55.6	11.7	40.3	78.4
50	8	34.4	−0.2	0.3	−2.1	−0.0	48.3	11.7	32.9	71.2
50	16	68.8	−0.7	0.6	−2.2	−0.4	41.7	11.7	26.3	64.6
80	2	13.8	−0.3	0.1	−1.9	−0.1	58.1	11.2	45.0	83.5
80	4	27.5	−0.9	0.3	−2.1	−0.5	48.5	11.2	35.4	74.6
80	8	55.0	−2.4	0.4	−3.0	−1.8	41.2	11.2	28.1	67.2
80	16	110.1	−3.4	0.2	−3.7	−2.3	34.5	11.2	21.4	60.7

*Results obtained from all the genres in dataset 'Ours'.

3.3 Robustness

The robustness of the proposed scheme was tested against some common audio attacks with different configurations. The attacks are namely content replacement (CR) which substitutes a certain percentage of samples with the same amount of random noise, re-quantization (RQ) which modifies the number of bits with which each sample is represented, re-sampling (RS) modifies the sampling frequency of the signal, re-coding (RC) changes the codification of the signals to MP4, and modification of the volume (Vol) of the signals indicated in decibels (dB). Table 4 presents the various configurations tested for each attack, the median (Med), interquartile range (IQR), minimum, and maximum values for the ODG measured between the host and recovered signals, and the bit error rate (BER) measured between the embedded and extracted watermarks. As it can be observed, the scheme is robust against content replacement attack with a replacement up to 70%. However, the scheme fails to correctly extract the watermarks for the rest of attacks. Future efforts must be directed towards the increase in robustness of the scheme.

3.4 Comparison against [18]

A comparison against the ODG results obtained after the encoding process of the scheme proposed by [18] and the scheme proposed in this work is given in Table 5. The median (Med), interquartile range (IQR), minimum, and maximum ODG values for the two schemes are presented. The bitrate inserted in both cases is 16.5 kbps. As it can be seen from the median values from the proposed scheme, the ODG results are higher than those of the scheme by [18]. Furthermore, the ODG values below the acceptable threshold of -2, and marked in bold red, occur in more cases for the scheme by [18] than for the proposed scheme, which occur only in one case.

4 DISCUSSION

In the proposed audio RWS, the embedding region in the frequency domain is determined by the psychoacoustic characteristics of every audio segment, therefore, this region self adapts to every particular

Table 4: Robustness results obtained from attacked signals with various configurations*.

Attack	Config	ODG				BER			
		Med	IQR	Min	Max	Med	IQR	Min	Max
CR	10%	−2.5	1.8	−3.9	−1.1	0.1	0.0	0.0	0.0
CR	20%	−3.0	1.1	−3.9	−1.3	0.1	0.0	0.1	0.1
CR	30%	−3.3	0.8	−3.9	−1.6	0.1	0.0	0.1	0.1
CR	40%	−3.4	0.7	−3.9	−2.3	0.2	0.0	0.2	0.2
CR	50%	−3.6	0.5	−3.9	−2.6	0.2	0.0	0.2	0.2
CR	60%	−3.6	0.3	−3.9	−2.9	0.3	0.0	0.3	0.3
CR	70%	−3.7	0.3	−3.9	−3.1	0.3	0.0	0.3	0.3
CR	80%	−3.7	0.2	−3.9	−3.1	0.4	0.0	0.4	0.4
CR	90%	−3.7	0.3	−3.9	−2.8	0.4	0.0	0.4	0.4
RQ	8 bits	−2.1	2.6	−3.9	0.1	0.5	0.0	0.5	0.5
RQ	24 bits	0.1	0.2	−0.3	0.2	0.4	0.0	0.4	0.4
RS	22,050 Hz	1.0	0.0	1.0	1.0	0.5	0.0	0.5	0.5
RC	128 kbps	−0.4	0.5	−2.6	0.0	0.5	0.0	0.5	0.5
RC	192 kbps	−0.4	0.4	−2.1	0.1	0.5	0.0	0.5	0.5
Vol	+60 dB	−3.9	0.0	−3.9	−1.4	0.5	0.0	0.5	0.5
Vol	−60 dB	−2.2	0.9	−3.9	−1.6	0.5	0.0	0.5	0.5

*Results obtained from dataset 'Ours'.

Table 5: Comparison on embedding quality against [18]*

DS	Scheme							
	Proposed				[18]			
	Med	IQR	Min	Max	Med	IQR	Min	Max
BALL	0.1	0.1	-2.0	0.2	−1.0	0.7	-2.3	0.0
MAB	0.2	0.0	−1.8	0.2	−0.6	0.4	-2.1	0.1
Ours	0.1	0.1	−1.8	0.1	−0.9	0.3	-2.1	−0.5

*Embedded bitrate = 16.5 kbps

signal. Because of this, the transparency of the scheme will maintain an ODG value over -2 for most natural audio signals. The embedding capacity of the scheme can be increased by the use of the PEE strategy with multi-bit, as the experimental results suggest.

The problem of underflow and overflow in the watermarked sample values occurs when these values fall beneath or above the adequate range in time domain. Since embedding of the watermark bits is done in the intDCT domain, there is not a direct way to detect which modifications in the frequency domain will result in an underflow/overflow problem in time domain sample values. In the proposed RWS scheme, this problem is addressed in a pre-processing stage of the signals, that adjusts the dynamic range of the time domain signals. The dynamic range of the audio signals is taken to an integer representation, and then this integer dynamic range is compressed to avoid overflow, in a similar way as in [8]. Most RWS construct a location map to indicate when these problems are present for a given audio sample. A strategy that constructs such location map has to be devised, and has to take into consideration which modifications in the intDCT domain will cause underflow or overflow in the time domain samples.

Experimental results show the robustness of the scheme against content replacement attacks up to 70%. Results also demonstrate the improvement of this scheme against [18] in terms of transparency given a fixed embedded bitrate. The PEE strategy in the intDCT domain with multi-bit embedding was explored testing various expansion factors and how this parameter affects the embedding capacity and transparency. Experimental results suggest that by using an e_f of 16 and modifying less frequencies, better transparency is obtained.

5 CONCLUSIONS AND FUTURE WORK

The embedding capacity of the proposed scheme can be increased through a multi-bit strategy, while a transparency constraint is fulfilled to allow the use of the scheme in practical applications. The effect of the expansion factor has to be further explored, to understand the trade-off between embedding capacity (determined by e_f) and transparency for more datasets.

The selection of frequencies for information hiding can be improved. Currently, the highest candidate FFT frequencies are used to carry information. An optimization technique, such as evolutionary algorithms could be used to identify which of the candidate frequencies are more suited.

An strategy which constructs a location map to control underflow and overflow problems has to be devised and incorporated to the scheme. The effect that the construction of such location map has against the final embedding capacity has to be studied, *i.e.* an analysis has to be made to measure the impact that the size of the location map has on the embedding capacity of the scheme. Future efforts should also explore strategies to improve the robustness of the scheme against various attacks.

The proposed scheme allows the insertion of 27.5 kbps while maintaining a transparency constraint over -2 ODG. These results are satisfactory for applications such as the ones mentioned in Section 1. Furthermore, a maximum 68.8 kbps with -0.9 ODG can be inserted using the modified PEE with multi-bit.

ACKNOWLEDGEMENTS

This work was supported by CONACyT under grant PDCPN2013-01-216689.

REFERENCES

[1] Durand Begault, Mark Anderson, and Mryan Mcclain. 2006. Spatially Modulated Auditory Alerts for Aviation, In 2003 International Conference on Auditory Display. *Journal on Audio Engineering Society* 54, 4 (2006), 276–282. http://www.aes.org/e-lib/browse.cfm?elib=13676

[2] Marinus M. Boone and Werner P. J. de Bruijn. 2003. Improving Speech Intelligibility in Teleconferencing by using Wave Field Synthesis. In *Audio Engineering Society Convention 114*. http://www.aes.org/e-lib/browse.cfm?elib=12559

[3] Brett Bradley and Adnan M. Alattar. 2005. High-capacity invertible data-hiding algorithm for digital audio, In SPIE Proceedings 5681, Security, Steganography, and Watermarking of Multimedia Contents VII. *SPIE Proceedings* 5681 (2005), 789–800. DOI: http://dx.doi.org/10.1117/12.586042

[4] W. H. Chang and T. Nguyen. 2007. Integer FFT with Optimized Coefficient Sets. In *IEEE International Conference on Acoustics, Speech and Signal Processing - ICASSP '07*, Vol. 2. II–109–II–112.

[5] Quan Chen, Shijun Xiang, and Xinrong Luo. 2013. Reversible Watermarking for Audio Authentication Based on Integer DCT and Expansion Embedding. In *Digital Forensics and Watermaking*, YunQ. Shi, Hyoung-Joong Kim, and Fernando Pérez-González (Eds.). Lecture Notes in Computer Science, Vol. 7809. Springer Berlin Heidelberg, 395–409. DOI: http://dx.doi.org/10.1007/978-3-642-40099-5_33

[6] D. Coltuc and A. Tudoroiu. 2012. Multibit versus multilevel embedding in high capacity difference expansion reversible watermarking. In *Proceedings of the 20th European Signal Processing Conference (EUSIPCO)*, 2012. 1791–1795.

[7] J.J. Garcia-Hernandez. 2012. Exploring Reversible Digital Watermarking in Audio Signals Using Additive Interpolation-error Expansion. In *Eighth International Conference on Intelligent Information Hiding and Multimedia Signal Processing (IIH-MSP)*, 2012. 142–145.

[8] J. J. Garcia-Hernandez. 2013. On a low complexity steganographic system for digital images based on interpolation-error expansion. In *IEEE 56th International Midwest Symposium on Circuits and Systems (MWSCAS)*. 1375–1378. DOI: http://dx.doi.org/10.1109/MWSCAS.2013.6674912

[9] Jerry D Gibson. 2002. *The communications handbook*. CRC press.

[10] Fabien Gouyon. 2006. Ballroom dataset. Online. (March 2006). http://mtg.upf.edu/ismir2004/contest/tempoContest/node5.html

[11] Helge Homburg, Ingo Mierswa, Bülent Möller, Katharina Morik, and Michael Wurst. 2005. A Benchmark Dataset for Audio Classification and Clustering.. In *ISMIR*, Vol. 2005. 528–31. http://www-ai.cs.uni-dortmund.de/audio.html

[12] Haibin Huang, S. Rahardja, Rongshan Yu, and Xiao Lin. 2006. Integer MDCT with enhanced approximation of the DCT-IV. *IEEE Transactions on Signal Processing* 54, 3 (March 2006), 1156–1159. DOI: http://dx.doi.org/10.1109/TSP.2005.862942

[13] Xuping Huang, Akira Nishimura, and Isao Echizen. 2011. A Reversible Acoustic Steganography for Integrity Verification. In *Digital Watermarking*, Hyoung-Joong Kim, YunQing Shi, and Mauro Barni (Eds.). Lecture Notes in Computer Science, Vol. 6526. Springer Berlin Heidelberg, 305–316. DOI: http://dx.doi.org/10.1007/978-3-642-18405-5_25

[14] Xuping Huang, Nobutaka Ono, Isao Echizen, and Akira Nishimura. 2014. *Reversible Audio Information Hiding Based on Integer DCT Coefficients with Adaptive Hiding Locations*. Springer Berlin Heidelberg, Berlin, Heidelberg, 376–389. DOI: http://dx.doi.org/10.1007/978-3-662-43886-2_27

[15] Yongjin Huo, Shijun Xiang, Shangyi Liu, Xinrong Luo, and Zhongliang Bai. 2013. Reversible audio watermarking algorithm using non-causal prediction. *Wuhan University Journal of Natural Sciences* 18, 5 (2013), 455–460. DOI: http://dx.doi.org/10.1007/s11859-013-0956-2

[16] Peter Kabal. 2002. *An examination and interpretation of ITU-R BS. 1387: Perceptual evaluation of audio quality*. Technical Report. McGill University. 1–89 pages.

[17] Yiqing Lin and Waleed H. Abdulla. 2015. . Springer. DOI: http://dx.doi.org/10.1007/978-3-319-07974-5

[18] Alejandra Menendez-Ortiz, Claudia Feregrino-Uribe, Jose Juan Garcia-Hernandez, and Zobeida Jezabel Guzman-Zavaleta. 2016. Self-recovery scheme for audio restoration after a content replacement attack. *Multimedia Tools and Applications* (2016), 1–28. DOI: http://dx.doi.org/10.1007/s11042-016-3783-6

[19] A. Nishimura. 2011. Reversible Audio Data Hiding Using Linear Prediction and Error Expansion. In *Seventh International Conference on Intelligent Information Hiding and Multimedia Signal Processing (IIH-MSP)*, 2011. 318–321.

[20] A. Nishimura. 2012. Controlling Quality and Payload in Reversible Data Hiding Based on Modified Error Expansion for Segmental Audio Waveforms. In *Eighth International Conference on Intelligent Information Hiding and Multimedia Signal Processing (IIH-MSP)*, 2012. 110–113.

[21] S. Oraintara, Y. J. Chen, and T. Q. Nguyen. 2002. Integer fast Fourier transform. *IEEE Transactions on Signal Processing* 50, 3 (Mar 2002), 607–618.

[22] B. Ou, X. Li, Y. Zhao, R. Ni, and Y. Q. Shi. 2013. Pairwise Prediction-Error Expansion for Efficient Reversible Data Hiding. *IEEE Transactions on Image Processing* 22, 12 (Dec 2013), 5010–5021. DOI: http://dx.doi.org/10.1109/TIP.2013.2281422

[23] Mark Owen. 2007. *Practical Signal Processing*. Cambridge University Press.

[24] Tony Poitschke, Florian Laquai, and Gerhard Rigoll. 2009. Guiding a Driver's Visual Attention Using Graphical and Auditory Animations. In *Engineering Psychology and Cognitive Ergonomics*, Don Harris (Ed.). Lecture Notes in Computer Science, Vol. 5639. Springer Berlin Heidelberg, 424–433. DOI: http://dx.doi.org/10.1007/978-3-642-02728-4_45

[25] Andreas Spanias, Ted Painter, and Venkatraman Atti. 2006. *Audio signal processing and coding*. John Wiley & Sons.

[26] Thilo Thiede, William C. Treurniet, Roland Bitto, Christian Schmidmer, Thomas Sporer, John G. Beerends, and Catherine Colomes. 2000. PEAQ - The ITU Standard for Objective Measurement of Perceived Audio Quality. *Journal of the Audio Engineering Society* 48, 1/2 (2000), 3–29. http://www.aes.org/e-lib/browse.cfm?elib=12078

[27] D.M. Thodi and J.J. Rodriguez. 2004. Reversible Watermarking by Prediction-Error Expansion. In *6th IEEE Southwest Symposium on Image Analysis and Interpretation, 2004*. 21–25. DOI: http://dx.doi.org/10.1109/IAI.2004.1300937

[28] Michiel van der Veen, Fons Bruekers, Arno van Leest, and Stephane Cavin. 2003. High capacity reversible watermarking for audio, In SPIE Proceedings 5020, Security and Watermarking of Multimedia Contents V. *SPIE Proceedings* 5020 (2003), 1–11. DOI: http://dx.doi.org/10.1117/12.476858

A Minimum Distortion – High Capacity Watermarking Technique for Relational Data

Maikel L. Pérez Gort
National Institute of Astrophysics,
Optics and Electronics
Puebla, Mexico
mlazaro2002es@inaoep.mx

Claudia Feregrino Uribe
National Institute of Astrophysics,
Optics and Electronics
Puebla, Mexico
cferegrino@inaoep.mx

Jyrki Nummenmaa
School of Information Sciences,
University of Tampere
Tampere, Finland
jyrki@cs.uta.fi

ABSTRACT

In this paper, a new multi-attribute and high capacity image-based watermarking technique for relational data is proposed. The embedding process causes low distortion into the data considering the usability restrictions defined over the marked relation. The conducted experiments show the high resilience of the proposed technique against tuple deletion and tuple addition attacks. An interesting trend of the extracted watermark is analyzed when, within certain limits, if the number of embedded marks is small, the watermark signal far from being compromised, discretely improves in the case of tuple addition attacks. According to the results, marking 13% of the attributes and under an attack of 100% of tuples addition, 96% of the watermark is extracted. Also, while previous techniques embed up to 61% of the watermark, under the same conditions, we guarantee to embed 99.96% of the marks.

KEYWORDS

Data usability; image-based watermarking; ownership proof; watermarking relational data

1 INTRODUCTION

The piracy of digital assets has been a concern for those who use them as business products over the web. Deploying an online company permits the use of the benefits of the internet, allowing the organization to go beyond the geographical obstacles and political borders. The problem is that, due to the easy access and distribution of digital data, piracy and illegal copies cause millionaire losses to these businesses.

IH&MMSec '17, June 20-22, 2017, Philadelphia, PA, USA
© 2017 Association for Computing Machinery.
ACM ISBN 978-1-4503-5061-7/17/06...$15.00
http://dx.doi.org/10.1145/3082031.3083241

The use of watermarks (WM) is a promising tool that allows owners to check the authenticity of digital assets in case of accusations of illegal copy [5, 6, 19, 20]. It works by introducing small changes called marks into the object of interest. All the marks together constitute the WM, and each one of them must have an insignificant impact on the data usability. Also, every mark should be embedded in such a way that a malicious user cannot destroy the WM without compromising the data quality. So, the watermarking technique is not the prevention of copying or distribution of the digital assets but a tool to be used in case of legal demands [3].

Several techniques have been proposed for allowing the wide distribution of multimedia data with embedded information that allows the verification of the copyright [4, 31, 32]. Although watermarking schemes for relational databases (RDB) have been created [8, 9, 10, 15, 16, 28] there are some problems still unsolved in this area, due to the nature of relational data and the lower maturity of these techniques compared to those created for videos, audios and images.

Watermarking methods proposed for multimedia data cannot be used for relational data due to the differences between these data types, which are [3, 14]: data redundancy, order of the data, frequency of updates and, data appreciation. Most of the watermarking techniques for multimedia data use the features of these data types for the generation, embedding and extraction of the WM. For example, the value of pixels in an image usually presents a high correlation with the value of their neighbors, an aspect that some techniques use [25]. The values of the attributes of the relation of a database should not present this feature at all according to the right RDB design (low redundancy: exception, the primary key of the relations). Also, multimedia data can change of domain using some transforms (e.g. Discrete Wavelet Transform (DWT)) and the WM can be embedded in the transformed domain, guaranteeing to scatter the marks all over the data [25]. If a similar operation is performed over the relational data, the usability may be severely compromised due to the spread of the distortion [3].

Watermarking relational data has proved to be a useful tool in various applications, the most common of them is for checking the copyright in ownership conflicts [18, 22, 26]. Also, embedding different WM in distinct copies of the data, called fingerprinting [14], is used to deter illegal copies and to trace traitor users [12, 13, 24]. These two applications use techniques classified as robust due to the requirement of the resilience of the WMs against attacks aimed to remove them. Also, classified as fragile, a WM can be used to control the integrity of the data and protect them against tampering and fraud [11, 21, 23, 33].

In this paper we present a robust watermarking technique for relational data copyright protection. The main objective of our proposal is to increase the embedding capacity of the watermark technique, diminishing the impact of the distortion and guaranteeing higher resilience to tuple deletion and tuple addition attacks. Our proposal uses an image for the WM generation, allowing a good WM restoration despite the severity of performed attacks.

The structure of this paper is as follows: In Section 2, the main theoretical elements of the research area are presented. In Section 3, the previous and related work are analyzed. Section 4 presents the proposed algorithm, and the experimental results are described in Section 5. The conclusions and future work constitute the last section.

2 BACKGROUND

Watermarking relational data consists of two general processes: embedding and extraction of the WM. The embedding process is formed by two main sub-processes, generation of the WM and embedding of the marks into the relation of the database. The simplest embedding process has at least one parameter, the Secret Key (SK), known only by the data owner (see Fig. 1).

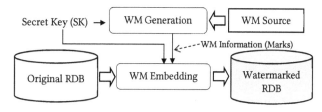

Figure 1: Structure of the watermark (WM) embedding process.

The extraction process is formed by three sub-processes: detection of the marks, extraction, and reconstruction of the WM. To be able to extract the WM, the value of each private parameter must be the same as the one used for the embedding process (see Fig. 2).

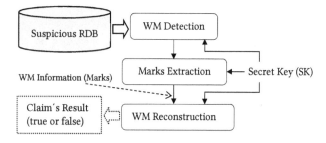

Figure 2: Structure of the watermark (WM) extraction process.

The watermarking techniques for relational data are classified according to the following criteria [3, 14]: The information used for generate the WM (e.g. image, text, etc.), if the technique causes distortion over the watermarked data or not, if the marked data are returned to its original unwatermarked version just after the WM extraction (reversibility or invertibility), and the intent of marking (e.g. tamper detection, localization, ownership proof, traitor detection, etc.).

Other classifications given to the watermarking techniques for relational data are [3, 14]: the cover type (depending on the type of attributes the marks are embedded into), the granularity level considering the process can be performed by modifying or adding information at bit level or higher level (e.g. the whole attribute value or tuple level), and the verifiability/detectability (the detection–verification process may be deterministic or probabilistic, and can be performed blindly or non-blindly, publicly (by anyone) or privately (by the owner only).

Watermarking techniques for relational databases must accomplish the requirements presented below [3, 14]:

- Capacity: The amount of embedded data should not compromise the database usability. Also, the embedding and extraction processes should be carried out without raising suspicion to potential attackers.

- Usability: It refers to how useful are the data for the environment in which they are being managed. Data usability cannot be degraded by the changes introduced during the WM embedding process. Tolerance to changes may vary according to the database purpose.

- Blindness: Extraction of the WM should not require either knowledge of the original database (unwatermarked copy) nor watermark information. On the contrary, when a scheme does not fulfill this requirement, the WM will be classified as non-blind.

- Security: Security of the watermarking process relies only on the private nature of their parameters (e.g. secret key) which should be kept completely secret by the users involved in the operation.

- Public System: The watermarking system should assume that the method used for inserting a watermark is public. The defense must be based on the privacy of its parameters [1].

- Incremental Watermarking: After the database has been watermarked, the watermarking algorithm should continue computing the watermarking values for the tuples that will be added or modified later on.

- Non-interference: If multiple WMs are inserted into the same relation of the RDB, their marks should not interfere with each other.

- False Positives and False Negatives: A false positive ratio is the probability of detecting a valid WM from unwatermarked data, whereas a false negative ratio is the probability of not detecting a valid WM from watermarked data that has been modified by malicious attacks or benign updates. False positives and false negatives ratios should not affect marks detection and should not influence the WM construction.

2.1 Commonly Used Notation

The main parameters defined by distortion-based techniques for watermarking RDBs are strongly linked to the table structure of the database relations. Their notation and a brief description for each one of them are presented below:

Table 1: Notation Given to the Parameters Used by Most of the Watermarking RDB Distortion-Based Techniques.

Symbol	Description
η	Number of tuples in the relation being watermarked.
ν	Number of attributes available for marking from the relation.
ξ	Number of less significant bits (lsb) available for marking in the binary representation of each attribute value.
$1/\gamma$	Tuple Fraction (TF), where $\gamma \in (1, \eta)$. Indicates the fraction of tuples to be marked. If the value of γ decreases more tuples will be considered for marking. Ignoring the usability constraints, if $\gamma = 1$ all tuples of the relation will be marked.
ω	Number of marked tuples from the η presented in the relation. Ignoring the usability constraints $\omega \approx \eta / \gamma$.

Usability will be controlled not only by the database constraints but also by the trade-off between the values of γ and ξ. These parameters will be responsible for an important part of the watermarking capacity, considering the distortion limits on the data to be marked.

Also, the relation to be marked will be identified as R with scheme $R(PK, A_0, ..., A_{\nu-1})$ where A_i: $i \in (0, \nu-1)$ are all the attributes available to mark and PK is the primary key of the relation. The tuples of the relation R will be identified as r_j where $r \in R$ and $j \in (0, \eta-1)$. So, the notation $r_j.A_i$ refers to the attribute i of the tuple r_j in the relation R where the primary key will be $r_j.PK$.

An important type of function to use in watermarking RDB is the one-way hash function which always guarantees the same output for the same input parameters. The function notation is H and for a given message M as input, the result will be h (operation represented as $h = H(M)$). As one-way function, will be hard to obtain M given h such that $M = H'(h)$. Also, given M will be hard to find another message M' that guarantees the same result h such that $H(M) = H(M')$ [2]. Common functions used for this purpose are MD5 and the SHA family (e.g. SHA-0, SHA-1, etc.).

Hash functions are very useful to obtain a unique and secret value that identifies a tuple given unique information about it (e.g. $r_j.PK$ or a unique combination of index values for seeking).

Also, combining $r_j.PK$ with the SK will improve the secrecy level of the operation.

3 RELATED WORK

The first watermarking technique for RDB was proposed in 2002 by Agrawal & Kiernan [2]. It was a scheme for marking numeric attributes at bit level and is classified as blind. The also called AHK algorithm mainly embeds a meaningless bit sequence into the relation to be watermarked by selecting the tuples to mark, the attributes and the bit of the attributes according to a value generated using a one-way hash function that takes as inputs SK and $r_j.PK$ (see Section 2.1). They define a Virtual Primary Key (VPK) as $F(r_j.PK) = H(SK \circ H(SK \circ r_j.PK))$ where the operator $\circ$ represents concatenation. So, the *desiderata* for watermarking relational data with random nature is defined by the *mod* operator. Tuple selection is performed if $F(r_j.PK) \bmod \gamma = 0$. In the same way, the attribute index for marking in the selected tuple will be obtained according to $F(r_j.PK) \bmod \nu$, and the bit position $F(r_j.PK) \bmod \xi$.

Agrawal & Kiernan [2] method's main limitations are given by a weak resilience against subset attacks and malicious updates such as data transformations. Also, the meaningless of the watermarking information may compromise the identification despite that the WM could survive the attacks. Finally, the usability control is based only on the parameters ξ and γ, and the constraints that may be implemented over the database are ignored.

In 2004, Sion *et al.* [29] presented a different approach for watermarking RDBs, also a blind technique that marks numeric attributes at bit level. They focused in do not compromising data usability, for that, they calculate data statistics and mark the selected tuple according to the database constraints and the range of allowed error for the data (using the Mean Squared Error (MSE) as metric). The limitation of this proposal is that a tuple sorting is required for defining subsets identifying some tuples as their bounds. Also called markers, each bound is selected similarly to the tuple selection in AHK Algorithms (if $H(SK \circ r_j.PK) \bmod e = 0$, where $e = attributes\_set.length / subset\_size$).

Creating subsets aims to take the watermarking problem into multiple simplified situations and embed marks with high redundancy, allowing error correction in the extraction process using majority voting. The problem is that some set attacks (e.g. adding or removing tuples) may add or remove some markers, which may compromise the detection of the same subset used in the embedding process and due to this, increment the probability of the synchronization errors. Sion *et al.* [29] introduce the idea of using maps for improving marks localization in the detection process, but this decreases the performance of watermarking embedding and extraction processes, and violates the blind principle of watermarking, not mentioning that this information may suffer losses in data actualization attacks, so the technique will have to add extra considerations for the maps robustness.

Other proposed technique classified as Image-Based Watermarking (IBW) was the presented in 2010 by Sardroudi &

Ibrahim [27]. This scheme uses an image for generating the WM and also checks the usability before modifying the data due to the mark insertion. The main idea is based on AHK algorithm, but there are some additional considerations to avoid data degradation.

The limitation of this proposal is given by the capability of the watermark and the random nature of the algorithm. The first IBW [34] considers a sequential nature for the marks in the embedding process. The problem is when a *subset-reverse order attack* (over tuples or/and attributes) is performed over the data. Since relational data do not have a fixed order, attributes and tuples can be reordered (operation known as *subset-reverse order attack*) without compromising the data use and the information recovered from them by information management systems. But if a WM is embedded considering a fixed order of the data being watermarked, performing a *subset-reverse order attack* causes serious WM synchronization problems, compromising its detection. Due to this, there may never be a way to recover the WM.

The solution of previous IBW techniques to be resilient against *subset-reverse order attack* was a random selection of the image pixels, but this solution often compromises embedding the entire watermark (some pixels are considered multiple times while others are ignored). The consequences of this are similar to performing tuple deletion attacks to the relation and their effects compromise more the entire embedding of the image if its size increases in comparison to the size of the relation to be watermarked, or if the relation is too small in comparison to the image size. Sardroudi & Ibrahim's technique presents better results that similar previous schemes, but the watermark still is not entirely embedded into the data even when all tuples of the relation are marked ($\gamma = 1$) causing a serious usability compromise and increasing the risk of providing evidence to the attackers about the locations of the marks.

There are other techniques focused in marking more than one attribute per tuple on the relation. At first glance, its main deficiency would be the increasing of data distortion compromising the usability. For example, Jawad, K. & Khan [17] use Genetic Algorithm (GA) for detecting a couple of attributes that combined will provoke less distortion over the tuple and the column (comparing the values of the same attribute two tuples up and two down). According to the studied multi-attribute techniques, a common limitation is that often they define a fixed number of attributes for embedding the marks.

Despite there are some multi-attribute WM techniques for RDBs, none of them seem to use images as WMs and try to reduce the distortion as our goal is, and at the same time increasing the considered pixels in the embedding process for the WM generation. IBW is chosen due to using images to generate WMs increases the resilience of watermarking techniques against malicious attacks. Even recovering attacked mark values in the WM extraction process, there is a set of algorithms that can be applied over images to enhance them despite noise addition or pixel loss. Considering the use of binary images, which unlike others store simpler values in their pixels, the information to embed as WM is modest so the

technique causes less distortion avoiding data quality degradation. Also, marking more than one attribute per tuple, considering the tuple tolerance for the embedding, make possible to increase the number of embedded pixels in spite of having been randomly selected from the image. Then, increasing the WM capacity we guarantee the technique resilience against *subset-reverse order attack*, tuple deletion and tuple addition attacks.

4 PROPOSED TECHNIQUE

Our proposal for watermarking relational data aims to improve the capability of the watermark using the idea of spatial image watermarking techniques (see Fig. 3). In conventional RDB watermarking techniques, the marks are embedded one per tuple so that the operation can be understood as a vertical process. But, we consider that if the marks were embedded in two directions (vertical-horizontal) then the capability of the watermarking would increase considerably.

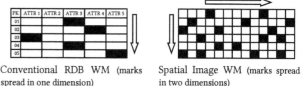

Conventional RDB WM (marks spread in one dimension)

Spatial Image WM (marks spread in two dimensions)

■ marked value
□ unmarked value

Figure 3: RDB embedding vs. 2D image embedding.

Also, subset attacks have a higher probability of compromising the WM detection if embedding is in one direction; if it is in two, this would improve WM robustness because of the marks redundancy. Then, it is probably better to embed more than one mark per tuple, simulating the image watermarking techniques that act over the spatial domain, although this may compromise much more the usability. Of course, the higher the number of marked values per tuple, the higher the distortion caused to data. That is why we include a module for data-quality control in our proposal (see Section 4.1). Adding more marks does not necessarily implies more distortion, this statement is backed up by the results we present in the next section.

Our scheme is based on AHK algorithm. Also, it is focused in marking numeric attributes at bit level without requiring the original data neither the WM source for the extraction process. The WM is generated from an image, and the marks are scattered more than one per tuple according to a new parameter we introduced. The idea is to create a scheme based on Sardroudi & Ibrahim´s proposal [27], adding a multi-attribute embedding factor called Attribute Fraction (*AF*: defined as $1/\varpi \in (1, \nu)$) that controls data distortion by considering the maximum error allowed. As with the tuple fraction, if $\varpi = 1$ all attributes of the tuple are marked, and if ϖ increases, fewer attributes are marked. Beside the parameters defined in Table 1, we use other secret parameters described in Table 2.

Table 2: Other Parameters Required by Our Scheme.

Notation	Description
AL	List of attributes for marking (*AL. size* = ν).
MSB	Range of most significant bits available for the random selection of the value identified as *msb*.
LSB	Range of less significant bits available for the random selection of the value identified as *lsb*.
IMG	Matrix that represents the array of pixels of the selected image for building the watermark.
H	Height of the image used for generating the WM. The randomly selected height position for the pixel extraction is denoted as *h*.
W	Width of the image used for generating the WM. The randomly selected width position for the pixel extraction is denoted as *w*.

The WM embedding process of our proposal is presented in Figure 4. We create a VPK for the analyzed tuple (VPK_j) using the function *Create_VPK*, taking as a parameter the PK of the tuple and the SK as mentioned in Section 3. Then, the tuple is considered for embedding a mark if $VPK_j \bmod \gamma = 0$, otherwise, we pass to the next tuple (see Tuple Selection block in Fig. 4).

For the considered tuple, we analyze each attribute only if it is included in the *AL* (see Attribute Selection block in Fig. 4). The Attribute Virtual Value (AVV) is generated by using the *Generate_AVV* function. If the attribute is selected to be marked, after embedding the mark his value could change, which results in LSB changes. Selecting the whole attribute binary value for the AVV creation causes contradiction, considering that the AVV generated could indicate mark embedding on the attribute. After being marked, the new AVV generated using the changed value could exclude the attribute for mark recovering on the WM extraction process. That is the reason why we use the values computed from the MSB of each attribute for generating the AVV, since MSBs do not change in the WM embedding process. Using the AVV and the VKP_j we generate the Attribute Virtual Hash (AVH) (function *Generate_AVH*) and we proceed to generate the values for the mark embedding on this attribute if $AVH_{ij} \bmod \varpi = 0$ and MSB and LSB parameters allow it (see Section 4.1).

As we mentioned, the WM is generated using an image where each randomly selected pixel (functions *GetPixelCoord and GetPixelVal*) will be *xored* with the *msb* (function *GenMark*). Then the created mark will be embedded in the *lsb* position selected from the range given as parameter (function *EmbeddingMark*). Mark embedding is carried out if the condition of the *lsb* position respect to the binary length (function *blength*) of the attribute value is met, and the changes are committed if the data constraints and the tolerated error allow it.

The WM extraction process follows the same steps of the WM embedding process and uses the same parameter values as well as the same functions. WM extraction process is deterministic, and majority voting is performed at the end of the

extraction to use redundancy of the embedded marks reducing the degree of negative impacts of attacks and benign updates.

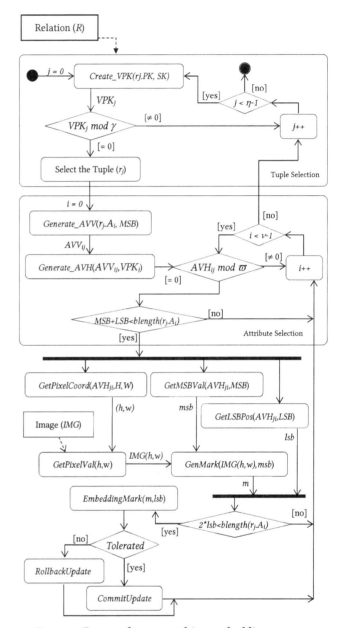

Figure 4: Proposed watermarking embedding process.

4.1 Avoiding Data Degradation

To avoid compromising data usability, we take into consideration not only the random values selected for attribute marking (e.g. *lsb*) but also the attribute value itself. So, if the attribute finally is marked or not, it gives to our technique a higher level of randomness, an aspect that improves it and makes it unpredictable for the attackers.

Similar to Sardroudi & Ibrahim's technique, we only mark an attribute if the length of its value in binary notation is at least twice the position of the LSB selected for marking. For example, for a binary number 111 (7 in decimal) when the second *lsb* is selected, we are provoking a change in the value of only 2 units, but respect the original value, this represents an alteration of 28.75% of its decimal value. With this restriction, we are making available the marking only if the *lsb* is 1 (distortion in one unit ≈ 14.29%, also the minimum available degradation) or forcing the selection of the second *lsb* only if the length of the binary value is 5 or higher. For example, a number 10111 (23 in decimal), changing the second *lsb* will provoke just an alteration of the 8.7% of its value.

The second consideration is that the selected positions for the *lsb* and the *msb* cannot overlap. For example, we can have numeric attribute values that require 10 digits for their binary representation and the available ranges for the random selection of 3 for the *lsb* and 4 for the *msb*. In this case the random positions selected for the *lsb* and the *msb* will never overlap, but if a number is represented by only 6 digits, there is the probability that the same selected value for the *msb* in the generation of the mark may be selected as the *lsb* to be modified (e.g. *msb* = 4, *lsb* = 3). Due to this, a wrong value could be obtained for the mark in the WM extraction process. Also, the number formed by the MSB range is used for deciding if the attribute will be marked according to the AF. If we change some value of the MSB, we may not consider this attribute in the WM extraction process.

One solution to this problem may be left zero padding of the binary representation to make all values of the same length, but this would provoke the detection of a lot of *msb* with same values, and it could make the technique predictable. The solution we propose is that the sum of the ranges indicated for the selection of the LSB and the MSB must be equal or higher to the length of the binary representation of the numeric value selected to mark.

Another consideration at bit level is the values change at the right of the selected *lsb* to reduce the difference between the new attribute value and the original. Other *lsb*'s will change their value to the opposite of the value inserted. For example, the binary value 1001101 (77 in decimal) when the 4th *lsb* is selected to be marked, the new value would be 1000101 (69 in decimal), but if the other *lsb*'s are changed according to this rule, the new value will be 1000111 (71 in decimal); so, the distortion will be lower. The number of *lsb* places to change will be indicated by a parameter, adding a higher random nature to our technique considering not all *lsb* have the same value compared with the marked one. Sardroudi & Ibrahim [27] apply the same concept but they act only over a single *lsb* (right next to the marked).

On the other hand, to avoid violating database constraints we work with transactions using *commit-rollback* classic blocks in case the operation requires to be reversed due to some constraint violations. In that way, we are also keeping the semantic of the data despite the marking process modifications.

The last consideration is similar to Sion *et al.*'s one [29], to allow clients (if they desire) to indicate the maximum amount of supported error for each attribute possibly marked. This value is a percentage of the attribute value before to be marked. In the case of exceeding the maximum allowed error, the data owner

can try to watermark the relation using different parameters. Also, a general amount of maximum allowed error is indicated to control the relation distortion as a whole.

5 EXPERIMENTAL RESULTS

The conducted experiments were performed using, as Sun *et al.* [30] and Sardroudi & Ibrahim [27], the *Forest Cover Type* relational dataset [7] available for public download. This dataset has 581,012 tuples with 54 attributes; we are using a subset of the original data with 30,000 tuples and 10 numeric attributes for a fair comparison of our results against previously reported ones in the literature. We are also using the Universiti Teknologi Malaysia (UTM) logo with size of 82*80 pixels (one bit per pixel) as the image for the watermark generation (see Fig. 5 a)).

Our watermarking system consists of a client-server architecture software. The client application was implemented using Java 1.8 as the programming language and Eclipse Mars.1 as Integrated Development Environment (IDE). The server technology was Oracle Database 12c with Oracle SQL Developer as Database Management Interface.

The metric for evaluating and comparing the results is called Correction Factor (CF) (see Formula 1), also used by Sardroudi & Ibrahim [27]. It compares each pixel value of the embedded image against the recovered one. The maximum value of this metric is 100 which means an exact similarity of the two images, while the minimum is 0 and indicates non-similarity between them.

$$CF = \frac{\sum_{i=1}^{x} \sum_{j=1}^{y} (Img_{org}(i,j) \bigoplus \overline{Img_{ext}(i,j)})}{x*y} * 100\% \quad (1)$$

To avoid visual confusion and appreciating better the *CF* obtained values, we assume 'Virtual Value' to the missed pixels (MP). Since our image is binary (in black and white), we do not assign any of these values but the red color (see Fig. 5), in that way it is clearer the distortion caused in the extracted image.

I-MP in red   II-MP in white   III-MP in black

a) Embedded image   b) Extracted image

Figure 5: Samples of images from the experiments.

5.1 Watermarking Capacity

The first analyzed feature of the proposed watermarking technique is the capacity. We consider more image pixels than previously proposed techniques for the WM generation although we are using a random method for their selection (see Fig. 6). A higher value of AF (AF = 9) guarantees almost the same results as the proposal of Sardroudi & Ibrahim [27]. When the AF value decreases, the number of embedded pixels increases, and when TF = 1, almost all pixels are considered.

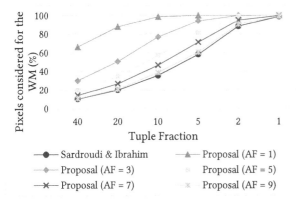

Figure 6: Percentage of image pixels considered for the WM generation.

For avoiding data quality degradation, we look at the parameters combination that allows WM identification even when not all pixels are embedded (see Table 3). Even so, we embed more pixels than similar techniques. Also, the average of selected attributes per tuple sometimes is similar to the considered in [27], this is due to attribute exclusion in some tuples for not being allowed to mark them (see Fig. 8).

Table 3: Embedded Image (with their corresponding CF) for Different Parameter Values.

Method	Tuple Fraction					
	40	20	10	5	2	1
Sardroudi & Ibrahim	10	19	35	58	88	98
Proposal (AF = 9)	10	20	38	60	90	99
Proposal (AF = 6)	16	30	50	75	97	99
Proposal (AF = 3)	30	50	76	94	99	99
Proposal (AF = 1)	66	87	98	99	99	99

From Figure 6 and Table 3 it can be seen the minimum number of pixels required for embedding, avoiding to mark a high number of attributes for not compromising the usability of the data. Even so, it is important to understand that embedding a higher number of pixels guarantees the robustness of the WM against malicious attacks and benign updates.

5.2 Detectability of the Marks

Our technique shows a very high confidentiality for mark detection. For the best-case scenario, when marks are extracted without having performed tuple additions or tuple deletions over the watermarked data, we can see a very similar *CF* distribution (see Fig. 7) to the graphic that represents the embedded pixels of the image (see Fig. 6).

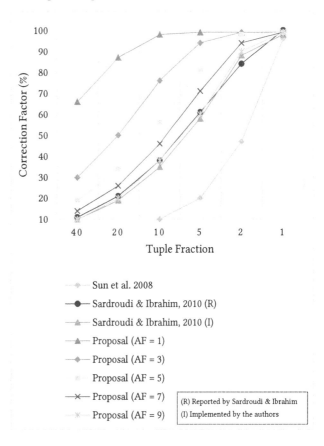

Figure 7: Distribution of the CF for different techniques.

Table 4 shows that for AF = 9 our technique gets similar results to Sardroudi & Ibrahim's. It is important to highlight that Sardroudi & Ibrahim report a CF of 100% for FT=1, but our implementation of their algorithm gets 99% as the highest value. It is interesting to note such good results even with the low number of embedded pixels. Our assumption is that it would be required a higher number of embedded pixels from the image to at least guarantee a higher value of CF (even so, not necessarily 100%).

Table 4: CF for previous techniques and to our Proposal.

Method / TF:	40	20	10	5	2	1
Sun et al.	2	5	10	20	47	96
Sardroudi & Ibrahim	11	21	38	61	84	100
Sardroudi & Ibrahim [*]	10	19	35	58	88	98
Proposal (AF = 1)	66	87	98	99	99	99
Proposal (AF = 3)	30	50	76	94	99	99
Proposal (AF = 5)	19	34	56	81	98	99
Proposal (AF = 7)	14	26	46	71	94	99
Proposal (AF = 9)	10	20	38	60	90	99

[*] Our implementation of Sardroudi & Ibrahim's technique.

On the other hand, it is important to check the WM detection after the tuples have been updated or attacked. In section 5.4 the results of performed experiments are presented.

5.3 Data Usability Tracking

It is possible to mark more than one attribute per tuple getting a low degradation in the data due to the careful selection of the elements that tolerate more changes. Also, it is important to understand that marking does not necessarily mean a value change. Often the value to embed and the already stored value by the *lsb* to mark is the same, allowing embedding the mark without causing any degradation.

Despite that, we may consider the average of marked attributes per tuple. In some tuples, the usability restrictions may exclude the possibility of marking while in others it may allow it in more than one attribute (depending on the AF). So, once again, the random nature increases and the average of attributes marked per tuple may be the same as previous techniques (see Fig. 8).

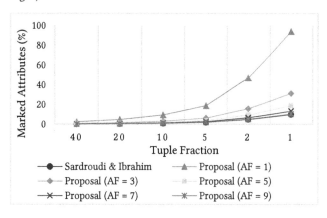

Figure 8: Marked attributes vs. tuple fraction.

For example, Figure 8 shows how using parameters like TF = 5 and AF = 5 do not include much more attributes for marking than Sardroudi & Ibrahim technique and also guarantees the consideration of more pixels (see Fig. 6, Table 3 and 4). The main

idea we bring is that it is not necessary to reduce too much the value of the parameter AF and TF for the marking, because this may compromise the data usability, but trying a medium value may guarantee a higher capability than previous techniques and a better identification of the WM after the extraction process.

5.4 Robustness Analysis

Robust WM schemes must be resilient against malicious attacks and benign updates, allowing the WM detection despite the data modification after marks embedding. Among the malicious attacks are the *Set Attacks*, operations trying to simulate the basic actions that form database transactions. The *Set Attacks* can be performed horizontally (tuple level), vertically (attribute level) or mixed (tuples and attributes), as well as at single level (one tuple or attribute) or massive level (multiple tuples or attributes). They are sub-classified as *subset attacks* (referring to deleting or updating tuples and/or attributes) and as *superset attacks* (referring to the insertion of new tuples and/or attributes).

The experiments carried out for the robustness analysis were focused on the tuples addition and deletion *Set Attacks*. The results show the resiliency of our proposal against them. Figures 9-14 show how even for a high percentage of alterations of the original watermarked data, the WM remains. It is important to understand that in some cases (e.g. *Tuple Addition*) the attacker may not try to modify the data at the same extreme level or higher to the used in our experiments. That will compromise the data quality and will make it useless for his purposes, even so, we stress the WM detection for some cases to see if it could be extracted and identified despite the excessive distortion caused by the attack.

For *Tuple Addition Attack* (see Fig. 9 and 10) the WM is easily identified despite the addition of even 200% of new tuples with values generated randomly inside the set and domain of the original values. For TF = 1 (highly aggressive embedding), using different values of the AF, our technique guarantees a better resilience than Sardroudi & Ibrahim (see Fig. 9). Even so, the main tendency is the degradation of the WM as the added tuples increases.

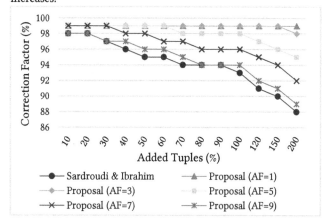

Figure 9: CF for tuples addition attack (TF = 1).

For TF = 40 (less aggressive embedding), the CF is close to the obtained for Sardroudi & Ibrahim in the case of AF = 9, but for other cases, it improves WM recognition (see Fig. 10). Despite the low values of the CF, the main tendency of the WM is to improve in a discrete way.

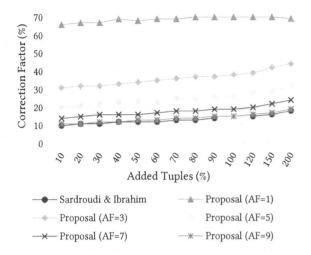

Figure 10: CF for tuples addition attack (TF = 40).

Considering that a TF of 40 is a very passive embedding, it is interesting to know at which level can be conducted the embedding to get better parameters, avoiding high data distortion. And even guaranteeing that tuple addition attacks, far for compromising the WM, contribute to its enhancement thanks to the random nature of the attacks and the majority voting used in the extraction process. Figure 11 shows the tendencies of the WM using different TF for the case of AF=7 (low embedding degree at attribute level). From this experiment, it is observed that the value of TF that may guarantee a change in the negative impact of the *Tuple Addition Attack* is between 5 and 10.

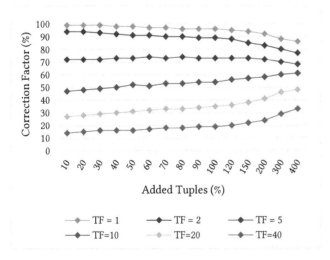

Figure 11: Tuples addition attack (AF = 7, different TF).

For *Tuple Deletion Attacks* (see Fig. 12-14), the WM degradation is directly linked to the TF and AF values. For example, for TF=1 (see Fig. 12) there is a high resilience of the WM. The different AF always guarantees a high CF. The problem begins when the dropped tuples are more than the 90%, which seriously compromise data usability.

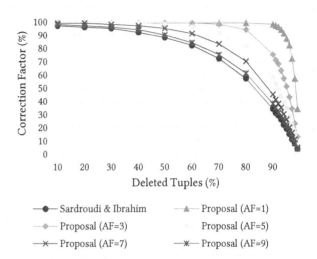

Figure 12: CF for tuples deletion attack (TF = 1).

For the case of TF=5 (see Fig. 13), Tuple Deletion Attack starts to compromise WM recognition for a lower modification than the used in the case of TF=1, but the WM still can be recognized by adding the 'Virtual Value' for the missed pixels. According to Table 3, even for a CF of 35, if the low value is due to missed values, the WM can be identified. So, the key value for compromising the WM robustness drops between the 60% and 70% of the tuples. That compromises the usability of the watermarked data once more, considering losing more than 50% of the information.

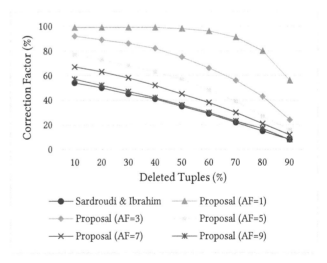

Figure 13: CF for tuples deletion attack (TF = 5).

Finally, for the case of the highest value of TF according to our experiments (see Fig. 14), the WM is seriously compromised. Here, a limit is clearly appreciated for the passivity of the embedding. So, if the data owner wants to guarantee the resilience of the WM against Tuple Deletion Attack, a TF value lower than 40 must be considered.

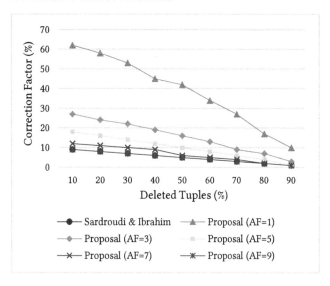

Figure 14: CF for tuples deletion attack (TF = 40).

6 CONCLUSIONS

In this paper, we present a robust watermarking technique that obtains the WM signal from an image. We include a new concept defined as the 'Attribute Fraction (AF)' used to reduce the number of marked tuples while guaranteeing a higher number of marks to be embedded. With this method we improve the embedding capacity causing less distortion over the watermarked data, allowing us to accept the rejection of marks by the data constraints with no major consequences.

The conducted experiments show the robustness of the proposed technique against attacks like addition and deletion of tuples. Also, they show how tuple addition attack, far from compromising the WM recognition, discretely helps to their improvement by considering the right parameters.

Watermarking techniques that depend on the primary key of the relation tuples are highly vulnerable to updating this attribute; so, as further work getting a new technique that does not depend on any unique attribute is desirable. Also, despite the distortion minimization, we propose to try new alternatives that cause less distortion of the data to be marked. Finally, we aim to increase the number of embedded marks, increasing their redundancy; seeking for the full inclusion of the WM and its robustness against another kind of attacks.

ACKNOWLEDGMENTS

This work was partially supported by a Ph.D. grant No. 714270 from CONACyT, Mexico and project PDCPN2013-01-216689.

REFERENCES

[1] Auguste, K., 1883. La cryptographie militaire. *Journal des sciences Militaires*, 9, p.538.

[2] Agrawal, R. and Kiernan, J., 2002, August. Watermarking relational databases. In *Proceedings of the 28th international conference on Very Large Data Bases* (pp. 155-166). VLDB Endowment.

[3] Agrawal, R., Haas, P.J. and Kiernan, J., 2003. Watermarking relational data: framework, algorithms and analysis. *The VLDB journal*, 12(2), pp.157-169.

[4] Bassia, P., Pitas, I. and Nikolaidis, N., 2001. Robust audio watermarking in the time domain. *Multimedia, IEEE Transactions on*, 3(2), pp.232-241.

[5] Cox, I.J. and Miller, M.L., 1997, June. Review of watermarking and the importance of perceptual modeling. In *Electronic Imaging'97* (pp. 92-99). International Society for Optics and Photonics.

[6] Cox, I., Miller, M., Bloom, J., Fridrich, J. and Kalker, T., 2007. *Digital watermarking and steganography*. Morgan Kaufmann.

[7] Forest CoverType, The UCI KDD Archive. Information and Computer Science. University of California, Irvine. Source:

http://kdd.ics.uci.edu/databases/covertype/covertype.html

[8] Franco-Contreras, J. and Coatrieux, G., 2015. Robust watermarking of relational databases with ontology-guided distortion control. *IEEE Transactions on Information Forensics and Security*, 10(9), pp.1939-1952.

[9] Franco-Contreras, J. and Coatrieux, G., 2016, September. Databases Traceability by Means of Watermarking with Optimized Detection. In International Workshop on Digital Watermarking (pp. 343-357). Springer, Cham.

[10] Gross-Amblard, D., 2011. Query-preserving watermarking of relational databases and xml documents. *ACM Transactions on Database Systems (TODS)*, 36(1), p.3.

[11] Guo, H., Li, Y., Liu, A. and Jajodia, S., 2006. A fragile watermarking scheme for detecting malicious modifications of database relations. *Information Sciences*, 176(10), pp.1350-1378.

[12] Guo, F., Wang, J. and Li, D., 2006, April. Fingerprinting relational databases. In *Proceedings of the 2006 ACM symposium on Applied computing* (pp. 487-492). ACM.

[13] Gursale, N. and Arti M., 2014. A Robust, Distortion Minimization Fingerprinting Technique for Relational Database. *International Journal on Recent and Innovation Trends in Computing and Communication (IJRITCC)*. (Vol. 2. Issue: 6, pp. 1737 – 1741, ISSN: 2321-8169).

[14] Halder, R., Pal, S. and Cortesi, A., 2010. Watermarking Techniques for Relational Databases: Survey, Classification and Comparison. *J. UCS*, 16(21), pp.3164-3190.

[15] Hanyurwimfura, D., Liu, Y. and Liu, Z., 2010, June. Text format based relational database watermarking for non-numeric data. In *Computer Design and Applications (ICCDA), 2010 International Conference on* (Vol. 4, pp. V4-312). IEEE.

[16] Hu, Z., Cao, Z. and Sun, J., 2009, April. An image based algorithm for watermarking relational databases. In *Measuring Technology and Mechatronics Automation, 2009. ICMTMA'09. International Conference on* (Vol. 1, pp. 425-428). IEEE.

[17] Jawad, K. and Khan, A., 2013. Genetic algorithm and difference expansion based reversible watermarking for relational databases. *Journal of Systems and Software*, 86(11), pp.2742-2753.

[18] Jiang, C., Chen, X. and Li, Z., 2009, August. Watermarking relational databases for ownership protection based on DWT. In *Information Assurance and Security, 2009. IAS'09. Fifth International Conference on* (Vol. 1, pp. 305-308). IEEE.

[19] Johnson, N.F., Duric, Z. and Jajodia, S., 2001. *Information Hiding: Steganography and Watermarking-Attacks and Countermeasures: Steganography and Watermarking: Attacks and Countermeasures* (Vol. 1). Springer Science & Business Media.

[20] Katzenbeisser, S. and Petitcolas, F., 2000. *Information hiding techniques for steganography and digital watermarking*. Artech house.

[21] Khan, A. and Husain, S.A., 2013. A fragile zero watermarking scheme to detect and characterize malicious modifications in database relations. *The Scientific World Journal*, 2013.

[22] Khanduja, V. and Verma, O.P., 2012. Identification and Proof of Ownership by Watermarking Relational Databases. *International Journal of Information and Electronics Engineering*, 2(2), p.274.

[23] Li, Y., Guo, H. and Jajodia, S., 2004, October. Tamper detection and localization for categorical data using fragile watermarks. In *Proceedings of the 4th ACM workshop on Digital rights management* (pp. 73-82). ACM.

[24] Li, Y., Swarup, V. and Jajodia, S., 2005. Fingerprinting relational databases: Schemes and specialties. *Dependable and Secure Computing, IEEE Transactions on*, 2(1), pp.34-45.

[25] Potdar, V.M., Han, S. and Chang, E., 2005, August. A survey of digital image watermarking techniques. In *Industrial Informatics, 2005. INDIN'05. 2005 3rd IEEE International Conference on* (pp. 709-716). IEEE.

[26] Rao, U.P., Patel, D.R. and Vikani, P.M., 2012. Relational database watermarking for ownership protection. *Procedia Technology*, 6, pp.988-995.

[27] Sardroudi, H.M. and Ibrahim, S., 2010, November. A new approach for relational database watermarking using image. In *Computer Sciences and Convergence Information Technology (ICCIT), 2010 5th International Conference on* (pp. 606-610). IEEE.

[28] Shehab, M., Bertino, E. and Ghafoor, A., 2008. Watermarking relational databases using optimization-based techniques. *Knowledge and Data Engineering, IEEE Transactions on*, 20(1), pp.116-129.

[29] Sion, R., Atallah, M. and Prabhakar, S., 2004. Rights protection for relational data. *Knowledge and Data Engineering, IEEE Transactions on*, 16(12), pp.1509-1525.

[30] Sun, J., Cao, Z. and Hu, Z., 2008, December. Multiple watermarking relational databases using image. In *MultiMedia and Information Technology, 2008. MMIT'08. International Conference on* (pp. 373-376). IEEE.

[31] Swanson, M.D., Zhu, B. and Tewfik, A.H., 1998. Multiresolution scene-based video watermarking using perceptual models. *Selected Areas in Communications, IEEE Journal on*, 16(4), pp.540-550.

[32] Swanson, M.D., Zhu, B. and Tewfik, A.H., 1996, September. Transparent robust image watermarking. In *Image Processing, 1996. Proceedings., International Conference on* (Vol. 3, pp. 211-214). IEEE.

[33] Tsai, M.H., Hsu, F.Y., Chang, J.D. and Wu, H.C., 2007, November. Fragile database watermarking for malicious tamper detection using support vector regression. In *Intelligent Information Hiding and Multimedia Signal Processing, 2007. IIHMSP 2007. Third International Conference on* (Vol. 1, pp. 493-496). IEEE.

[34] Zhang, Z.H., Jin, X.M., Wang, J.M. and Li, D.Y., 2004, August. Watermarking relational database using image. In *Machine Learning and Cybernetics, 2004. Proceedings of 2004 International Conference on* (Vol. 3, pp. 1739-1744). IEEE.

A Steganalytic Algorithm to Detect DCT-based Data Hiding Methods for H.264/AVC Videos

Peipei Wang

State Key Laboratory of Information Security,
Institute of Information Engineering, Chinese
Academy of Sciences, Beijing, China 100093
School of Cyber Security, University of Chinese
Academy of Sciences, Beijing, China 100093
wangpeipei@iie.ac.cn

Yun Cao

State Key Laboratory of Information Security,
Institute of Information Engineering, Chinese
Academy of Sciences, Beijing, China 100093
School of Cyber Security, University of Chinese
Academy of Sciences, Beijing, China 100093
caoyun@iie.ac.cn

Xianfeng Zhao*

State Key Laboratory of Information Security,
Institute of Information Engineering, Chinese
Academy of Sciences, Beijing, China 100093
School of Cyber Security, University of Chinese
Academy of Sciences, Beijing, China 100093
zhaoxianfeng@iie.ac.cn

Meineng Zhu

Beijing Institute of Electronics Technology
and Application
No. 15 Xinjiangongmen Rd
Beijing, China 100091
zmneng@163.com

ABSTRACT

This paper presents an effective steganalytic algorithm to
detect Discrete Cosine Transform (DCT) based data hiding
methods for H.264/AVC videos. These methods hide covert
information into compressed video streams by manipulating
quantized DCT coefficients, and usually achieve high payload and low computational complexity, which is suitable
for applications with hard real-time requirements. In contrast to considerable literature grown up in JPEG domain
steganalysis, so far there is few work found against DCT-
based methods for compressed videos. In this paper, the embedding impacts on both spatial and temporal correlations
are carefully analyzed, based on which two feature sets are
designed for steganalysis. The first feature set is engineered
as the histograms of noise residuals from the decompressed
frames using 16 DCT kernels, in which a quantity measuring residual distortion is accumulated. The second feature
set is designed as the residual histograms from the similar
blocks linked by motion vectors between inter-frames. The
experimental results have demonstrated that our method can
effectively distinguish stego videos undergone DCT manipulations from clean ones, especially for those of high qualities.

---

*Corresponding author

KEYWORDS

Steganalysis; data hiding; video; DCT; H.264/AVC

ACM Reference format:
Peipei Wang, Yun Cao, Xianfeng Zhao, and Meineng Zhu. 2017.
A Steganalytic Algorithm to Detect DCT-based Data Hiding
Methods for H.264/AVC Videos. In *Proceedings of IH&MMSec
'17, June 20–22, 2017, Philadelphia, PA, USA, ,* 11 pages.
DOI: http://dx.doi.org/10.1145/3082031.3083245

1 INTRODUCTION

The goal of steganalysis is to reveal the existence of secret
information embedded into innocent-looking media. Relevant techniques are developed to cope with the abuse of
steganography. Nowadays, facilitated by the advanced video
compression and network technology, the compressed digital
video has become one of the most influential media and also
one of the most suitable cover for data hiding. Hence video
targeted steganalysis has attracted much attention recently.

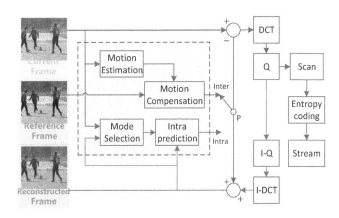

Figure 1: The compression process of H.264/AVC.

H.264/AVC [1] is developed in the pursuit of better compression performance and has become one of the most commonly practiced video coding standards. Up to date data hiding methods are usually integrated into the video compression process (Figure 1). Such approaches hide information by modifying certain output coefficients during compression procedure, such as motion vectors (MV) [3, 17, 20], inter prediction modes [8, 21], quantized DCT coefficients [11–14, 18] and variable length codes [9, 10].

This paper focuses on attacking DCT-based data hiding methods which are designed to satisfy hard real-time requirements. By directly modifying the quantized DCT coefficients of compressed video, the computationally expensive of full decoding and re-compression processes can be avoided. Several typical DCT-based methods [11–14, 18] have been proposed in video data hiding. By embedding information into the non-zero quantized DCT coefficients after zigzag scanning, Nakajima et al. [14] proposed the high capacity data hiding method. And in [18], both of the Mquant and quantized DCT coefficients are simultaneously manipulated with the attempt of preserving video quality. However, above methods all suffer from distortion drift of intra-frame. In order to avoid this problem, Ma et al. [12] utilized several paired-coefficients of each 4×4 DCT block for data embedding and the intra-frame distortion compensation was also implemented. And in [13], they further accumulated the distortion introduce by paired-coefficients' modifications and employed the directions of intra-frame prediction to avert the distortion drift. Recently, Lin et al. [11] proposed an improved method by perturbing the coefficient-pairs defined by a new set of sifted 4×4 blocks. In contrast to [13], this algorithm preserved the stego video's visual quality as well as increased the embedding capacity greatly. The problem of above DCT-based data hiding methods is that, the modifications of quantized DCT coefficients will lead to certain pixels' change in uncompressed stream, which leaves the opportunity of being detected by steganalysis.

A series of steganalytic methods [5, 15, 19] have been developed by exploiting the spatial or temporal correlation in video stream. Pankajakshan et al. [15] investigated the temporal correlation by extracting features from residual frames after temporal prediction. And Zarmehi et al. [19] estimated the cover frames and computed features both from video frames and residual matrix. In [5], in order to combine spatial correlation with temporal correlation among frames, the gray-level co-occurrence matrix between blocks was utilized to establish markov model of inter-frames. However, all above steganalytic approaches are not specialized in detecting DCT-based data hiding methods. Although they perform poorly in DCT-based steganalysis, these methods guide our approach against video data hiding. Moreover, the research of data hiding using quantized DCT coefficients has been well studied in image steganography. The effective schemes in JPEG image steganalysis [6, 7] also inspire the design of the proposed steganalytic feature.

The main contribution of this paper is the proposal of the first targeted steganalytic approach for data hiding in H.264/AVC videos by directly manipulating quantized DCT coefficients. By considering both the embedding impact on both spatial and temporal correlation, two feature sets are designed for training and classification. The intra-frame feature set is engineered as the residual histograms using DCT kernels and a quantity measuring embedding distortion is accumulated in the histograms. Considering the correlation of blocks between inter-frames, the second feature set is computed from the similar blocks linked by MVs.

The rest of this paper is organized as follows. The preliminaries are introduced in Section 2 and the methods of DCT-based data hiding are modeled is Section 3. In Section 4, the spatial and temporal correlations are elaborated and the design of final feature is also presented. Section 5 shows the experimental results and followed by the conclusions and future works given in Section 6.

2 PRELIMINARIES

2.1 Intra-Frame Coding

As the integral part of H.264/AVC compression [1], intra-frame prediction is employed to reduce the spatial redundancy in video frames. Intra-frame prediction algorithm used in H.264/AVC provides two sizes of luminance block: 4×4 and 16×16. Because 16×16 luminance block usually varies smoothly and human eyes are very sensitive to the change of luminance values, the existing data hiding methods only consider the 4×4 blocks in I frames. There are nine prediction modes for each 4×4 luminance block, which is shown in Figure 2. During intra-frame prediction, each current block is predicted based on the previously encoded adjacent block. As shown in Figure 3, $B_{i,j}$ is the current 4×4 block with pixels labeled as a to p. By using an optimal prediction mode of the nine modes, the prediction block $B_{i,j}^p$ is obtained. The reference pixels (A to M) located in the reconstructed neighboring blocks are utilized for prediction. The difference matrix between prediction block and original block constructs the residual block $R_{i,j}$, which undergoes the following compression process.

The integer DCT and quantization operation applied to $R_{i,j}$ can be formulized as follows.

$$\boldsymbol{R}_{i,j}^{QDCT} = (\boldsymbol{C}_f \boldsymbol{R}_{i,j} \boldsymbol{C}_f^T) \otimes \frac{\boldsymbol{E}_f}{Q_{step}} = \begin{bmatrix} r_{00} & r_{01} & r_{02} & r_{03} \\ r_{10} & r_{11} & r_{12} & r_{13} \\ r_{20} & r_{21} & r_{22} & r_{23} \\ r_{30} & r_{31} & r_{32} & r_{33} \end{bmatrix}$$
(1)

where

$$\boldsymbol{C}_f = \begin{bmatrix} 1 & 1 & 1 & 1 \\ 2 & 1 & -1 & -2 \\ 1 & -1 & -1 & 1 \\ 1 & -2 & 2 & -1 \end{bmatrix}$$

$$\boldsymbol{E}_f = \begin{bmatrix} a^2 & ab/2 & a^2 & ab/2 \\ ab/2 & b^2/4 & ab/2 & b^2/4 \\ a^2 & ab/2 & a^2 & ab/2 \\ ab/2 & b^2/4 & ab/2 & b^2/4 \end{bmatrix}$$

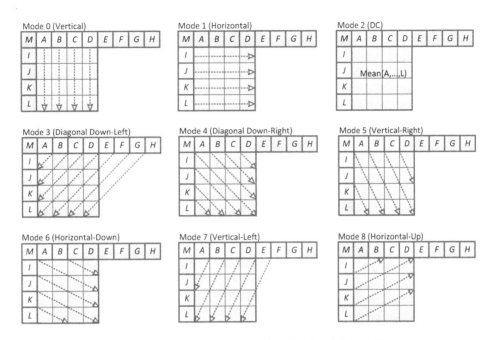

Figure 2: Nine prediction modes for 4×4 luma block.

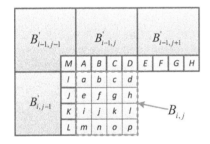

Figure 3: The predicted 4×4 luma block and the reference pixels in neighboring blocks.

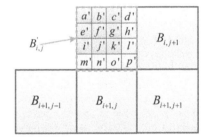

Figure 4: The reconstructed 4×4 luma block and neighboring blocks affected by intra-frame prediction.

and $\otimes$ denotes the product operation of the corresponding elements, Q_{step} is the quantizer step size determined by quantization parameter (QP), a and b are real numbers assigned by $a = 1/2$ and $b = \sqrt{2/5}$ respectively.

2.2 Distortion Drift

Current DCT-based data hiding methods [11–14, 18] embed information by perturbing $R_{i,j}^{QDCT}$ parameter, which is the quantized DCT coefficient of $R_{i,j}$. The reconstructed block is derived by $B'_{i,j} = B^p_{i,j} + R'_{i,j}$. $R'_{i,j}$ denotes the reconstructed residual block, which is obtained by inverse DCT transforming and dequantizing $R_{i,j}^{QDCT}$. As depicted in Figure 4, four neighboring blocks are affected by current reconstructed block because the pixels in bottom row and right column of $B'_{i,j}$ are utilized for their intra-frame predictions. After embedding information into $R_{i,j}^{QDCT}$, $R_{i,j}^{QDCTs}$ is obtained and the corresponding reconstructed block is $B'^s_{i,j}$. If $\{m', n', o', p'\}$ of $B'^s_{i,j}$ are changed and the prediction mode

of neighboring block $B_{i+1,j}$ is Mode 0, the distortion will drift to $B'_{i+1,j}$.

3 MODELING OF DCT-BASED DATA HIDING METHODS

In order to avoid the distortion drift, the existing data hiding methods [11–13] classify the 4×4 blocks according to their neighboring blocks' prediction modes and then provide the qualified paired-coefficients under different conditions. The distortion drift occurs only if $\{d', h', l', p', m', n', o', p'\}$ are reference pixels in neighboring blocks' prediction. If the prediction mode of $B_{i,j+1}$ satisfies $PM_{i,j+1} = \{1, 2, 4, 5, 6, 8\}$, $\{d, h, l, p\}$ are used in prediction process. $\{m, n, o, p\}$ are reference pixels if $PM_{i+1,j} = \{0, 2, 3, 4, 5, 6, 7\}$ and $PM_{i+1,j-1} = \{3, 7\}$. And $PM_{i+1,j+1} = \{4, 5, 6\}$ indicates that pixel p is referred for the prediction of $B_{i+1,j+1}$. The currently optimal approach [11] of categorizing the 4×4 blocks is recorded

Table 1: Five categories of 4×4 block used in DCT-based data hiding

Category	$PM_{i,j+1}$	$PM_{i+1,j}$	$PM_{i+1,j-1}$	$PM_{i+1,j+1}$
1st	{1,2,4,5,6,8}	{1,8}	{0,1,2,4,5,6,8}	ANY
2st	{0,3,7}	{0,2,3,4,5,6,7}	{3,7}	ANY
3st	{0,3,7}	{1,8}	{0,1,2,4,5,6,8}	{4,5,6}
4st	{1,2,4,5,6,8}	{0,2,3,4,5,6,7}	{3,7}	ANY
5st	{0,3,7}	{1,8}	{0,1,2,4,5,6,8}	{0,1,2,3,7,8}

in Table 1. Based on whether the seven pixels are used in intra-prediction of neighboring blocks, every block to be embedded is classified to one of the five categories.

In DCT-based data hiding methods, different coefficient-pairs of matrix $R_{i,j}^{QDCT}$ are modified in different categories. For the first category, the $\{d', h', l', p'\}$ of $B'_{i,j}$ are reference pixels in prediction. In order to prevent distortion drift, the modifications of $R_{i,j}^{QDCT}$'s coefficients should not perturb the right column pixels. The paired-coefficients of $\{(r_{00}, r_{02}), (r_{10}, r_{12}), (r_{20}, r_{22}), (r_{30}, r_{32})\}$ are qualified for embedding. Similarly, if $B_{i,j}$ belongs to second category, $\{m', n', o', p'\}$ will be employed in prediction and $(r_{01}, r_{21}), (r_{02}, r_{22}), (r_{03}, r_{23}), (r_{00}, r_{20})$ are modified to embed information. Because only p' is referred in prediction of the block in category three, the coefficient-pairs can also be obtained through the above method. For category four, restricted by the circumstance that all seven related pixels will be used in prediction, one bit can only be embedded through modifying $(r_{00}, r_{02}, r_{20}, r_{22})$ to $(r_{00} + 1, r_{02} - 1, r_{20} - 1, r_{22} + 1)$. In the fifth category, it is unnecessary to consider distortion drift because none of $\{d', h', l', m', n', o', p'\}$ is reference pixel. And all of the parameters of $R_{i,j}^{QDCT}$ can be used to embed sixteen bits. Thus the information can be embedded through above manipulations, and the distortion drift is averted in DCT-based data hiding.

However, the modifications of quantized DCT coefficients will reflect on the pixels' values of decompressed stream. The dequantization and integer inverse DCT are operated to $R_{i,j}^{QDCT}$ during decompression process, which can be demonstrated by following formulate.

$$R'_{i,j} = C_r^T (R_{i,j}^{QDCT} \times Q_{step} \otimes E_r) C_r \qquad (2)$$

where

$$C_r = \begin{bmatrix} 1 & 1 & 1 & 1 \\ 1 & 1/2 & -1/2 & -1 \\ 1 & -1 & -1 & 1 \\ 1/2 & -1 & 1 & -1/2 \end{bmatrix}$$

$$E_r = \begin{bmatrix} a^2 & ab & a^2 & ab/2 \\ ab & b^2 & ab & b^2 \\ a^2 & ab & a^2 & ab/2 \\ ab & b^2 & ab & b^2 \end{bmatrix}$$

For example, one bit is embedded by modifying (Y_{00}, Y_{02}) to $(Y_{00} + 1, Y_{02} - 1)$ in the first category. The difference

matrix between $R_{i,j}^{QDCT}$ and $R_{i,j}^{QDCTs}$ is

$$\triangle R_{i,j}^{QDCT} = R_{i,j}^{QDCTs} - R_{i,j}^{QDCTc} = \begin{bmatrix} 1 & 0 & -1 & 0 \\ 0 & 0 & 0 & 0 \\ 0 & 0 & 0 & 0 \\ 0 & 0 & 0 & 0 \end{bmatrix} \qquad (3)$$

And the corresponding difference between $R'_{i,j}$ and $R'^{s}_{i,j}$ equals

$$\triangle R'_{i,j} = R'^{s}_{i,j} - R'^{c}_{i,j} = C_r^T (\triangle R_{i,j}^{QDCT} \times Q_{step} \otimes E_r) C_r$$

$$= Q_{step} \times \begin{bmatrix} 0 & 2a^2 & 2a^2 & 0 \\ 0 & 2a^2 & 2a^2 & 0 \\ 0 & 2a^2 & 2a^2 & 0 \\ 0 & 2a^2 & 2a^2 & 0 \end{bmatrix} \qquad (4)$$

The reconstructed block after embedding is calculated by $B'^{s}_{i,j} = B'_{i,j} + R'_{i,j} + \triangle R'_{i,j}$. Although the right column of $B'^{s}_{i,j}$ is not perturbed by modifications, the pixels' values in the middle two columns are all changed due to DCT-based data hiding.

4 PROPOSED STEGANALYSTIC FEATURE SETS

4.1 Spatial Correlation in Intra-Frame

Video stream is actually composed of continuous frames and every frame can be viewed as an image in spatial domain. In this section, we analyze the spatial correlation in intra-frame and propose the intra-frame feature with residual distortion measure.

4.1.1 Feature based on H.264 phase. In H.264/AVC[1], in order to reduce computation complexity during video compression, the 4×4 integer DCT and quantization is reformed from the following transformation formula

$$R^{QDCT} = ARA^T \qquad (5)$$

where A is the identity orthogonal matrix defined by

$$A = \begin{bmatrix} \frac{1}{2}\cos(0) & \frac{1}{2}\cos(0) & \frac{1}{2}\cos(0) & \frac{1}{2}\cos(0) \\ \sqrt{\frac{1}{2}}\cos(\frac{\pi}{8}) & \sqrt{\frac{1}{2}}\cos(\frac{3\pi}{8}) & \sqrt{\frac{1}{2}}\cos(\frac{5\pi}{8}) & \sqrt{\frac{1}{2}}\cos(\frac{7\pi}{8}) \\ \sqrt{\frac{1}{2}}\cos(\frac{2\pi}{8}) & \sqrt{\frac{1}{2}}\cos(\frac{6\pi}{8}) & \sqrt{\frac{1}{2}}\cos(\frac{10\pi}{8}) & \sqrt{\frac{1}{2}}\cos(\frac{14\pi}{8}) \\ \sqrt{\frac{1}{2}}\cos(\frac{3\pi}{8}) & \sqrt{\frac{1}{2}}\cos(\frac{9\pi}{8}) & \sqrt{\frac{1}{2}}\cos(\frac{15\pi}{8}) & \sqrt{\frac{1}{2}}\cos(\frac{21\pi}{8}) \end{bmatrix}$$

And the inverse quantization and inverse integer DCT is calculated by

$$R = A^T R^{QDCT} A \qquad (6)$$

These formulas are actually derived from 2-D DCT and inverse DCT transformation. For every frame with the size

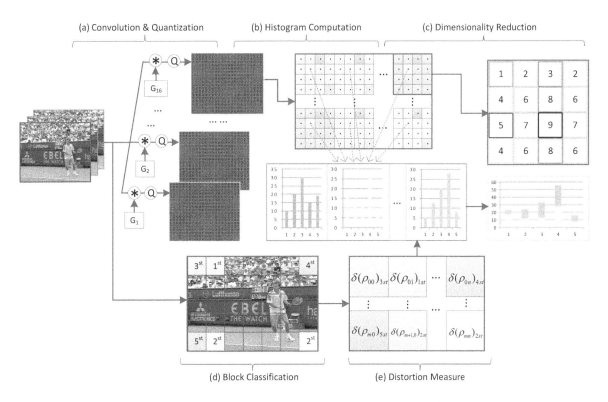

Figure 5: The extraction process of intra-frame feature based on H.264 phase with distortion measure.

of $M \times N$, the (i,j)th 4×4 residual block, $1 \leq i \leq M/4$, $1 \leq j \leq N/4$, is formed by $R_{ij}(m,n)$, which is restricted to $0 \leq m \leq 3$ and $0 \leq n \leq 3$. The DCT coefficient matrix of residual block is composed of $R_{ij}^{DCT}(u,v)$, where $0 \leq u \leq 3$ and $0 \leq v \leq 3$. The 2-D DCT and IDCT transformation can be formulated by

$$R_{ij}^{DCT}(u,v) = \frac{w_u w_v}{2} \sum_{m=0}^{3} \sum_{n=0}^{3} R_{ij}(m,n) \cdot \\ cos\frac{(2m+1)u\pi}{8} \cdot cos\frac{(2n+1)v\pi}{8} \quad (7)$$

$$R_{ij}(m,n) = \sum_{u=0}^{3} \sum_{v=0}^{3} \frac{w_u w_v}{2} R_{ij}^{DCT}(u,v) \cdot \\ cos\frac{(2m+1)u\pi}{8} \cdot cos\frac{(2n+1)v\pi}{8} \quad (8)$$

where $w_0 = 1/\sqrt{2}$ and $w_u = 1, w_v = 1$ if $u > 0, v > 0$.

As described in Section 3, the modifications of residual blocks' quantized DCT coefficients will perturb the pixels in reconstructed blocks, which inspires us to detect the DCT-based data hiding methods in our algorithm. In image steganalysis, JPEG phase based methods [6, 7] perform effectively to detect JPEG stegnanography. Derived from the principle of JPEG phase feature, video steganalysis based on H.264 phase is proposed, in which the H.264 phase is defined as the locations of the 4×4 pixel grid in every block.

In order to compute the steganalytic feature based on H.264 phase, the compressed video is first decompressed to spatial domain. And as the result, a series of frames $\boldsymbol{F}$ which consist of pixels are obtained. Then the noise residuals are calculated by convolving $\boldsymbol{F}$ with DCT kernels.

$$\boldsymbol{U}(\boldsymbol{F}, \boldsymbol{G}) = \{\boldsymbol{U}^{(u,v)}|0 \leq u, v \leq 3\} \quad (9)$$
$$\boldsymbol{U}^{(u,v)} = \boldsymbol{F} * \boldsymbol{G}^{(u,v)}$$

where $\boldsymbol{U}^{(u,v)} \in \mathbb{R}^{(M-3)\times(N-3)}$ and the operator * denotes the convolution without padding. The DCT kernels are formed as follows.

$$\boldsymbol{G}^{(u,v)} = \{G_{mn}^{(u,v)}|0 \leq m, n \leq 3\} \quad (10)$$

$$G_{mn}^{(u,v)} = \frac{w_u w_v}{2} \cdot cos\frac{(2m+1)u\pi}{8} \cdot cos\frac{(2n+1)v\pi}{8} \quad (11)$$

where every DCT basis $G_{uv}^{(m,n)}$ is 4×4 matrix and there are 16 DCT bases in this operation. Consequently, a set of 16 residual matrices are formed after convolutions. Subsequently the residual matrix is quantized by

$$\boldsymbol{U}(\boldsymbol{F}, \boldsymbol{G}, Q) = Q(\boldsymbol{U}(F, G)/q) \quad (12)$$

where q is a fixed quantization step, Q is a quantizer with $\{0, 1, 2, ...T_r\}$ as the centroids and T_r is the truncation threshold. The convolution and quantization process is depicted in Figure 5(a). After these two step, each of the 16 quantized residual matrices is used to compute histograms as follows.

$$h_\tau^{(u,v)}(\boldsymbol{F}, \boldsymbol{G}, Q) = \sum_{i=1}^{\lfloor M/4 \rfloor} \sum_{j=0}^{\lfloor N/4 \rfloor} [U_{ij}^{(u,v)}(F, G, Q) = \tau] \quad (13)$$

As indicated in Figure 5(b), there are 16 histograms that can be obtained for each residual matrix and every histogram consists T_r+1 values. Based on the symmetries of the kernel and DCT basis, the number of histograms can be reduced by merging certain bins of the histograms. As shown in Figure 5(c), the histograms of the phases labeled with the same number can be merged and the number of histograms is reduced from 16 to 9. Therefore, for each frame, the dimensionality of the H.264 phase-based feature can be calculated by $16 \times 9 \times (T_r + 1) = 144 \times (T_r + 1)$.

4.1.2 Residual distortion measure. In order to better detect the current DCT-based data hiding methods, the residual distortion is measured and incorporated into the design of the proposed feature.

For the frames of cover videos, the quantized DCT coefficients in the (i, j) residual block is denoted by $R_{ij}^{QDCTc}(u, v)$. Deduced from Eq.2, Eq.8 and Eq.11, the decompressed residuals can be calculated by $R_{ij}^{'c}(m, n) = \sum_{u,v=0}^{3} G_{mn}^{(u,v)} \cdot q_{mn} \cdot R_{ij}^{QDCTc}(u, v)$, where q_{mn} is the quantization step. The quantized DCT residuals after embedding $s_{i,j}(u, v)$ are $R_{ij}^{QDCTs}(u, v) = R_{ij}^{QDCTc}(u, v) + s_{i,j}(u, v)$. And the corresponding decompressed residual block is $R_{ij}^{'s}(m, n) = \sum_{u,v=0}^{3} G_{mn}^{(u,v)} \cdot q_{mn} \cdot R_{ij}^{QDCTs}(u, v)$. Thus the difference between decompressed stego block and cover block is computed by

$$B_{i,j}^{'s}(m, n) = B_{i,j}^{'}(m, n) + R_{ij}^{'s}(m, n)$$

$$B_{i,j}^{'c}(m, n) = B_{i,j}^{'}(m, n) + R_{ij}^{'c}(m, n)$$

$$\triangle B_{i,j}^{'}(m, n) = \triangle R_{i,j}^{'}(m, n) = R_{ij}^{'s}(m, n) - R_{ij}^{'c}(m, n)$$

$$= \sum_{u,v=0}^{3} G_{mn}^{(u,v)} \cdot q_{mn} \cdot s_{i,j}(u, v) \tag{14}$$

Based on the linearity of convolution, the difference between $R_{ij}^{'s}$ and $R_{ij}^{'c}$ is used as the accumulated quantity in the feature calculation. Thus the residual distortion is defined by

$$\rho(s) = \boldsymbol{R}^s * \boldsymbol{G} - \boldsymbol{R}^c * \boldsymbol{G} = \boldsymbol{s} * \boldsymbol{G} \tag{15}$$

where $\rho(s) = \{\rho_{ij}(s) | 1 \le i \le M/4, 1 \le j \le N/4\}$. After modifying the quantized DCT coefficients, the difference between the stego and cover decompressed residual is denoted as

$$\triangle R_{i,j}^{'} = \begin{bmatrix} \triangle R_{0,0}^{'} & \triangle R_{0,1}^{'} & \triangle R_{0,2}^{'} & \triangle R_{0,3}^{'} \\ \triangle R_{1,0}^{'} & \triangle R_{1,1}^{'} & \triangle R_{1,2}^{'} & \triangle R_{1,3}^{'} \\ \triangle R_{2,0}^{'} & \triangle R_{2,1}^{'} & \triangle R_{2,2}^{'} & \triangle R_{2,3}^{'} \\ \triangle R_{3,0}^{'} & \triangle R_{3,1}^{'} & \triangle R_{3,2}^{'} & \triangle R_{3,3}^{'} \end{bmatrix} \tag{16}$$

Based on the theorem in [16], the sum of square errors is utilized as the measure of distortion

$$\delta(\rho_{ij}) = \sum_{m=0}^{3} \sum_{n=0}^{3} \triangle R_{m,n}^{'2} \tag{17}$$

As described in Section 3, the secret information is embedded to quantized DCT paired-coefficients according to the 4×4 blocks' classification. Take the first category as example, the four vertical coefficient-pairs in $\{(r_{00}, r_{02}), (r_{10}, r_{12}),$

$(r_{20}, r_{22}), (r_{30}, r_{32})\}$ are the suggested parameters for modifications. If the pair (r_{10}, r_{12}) is perturbed to $(r_{10}+1, r_{12}-1)$, the difference between R_{ij}^{QDCTs} and R_{ij}^{QDCTc} is computed by

$$\triangle R_{ij}^{QDCT} = R_{ij}^{QDCTs} - R_{ij}^{QDCTc} = \begin{bmatrix} 0 & 0 & 0 & 0 \\ 1 & 0 & -1 & 0 \\ 0 & 0 & 0 & 0 \\ 0 & 0 & 0 & 0 \end{bmatrix} \tag{18}$$

And difference between decompressed cover block $R_{ij}^{'c}$ and stego block $R_{ij}^{'s}$ can be derived from Eq. 2 as follows.

$$\triangle \boldsymbol{R}_{i,j}^{'} = \boldsymbol{R}_{i,j}^{'s} - \boldsymbol{R}_{i,j}^{'c} = \boldsymbol{C}_r^T (\triangle \boldsymbol{R}_{i,j}^{QDCT} \times Q_{step} \otimes \boldsymbol{E}_r) \boldsymbol{C}_r$$

$$= Q_{step} \times \begin{bmatrix} 0 & 2ab & 2ab & 0 \\ 0 & ab & ab & 0 \\ 0 & -ab & -ab & 0 \\ 0 & -2ab & -2ab & 0 \end{bmatrix} \tag{19}$$

where $a = 1/2, b = \sqrt{2/5}$ and Q is the step size of a quantizer determined by QP. Then the distortion induced by perturbing (r_{10}, r_{12}) is measured by

$$\delta(\rho_{ij})(r_{10}, r_{12}) = \sum_{m=0}^{3} \sum_{n=0}^{3} \triangle R_{m,n}^{'2}$$

$$= (4 \times (2ab)^2 + 4 \times (ab)^2) \times Q^2 \tag{20}$$

$$= 20 \times (ab)^2 \times Q^2 = 2Q^2$$

Similarly the residual distortions of other pairs are obtained $\delta(\rho_{ij})(r_{00}, r_{02}) = \delta(\rho_{ij})(r_{20}, r_{22}) = \delta(\rho_{ij})(r_{30}, r_{32}) = 2Q^2$. And the total distortion of first category equals $8Q^2$, which is the sum of these four sub-distortions. By the same derivation, the distortion of second and third category is also $8Q^2$. In category four, $(r_{00}, r_{02}, r_{20}, r_{22})$ is modified to $(r_{00}+1, r_{02}-1, r_{20}-1, r_{22}+1)$ and the corresponding distortion is

$$\delta(\rho_{ij})(r_{00}, r_{02}, r_{20}, r_{22}) = \sum_{m=0}^{3} \sum_{n=0}^{3} \triangle R_{m,n}^{'2}$$

$$= 4 \times (4a^2)^2 \times Q^2 = 64a^4 \times Q^2 \tag{21}$$

$$= 4Q^2$$

Because all of the sixteen bits can be utilized for embedding in the fifth category, the overall distortion is $16Q^2$. Thus the distortion measure of DCT-based data hiding can be presented by $\delta(\rho_{ij}) = \{\delta(\rho_{ij})_{1st}, \delta(\rho_{ij})_{2st}, \delta(\rho_{ij})_{3st}, \delta(\rho_{ij})_{4st}, \delta(\rho_{ij})_{5st}\} = \{8Q^2, 8Q^2, 8Q^2, 4Q^2, 16Q^2\}$. And the H.264 phase based histogram with this distortion measure is formulized as

$$\dot{h}_\tau^{(u,v)}(\boldsymbol{F}, \boldsymbol{G}, Q) = \sum_{i=1}^{\lfloor M/4 \rfloor} \sum_{j=0}^{\lfloor N/4 \rfloor} [U_{ij}^{(u,v)}(\boldsymbol{F}, \boldsymbol{G}, Q) = \tau] \cdot \delta(\rho_{ij}) \tag{22}$$

As shown in 5(e)(d), the residual distortion induced by modifications is measured based on the block classification in DCT-based data hiding methods. Then it can cooperate with the histogram computation to extract the intra-frame feature.

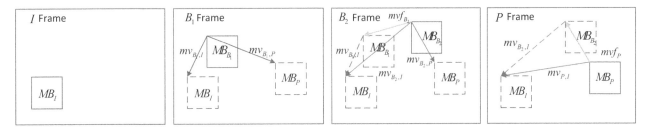

Figure 6: Compute SMV based on Inter-frame prediction in GOP.

4.2 Temporal Correlation between Inter-Frames

Due to the continuity in time, strong correlation usually exists between the blocks of adjacent frames, which is probable to be disturbed by embedding manipulation. Thus we exploit the correlation of similar blocks between adjacent frames, from which the inter-frame feature is extracted.

4.2.1 4×4 block link using motion vectors. Motion estimation is designed to reduce the temporal redundancy between video frames. This is achieved by allowing blocks of pixels from currently coded frame to be matched with those from reference frame(s). As the result of motion estimation, MV represents the spatial displacement offset between a block and its prediction.

Therefore, the similar blocks along the time-axis can be linked by the MVs. However, MVs' values are greatly determined by the performance of motion estimation. In order to decide whether the block pointed by MV is the similar one of current block, the MVs are screened by

$$|SAD - \frac{SAD_1 + \cdots + SAD_{\mathbb{N}^2-1}}{\mathbb{N}^2 - 1}| < \mu \qquad (23)$$

Here, SAD is the sum of absolute difference between the block and its prediction, μ is the standard deviation of SAD. This formula computes the difference between the current SAD and the average SAD of its neighbors. Because 4×4 is the size of the investigated blocks, the motion of neighboring blocks is homogeneous. If the SAD of this MB is distinctly large compared with its neighbors, it is a singularity in prediction and the reference block is not the similar block. All of the inaccurate MVs would be screened out after this procedure, leaving those pointing to similar blocks.

There are three types of frames including I,P and B frame in group of pictures (GOP). A GOP usually starts with an I frame and consists of several P and B frames. In the inter-prediction, I frame conducts as the reference frame, one frame is used to predict P frame and two frames are referred when predicting B frame. Therefore, in video compression, the MVs point to the reference blocks in disorder. In order to link the similar blocks in chronological order along the time axis, we need to calculate the sequential MVs (SMV). The set of SMVs in frame F_t is denoted by $\{smv_t\}$, in which every SMV points to the prediction block in $(t-1)$th frame.

As shown in Figure 6, in every frame, the smv_t can be computed from their original MVs. In frame F_{B_1}, smv_{B_1} equals $mv_{B_1,I}$, which is the MV obtained by referring to the corresponding MB_I in frame I. In frame F_{B_2}, according to the operation rule of vector (the Triangle Rule), we can get $smv_{B_2} = mv_{B_2,I} - mv_{B_1,I}$. And similarly $smv_P = mv_{P,I} - mv_{B_2,I}$ can be obtained in frame F_P by analyzing the constraints of the original MVs.

For a given video sequence $\{F_t\}_{t=1}^T$, the SMV set $\{smv_t\}$ of every frame can be constructed by above computation and smv_t points to the location of corresponding similar block in frame F_{t-1}. All of the similar blocks in GOP can be linked by smv_t, which is diagrammatically expressed in Figure 7. If the location of predicted block crosses the boundary in reference frame, the one with largest overlapping area is selected as the linked block. Besides 4×4 luma block, 16×16 luma block also exists in H.264/AVC. In order to link the associated blocks which are similar to the 4×4 block in I frame, the block of larger size is divided into 4×4 sub-blocks. Consequently, all of the similar 4×4 blocks are linked in sequence with the head of 4×4 block in I frame.

4.2.2 Feature based on block link. Besides the intra-frame feature which is extracted based on the spatial correlation, we also extract feature by exploiting the correlation between inter-frames.

After above manipulation, the temporal correlation is exploited by linking the similar blocks in video GOP. In order to extract feature based on such correlation, we construct the temporal pattern by splicing the linked blocks, which is illustrated in Figure 8. Every row of the pattern consists of T linked 4×4 blocks which are similar to the same one in I frame, where T is the frame number of this GOP. Supposing

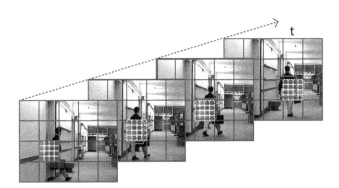

Figure 7: 4×4 block link by SMVs.

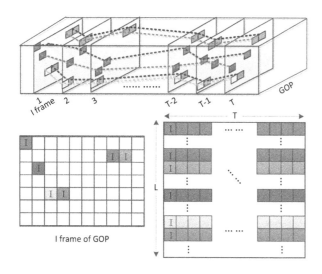

Figure 8: Construct pattern using linked blocks.

L 4×4 blocks in I frames can be linked, the number of links in this GOP is L. Thus L rows of the linked 4×4 blocks compose the temporal pattern of this GOP.

Then features are extracted from the pattern using the same method described in Subsection 4.1. The temporal histogram is calculated by

$$\ddot{h}_\tau^{(u,v)}(\boldsymbol{P}, \boldsymbol{G}, Q) = \sum_{i=1}^{T} \sum_{j=0}^{L} [U_{ij}^{(u,v)}(\boldsymbol{P}, \boldsymbol{G}, Q) = \tau] \cdot \delta(\rho_i) \quad (24)$$

where T and L is the width and height of the constructed pattern in 4×4 block unit, $\boldsymbol{P}$ is the decompressed pattern, $\delta(\rho_i)$ is the distortion of the block in ith row. It is noticeable that the linked block's distortion in one row is identical, which equals to the distortion of the similar block in I frame. And for each constructed pattern, the dimensionality of temporal feature can also be calculated by $16 \times 9 \times (T_r + 1) = 144 \times (T_r + 1)$.

4.3 Final Feature Design

As described in Subsection 4.1 and 4.2, the intra-frame and inter-frame correlations of video sequence are exploited to detect DCT-based data hiding. In order to improve the steganalytic performance, we utilize the distortion measure to optimize the feature extraction in spatial and temporal domain. Based on above analysis, we design the final feature and summarize the implementation in pseudo-code. In the below pseudo-code, the kernels of convolution in $\boldsymbol{G}$ are formed by 16 DCT bases, and Q is the quantizer step size determined by QP.

1. Divide the compressed video into K GOPs and the head of every GOP is I frame.
2. For every GOP,
   1) decompress the I frame under investigation to the spatial domain. For every spatial frame $\boldsymbol{F}_\kappa$,

a) compute the noise residual $U(\boldsymbol{F}_\kappa, \boldsymbol{G})$ and quantize it to get $U(\boldsymbol{F}_\kappa, \boldsymbol{G}, Q)$;
b) evaluate $\delta(\rho_{ij}) \in \{8Q^2, 8Q^2, 8Q^2, 4Q^2, 16Q^2\}$ for every (i,j)th 4×4 block by classifying it to one of the five categories;
c) calculate the histogram $\dot{h}_\tau^{(u,v)}(\boldsymbol{F}_\kappa, \boldsymbol{G}, Q)$ by $\sum_{i=1}^{\lfloor M/4 \rfloor} \sum_{j=0}^{\lfloor N/4 \rfloor} [U_{ij}^{(u,v)}(\boldsymbol{F}_\kappa, \boldsymbol{G}, Q) = \tau] \cdot \delta(\rho_{ij})$, where $0 \leq \tau \leq T_r, 0 \leq u, v \leq 3$.
2) decompress the P and B frames in this GOP, and during the decompression,
   a) construct the temporal pattern $\boldsymbol{P}_\kappa$ by linking the spatial blocks similar to the same one in $\boldsymbol{F}_\kappa$;
   b) compute the noise residual $U(\boldsymbol{P}_\kappa, \boldsymbol{G})$ and quantize it to get $U(\boldsymbol{P}_\kappa, \boldsymbol{G}, Q)$;
   c) compute the histogram values in $\ddot{h}_\tau^{(u,v)}(\boldsymbol{P}_\kappa, \boldsymbol{G}, Q)$ $\sum_{i=1}^{T} \sum_{j=0}^{L} [U_{ij}^{(u,v)}(\boldsymbol{P}_\kappa, \boldsymbol{G}, Q) = \tau] \cdot \delta(\rho_i)$, here $\delta(\rho_i)$ is the block's distortion in $\boldsymbol{F}_\kappa$.
3) merge the bins of $\dot{h}_\tau^{(u,v)}(\boldsymbol{F}_\kappa, \boldsymbol{G}, Q)$ and $\ddot{h}_\tau^{(u,v)}(\boldsymbol{P}_\kappa, \boldsymbol{G}, Q)$ using symmetrization rules, then concatenate two merg -ed histograms to construct the final feature set.
3. manipulate every $GOP_\kappa, 1 \leq \kappa \leq K$ as Step 2 until the end of the compressed video.

After the above process, K features are extracted from the video. Because the feature dimensionality of intra-frame or inter-frame correlation equals $144 \times (T_r + 1)$, the concatenated feature's dimension is supposed to be $2 \times 144 \times (T_r + 1) = 288 \times (T_r + 1)$. And there are 1440 values in the final feature set with T_r set as 4. In the next section, the extracted features will be further subjected to classifier for experimental evaluation.

5 EXPERIMENTS

5.1 Experimental Setup

As the well-known H.264/AVC codec, x264 [2] is utilized to implement the data hiding and steganalytic algorithms in our experiments. The video database consists of 100 standard CIF sequences in YUV 4:2:0 format. These sequences vary from 100 to 2000 frames in length and are all coded at the frame rate of 30*fps*.

In order to evaluate steganalytic method against existing DCT-based data hiding schemes, Ma's [13] and Lin's [11] methods are realized to embed information. The embedding

Table 2: Percentage of 4×4 blocks in each category under different QPs

QP	1st	2st	3st	4st	5st
20	24.72%	26.63%	1.60%	43.91%	3.14%
24	23.15%	26.17%	1.10%	45.78%	3.80%
28	23.03%	24.59%	1.20%	47.18%	4.00%
32	22.18%	23.31%	0.90%	50.11%	3.50%
36	18.26%	19.91%	1.30%	57.73%	2.80%
40	15.62%	17.13%	1.10%	63.95%	2.20%

Table 3: Detection accuracies (%) of Da's method, DCTR feature and proposed steganalytic algorithm against DCT-based data hiding methods

DCT-based Data Hiding	QP	ER (*bpnc*)	Da's method		DCTR feature		Proposed algorithm	
			Ensemble Classifier	SVM	Ensemble Classifier	SVM	Ensemble Classifier	SVM
Ma's method	28	0.05	53.30	62.79	64.27	67.70	66.59	76.90
		0.1	58.16	75.23	74.19	76.93	84.72	95.81
	32	0.05	53.01	61.19	58.64	63.64	60.78	70.68
		0.1	58.09	73.54	70.61	74.53	80.29	86.70
	36	0.05	52.04	58.74	54.34	59.42	57.20	64.24
		0.1	56.87	71.51	65.93	68.98	73.02	79.13
Lin's method	28	0.05	57.03	74.20	74.82	81.70	89.38	95.71
		0.1	66.87	87.58	83.07	85.67	94.29	98.41
		0.15	69.75	91.11	81.80	86.04	95.81	99.13
	32	0.05	53.99	68.53	70.32	76.77	82.64	89.12
		0.1	64.15	84.02	87.84	90.32	96.13	98.37
		0.15	69.49	90.53	89.91	90.98	96.96	98.69
	36	0.05	50.68	50.25	56.68	59.99	67.46	64.97
		0.1	59.80	78.62	79.45	81.81	92.38	97.85
		0.15	68.36	88.79	87.44	88.97	95.54	98.62

rate (ER) is measured by the number of bits embedded per non-zero coefficient (*bpnc*). We test the percentage distribution of blocks in each categories and calculate the maximum embedding rate that can be achieved under different QPs. As shown in Table 2 and Figure 9, the maximum embedding rate reduces with the increase of QP and the embedding capacity of Lin's method is larger than that of Ma's. In our experiments, the videos are compressed with common QP set (28, 32, 36) and the different embedding rates are respectively considered for Ma's and Lin's methods (0.05 *bpnc*, 0.1 *bpnc* for Ma's method and 0.05 *bpnc*, 0.1 *bpnc*, 0.15 *bpnc* for Lin's method).

Because there are not any approaches which are specifically designed to detect DCT-based data hiding methods, Da's video steganalytic approach [5] and the DCTR feature [6] in image steganalysis are leveraged for comparisons. In order to compute DCTR feature using video stream, every YUV frame decompressed from cover or stego video is

treated as an image in spatial domain and the kernels used in feature computation are 4×4 DCT bases.

Both of Ensemble Classifier and LibSVM toolbox (SVM) [4] are utilized as classifiers. 50 percent cover-stego pairs are randomly selected for training and the remaining ones for testing. The true negative (TN) rate and the true positive (TP) rate are computed by counting the number of detections in the test sets. By averaging TN and TP, the detection accuracy is obtained. After repeating 20 times, the average detection accuracies are used to evaluate the final performance.

5.2 Results and Discuss

In the experiments, Da's method, DCTR feature and the proposed algorithm are utilized to detect data hiding methods under different cases. The detection accuracies against DCT-based data hiding methods are recorded in Table 3. Figure 10 depicts the comparison of their performances in detecting Ma's and Lin's methods respectively. It can be observed that the proposed approach performs best among the three steganalytic approaches. And in most cases, the steganalytic scheme using DCTR feature performs better than Da's method. The steganalytic performance meliorates with the decrease of QP. It is because less loss is induced in higher quality videos which are compressed with lower QP values, and the features extracted from these streams are more effective. Due to the low dimension of extracted features, the SVM outperforms Ensemble Classifier for all of the three steganalytic methods in classification.

In order to compare the detection accuracies against Ma's and Lin's methods, Figure 11 illustrates the steganalytic performances of the three steganalytic algorithms respectively. As the expense of large embedding capacity, the security

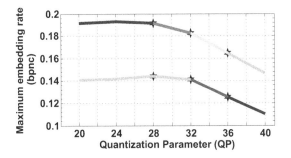

Figure 9: Maximum embedding rate of DCT-based data hiding methods under different QPs.

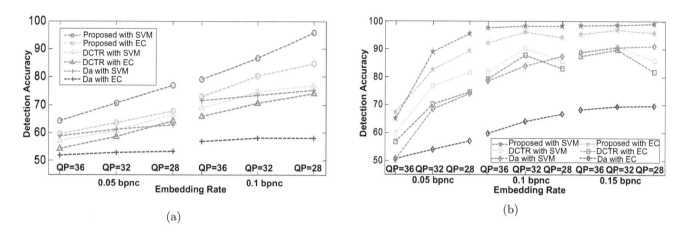

Figure 10: Detection accuracies (%) against (a) Ma's and (b) Lin's DCT-based data hiding methods.

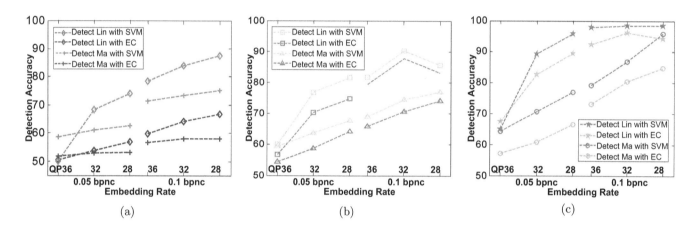

Figure 11: Steganalytic performances (%) of (a) Da's (b) DCTR and (c) proposed algorithms.

level of Lin's is inferior to Ma's method. Although the Da's approach and DCTR feature can detect the DCT-based data hiding to some extent, the proposed approach improves the detection accuracy significantly. Our method achieves the detection accuracy of 99.13% when detecting Lin's scheme with 0.15 *bpnc* and QP=28. And the detection accuracy against Ma's method is up to 95.81% with 0.1 *bpnc* and QP = 28. Overall, our proposed method can effectively detect the existing DCT-based data hiding methods.

6 CONCLUSIONS

In this paper, an effective steganalytic approach is proposed for H.264/AVC videos to detect covert information hidden in the quantized DCT coefficients. Both the intra-frame and inter-frame correlations are considered in the design of steganalytic features. Considering the temporal correlation of blocks in intra-frame, the first feature set using 16 DCT kernels is proposed. Moreover, the residual distortion incorporated into the feature design is defined by analyzing the

state-of art embedding strategy. In order to exploit the temporal correlation, the similar blocks between inter-frames are linked using MVs, from which the second feature set is extracted. The experimental results have demonstrated that our method can effectively distinguish stego H.264 videos undergone DCT manipulations from clean ones, especially for those compressed using low QP values.

As part of our future work, the steganalytic approach to detect data hiding methods in low quality videos is to be exploited. Moreover, the steganalysis with light computation is also to be further studied in practical applications.

ACKNOWLEDGMENTS

This work was supported by the NSFC under U1636102 and U1536105, and National Key Technology R&D Program under 2014BAH41B01, 2016YFB0801003 and 2016QY15Z2500.

REFERENCES

[1] 2003. Draft ITU-T Recommendation and Final Draft International Standard of Joint Video Specification, document ITU-T Rec. H.264/ISO/IEC 14496-10 AVC, Joint Video Team (JVT) of ISO/IEC MPEG and ITU-T VCEG,JVTG050. (May 2003).

[2] 2014. VideoLAN. x264. (2014). Available: http://www.videolan.org/developers/x264.html.

[3] Y. Cao, H. Zhang, X. Zhao, and H. Yu. 2015. Video Steganography Based on Optimized Motion Estimation Perturbation. In *Proceedings of the 3rd ACM Workshop on Information Hiding and Multimedia Security (IH&MMSec '15)*. ACM, New York, NY, USA, 25–31. DOI: http://dx.doi.org/10.1145/2756601.2756609

[4] C.Chang and C.Lin. 2001 [online]. LIBSVM: A Library for Support Vector Machines. (2001 [online]). Available: http://www.csie.ntu.edu.tw/cjlin/libsvm.

[5] Ting Da, ZhiTang Li, and Bing Feng. 2015. *A Video Steganalysis Algorithm for H.264/AVC Based on the Markov Features*. Springer International Publishing, Cham, 47–59. DOI: http://dx.doi.org/10.1007/978-3-319-22186-1_5

[6] V. Holub and J. Fridrich. 2015. Low-Complexity Features for JPEG Steganalysis Using Undecimated DCT. *IEEE Transactions on Information Forensics and Security* 10, 2 (Feb 2015), 219–228. DOI:http://dx.doi.org/10.1109/TIFS.2014.2364918

[7] V. Holub and J. Fridrich. 2015. Phase-aware projection model for steganalysis of JPEG images. (2015). DOI: http://dx.doi.org/10.1117/12.2075239

[8] S. Kapotas and A. Skodras. 2008. A new data hiding scheme for scene change detection in H.264 encoded video sequences. In *2008 IEEE International Conference on Multimedia and Expo*. 277–280. DOI:http://dx.doi.org/10.1109/ICME.2008.4607425

[9] S. Kim, S. Kim, Y. Hong, and C. Won. 2007. *Data Hiding on H.264/AVC Compressed Video*. Springer Berlin Heidelberg, Berlin, Heidelberg, 698–707. DOI: http://dx.doi.org/10.1007/978-3-540-74260-9_62

[10] K. Liao, S. Lian, Z. Guo, and J. Wang. 2012. Efficient Information Hiding in H.264/AVC Video Coding. *Telecommun. Syst.* 49, 2 (Feb. 2012), 261–269. DOI: http://dx.doi.org/10.1007/s11235-010-9372-5

[11] T. Lin, K. Chung, P. Chang, Y. Huang, H. Liao, and C. Fang. 2013. An improved DCT-based perturbation scheme for high capacity data hiding in H.264/AVC intra frames. *Journal of Systems and Software* 86, 3 (2013), 604–614. DOI: http://dx.doi.org/10.1016/j.jss.2012.10.922

[12] X. Ma, Z. Li, J. Lv, and W. Wang. 2009. Data Hiding in H.264/AVC Streams with Limited Intra-Frame Distortion Drift. In *2009 International Symposium on Computer Network and Multimedia Technology*. 1–5. DOI: http://dx.doi.org/10.1109/CNMT.2009.5374766

[13] X. Ma, Z. Li, H. Tu, and B. Zhang. 2010. A Data Hiding Algorithm for H.264/AVC Video Streams Without Intra-Frame Distortion Drift. *IEEE Transactions on Circuits and Systems for Video Technology* 20, 10 (Oct 2010), 1320–1330. DOI: http://dx.doi.org/10.1109/TCSVT.2010.2070950

[14] K. Nakajima, K. Tanaka, T. Matsuoka, and Y. Nakajima. 2005. Rewritable Data Embedding on MPEG Coded Data Domain. In *2005 IEEE International Conference on Multimedia and Expo*. 682–685. DOI:http://dx.doi.org/10.1109/ICME.2005.1521515

[15] V. Pankajakshan and A. Ho. 2007. Improving Video Steganalysis Using Temporal Correlation. In *Proceedings of the Third International Conference on International Information Hiding and Multimedia Signal Processing (IIH-MSP 2007) - Volume 01 (IIH-MSP '07)*. IEEE Computer Society, Washington, DC, USA, 287–290. http://dl.acm.org/citation.cfm?id=1336956.1337487

[16] Athanasios Papoulis and A. A. Maradudin. 1962. The Fourier Integral and Its Applications. 51, 1 (1962), 159–161.

[17] P. Wang, Hong Zhang, Yun Cao, and Xianfeng Zhao. 2016. A Novel Embedding Distortion for Motion Vector-Based Steganography Considering Motion Characteristic, Local Optimality and Statistical Distribution. In *Proceedings of the 4th ACM Workshop on Information Hiding and Multimedia Security (IH&MMSec '16)*. ACM, New York, NY, USA, 127–137. DOI: http://dx.doi.org/10.1145/2909827.2930801

[18] K. Wong, K. Tanaka, K. Takagi, and Y. Nakajima. 2009. Complete Video Quality-Preserving Data Hiding. *IEEE Transactions on Circuits and Systems for Video Technology* 19, 10 (Oct 2009), 1499–1512. DOI: http://dx.doi.org/10.1109/TCSVT.2009.2022781

[19] N. Zarmehi and M. Akhaee. 2016. Digital video steganalysis toward spread spectrum data hiding. *IET Image Processing* 10, 1 (2016), 1–8. DOI:http://dx.doi.org/10.1049/iet-ipr.2014.1019

[20] H. Zhang, Y. Cao, and X. Zhao. 2017. A Steganalytic Approach to Detect Motion Vector Modification Using Near-Perfect Estimation for Local Optimality. *IEEE Transactions on Information Forensics and Security* 12, 2 (Feb 2017), 465–478. DOI: http://dx.doi.org/10.1109/TIFS.2016.2623587

[21] H. Zhang, Y. Cao, X. Zhao, W. Zhang, and N. Yu. 2014. Video Steganography with Perturbed Macroblock Partition. In *Proceedings of the 2Nd ACM Workshop on Information Hiding and Multimedia Security (IH&MMSec '14)*. ACM, New York, NY, USA, 115–122. DOI:http://dx.doi.org/10.1145/2600918.2600936

Combined and Calibrated Features for Steganalysis of Motion Vector-Based Steganography in H.264/AVC

Liming Zhai
School of Computer,
Wuhan University
Wuhan 430072, China
limingzhai@whu.edu.cn

Lina Wang
School of Computer,
Wuhan University
Wuhan 430072, China
lnwang@whu.edu.cn

Yanzhen Ren
School of Computer,
Wuhan University
Wuhan 430072, China
renyz@whu.edu.cn

ABSTRACT

This paper presents a novel feature set for steganalysis of motion vector-based steganography in H.264/AVC. First, the influence of steganographic embedding on the sum of absolute difference (SAD) and the motion vector difference (MVD) is analyzed, and then the statistical characteristics of these two aspects are combined to design features. In terms of SAD, the macroblock partition modes are used to measure the quantization distortion, and by using the optimality of SAD in neighborhood, the partition based neighborhood optimal probability features are extracted. In terms of MVD, it has been proved that MVD is better in feature construction than neighboring motion vector difference (NMVD) which has been widely used by traditional steganalyzers, and thus the inter and intra co-occurrence features are constructed based on the distribution of two components of neighboring MVDs and the distribution of two components of the same MVD. Finally, the combined features are enhanced by window optimal calibration, which utilizes the optimality of both SAD and MVD in a local window area. Experiments on various conditions demonstrate that the proposed scheme generally achieves a more accurate detection than current methods especially for videos encoded in variable block size and high quantization parameter values, and exhibits strong universality in applications.

KEYWORDS

Video steganalysis; sum of absolute difference (SAD); partition modes; motion vector difference (MVD); calibration; combined and calibrated features (CCF)

1 INTRODUCTION

Steganalysis is the counter measure to steganography. Its main purpose is to determine if there is a secret message hidden in digital media such as image, video and audio. Most current steganalysis focuses on image steganography, while the steganalysis for digital video has received relatively limited attention. With the popularity of video capture devices and internet video applications, digital video has become a readily available information hiding carrier. Besides, the video volume is usually large and can provide enough space for secret messages. More seriously, the digital video, especially the compressed video, has rich and varied components, which are favorable to design various steganographic methods, such as motion vector (MV) [1, 3, 6, 10, 27, 29], transformed coefficients [14, 19], prediction modes [9, 28], partition modes [11, 30] and entropy encoded bitstream [13, 18]. As a result, steganography tools or algorithms based on digital video have been gradually increasing recently, and they pose a severe challenge to video steganalysis.

Among all video steganography, the MV based steganography in H.264/AVC is chosen as the target for steganalysis for two reasons: First, MV based steganography is prevailing owing to its security and high embedding capacity [29]. Second, H.264/AVC is currently the most widely used video coding standard, and is likely to be the carrier of video steganography in many practical applications [22].

The MV based steganography is usually accomplished by modifying the MVs and adjusting the corresponding prediction errors (PEs) simultaneously. There are many MV based steganography using different ideologies. Some early methods use predefined selection rules (SRs) to select candidate MVs for embedding. Jordan [10] firstly proposed a MV based embedding method by replacing the least significant bits (LSBs) of the horizontal and vertical components of all MVs with secret message bits. Xu [27] proposed to select the MVs that satisfy a certain threshold, and modify the MV components with larger magnitude to embed messages. In [6], Fang suggested hiding messages by the phase angle between two components of MVs. However, the fixed SRs above will bring some potential risks, so the steganography later introduces adaptive mechanisms or steganographic codes to improve the steganographic security. Aly [1] designed an adaptive PE threshold selection scheme, and embedded secret messages into both components of MVs associated with larger PEs. A steganographic method with perturbed motion estimation was presented in [3], where the embedding is implemented by incorporating wet paper code (WPC). Moreover, Zhang [29] proposed to modify MVs with preserved local optimality, and syndrome-trellis code (STC) is employed to minimize the embedding distortion.

IH&MMSec '17, June 20-22, 2017, Philadelphia, PA, USA
© 2017 ACM. ISBN 978-1-4503-5061-7/17/06. . . $15.00
DOI: http://dx.doi.org/10.1145/3082031.3083237

To detect the MV based steganography, some feature-based steganalytic methods have been proposed in recent years, and they can be approximately divided into three types. The first type of steganalytic methods constructs features based on neighboring motion vector difference (NMVD). Su [20] proposed to use the features derived from the statistical characteristics of NMVDs in spatial and temporal domain. Wu [26] used the joint distribution of the NMVDs between one macroblock (MB) and the other two MBs as features. The NMVD, which is obtained by the subtraction between two neighboring MVs, is the key point for the construction of these features. However, in H.264/AVC and other advanced video coding standards, when two neighboring MBs have different partition modes or neighboring MV does not exist, it is difficult to calculate the NMVD.

The second type of steganalytic methods uses the statistics of sum of absolute differences (SADs) to design features. In Wang's work [24], a feature set called AoSO (Add-or-Subtract-One), which bases on the assumption that the local optimality of SAD will be changed if the corresponding MV is modified, was proposed for steganalysis. Ren [16] also proposed a SPOM (Subtractive Probability of Optimal Matching) feature by using the local optimal SAD. The ideologies of AoSO and SPOM are similar, but they all face the same problem: When the quantization parameter (QP) value is high or the distribution of PE is smooth, the stability of the local optimality of SAD will decrease due to the quantization distortion, thus leading to deteriorated detection performance. Also, for some steganography that considers preserving the statistics of SADs during embedding [3, 29], the performance of AoSO and SPOM are also not ideal.

The third type of steganalytic methods uses calibrations to enhance the features. Cao [2] presented a recompressed calibration method, and then the motion vector reversion-based (MVRB) features were drawn from the difference of MVs and SADs before and after calibration. However, the coding parameters for two compression processes need to be the same, otherwise the detection performance will deteriorate. Deng [5] proposed another calibration using local polynomial kernel regression model (LPKRM) to recover original MVs. The LPKRM depends on the correlation among neighboring MVs; however, like NMVD features [20, 26], the locations and existence of neighboring MVs were also not considered.

To sum up, the current steganalytic features are mainly designed from MVs/NMVDs and PEs/SADs, or supplemented by certain calibration techniques, but they all have their own limitations. In addition, MV based steganography simultaneously modifies the MVs and PEs, both statistics of which are disturbed to some extent. However, apart from [2], all the features above are derived either from MVs or from PEs separately. It is necessary that both statistics of MVs and PEs should be combined for steganalysis.

In this paper, we propose a feature set, named combined and calibrated features (CCF), to detect MV based steganography. The CCF is derived from the statistical characteristics of SADs and motion vector differences (MVDs) and further improved by calibration. The rationale are as follows: For

SAD features, we found that the quantization distortion of SAD is often associated with partition modes, which can be used to measure the quantization distortion. Moreover, the steganographic embedding not only changes the local optimality of SAD, but also the neighborhood optimality. So the partition based neighborhood optimal probability (PB-NOP) features are extracted. For MVD features, we found that there exists an inter distribution of components of neighboring MVDs and an intra distribution of components of the same MVD. These two distributions of MVDs are more sensitive to embedding and more tractable to feature design than those of NMVDs. Then the inter and intra co-occurrence (IIC) features of MVD are constructed as a new statistical representation based on the above two distributions. For calibration, a new calibration method called window optimal calibration (WOC) is proposed by using the optimality of both SAD and MVD in a local window area.

The contribution of this paper is three fold: First, we propose a partition based quantization method, and the influence of quantization distortion on SAD features is greatly reduced. Second, we for the first time propose to construct features based on MVD, which is superior to the traditional NMVD. Third, we propose a highly universal calibration that can be applied to various coding conditions without any restriction.

This paper is organized as follows. Section 2 introduces the encoding process of H.264/AVC and then describes the effects of MV based steganography on video statistics. Section 3 elaborates the relation between quantization distortion and partition modes, followed by the construction of PB-NOP features. The subsequent Section 4 contrasts the statistical characteristics of MVDs and NMVDs, and then presents the IIC features. The description for WOC appears in Section 5. In Section 6, the experimental results are given. Finally, the paper is concluded in Section 7.

Throughout the paper, calligraphic font is reserved for sets. For a finite set $\mathcal{X}$, $|\mathcal{X}|$ denotes the cardinality. Macroblock (MB) specifically refers to the block of size 16×16. "Block" and "partition" have the same meaning and are used in different contexts. "Block" generally refers to the blocks of various sizes. "Partition" refers to the subblocks of MB, it is used to emphasize the division of a MB.

2 PRELIMINARIES

2.1 Basics of H.264/AVC

The H.264/AVC adopts a block-based predictive/transform coding model. For an inter block of size $M \times N$ in the current frame, it searches a similar and best matching region in the encoded reference frame through a block matching algorithm. The best matching region is called reference block, and the offset from the current block to the reference block is called motion vector (MV). This process is known as motion estimation (ME), which reduces temporal redundancy between neighboring frames. The reference block is subtracted from the current block to form a residual block (i.e., PE), and then the PE is subjected to transform and quantization to

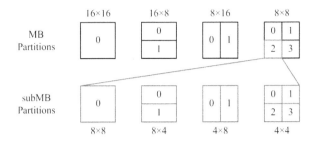

Figure 1: MB partitions and subMB partitions.

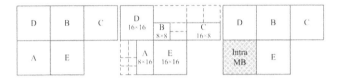

Figure 2: Current and neighboring partitions. Left: Same partition mode. Middle: Different partition modes. Right: Discontinuous inter-partitions.

further reduce spatial redundancy. Finally, the transformed and quantized PE together with motion vector difference (MVD) is entropy encoded to reduce statistical redundancy. To make this paper self-contained, the following concepts on inter coding need to be further introduced.

2.1.1 Partition Modes. The size of a MB is fixed at 16×16. In order to achieve a more accurate ME, the MB is often divided into some subblocks, and this is so called variable block size (VBS); while the opposite case is fixed block size (FBS). For the VBS, a MB can be divided into one 16×16 partition, two 16×8 partitions, two 8×16 partitions, or four 8×8 partitions; they are all called MB partitions. The 8×8 partition, also named subMB, can be further divided into one 8×8 partition, two 8×4 partitions, two 4×8 partitions, or four 4×4 partitions; they are all called subMB partitions. Figure 1 illustrates the partitioning of a MB.

2.1.2 Motion vector prediction and Motion vector difference. The motion of neighboring blocks is often similar, so the MV of neighboring block is served as a starting point for ME. This starting MV is called predicted motion vector (PMV), whose forming depends on the partition modes of neighboring partitions and the availability of neighboring MVs.

Let E be the current partition, and A, B, C, and D be the left, top, top-right and top-left partition immediately next to E respectively. Figure 2 shows examples of the positions of A, B, C, D and E in different cases. In general, the PMV of E is the median of the MVs of A, B and C. If the MV of C does not exist (the partition beyond the frame boundary or belongs to an intra MB), the MV of D is taken instead. If other neighboring MVs do not exist, the forming of PMV will change accordingly [21].

$$V^{(0,+1)} \qquad\qquad S^{(+1,+1)}$$

Figure 3: The structures of $\mathcal{V}_l$ (left) and the corresponding $\mathcal{S}_l$ (right) in 3×3 window.

For saving bitstream, the motion vector difference (MVD) instead of MV will be entropy encoded and transmitted. MVD is the difference between MV and PMV defined by

$$\bar{D} = V - P \tag{1}$$

where $\bar{D}$, V, and P denote the MVD, MV, and PMV respectively.

2.1.3 Block Matching Criterion. The ME locates the best matching block in the reference frame using a rate-distortion criterion [17]: minimizing the loss of video quality under the constraint of bit rate. This criterion is usually fulfilled by minimizing the following Lagrangian cost function:

$$J = S + \lambda \cdot B(\bar{D}) \tag{2}$$

where J is the Lagrangian cost; S denotes the SAD; $\bar{D}$ is the MVD calculated by (1); $B(\bar{D})$ refers to the bits required for coding $\bar{D}$; λ is the Lagrangian multiplier, whose recommended value is obtained by the following expression [25]:

$$\lambda = \sqrt{0.85 \times 2^{(Q-12)/3}} \tag{3}$$

where Q stands for quantization parameter (QP).

2.2 Effects of MV Based Steganography on Video Statistics

According to current MV based steganography [1, 3, 6, 10, 27, 29], one or two components of a MV can be modified during emmbeding. Let $V_l = \left(V_l^h, V_l^v\right)$ be the l-th MV in a cover video frame, V_l^h and V_l^v are the horizontal component and vertical component of V_l. For LSB embedding, the possible variations of V_l will form a 3×3 window area

$$\mathcal{W}_9 = \{(\Delta h, \Delta v) \,|\, \Delta h, \Delta v = -1, 0, +1\} \tag{4}$$

where Δh and Δv denote the modification amplitude of V_l^h and V_l^v respectively.

Focusing only on the actual modifications of V_l, namely $\Delta h, \Delta v = \pm 1$, a local 8-neighborhood will be defined as

$$\mathcal{N}_8 = \mathcal{W}_9 \setminus \{(0,0)\} \tag{5}$$

where $(0,0) \in \mathcal{W}_9$ means no modification of V_l.

The $\mathcal{W}_9$ corresponds to a set consisting of possible MVs as follows

$$\mathcal{V}_l = \Big\{ V_l^{(\Delta h, \Delta v)} \Big| V_l^{(\Delta h, \Delta v)} = \left(V_l^h + \Delta h, \ V_l^v + \Delta v\right), \\ (\Delta h, \Delta v) \in \mathcal{W}_9 \Big\} \tag{6}$$

among which $V_l^{(0,0)}$ denotes the original MV, and $V_l^{(\Delta h, \Delta v)}$, $(\Delta h, \Delta v) \in \mathcal{N}_8$ refers to the modified MVs. During embedding, not only the MVs but also the PEs are modified, so $\mathcal{W}_9$ corresponds to a set $\mathcal{S}_l = \left\{ S_l^{(\Delta h, \Delta v)} \right\}$ for possible SADs as well ($S_l^{(\Delta h, \Delta v)}$ denotes the SAD corresponding to $V_l^{(\Delta h, \Delta v)}$). The structures of $\mathcal{V}_l$ and $\mathcal{S}_l$ are shown in Figure 3.

According to Section 2.1, some statistical properties of PEs/SADs and MVs/MVDs can be easily observed. For example, most SADs of PEs are local optimal for the cover videos, i.e., $S_l^{(0,0)} \leq S_l^{(\Delta h, \Delta v)}, (\Delta h, \Delta v) \in \mathcal{N}_8$. The MVs of neighboring blocks in cover videos are highly correlated because of motion similarity. However, the above statistical properties are often disturbed by MV based steganography, e.g., the SADs of PEs will be changed from local optimal to suboptimal, and the strength of the correlations between neighboring MVs will be weakened and thus the distributions of MVDs will also be changed. All of these leave detectable traces for steganalysis.

In the following sections, we will construct steganalytic features and then calibrate the features by using the statistical characteristics of both SADs and MVDs.

3 PB-NOP: PARTITION BASED NEIGHBORHOOD OPTIMAL PROBABILITY FEATURES

3.1 Relation between Quantization Distortion and Partition Modes

The SAD of PE is modified along with MV during message embedding. Both [24] and [16] pointed out that the proportion of local optimal SADs will be changed before and after embedding, and this is the basis for AoSO and SPOM features. Since the local optimality of SAD is affected by quantization distortion [24], the performance of AoSO and SPOM will also be affected inevitably.

Reference [24] assumed that the 2D-DCT (discrete cosine transform) coefficients of PE follow a Laplace distribution. Furthermore, [24] also proved that the quantization distortion is determined by QP and α, where α is the parameter of the Laplace distribution.

QP represents the compression degree, and α refers to the shape of the Laplace distribution. However, for the video compressed in constant bit rate, the value of QP is dynamic. The α is related to the movement of video content, texture complexity, and ME method [24]. So both QP and α are not easy to determine and measure. This also means that the degree of quantization distortion for blocks exhibits variability and uncertainty, which are harmful to the steganalytic features based on the local optimality of SAD (experiments for AoSO in Section 6 prove this point). If the quantization distortion can be quantized to a definite and tractable form, it will help to improve the features' performance.

For the ME using variable block size (VBS), we found that the quantization distortion is often associated with partition modes, and this can be demonstrated experimentally. Two video sequences, akiyo (slow moving and flat texture) and

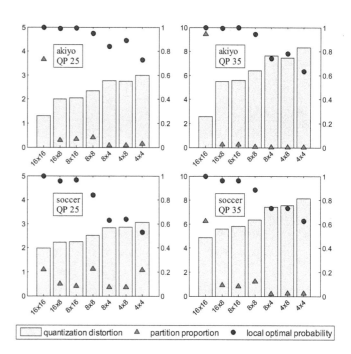

Figure 4: The quantization distortion, partition proportion, and local optimal probability for different partition modes and different QPs.

soccer (fast moving and complex texture), are selected for this experiment. The quantization distortion[1], partition proportion, and local optimal probability[2] (LOP) for different partition modes and different QPs are shown in Figure 4. It is shown that the smaller the partition size, the larger the quantization distortion, and the smaller the LOP. Moreover, with the increase of QP value, the quantization distortion also increases.

The relationship between quantization distortion and partition modes can be analyzed with QP and α. From (2) and (3), the λ (also the QP) controls the tradeoff between rate and distortion. For a high QP, the cost in (2) will be dominated by MVD, and a larger partition size will limit the number of MVs/MVDs for a MB and hence reduces the bitstream [17]. For the example shown in Figure 4, the proportion of 16×16 sized partitions is larger for a higher QP value. As for the α, it reflects the variance of the DCT coefficients of PE. In addition to ME method that is hard to interpret, the fast moving objects and textured areas (i.e. small α) are more in need of small partitions to fit the details [17]. As shown in Figure 4, the proportion of small partitions is larger for soccer than akiyo. Since the partition modes are related to QP and α, so we use partition modes instead of QP and α to quantize the quantization distortion.

---

[1] The quantization distortion is represented by the difference between current block and reconstructed block, and it is normalized by dividing by its block area for a fair comparison.
[2] The probability of occurrence of local optimal SADs is defined as local optimal probability (LOP), which is represented by the proportion of blocks with local optimal SADs in a video.

In the next subsection, we will extract features from separate partition modes to reduce the influence of quantization distortion, and we call it the partition based quantization method.

3.2 Neighborhood Optimal Probability of SAD

As described in Section 2.2, in cover videos, there always exists $S_l^{(0,0)} \leq S_l^{(\Delta h, \Delta v)}, (\Delta h, \Delta v) \in \mathcal{N}_8$ because of the local optimality of SAD; such a SAD is defined as local optimal SAD (LO-SAD). On the other hand, in stego videos, for the MV whose LSB has been modified, its corresponding original MV remains in 8-neighborhood, and thus may result in $S_l^{(\Delta h, \Delta v)} \leq S_l^{(0,0)}, (\Delta h, \Delta v) \in \mathcal{N}_8$; such a SAD is defined as neighborhood optimal SAD (NO-SAD). This is the case at the encoder side, and the situation will be maintained to some extent at the decoder side [24]. Therefore, it is obvious that the probability of a block that has at least one NO-SAD in stego videos is usually larger than that in cover videos.

Let the set of NO-SADs for a block be defined as

$$\mathcal{S}_l^{no} = \left\{ S_l^{(\Delta h, \Delta v)} \middle| S_l^{(\Delta h, \Delta v)} \leq S_l^{(0,0)}, (\Delta h, \Delta v) \in \mathcal{N}_8 \right\} \quad (7)$$

The NO-SADs in cover videos are mainly caused by quantization distortion, while the NO-SADs in stego videos mostly result from steganographic embedding other than quantization distortion, so the number of NO-SADs for a block, i.e., $|\mathcal{S}_l^{no}|$, in stego videos is usually larger than that in cover videos. The probability of a block that has a specified number of NO-SADs is called neighborhood optimal probability (NOP) and is denoted as $\Pr\left(|\mathcal{S}_l^{no}| = i\right), i = 0, 1, \cdots, 8$, where $i = 0$ means that the block does not have NO-SADs, but has a LO-SAD instead.

The comparison of NOP $\Pr\left(|\mathcal{S}_l^{no}| = i\right)$ for different partition modes in cover and stego videos is shown in Figure 5. The stego videos are created by random LSB matching embedding on the larger component of all MVs, and the QP value is 25. It is evident that the $\Pr\left(|\mathcal{S}_l^{no}| = i\right)$ of stego is less than that of cover for $i = 0$, but larger for $i > 0$ (especially for $i = 1, 2, 3, 4$). In addition, no matter whether it is cover or stego, partitions of smaller size tend to have more NO-SADs, demonstrating the fact that the influence of quantization distortion on SAD varies with different partition modes (it is consistent with the LOP shown in Figure 4).

Following the steganalytic features are designed by using NOP incorporated with partition based quantization method.

Let $P_{16\times16}, P_{16\times8}, P_{8\times16}, P_{8\times8}, P_{8\times4}, P_{4\times8}, P_{4\times4}$ be the seven original partition modes mentioned in Section 2.1, then four sets containing new partition modes are defined as follows

$$
\begin{aligned}
\mathcal{P}_1 &= \{P_{16\times16} \vee P_{16\times8} \vee P_{8\times16} \vee P_{8\times8} \vee P_{8\times4} \vee P_{4\times8} \vee P_{4\times4}\} \\
\mathcal{P}_2 &= \{P_{16\times16} \vee P_{16\times8} \vee P_{8\times16} \vee P_{8\times8}, P_{8\times4} \vee P_{4\times8} \vee P_{4\times4}\} \\
\mathcal{P}_5 &= \{P_{16\times16}, P_{16\times8} \vee P_{8\times16}, P_{8\times8}, P_{8\times4} \vee P_{4\times8}, P_{4\times4}\} \\
\mathcal{P}_7 &= \{P_{16\times16}, P_{16\times8}, P_{8\times16}, P_{8\times8}, P_{8\times4}, P_{4\times8}, P_{4\times4}\}
\end{aligned}
\quad (8)
$$

where the symbol '$\vee$' means merging original partition modes into a new partition mode, $\mathcal{P}_1$ has only one new partition mode without considering the sizes of the original partitions

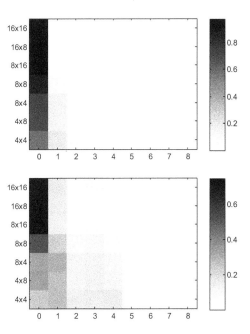

Figure 5: The NOP $\Pr\left(|\mathcal{S}_l^{no}| = i\right)$ for different partition modes in cover (top) and stego (bottom) videos.

(AoSO and SPOM belong to this type), $\mathcal{P}_2$ has two new partition modes based on MB partitions and subMB partitions, $\mathcal{P}_5$ forms five new partition modes according to the area of the original partitions, $\mathcal{P}_7$ contains all original partition modes without any merging.

Based on the new partition modes, the set of NO-SADs for a partition is redefined as

$$\mathcal{S}_{p,l}^{no} = \left\{ S_{p,l}^{(\Delta h, \Delta v)} \middle| S_{p,l}^{(\Delta h, \Delta v)} \leq S_{p,l}^{(0,0)}, (\Delta h, \Delta v) \in \mathcal{N}_8 \right\} \quad (9)$$

where $p = 1, \cdots, P$ is the index of the new partition modes in $\mathcal{P}_i$, $P = |\mathcal{P}_i|$, $i \in \{1, 2, 5, 7\}$. $l = 1, 2, \cdots, L_p$ is the index of partitions with new partition mode p in a frame. Then the partition based neighborhood optimal probability (PB-NOP) features are defined as

$$f_{p,i} = \Pr\left(|\mathcal{S}_{p,l}^{no}| = i\right) = \frac{1}{L_p} \sum_{l=1}^{L_p} \delta\left(|\mathcal{S}_{p,l}^{no}|, i\right), \ i = 0, 1, \cdots, 8 \quad (10)$$

where $\delta(x, y) = 1$ if $x = y$ and 0 otherwise.

As can be seen from Figure 4 and Figure 5, the partitions with the same area have a similar LOP or NOP, so $\mathcal{P}_5$ is adopted to measure the quantization distortion (see Section 6.2 for more discussions). It can also be seen from Figure 5 that when $|\mathcal{S}_{p,l}^{no}|$ has large values ($i > 5$), the $f_{p,i}$ is all very small, and their difference is negligible. To get a more compact and robust form, a threshold is used to merge the underpopulated features together. Then the final PB-NOP features are as follows

$$F_{p,i} = \begin{cases} f_{p,i}, & if \ i = 0, 1, \cdots, T_1 - 1 \\ \sum_{j=T_1}^{8} f_{p,j}, & if \ i = T_1 \end{cases} \quad (11)$$

where T_1 is the threshold. In this paper we set $T_1 = 5$ (the discussion of T_1 is postponed to Section 6.2), so the dimensionality of PB-NOP features is $P \times (T_1 + 1) = 30$.

4 IIC: INTER AND INTRA CO-OCCURRENCE FEATURES

4.1 MVD vs. NMVD

As described in Section 2.2, the statistics of MVs are disturbed by MV based steganography. Like some classic steganalytic features for image [8, 15], MV steganalytic features [20, 26] are usually constructed by the subtraction of neighboring elements, i.e., NMVD, to reveal the statistical anomalies. The MVD, which can be viewed as a special case of NMVD, shows more superiority than NMVD on feature construction.

4.1.1 Compactness of Distribution.
Owing to the correlation between neighboring MVs, the distribution of NMVDs exhibits zero-mean and symmetry. As mentioned in Section 2.1, the PMV is the median value of three neighboring MVs. So according to (1), MVD is also the median of three corresponding NMVDs. In order to better describe the characteristics of NMVDs and MVDs and compare their difference, the distributions of NMVDs and MVDs are analyzed experimentally.

Figure 6(a) shows the histogram of the horizontal components of MVDs and the histogram of the horizontal components of NMVDs calculated from neighboring MVs in horizontal direction. As shown, the two histograms are both Laplacian-like, but the histogram of MVDs is much steeper. So it can be concluded that the distribution of MVDs is more compact than that of NMVDs. As for the joint distributions of MVDs/NMVDs, i.e., the co-occurrence for two components of neighboring MVDs/NMVDs, and the co-occurrence for two components of the same MVD/NMVD, the argument is also tenable (this can also be demonstrated experimentally but is not shown here due to lack of space).

For steganalytic features based on residual signals in image [8, 15] or video [26], a thresholding technique is often used to reduce feature dimensionality. Since the threshold in practice usually takes a small value, it will lose some useful statistical information to an extent. Therefore, a compact distribution will be helpful to capture more statistical information with a small threshold. From this point of view, MVD is more favorable than NMVD.

4.1.2 Inter Distribution.
The features in [20] and [26] are based on the first-order distributions (histograms) of NMVDs and the joint distributions of NMVDs. The NMVD features are under the assumption that all blocks are of the same size (i.e., FBS) and all neighboring blocks have their own MVs. However, this assumption is unsuitable for many advanced video coding standards, thus limiting the construction and application of NMVD features. In contrast, the MVD is automatically generated by the video encoder without considering the consistency of neighboring partitions and the continuity of MVs. So the features based on MVD can be easily applied to various coding conditions.

The joint distribution of horizontal or vertical components of neighboring MVDs is defined as inter distribution. The inter distribution can be denoted by $\Pr(x^{\mathrm{E}}, x^{\mathrm{N}})$, where x^{E} and x^{N} are the horizontal or vertical components of MVDs for current block and neighboring block respectively.

Like the joint distributions of NMVDs [26], the inter distributions will also be changed by MV based steganography. There are four inter distributions of MVDs can be used for steganalysis. Let A, B, C and D be four neighboring blocks next to current block E as shown in Figure 2, the inter distributions of current MVD and neighboring MVDs in location A (horizontal), B (vertical), C (minor diagonal) and D (main diagonal) are concerned, i.e., $\mathrm{N} \in \{\mathrm{A, B, C, D}\}$ in x^{N}. Note that the nonexistent neighboring MVD pairs are not counted. Figure 6(b) shows the $\Pr(x^{\mathrm{E}}, x^{\mathrm{A}})$ of two neighboring horizontal components of MVDs, it is observed that most of the neighboring MVD components have similar values, and are located around the origin. The inter distributions $\Pr(x^{\mathrm{E}}, x^{\mathrm{B}})$, $\Pr(x^{\mathrm{E}}, x^{\mathrm{C}})$ and $\Pr(x^{\mathrm{E}}, x^{\mathrm{D}})$ are also similar.

4.1.3 Intra Distribution.
The NMVD features are derived from the statistical characteristics of components of neighboring MVs [20, 26]. However, both NMVD and MVD have two components, and the statistical characteristics of components of the same NMVD or MVD have not yet been fully studied for steganalysis.

The joint distribution of two components of the same MVD is defined as intra distribution, which can also be denoted by $\Pr(x^h, x^v)$, where x^h and x^v are the horizontal and vertical components of the same MVD. The intra distribution can be interpreted from a coding point of view. The $B(\bar{D})$ in (2) indicates that the coding weights of two components of a MVD are equal, so the two components of a MVD will have a higher probability to obtain similar values. Figure 6(c) shows the $\Pr(x^h, x^v)$, it is observed that the distributional characteristics of $\Pr(x^h, x^v)$ are similar to that of $\Pr(x^{\mathrm{E}}, x^{\mathrm{A}})$. $\Pr(x^h, x^v)$ is also affected by steganographic embedding, and can be used for steganalysis.

4.1.4 Statistical Discriminability.
Statistical discriminability is the key factor that has to be considered for feature design. To compare the statistical discriminability of MVD and NMVD, the K-L divergence between the cover and stego distributions is adopted as a benchmark. The K-L divergence between the histograms of MVDs and NMVDs and the K-L divergence between the joint distributions of MVDs and NMVDs are shown in Figure 6(d) and (e) respectively. The stego videos are created by random LSB matching embedding on the larger component of all MVs. To get the joint distributions of NMVDs, the videos for Figure 6(e) are only encoded in 16×16 partitions (i.e., FBS). The NMVD-A, NMVD-B, NMVD-C and NMVD-D are the NMVDs calculated from horizontal, vertical, minor diagonal and main diagonal directions respectively.

As shown in Figure 6(d) and (e), in all cases, the divergence value of MVD is greater than that of NMVD. Greater K-L divergence value represents larger statistical distortion in the

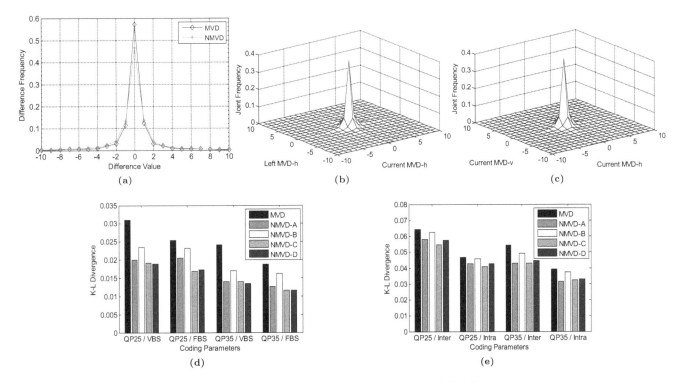

Figure 6: (a) Histograms of MVDs and NMVDs. (b) Inter distribution $\Pr(x^{\mathbf{E}}, x^{\mathbf{A}})$ **of MVDs. (c) Intra distribution** $\Pr(x^h, x^v)$ **of MVDs. (d) K-L divergence between histograms of MVDs and NMVDs. (e) K-L divergence between joint distributions of MVDs and NMVDs. Histograms and inter distributions only use horizontal components.**

stego, that is to say, the statistical representation of MVD is better at revealing the traces of steganographic embedding than that of NMVD.

4.2 Inter and Intra Co-occurrences of MVD

From the above comparative analysis, the MVD is exploited to construct features based on inter and intra distributions, which are represented by co-occurrence matrices.

4.2.1 Inter Co-occurrence. Let $D_l(h)$ and $D_l(v)$ denote the horizontal and vertical components of the l-th MVD in a frame. $D_l^*(x)$ is a neighboring MVD component to $D_l(x)$, where $* \in \{\leftarrow, \uparrow, \nearrow, \nwarrow\}$ stands for the neighboring relation in horizontal, vertical, minor diagonal, or main diagonal direction corresponding to location A, B, C, or D in Figure 2. $x \in \{h, v\}$ stands for the horizontal or vertical component of MVD. The inter co-occurrence matrix of $D_l(h)$ and $D_l^{\leftarrow}(h)$, for example, is defined as follows:

$$C_{m,n}^{\leftarrow}(h) = \frac{1}{Z_1} \left| \{(D_l(h), D_l^{\leftarrow}(h)) \,|\, D_l(h) = m, D_l^{\leftarrow}(h) = n\} \right| \quad (12)$$

where Z_1 is a normalization factor ensuring that $\sum_{m,n} C_{m,n}^{\leftarrow}(h) = 1$.

By analogy, a total of 8 inter co-occurrence matrices $C_{m,n}^*(x)$ can be obtained.

4.2.2 Intra Co-occurrence. Similar to the $C_{m,n}^*(x)$, the intra co-occurrence matrix of $D_l(h)$ and $D_l(v)$ is defined as

$$C_{m,n}^{ia} = \frac{1}{Z_2} \left| \{(D_l(h), D_l(v)) \,|\, D_l(h) = m, D_l(v) = n\} \right| \quad (13)$$

where the normalization factor Z_2 ensures that $\sum_{m,n} C_{m,n}^{ia} = 1$.

4.2.3 Co-occurrence Concentration. As shown in Figure 6(b) and (c), most of the MVDs are located around the bin zero. To make the co-occurrence bins well populated, a threshold is utilized to compactify the co-occurrences. For a predefined threshold T_2, only the bins of $C_{m,n}^*(x)$ and $C_{m,n}^{ia}$ belonging to $[-T_2, T_2]$ are selected for features.

The Figure 6(b) and (c) also show that the joint distributions of MVDs are symmetrical about the origin. For the sake of robustness and lower dimensionality, the co-occurrence matrices are symmetrized by both direction and sign inspired by [8]. The directional symmetry is under the assumption that the inter and intra distributions do not change after swapping two elements' positions. From a coding perspective, the coding cost of MVD is also independent of the sign. Then the symmetrizations by direction and sign for an inter co-occurrence matrix in the horizontal direction, for example, are defined as follows:

$$\overleftrightarrow{C}_{m,n}^{\leftarrow}(h) \Leftarrow C_{m,n}^{\leftarrow}(h) + C_{n,m}^{\leftarrow}(h) \quad (14)$$

$$\bar{C}_{m,n}^{\leftarrow}(h) \Leftarrow \overset{\leftrightarrow}{C}_{m,n}^{\leftarrow}(h) + \overset{\leftrightarrow}{C}_{-m,-n}^{\leftarrow}(h) \tag{15}$$

The symmetrizations of the other inter and intra co-occurrence matrices are defined analogically.

In our additional experiments, we observed that the statistical properties of 8 inter co-occurrences are quite similar despite their components or directions are different. To further decrease the feature dimensionality and improve the robustness, the inter co-occurrence matrices are averaged by components and directions as follows:

$$\bar{C}_{m,n}^{\leftarrow} = \frac{1}{2}\left[\bar{C}_{m,n}^{\leftarrow}(h) + \bar{C}_{m,n}^{\leftarrow}(v)\right] \tag{16}$$

$$\bar{C}_{m,n}^{ir} = \frac{1}{4}\left[\bar{C}_{m,n}^{\leftarrow} + \bar{C}_{m,n}^{\uparrow} + \bar{C}_{m,n}^{\nearrow} + \bar{C}_{m,n}^{\nwarrow}\right] \tag{17}$$

Note that the direction used for symmetrization and averaging are different. After a series of concentration (thresholding, symmetrization, and averaging), the final inter and intra co-occurrence (IIC) features will be obtained as

$$F_{1,\cdots,k} = unique\left(\bar{C}_{\cdot}^{ir}\right) \tag{18}$$

$$F_{k+1,\cdots,2k} = unique\left(\bar{C}_{\cdot}^{ia}\right) \tag{19}$$

where $unique\left(\cdot\right)$ represents eliminating the duplicates produced by symmetrization from a co-occurrence matrix, and $k = \left(T_2 + 1\right)^2$ is the feature dimensionality for a concentrated co-occurrence matrix. In this paper we use $T_2 = 3$ (see Section 6.2 for the selection of T_2), obtaining thus 16-dimensional features for inter co-occurrence and intra co-occurrence respectively.

5 WOC: WINDOW OPTIMAL CALIBRATION

Calibration, which enhances the feature sensitivity and thus improves the detection accuracy, has been frequently applied to image steganalysis [7, 12] and video steganalysis [2, 5].

Calibration of narrow sense is to estimate the statistical properties of a cover from a stego object [7]. Existing calibration methods in video steganalysis [2, 5] all attempt to recover the original MVs. Following this idea, assuming the MV based steganography only modifies the LSB of MV component, i.e., the modified MV is located in $\mathcal{W}_9$ of original MV, then the calibrated (original) MV should also be located in $\mathcal{W}_9$ of the modified MV. More specifically, for the MV that has not been modified, the calibrated MV is likely to be the $V_l^{(0,0)}$ in $\mathcal{W}_9$; while for the modified MV, the calibrated MV is probably the $V_l^{(\Delta h, \Delta v)}, (\Delta h, \Delta v) \in \mathcal{N}_8$. If the calibrated MV can be obtained, then the calibrated features for the proposed PB-NOP and IIC can also be extracted. Therefore, the key is how to get the calibrated MV.

The SAD with minimal value in $\mathcal{W}_9$ is defined as window optimal SAD (WO-SAD), which forms the following set

$$\mathcal{S}_{p,l}^{wo} = \left\{ \left. S_{p,l}^{(\Delta h, \Delta v)} \right| S_{p,l}^{(\Delta h, \Delta v)} \leq S_{p,l}^{(\Delta \bar{h}, \Delta \bar{v})}, \right.$$
$$\left. (\Delta h, \Delta v) \in \mathcal{W}_9, \left(\Delta \bar{h}, \Delta \bar{v}\right) \in \mathcal{W}_9 \right\} \tag{20}$$

The MV that corresponds to a WO-SAD and has minimal bitstream size for coding MVD is defined as window optimal MV (WO-MV). The set of WO-MVs is as follows

$$\mathcal{V}_{p,l}^{wo} = \left\{ \left. V_{p,l}^{(\Delta h, \Delta v)} \right| B\left(D_{p,l}^{(\Delta h, \Delta v)}\right) \leq B\left(D_{p,l}^{(\Delta \bar{h}, \Delta \bar{v})}\right), \right.$$
$$\left. S_{p,l}^{(\Delta h, \Delta v)} \in \mathcal{S}_{p,l}^{wo}, S_{p,l}^{(\Delta \bar{h}, \Delta \bar{v})} \in \mathcal{S}_{p,l}^{wo} \right\} \tag{21}$$

where $D_{p,l}^{(\Delta h, \Delta v)}$ is the MVD corresponding to $S_{p,l}^{(\Delta h, \Delta v)}$ and $V_{p,l}^{(\Delta h, \Delta v)}$, $B\left(\cdot\right)$ refers to the bitstream size of MVD.

Let $\widehat{V}_{p,l}$ be the calibrated MV. In most cases, $\left|\mathcal{V}_{p,l}^{wo}\right| = 1$, then $\widehat{V}_{p,l} = V_{p,l}^{(\Delta h, \Delta v)}$, $V_{p,l}^{(\Delta h, \Delta v)} \in \mathcal{V}_{p,l}^{wo}$. If $\left|\mathcal{V}_{p,l}^{wo}\right| > 1$, the $\widehat{V}_{p,l}$ will be selected from $\mathcal{V}_{p,l}^{wo}$ randomly or in a certain order[3]. According to Section 2.2 and Section 3.2, the $\widehat{V}_{p,l}$ is most likely the original MV generated during ME owing to the optimality of SAD and MVD in a local window area. So this calibration is called window optimal calibration (WOC). The detailed steps of WOC for a video frame are as follows:

Step 1. For a MV $V_{p,l}$ in a video frame, get its calibrated MV $\widehat{V}_{p,l}$ using (20) and (21).

Step 2. Get the SAD corresponding to $\widehat{V}_{p,l}$ and take it as the calibrated SAD denoted as $\widehat{S}_{p,l}$.

Step 3. Repeat Step 1 and Step 2, and calibrate all the MVs in the frame in a coding order, thus forming a calibrated frame consisting of blocks with calibrated SADs and calibrated MVs.

Step 4. For each $\widehat{S}_{p,l}$, form a local window $\mathcal{W}_9$ centered at $\widehat{S}_{p,l}$, and then compute the $\widehat{S}_{p,l}^{no}$ for $\widehat{S}_{p,l}$ based on $\mathcal{W}_9$ using (9).

Step 5. Repeat Step 4 until all $\widehat{S}_{p,l}^{no}$ has been calculated, and then compute the PB-NOP features for the calibrated frame according to Section 3.2.

Step 6. For each $\widehat{V}_{p,l}$, update its PMV by the neighboring calibrated MVs in the calibrated frame, and then compute the calibrated MVD corresponding to $\widehat{V}_{p,l}$ using (1).

Step 7. Repeat Step 6 until all calibrated MVDs have been calculated, and then compute the IIC features for the calibrated frame according to Section 4.2.

Unlike the difference calibration [7] used in [2, 5], the calibrated features in this paper are processed as a Cartesian form [12]. The main reasons for that are as follows. The difference calibrated features can be completely derived from Cartesian calibrated features, but not vice versa. In other words, the Cartesian calibrated features contain more discriminative information than difference calibrated features.

Even though the Cartesian calibration doubles the feature dimensionality, it is not difficult for classifier training owing to the low dimensionality of original features. Table 1 shows the dimensionalities of all feature components. The total dimensionality of the combined and calibrated features (CCF) is $(30 + 32) \times 2 = 124$.

---

[3]In this paper, the $V_{p,l}^{(\Delta h, \Delta v)}$ in $\mathcal{W}_9$ is scanned in a top-to-bottom, and left-to-right order, and the first $V_{p,l}^{(\Delta h, \Delta v)}$, $V_{p,l}^{(\Delta h, \Delta v)} \in \mathcal{V}_{p,l}^{wo}$, is selected as $\widehat{V}_{p,l}$.

Table 1: Feature dimensionality of PB-NOP and IIC with and without WOC

Calibration	Feature	Threshold	Dimensionality
Non-WOC	PB-NOP	5	30
	IIC	3	32
WOC	PB-NOP	5	30
	IIC	3	32

Compared with the existing MV calibration methods, the window optimal calibration (WOC) is more universal. As mentioned before, the calibration methods in [2, 5] are used under some particular conditions. While the WOC has no additional constraints, its calibration process only depends on the MVs and SADs in a local window $\mathcal{W}_9$ which is independent of any coding parameters, so WOC can be applied to a variety of coding conditions without any restriction.

6 EXPERIMENTS

6.1 Experimental Setup

6.1.1 Video Sequences. A video database consisting of 36 standard test sequences downloaded from the internet is used for experiments. All video sequences are stored in 4:2:0 YUV format and have the size of CIF (352×288). The original video sequences have various scenes and various frames (mostly 300 frames), in order to uniformly disperse the video sequences, only the first 240 frames of each video sequence are utilized, thus forming trimmed sequences.

6.1.2 Steganographic Methods. To evaluate the detection performance of the steganalytic features, four typical MV based steganography, i.e., Xu's method [27], Aly's method [1], Cao's method [3] and Zhang's method [29], are included. These steganographic methods are implemented using a well-known H.264/AVC codec named x264 [23] to generate the stego videos, and the basic profile is adopted for simplicity.

The random bit stream is used for embedding, and the embedding rate or payload is denoted by bpnsmv (bits per non-skip MV), which represents the ratio of embedded bits' number to the total number of non-skip MVs in each frame (excluding the MV of a skip MB is due to the fact that zero-valued SAD and MVD are susceptible to steganographic embedding, which leads to deteriorated steganographic security and compression efficiency).

6.1.3 Training and Classification. For stability, the steganalytic features are extracted from the frames within a fixed size sliding window which scans each trimmed sequence without overlapping. The sliding window size is set to be 6 based on experimental experiences.

The soft-margin support vector machine (C-SVM) with Gaussian kernel [4] is used as classifier, and the penalty parameter C and kernel parameter γ of the C-SVM are optimized using five-fold cross-validation on the following grid space $(C, \gamma) \in \left\{ \left(2^i, 2^j\right) | i = -5, -4, \cdots, 15, j = -15, -14, \cdots, 3 \right\}$.

Table 2: Effect of the partition mode sets $\mathcal{P}_i$ on the detection accuracy rate of PB-AoSO

$\mathcal{P}_i$	$i = 1$	$i = 2$	$i = 5$	$i = 7$
AR	0.7570	0.7953	0.7952	0.7796

Table 3: Effect of the partition mode sets $\mathcal{P}_i$ on the detection accuracy rate of PB-NOP

$\mathcal{P}_i$	$i = 1$	$i = 2$	$i = 5$	$i = 7$
AR	0.6126	0.6441	0.6879	0.6869

Table 4: Effect of the threshold T_1 on the detection accuracy rate of PB-NOP

T_1	4	5	6	7	8
AR	0.6876	0.6879	0.6789	0.6834	0.6817

Table 5: Effect of the threshold T_2 on the detection accuracy rate of IIC

T_2	2	3	4	5
AR	0.7235	0.7256	0.7277	0.7132

A binary classifier is trained for each specific feature set, steganographic method, and embedding rate. For each binary classifier, half of cover and the corresponding half of stego are randomly selected for training, and the remaining half pairs of the cover and stego are used for testing. The detection performance is measured by accuracy rate (AR) computed as $AR = (TPR + TFR)/2$, where TPR and TNR represent the true positive rate and true negative rate respectively. The training and testing process is repeated 50 times, and the mean value of all results is calculated as the final AR.

6.2 Parameters Selection

To promote the effectiveness of the steganalytic features, some parameters should be tuned before feature extraction. In this subsection, a total of four parameters, the partition mode sets $\mathcal{P}_i$ for AoSO and PB-NOP, the threshold T_1 for PB-NOP, and the threshold T_2 for IIC, are discussed through experiments. The videos are encoded in VBS for QP 25. For simplicity, we only detect Xu's method at 0.1 bpnsmv.

6.2.1 Partition Mode Sets $\mathcal{P}_i$. The partition based quantization method uses partition mode sets $\mathcal{P}_i$, $i \in \{1, 2, 5, 7\}$ to reduce the quantization distortion and thus enhances the SAD features, but different $\mathcal{P}_i$ have different effects on features' detection performance. Moreover, to evaluate the universality of partition based quantization method, the AoSO [24] is extended by the $\mathcal{P}_i$ and we call it partition based AoSO (PB-AoSO). In Table 2 and Table 3, the effects of the different $\mathcal{P}_i$ on the detection AR of PB-AoSO and PB-NOP are given. Note that the PB-AoSO with $\mathcal{P}_1$ is the original AoSO.

Table 6: Accuracy rate of AoSO, PB-AoSO and CCF for videos encoded in VBS and QP 25

Method	bpnsmv	AoSO	PB-AoSO	CCF
Xu's	0.05	0.6654	0.6947	0.6751
	0.1	0.7570	0.7953	0.7750
	0.2	0.8359	0.8691	0.8713
	0.3	0.8708	0.9090	0.9319
Aly's	0.05	0.8481	0.9085	0.9264
	0.1	0.9139	0.9477	0.9641
	0.2	0.9426	0.9691	0.9794
	0.3	0.9547	0.9731	0.9817
Cao's	0.05	0.5211	0.5181	0.5832
	0.1	0.5173	0.5171	0.6492
	0.2	0.5227	0.5106	0.7678
	0.3	0.5515	0.5344	0.8426
Zhang's	0.05	0.5182	0.5106	0.6095
	0.1	0.5219	0.5383	0.6796
	0.2	0.5531	0.5903	0.7596
	0.3	0.5739	0.6553	0.8301

Table 7: Accuracy rate of AoSO, PB-AoSO and CCF for videos encoded in VBS and QP 35

Method	bpnsmv	AoSO	PB-AoSO	CCF
Xu's	0.05	0.5127	0.5202	0.5570
	0.1	0.5279	0.5664	0.6179
	0.2	0.5722	0.6238	0.7268
	0.3	0.6027	0.6610	0.7998
Aly's	0.05	0.5967	0.6869	0.7307
	0.1	0.6607	0.7543	0.8457
	0.2	0.7148	0.8072	0.8968
	0.3	0.7149	0.8179	0.9054
Cao's	0.05	0.5072	0.5043	0.5436
	0.1	0.5116	0.5090	0.6031
	0.2	0.5149	0.5126	0.7009
	0.3	0.5150	0.5153	0.7602
Zhang's	0.05	0.5119	0.5103	0.5727
	0.1	0.5185	0.5196	0.6322
	0.2	0.5321	0.5375	0.7357
	0.3	0.5342	0.5605	0.7951

Table 8: Accuracy rate of Su's feature, MVRB, AoSO and CCF for videos encoded in FBS and QP 25

Method	bpnsmv	Su	MVRB	AoSO	CCF
Xu's	0.05	0.5125	0.7088	0.7772	0.6822
	0.1	0.5338	0.7611	0.8272	0.7194
	0.2	0.5929	0.8631	0.8877	0.8195
	0.3	0.6340	0.9137	0.8815	0.8603
Aly's	0.05	0.5490	0.8273	0.9442	0.8886
	0.1	0.5911	0.8994	0.9678	0.9539
	0.2	0.6714	0.9454	0.9797	0.9816
	0.3	0.6978	0.9715	0.9825	0.9854
Cao's	0.05	0.5141	0.5219	0.5236	0.6176
	0.1	0.5283	0.5615	0.5231	0.6356
	0.2	0.5643	0.6095	0.5412	0.6507
	0.3	0.5861	0.6668	0.5782	0.6823
Zhang's	0.05	0.5037	0.5047	0.5456	0.6337
	0.1	0.5126	0.5165	0.5465	0.6333
	0.2	0.5396	0.5519	0.5490	0.6635
	0.3	0.5673	0.5671	0.5577	0.6994

Table 9: Accuracy rate of Su's feature, MVRB, AoSO and CCF for videos encoded in FBS and QP 35

Method	bpnsmv	Su	MVRB	AoSO	CCF
Xu's	0.05	0.5106	0.5087	0.5333	0.5160
	0.1	0.5289	0.5332	0.5726	0.5786
	0.2	0.5805	0.5766	0.6344	0.6644
	0.3	0.6314	0.6131	0.6501	0.7334
Aly's	0.05	0.5173	0.5880	0.7079	0.6742
	0.1	0.5538	0.6609	0.7757	0.7583
	0.2	0.6144	0.7379	0.8213	0.8418
	0.3	0.6410	0.7817	0.8467	0.8641
Cao's	0.05	0.5142	0.5025	0.5129	0.5323
	0.1	0.5349	0.5091	0.5061	0.5758
	0.2	0.5597	0.5216	0.5192	0.6235
	0.3	0.5690	0.5322	0.5090	0.6684
Zhang's	0.05	0.5044	0.5048	0.5133	0.5658
	0.1	0.5133	0.5145	0.5110	0.6143
	0.2	0.5322	0.5300	0.5237	0.6766
	0.3	0.5683	0.5332	0.5208	0.7284

From Table 2 and Table 3, it can be seen that the $\mathcal{P}_2$ is more appropriate to PB-AoSO while the $\mathcal{P}_5$ is best suited for PB-NOP. So we select $\mathcal{P}_2$ for PB-AoSO and $\mathcal{P}_5$ for PB-NOP respectively in this paper.

6.2.2 Threshold T_1. The threshold T_1 is another parameter for PB-NOP. In Table 4, the effects of the threshold T_1 on the detection AR of PB-NOP are shown.

From Table 4, it can be seen that the detection performance of PB-NOP is insensitive to threshold T_1. When T_1 is larger than 5, the detection AR is no longer increasing. So the T_1 is set to be 5 in this paper.

6.2.3 Threshold T_2. The threshold T_2 is used to curb the dynamic range of MVD. A larger T_2 keeps more statistical

information, whereas the dimension of IIC will increases sharply. In Table 5, the effects of the threshold T_2 on the detection AR of IIC are given.

As shown in Table 5, when the T_2 increases, the detection AR of IIC does not improve obviously. So we set $T_2 = 3$ for a balance between feature dimensionality and detection performance.

6.3 Comparison With Prior Art

6.3.1 Comparison on VBS and QP. To evaluate various steganalytic features on the videos encoded in VBS and different QPs, the MBs are allowed to be divided into small partition sizes as shown in Figure 1, and the QP values are set to be 25 (high bit rate) and 35 (low bit rate). The reason why we use constant QP instead of constant bit rate is that the constant QP is easier to measure the influence of compression degree on steganalytic features than dynamic QP. The current steganalytic features that can be fully applicable to the VBS videos are AoSO [24] and SPOM [16], and the AoSO has the best performance, so AoSO is chosen for comparison. Moreover, the PB-AoSO with $\mathcal{P}_2$ is also included, and its feature dimensionality is 36. The AR of AoSO, PB-AoSO and CCF on VBS videos with QP 25 and 35 are reported in Table 6 and Table 7 respectively.

It is observed that for low QP, the proposed CCF generally performs better than AoSO and PB-AoSO (the AR of CCF is slightly lower than that of PB-AoSO on detecting Xu's method at low payloads). For high QP, CCF delivers the best performance across all tested steganographic methods and all embedding rates.

By comparing AoSO and PB-AoSO, the PB-AoSO outperforms AoSO especially under the condition of high QP. When detecting Aly's method for QP 35, the PB-AoSO can even increase AR by about 10%. This demonstrates that the partition based quantization method can effectively deal with the issue of quantization distortion, and can also be applied to other steganalytic features that are based on LO-SAD or NO-SAD.

As for the Cao's method and Zhang's method, the AoSO is basically invalid, and the PB-AoSO does not work either. Cao's method replaces original optimal MV with suboptimal MV. Both SADs corresponding to optimal MV and suboptimal MV are quite close, and the local optimality of these two SADs are likely to be consistent with each other at the decoder side. In other words, their differences are more easily obscured by quantization distortion. Zhang's method preserves the local optimality of SADs at the decoder side during embedding. So both mechanisms lead to the failure of AoSO that is based on LO-SAD. The PB-NOP also faces the same problem against these two methods (see Table 10), but owing to the robustness of IIC, the CCF can still detect Cao's method and Zhang's method.

It can also be seen from Table 6 and Table 7 that the AR of three feature sets decreases with the increase of QP. This is mainly caused by the aggravation of quantization distortion. In addition, for higher QP, more MBs tend to choose larger partition size (see the partition proportion in Figure 4), which can be viewed as a transition from VBS to FBS (see experiments below), thus weakening the effectiveness of partition based quantization method used in PB-AoSO and PB-NOP.

6.3.2 Comparison on FBS and QP. To evaluate various steganalytic features on the videos encoded in FBS and different QPs, all MBs are of size 16×16, and the QP values are also set to be 25 and 35. The feature sets for comparison are Su's feature [20] (features are derived only from MVs), MVRB [2] (features are derived from MVs and SADs), and AoSO [24] (features are derived only from SADs). The [5, 16, 26] are omitted, because their ideologies are similar to [2, 20, 24] and the latter are more representative. All coding

Table 10: Accuracy rate of CCF and its components for four methods with 0.1 bpnsmv on VBS videos

QP	Method	Calibrated PB-NOP	Calibrated IIC	PB-NOP and IIC	CCF
25	Xu's	0.6879	0.7256	0.6929	0.7750
	Aly's	0.9349	0.9275	0.9181	0.9641
	Cao's	0.5076	0.6453	0.5806	0.6492
	Zhang's	0.5662	0.6784	0.6209	0.6796
35	Xu's	0.5609	0.5992	0.5972	0.6179
	Aly's	0.7948	0.7534	0.7969	0.8457
	Cao's	0.5031	0.6017	0.5959	0.6031
	Zhang's	0.5203	0.6313	0.6215	0.6322

parameters are kept the same for two compressions of MVRB. The dimensionality of PB-NOP is only 6 due to the FBS, so the total dimensionality of CCF is $(6 + 32) \times 2 = 76$. The AR of Su, MVRB, AoSO and CCF on FBS videos with QP 25 and 35 are reported in Table 8 and Table 9 respectively.

As seen from Table 8, for the steganography with high security (Cao's method and Zhang's method), CCF achieves the best detection performance. For other steganography, AoSO provides the highest AR, CCF and MVRB have comparable performance (CCF is better in detecting steganography that modifies two components of MV, while MVRB can better detect steganography that modifies one component of MV), and Su performs worst in most tested cases.

The Table 9 shows that for the VBS videos with high QP, CCF is the best performer in most cases. Of particular note is the Su's feature, which achieves a higher AR for Cao's method and Zhang's method than AoSO and MVRB owing to the robustness of NMVD features.

By the comprehensive comparison from Table 6 – Table 9, it can be concluded that CCF is better suited to detect videos encoded in VBS and high QP values. This is because for the VBS video, the various partition modes can be fully utilized to quantize the quantization distortion, and it can also be considered to increase the feature diversity. As for the QP, the SAD features are more sensitive to QP due to quantization distortion, so MVRB and AoSO perform worse for the higher QP. While CCF is combined by the SAD features and MVD features, and the latter is robust to QP, so CCF is still in effect for high QP owing to IIC.

6.4 Feature Component Analysis

The CCF consists of three components: PB-NOP, IIC, and WOC. To evaluate the performance of different components and to validate the importance of combining all components together, calibrated PB-NOP features (60-D)[4], calibrated IIC features (64-D), combined PB-NOP and IIC features (62-D), and CCF (124-D) are subject to test. The videos are encoded in VBS for QP 25 and 35, and only embedding rate of 0.1 bpnsmv is considered for simplicity. The detection AR of CCF and its components are shown in Table 10.

---

[4]The number in bracket denotes a feature dimensionality, see Table 1 for details. The same below.

As expected, the detection performance of CCF is superior to any single component for all tested steganographic methods. The comparison among CCF, calibrated PB-NOP and calibrated IIC validates the viewpoint that the statistical characteristics of different aspects should be combined to improve the detection capability. Besides, the performance of combined features with and without calibration also proves the effectiveness of WOC.

7 CONCLUSION

The steganographic embedding in MVs changes the statistical characteristics of both SADs and MVDs. According to this phenomenon, the combined and calibrated features (CCF) for steganalysis of MV based steganography in H.264/AVC is introduced in this paper.

The CCF consists of three components: partition based neighborhood optimal probability (PB-NOP) features, inter and intra co-occurrence (IIC) features, and window optimal calibration (WOC). The performance of CCF was carefully examined by various experiments. The experimental results show that CCF achieves in general a higher accuracy than current steganalytic methods especially for videos encoded in VBS and high QP values. Although it has been emphasized that CCF is applied to H.264/AVC videos, owing to the universality of PB-NOP, IIC and WOC, CCF can be easily extended to other video coding standards, such as MPEG-4 and MPEG-2.

For future work, the CCF will be further optimized. For instance, the new partition modes in partition based quantization method will be formed in an adaptive way. In addition, testing of more MV based steganography and comparison of CCF with more steganalytic methods are also on our agenda of future research.

ACKNOWLEDGMENTS

This work was supported by the National Natural Science Foundation of China (Nos. U1536204, U1536114), and the National Key Technologies R&D Program of the Ministry of Science and Technology of China (No. 2014BAH41B00).

REFERENCES

[1] Hussein A Aly. 2011. Data hiding in motion vectors of compressed video based on their associated prediction error. *IEEE Trans. Inf. Forensics Security* 6, 1 (Mar. 2011), 14–18.

[2] Yun Cao, Xianfeng Zhao, and Dengguo Feng. 2012. Video steganalysis exploiting motion vector reversion-based features. *IEEE Signal Process. Lett.* 19, 1 (Jan. 2012), 35–38.

[3] Yun Cao, Xianfeng Zhao, Dengguo Feng, and Rennong Sheng. 2011. Video steganography with perturbed motion estimation. In *Proc. 13th Int. Conf. IH*, Vol. 6958. 193–207.

[4] Chih-Chung Chang and Chih-Jen Lin. 2015. LIBSVM: A Library for Support Vector Machines. (Feb. 2015). http://www.csie.ntu.edu.tw/~cjlin/libsvm

[5] Yu Deng, Yunjie Wu, and Linna Zhou. 2012. Digital video steganalysis using motion vector recovery-based features. *Appl. Opt.* 51, 20 (Jul. 2012), 4667–4677.

[6] Ding-Yu Fang and Long-Wen Chang. 2006. Data hiding for digital video with phase of motion vector. In *Proc. IEEE Int. Symp. Circuits Syst.* 1422–1425.

[7] Jessica Fridrich. 2004. Feature-based steganalysis for JPEG images and its implications for future design of steganographic schemes. In *Proc. 6th Int. Conf. IH.* 67–81.

[8] Jessica Fridrich and Jan Kodovský. 2012. Rich models for steganalysis of digital images. *IEEE Trans. Inf. Forensics Security* 7, 3 (Jun. 2012), 868–882.

[9] Yang Hu, Chuntian Zhang, and Yuting Su. 2007. Information hiding based on intra prediction modes for H.264/AVC. In *Proc. IEEE Int. Conf. Multimedia Expo.* 1231–1234.

[10] Fred Jordan, Martin Kutter, and Touradj Ebrahimi. 1997. Proposal of a watermarking technique for hiding/retrieving data in compressed and decompressed video. *ISO/IEC Doc. JTC1/SC29/WG11 MPEG97/M2281* (Jul. 1997).

[11] Spyridon K Kapotas and Athanassios N Skodras. 2008. A new data hiding scheme for scene change detection in H.264 encoded video sequences. In *Proc. IEEE Int. Conf. Multimedia Expo.* 277–280.

[12] Jan Kodovský and Jessica Fridrich. 2009. Calibration revisited. In *Proc. 11th ACM Multimedia Security Workshop.* 63–74.

[13] Ke Liao, Shiguo Lian, Zhichuan Guo, and Jinlin Wang. 2012. Efficient information hiding in H.264/AVC video coding. *Telecomm. Syst.* 49, 2 (2012), 261–269.

[14] Xiaojing Ma, Zhitang Li, Hao Tu, and Bochao Zhang. 2010. A data hiding algorithm for H.264/AVC video streams without intra-frame distortion drift. *IEEE Trans. Circuits Syst. Video Technol.* 20, 10 (Oct. 2010), 1320–1330.

[15] Tomáš Pevný, Patrick Bas, and Jessica Fridrich. 2010. Steganalysis by subtractive pixel adjacency matrix. *IEEE Trans. Inf. Forensics Security* 5, 2 (Jun. 2010), 215–224.

[16] Yanzhen Ren, Liming Zhai, Lina Wang, and Tingting Zhu. 2014. Video steganalysis based on subtractive probability of optimal matching feature. In *Proc. 2nd ACM Workshop Inf. Hiding Multimedia Security.* 83–90.

[17] Iain E Richardson. 2011. *The H.264 advanced video compression standard.* John Wiley & Sons.

[18] Young-Ho Seo, Hyun-Jun Choi, Chang-Yeul Lee, and Dong-Wook Kim. 2008. Low-complexity watermarking based on entropy coding in H.264/AVC. *IEICE Trans. Fundamentals Electron. Commun. Comput. Sci.* E91.A, 8 (Aug. 2008), 2130–2137.

[19] Zafar Shahid, Marc Chaumont, and William Puech. 2013. Considering the reconstruction loop for data hiding of intra-and inter-frames of H.264/AVC. *Signal Image Video Process.* 7, 1 (Jan. 2013), 75–93.

[20] Yuting Su, Chengqian Zhang, and Chuntian Zhang. 2011. A video steganalytic algorithm against motion-vector-based steganography. *Signal Process.* 91, 8 (Aug. 2011), 1901–1909.

[21] Joint Video Team. 2003. Advanced video coding for generic audiovisual services. *ITU-T Rec. H.264 and ISO/IEC 14496-10 AVC* (May 2003).

[22] Yiqi Tew and KokSheik Wong. 2014. An overview of information hiding in H.264/AVC compressed video. *IEEE Trans. Circuits Syst. Video Technol.* 24, 2 (Feb. 2014), 305–319.

[23] VideoLAN. 2015. x264. (Feb. 2015). http://www.videolan.org/developers/x264.html

[24] Keren Wang, Hong Zhao, and Hongxia Wang. 2014. Video steganalysis against motion vector-based steganography by adding or subtracting one motion vector value. *IEEE Trans. Inf. Forensics Security* 9, 5 (May 2014), 741–751.

[25] Thomas Wiegand, Heiko Schwarz, Anthony Joch, Faouzi Kossentini, and Gary J Sullivan. 2003. Rate-constrained coder control and comparison of video coding standards. *IEEE Trans. Circuits Syst. Video Technol.* 13, 7 (Jul. 2003), 688–703.

[26] Hao-Tian Wu, Yuan Liu, Jiwu Huang, and Xin-Yu Yang. 2014. Improved steganalysis algorithm against motion vector based video steganography. In *Proc. IEEE Int. Conf. Image Processing (ICIP).* 5512–5516.

[27] Changyong Xu, Xijian Ping, and Tao Zhang. 2006. Steganography in compressed video stream. In *Proc. 1st Int. Conf. Innov. Comput., Inf. Control*, Vol. 1. 269–272.

[28] Gaobo Yang, Junjie Li, Yingliang He, and Zhiwei Kang. 2011. An information hiding algorithm based on intra-prediction modes and matrix coding for H.264/AVC video stream. *AEU Int. J. Electron. Commun.* 65, 4 (Apr. 2011), 331–337.

[29] Hong Zhang, Yun Cao, and Xianfeng Zhao. 2016. Motion vector-based video steganography with preserved local optimality. *Multimedia Tools and Applications* 75, 21 (2016), 13503–13519.

[30] Hong Zhang, Yun Cao, Xianfeng Zhao, Weiming Zhang, and Nenghai Yu. 2014. Video steganography with perturbed macroblock partition. In *Proc. 2nd ACM Workshop Inf. Hiding Multimedia Security.* 115–122.

A Generic Approach Towards Image Manipulation Parameter Estimation Using Convolutional Neural Networks

Belhassen Bayar
Drexel University
Dept. of Electrical & Computer Engineering
Philadelphia, PA, USA
bb632@drexel.edu

Matthew C. Stamm
Drexel University
Dept. of Electrical & Computer Engineering
Philadelphia, PA, USA
mstamm@coe.drexel.edu

ABSTRACT

Estimating manipulation parameter values is an important problem in image forensics. While several algorithms have been proposed to accomplish this, their application is exclusively limited to one type of image manipulation. These existing techniques are often designed using classical approaches from estimation theory by constructing parametric models of image data. This is problematic since this process of developing a theoretical model then deriving a parameter estimator must be repeated each time a new image manipulation is derived. In this paper, we propose a new data-driven generic approach to performing manipulation parameter estimation. Our proposed approach can be adapted to operate on several different manipulations without requiring a forensic investigator to make substantial changes to the proposed method. To accomplish this, we reformulate estimation as a classification problem by partitioning the parameter space into disjoint subsets such that each parameter subset is assigned a distinct class. Subsequently, we design a constrained CNN-based classifier that is able to extract classification features directly from data as well as estimating the manipulation parameter value in a subject image. Through a set of experiments, we demonstrated the effectiveness of our approach using four different types of manipulations.

KEYWORDS

Image forensics; manipulation parameter estimation; convolutional neural networks; quantization

1 INTRODUCTION

Digital images play an important role in a wide variety of settings. They are used in news reporting, as evidence in criminal investigations and legal proceedings, and as signal intelligence in governmental and military scenarios. Unfortunately, widely available photo editing software makes it possible for information attackers to create image forgeries capable of fooling the human eye. In order to regain trust in digital images, researchers have developed a wide variety of techniques to detect image editing and trace an image's processing history [36].

IH&MMSec '17, June 20–22, 2017, Philadelphia, PA, USA
© 2017 ACM. ISBN 978-1-4503-5061-7/17/06…$15.00.
DOI: http://dx.doi.org/10.1145/3082031.3083249

An important part of characterizing an image's processing history involves determining specifically how each editing operation was applied. Since several editing operations used to manipulate an image are parameterized, this involves estimating these manipulation parameters. For example, a user must choose a scaling factor when resizing an image, a quality factor when compressing an image, or blur kernel parameters (e.g. kernel size, blur variance) when smoothing an image.

Estimating manipulation parameter values may also be important when performing several other forensics and security related tasks. In some cases, it is useful or necessary to determine manipulation parameter values when detecting the use of multiple editing operations and tracing processing chains [10, 32]. Manipulation parameter estimates can be used to undo the effects of editing or provide an investigator with information about an image before it was edited. They can also be used to improve camera identification algorithms [16] or used as camera model identification features [21]. Additionally, manipulation parameter estimates can be used to increase the performance of some steganographic algorithms [26] and watermark detectors [11, 30].

Existing manipulation parameter estimation algorithms are often designed using classical approaches from estimation theory. This is typically done by first constructing a theoretical model to describe a manipulated image or some image statistic (e.g. pixel value or DCT coefficient histograms) that is parameterized by the manipulation parameter that is to be estimated. Next, an estimator for the manipulation parameter is theoretically derived from the statistical model. Algorithms have been developed to estimate the scaling factor used when resizing an image [27, 28], the contrast enhancement mapping applied to an image [13, 33, 34], the quality factor or quantization matrix used when compressing an image [6, 12, 26, 37], the size of the filter window used when median filtering an image [20], and blurring kernel parameters [1, 7, 9].

While classical approaches from estimation theory have led to the development of several successful manipulation parameter estimation algorithms, developing estimation algorithms for new manipulations or improving upon existing algorithms can be quite challenging. It is frequently difficult to develop accurate parametric models of image data that can be used for manipulation parameter estimation. Once a model is constructed, deriving a manipulation parameter estimator from this model may also be both difficult and time consuming. Furthermore, this process of developing a theoretical model then deriving a parameter estimator must be repeated each time a new image manipulation is developed.

In light of these challenges, it is clear that forensic researchers can benefit from the development of a *generic* approach to performing manipulation parameter estimation. By generic, we mean an approach that can be easily adapted to perform parameter estimation for different manipulations without requiring an investigator to make anything other than minor changes to the estimation algorithm. Instead of relying on theoretical analysis of parametric models, this approach should be data-driven. In other words, this approach should be able to *learn* estimators directly from a set of labeled data.

Recent work in multimedia forensics suggests that this goal may be accomplished by using convolutional neural networks (CNNs). CNNs have already been developed to learn image manipulation detectors directly from data. For example, we showed in our previous work that by incorporating a "constrained convolutional layer" into the beginning of a CNN architecture, we could train this fixed architecture to detect several different image manipulations [2, 3]. Similarly, Chen et al. showed that a CNN can be trained to perform median filtering detection using an image's median filter residual [8].

In this paper, we propose a new, generic data-driven approach to performing manipulation parameter estimation. Our approach does not require researchers to develop a parametric model of a particular manipulation trace in order to construct an estimator. Instead, manipulation parameter estimation features are learned directly from training data using a constrained convolutional neural network. Furthermore, our CNN can be re-trained to perform parameter estimation for different manipulations without requiring changes to the CNN's architecture except for the output classes. Our approach operates by first approximately reformulating manipulation parameter estimation as a classification problem. This is done by dividing the manipulation parameter set into different subsets, then assigning a class to each subset. After this, our specially designed CNN is used to learn traces left by a desired manipulation that has been applied using parameter values in each parameter subset. We experimentally evaluated our proposed CNN-based estimation approach using four different parameterized manipulations. The results of our experiments show that our proposed approach can correctly identify the manipulation parameter subset and provide an approximate parameter estimate for each of these four manipulations with estimation accuracies typically in the 95% to 99% range.

The remainder of this paper is organized as follows. In Section 2, we provide an overview of our proposed generic parameter estimation approach, including details on class formation and high-level classifier design. Our parameter estimation CNN architecture is described in detail in Section 3. In Section 4, we experimentally evaluate the performance of our proposed approach when performing parameter estimation for four different manipulations: resizing, JPEG compression, median filtering, and Gaussian blurring. Section 5 concludes this paper.

2 PROPOSED ESTIMATION APPROACH

To develop our CNN-based approach to performing manipulation parameter estimation, we begin by assuming that an image under investigation I is a manipulated version of some original image I'

such that

$$I = m(I', \theta) \qquad (1)$$

where $m(\cdot)$ is a known image editing operation that is parameterized by parameter θ. We assume that the set of possible parameter values Θ is totally ordered and is known to the forensic investigator. In this paper, we assume that θ is one dimensional (e.g. a scaling factor or JPEG compression quality factor), however it is simple to extend our approach to the case of multidimensional θ's.

While the editing operation m is known to an investigator, we do not assume that the investigator knows the specific traces left by m. We do assume, however, that m leaves behind traces that are learnable by some classifier g. Prior research has shown that traces left by several manipulations can be learned using CNNs constructed using a constrained convolutional layer [3] or by an ensemble classifier provided with rich model features [14, 29]. Furthermore, we assume that the specific nature of these traces changes depending on the choice of the manipulation parameter θ. Additionally, we assume that an investigator has access to a large corpus of images and can modify them with m using different values of θ in order to create training data for our parameter estimator.

2.1 Formulating parameter estimation as a classification problem

In order to leverage the power of CNNs that are able to learn manipulation traces, we first approximately reformulate our parameter estimation problem as a classification problem. To do this, we partition the parameter set Θ into K disjoint subsets ϕ_k such that

$$\phi_k = \{\theta : t_k \le \theta < t_{k+1}\}, \qquad (2)$$

for $k = 1, \dots, K - 1$ and

$$\phi_K = \{\theta : t_K \le \theta \le t_{K+1}\}, \qquad (3)$$

where t_1 is the smallest element in Θ, t_{K+1} is the largest element in Θ, and the t_k's form upper and lower boundaries for each of the parameter subsets. Taken together, the set Φ of all subsets ϕ_k form a minimal cover for Θ, i.e.,

$$\bigcup_{k=1}^{K} \phi_k = \Theta. \qquad (4)$$

When constructing our CNN-based classifier g, each parameter subset is assigned a distinct class label c_k such that

$$g(I) = c_k \quad \Rightarrow \quad \theta \in \phi_k. \qquad (5)$$

Figure 1 shows an overview of how parameter subsets and their corresponding classes are formed by partitioning the parameter space. If we wish to include the possibility that the image is unaltered (i.e. no parameter value can be estimated because m hasn't been used to modify I), then an additional class c_0 can be added to the classifier to represent this possiblity.

To produce parameter estimates, we construct an additional function $h(\cdot)$ that maps each class to an estimated parameter value $\hat{\theta}$. The function h can be constructed in multiple ways depending on the nature of the paramter subsets ϕ_k.

For some estimation problems where Θ is finite and countable, each parameter subset can be chosen to contain only one element. Examples of this include estimating the window size of a median filter or the quality factor used when performing JPEG compression.

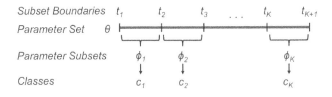

Figure 1: Overview of how classes are formed by partitioning the parameter set.

Since each parameter subset contains only one element, the parameter estimate is chosen to be the lone element of the parameter subset that corresponds to the class chosen by the classifier, i.e.

$$\hat{\theta} = \theta_k \quad \text{given } \phi_k = \{\theta_k\}. \tag{6}$$

In other estimation scenarios, each parameter subset may be chosen to contain multiple elements or may be uncountable. Estimating the scaling factor used when resizing an image is a typical example of this, since the set of possible scaling factors itself is uncountable. In these cases, a parameter estimate produced by the equation

$$\hat{\theta} = \frac{t_k + t_{k+1}}{2}. \tag{7}$$

This is equivalent to choosing the parameter estimate as the centroid of the parameter subset that corresponds to the class chosen by the classifier.

Both rules (6) and (7) can be taken together to produce the parameter estimation function

$$\hat{\theta} = h(c_k) = \begin{cases} \theta_k & \text{if } \phi_k = \{\theta_k\}, \\ \frac{t_k + t_{k+1}}{2} & \text{if } |\phi_k| \neq 1. \end{cases} \tag{8}$$

We note that our approach can be roughly interpreted as choosing between several quantized values of the manipulation parameter θ. While quantization will naturally introduce some error into the final estimate produced, it allows us to define a finite number of classes for our classifier to choose between. The estimation error introduced by this quantization can be controlled by decreasing the distance between the class boudaries t_k at the expense of increasing the number of classes.

2.2 Classifier design

For the estimation approach outlined in Section 2.1 to be truly generic, we need to construct a classifier $g(\cdot)$ that is able to directly learn from data some parameter specific traces left by a manipulation m. This requires the use of some generic low-level feature extractors that can expose traces of many different manipulations. While CNNs are able to learn feature extractors from training data, CNNs in their standard form tend to learn features that represent an image's content. As a result, they must be modified in order to become suitable for forensic applications. To create our CNN for performing manipulation parameter estimation, we leverage significant prior research that shows that traces left by many different manipulations can be learned from sets of prediction residuals [8, 19, 22, 24, 29].

Prediction residual features are formed by using some function $f(\cdot)$ to predict the value of a pixel based on that pixel's neighbors within a local window. The true pixel value is then subtracted from the predicted value to obtain the prediction residual r such that

$$r = f(I) \quad I \tag{9}$$

Frequently, a diverse set of L different prediction functions are used to obtain many different residual features. Many existing generic feature sets used in forensics take this form, including rich model features [14, 29], SPAM features [24, 25], and median filter residual features [8, 19]. These prediction residual features suppress an image's contents but still allow traces in the form of content-independent pixel value relationships to be learned by a classifier.

To provide our CNN-based classifier g with low-level prediction residual features, we make our CNN's first layer a *constrained convolutional layer* [3]. This layer is formed by using L different convolutional filters w_ℓ that are adaptively learned, but are constrained to be prediction error filters. These filters are initially seeded with random values, then their filter weights are iteratively learned through a stochastic gradient descent update during the backpropagation step of training. Since this update may move each filter outside of the set of prediction error filters, the following constraints

$$\begin{cases} w_\ell(0,0) = 1, \\ \sum_{m,n \neq 0} w_\ell(m,n) = 1, \end{cases} \tag{10}$$

are enforced upon each filter immediately after the backpropagation step to project the updated filter back into the set of prediction error filters.

It can easily be shown that the L feature maps produced by a constrained convolutional layer are residuals of the form (9). A simple way to see this is to define a new filter $\tilde{w}_\ell$ as

$$\tilde{w}_\ell(m,n) = \begin{cases} w(m,n) & \text{if } (m,n) \neq (0,0), \\ 0 & \text{if } (m,n) = (0,0). \end{cases} \tag{11}$$

As a result, the feature map produced by convolving an image with the filter w_ℓ is

$$r_\ell = w * I = \tilde{w}_\ell * I \quad I. \tag{12}$$

By defining $f(I) = \tilde{w}_\ell * I$, we can see these residuals are of the same form as in (9).

By using a constrained convolutional layer, our CNN can be trained to learn appropriate residual features for estimating parameter values associated with different manipulations instead of relying on fixed residual features. Associations between these features are learned by higher layers of our CNN, whose full architecture is described below in Section 3.

The final layer of our CNN consists of K neurons with a softmax activation function. Each neuron corresponds to a unique class (and its associated parameter set) defined in Section 2.1. A class c is chosen by our CNN according to the rule

$$c = \arg \max_k \lambda_k, \tag{13}$$

where λ_k is the activation level of the neuron corresponding to the kth class. Since we use a softmax activation function, the activation levels in the last layer can be loosely interpreted as a probability distribution over the set of classes. As a result, (13) can be loosely interpreted as choosing the most probable class.

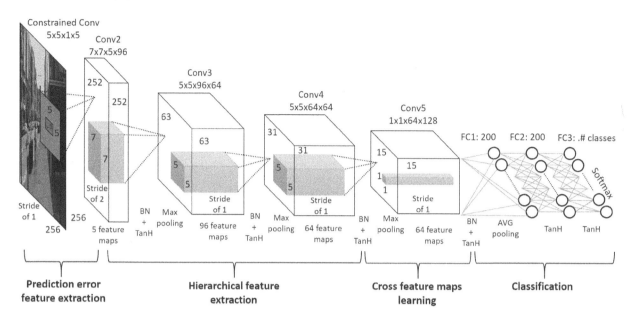

Figure 2: CNN proposed architecture; BN:Batch-Normalization Layer; TanH: Hyperbolic Tangent Layer

Parameter estimation steps. Our proposed method is summarized below.

Input: Image I manipulated by $m(\cdot)$ and parameter set Θ.

Output: Estimated parameter $\hat{\theta}$.

Step 1   Partition the parameter space Θ into a set of disjoint subsets ϕ_k defined in Eqs. (2) and (3) to form a cover for Θ.

Step 2   Define a CNN-based classifier g in Eq. (5) such that each parameter subset is assigned a distinct class c_k.

Step 3   Define the estimate $\hat{\theta}$ as denoted in Eq. (8).

Step 4   Train a constrained CNN to classify input images into the set of classes c_k's.

Step 5   Estimate $c = \arg\max_k \lambda_k$ where λ_k is the activation level of the neuron corresponding to the kth class in CNN.

Step 6   Assign $\hat{\theta} = h(c)$.

3   NETWORK ARCHITECTURE

In this section, we give an overview of the constrained CNN architecture used in our generic parameter estimation approach. We note that our CNN architecture differs significantly from the architecture proposed in [3]. Fig. 2 depicts the overall architecture of our CNN. One can observe that we use four conceptual blocks to build a CNN's architecture capable of distinguishing between different manipulation parameters.

Our proposed CNN has different conceptual blocks designed to: (1) jointly suppress an image's content and learn low-level pixel-value dependency features while training the network, (2) learn higher-level classification features through deeper convolutional layers and (3) learn associations across feature maps using 1×1 convolutional filters. These 1×1 filters are used to learn linear combination between features located at the same spatial location

but belong to different feature maps [4]. The input to the CNN is a grayscale image (or a green color layer of an image) patch sized 256×256 pixels. In what follows, we give more details about each block.

3.1   Pixel-value dependency feature extraction

As mentioned in Section 2.2, CNNs in their existing form tend to learn features related to an image's content. If CNNs of this form are used to identify parameters of an image manipulation, this will lead to a classifier that identifies scene content associated with the training data. To address this problem, in our architecture we make use of a constrained convolutional layer [3] ("Constrained Conv") which is able to jointly suppress an image's content and learn pixel-value dependency traces induced by one particular manipulation's parameter. This layer consists of five constrained convolutional prediction-error filters of size 5×5 adaptively learned while training the CNN and operates with a stride of size 1. The output of this "Constrained Conv" layer will take the form of prediction-error feature maps of size 252×252×5. These residual features are vulnerable to be destroyed by nonlinear operations such as, activation function and pooling layer. Therefore, they are directly passed to a regular convolutional layer.

3.2   Hierarchical feature extraction

In our second conceptual block, we use a set of three regular convolutional layers to learn new associations and higher-level prediction-error features. From Fig. 2, one can notice that all convolutional layers in the network operate with a stride of 1 except "Conv2 layer which uses a stride of 2. We also can notice that all the three convolutional layers are followed by a batch normalization (BN) layer. Specifically, this type of layer minimizes the internal covariate shift, which is the change in the input distribution to a learning system by applying a zero-mean and unit-variance transformation of the data while training the CNN model.

The output of the BN layer after every regular convolutional layer is followed by a nonlinear mapping called an activation function. This type of function is applied to each value in the feature maps of every convolutional layer. In our CNN, we use hyperbolic tangent (TanH) activation functions. Furthermore, to reduce the dimension of the activated large feature map volumes we use a max-pooling layer with a sliding window of size 3×3 and stride of 2. Fig. 2 depicts the size of filters in each convolutional layer as well as the dimension of their corresponding output feature maps.

3.3 Cross feature maps learning

To enhance the learning ability of our CNN, we use a cross feature maps learning block in our proposed architecture. From Fig. 2, we can notice that this block contains 128 1×1 convolutional filters in layer "Conv5" followed by a BN layer. These filters are used to learn a new association between the highest-level residual feature maps in the network. Additionally, this convolutional layer is the last layer before the classification block. Therefore, in order to keep the most representative features, we use an average-pooling layer that operates with a sliding window of size 3×3 and stride of 2. The output of this conceptual block is a feature maps volume of size 7×7×128 which takes the form of a fully-connected layer that is directly passed to a regular neural network.

3.4 Classification

To perform classification, we use a conceptual block that consists of three fully-connected layers. The first two layers contain 200 neurons followed by a TanH activation function. These two layers are used to learn deeper classification features in CNN. Finally, the number of neurons in the last fully-connected layer, also called classification layer, corresponds to the number of classes defined in Section 2.1. The classification layer is followed by a softmax activation function which maps the deepest features of the network learned by this layer to probability values. Input images to our CNN will be assigned to the class associated with the highest activation value using an arg max operator.

4 EXPERIMENTS
4.1 General experimental setup

We evaluated the performance of our proposed generic approach to perform manipulation parameter estimation through a set of experiments. In total, we considered four different tampering operations: JPEG compression, resampling, median filtering and gaussian blurring. The goal of these experiments is to show that using our generic data-driven approach we can forensically estimate the parameter of different types of manipulations. This is done without requiring a forensic investigator to make substantial changes to our generic approach. To extract classification features directly from data, we used our proposed constrained CNN architecture depicted in Fig. 2.

To create our training and testing databases, we downloaded images from the publicly available Dresden Image Database [15]. We then created different experimental databases where each corresponds to one particular manipulation with different parameter values applied to images. Since in general, a CNN's performance is

dependent of the size and quality of the training set [5, 31], we created a large dataset for every experiment. The smallest dataset used in any of these experiments consisted of 438, 112 grayscale images of size 256×256. To do this, for every experimental database, the training and testing data were collected from two separate sets of images where the green layer of the nine central 256×256 patches of every image was retained. These patches are then processed using the four underlying types of manipulations with different parameters.

When training each CNN, we set the batch size equal to 64 and the parameters of the stochastic gradient descent as follows: $momentum = 0.95$, $decay = 0.0005$, and a learning rate $\epsilon = 10^{-3}$ that decreases every 3 epochs, which is the number of times that every sample in the training data was trained, by a factor $\gamma = 0.5$. We trained the CNN in each experiment for 36 epochs. Note that training and testing are disjoint and CNNs were tested on separate testing datasets. Additionally, while training CNNs, their testing accuracies on a separate testing database were recorded every 1, 000 iterations to produce tables in this section. In all tables, unaltered images are denoted by the uppercase letter U.

We implemented all of our CNNs using the Caffe deep learning framework [18]. We ran our experiments using one Nvidia GeForce GTX 1080 GPU with 8GB RAM. The datasets used in this work were all converted to the lmdb format. In what follows, we present the results of all our experiments.

4.2 Resampling: Scaling factor estimation

Resampling editing operation is often involved in creating composite image forgeries, where the size or angle of one source image needs to be adjusted. In this set of experiments, we evaluated the ability of our CNN-based approach to estimating the scaling factor in resampled images. We rescaled these images using a bilinear interpolation. We consider two practical scenarios where an investigator can estimate either a scaling factor from a given known candidate parameter set or an arbitrary scaling factor in more realistic scenario.

4.2.1 Scaling factor estimation given known candidate set. In this experiment, we assume that the investigator knows that the forger used one of scaling factor values in a fixed set. Here, this set is $\Theta = \{50\%, 60\%, 70\%, \cdots, 150\%\}$. Note that 100% means no scaling applied to an image. Our estimate θ is the scaling factor denoted by s. In this simplified scenario, we cast the problem of estimating the scaling factor in resampled images as a classification problem. Thus, we assign each scaling factor to a unique class c_k. We used our CNN to distinguish between these different scaling factors. The output layer of CNN in Fig. 2 consists of 11 neurons.

Next, we created a training database that consisted of 1, 465, 200 grayscale patches of size 256×256 . To accomplish this, we randomly selected 14, 800 image from the Dresden database. These images were divided into 256×256 grayscale blocks as described in Section 4.1. We then used the above defined scaling factors s to generate the corresponding resampled images of each grayscale patch. Subsequently, we selected 505 images not used for the training to build our testing database that consisted of 49, 995 grayscale patches of size 256×256 in the same manner described above.

Table 1: Confusion matrix showing the parameter identification accuracy of our constrained CNN for resampling manipulation with different scaling factors s; True (rows) versus Predicted (columns).

Acc=98.40%	s=50%	s=60%	s=70%	s=80%	s=90%	s=100%	s=110%	s=120%	s=130%	s=140%	s=150%
s=50%	**95.89%**	3.34%	0.68%	0.07%	0.00%	0.02%	0.00%	0.00%	0.00%	0.00%	0.00%
s=60%	4.91%	**92.19%**	2.68%	0.13%	0.02%	0.00%	0.02%	0.02%	0.00%	0.00%	0.02%
s=70%	0.53%	2.40%	**96.68%**	0.26%	0.02%	0.00%	0.00%	0.00%	0.00%	0.09%	0.02%
s=80%	0.04%	0.15%	0.33%	**99.36%**	0.00%	0.00%	0.00%	0.02%	0.02%	0.07%	0.00%
s=90%	0.00%	0.00%	0.15%	0.02%	**99.71%**	0.00%	0.00%	0.04%	0.02%	0.04%	0.00%
s=100%	0.02%	0.00%	0.00%	0.02%	0.00%	**99.87%**	0.00%	0.00%	0.00%	0.09%	0.00%
s=110%	0.00%	0.00%	0.00%	0.04%	0.00%	0.00%	**99.74%**	0.02%	0.02%	0.15%	0.02%
s=120%	0.00%	0.00%	0.00%	0.00%	0.00%	0.00%	0.02%	**99.56%**	0.04%	0.31%	0.07%
s=130%	0.00%	0.00%	0.00%	0.00%	0.00%	0.00%	0.00%	0.00%	**99.71%**	0.24%	0.04%
s=140%	0.00%	0.00%	0.00%	0.00%	0.00%	0.00%	0.00%	0.00%	0.00%	**100%**	0.00%
s=150%	0.02%	0.00%	0.00%	0.00%	0.08%	0.00%	0.00%	0.00%	0.00%	0.33%	**99.65%**

Table 2: Confusion matrix showing the parameter identification accuracy of our constrained CNN for resampling manipulation with different scaling factor intervals; True (rows) versus Predicted (columns).

Acc=95.45%	$I_{45-55\%}$	$I_{55-65\%}$	$I_{65-75\%}$	$I_{75-85\%}$	$I_{85-95\%}$	$I_{95-105\%}$	$I_{105-115\%}$	$I_{115-125\%}$	$I_{125-135\%}$	$I_{135-145\%}$	$I_{145-155\%}$
$I_{45-55\%}$	**93.89%**	5.33%	0.38%	0.20%	0.02%	0.09%	0.02%	0.00%	0.02%	0.00%	0.04%
$I_{55-65\%}$	3.80%	**86.27%**	7.82%	1.98%	0.04%	0.09%	0.00%	0.00%	0.00%	0.00%	0.00%
$I_{65-75\%}$	0.29%	4.82%	**85.98%**	8.24%	0.40%	0.04%	0.00%	0.09%	0.09%	0.02%	0.02%
$I_{75-85\%}$	0.02%	0.24%	3.40%	**93.98%**	1.87%	0.04%	0.02%	0.16%	0.27%	0.00%	0.00%
$I_{85-95\%}$	0.00%	0.00%	0.04%	1.18%	**97.67%**	0.04%	0.87%	0.09%	0.04%	0.07%	0.00%
$I_{95-105\%}$	0.07%	0.00%	0.07%	0.18%	0.22%	**99.38%**	0.02%	0.00%	0.07%	0.00%	0.00%
$I_{105-115\%}$	0.00%	0.00%	0.00%	0.00%	0.09%	0.00%	**99.11%**	0.27%	0.47%	0.07%	0.00%
$I_{115-125\%}$	0.00%	0.00%	0.00%	0.07%	0.02%	0.07%	0.09%	**98.69%**	1.00%	0.07%	0.00%
$I_{125-135\%}$	0.00%	0.00%	0.00%	0.02%	0.00%	0.02%	0.00%	0.04%	**99.56%**	0.31%	0.04%
$I_{135-145\%}$	0.00%	0.00%	0.00%	0.00%	0.00%	0.00%	0.00%	0.00%	1.47%	**97.24%**	1.29%
$I_{145-155\%}$	0.00%	0.00%	0.00%	0.00%	0.02%	0.00%	0.00%	0.00%	0.33%	1.44%	**98.20%**

We then used our trained CNN to estimate the scaling factor associated with each image in our testing database. We present our experimental results in Table 1 where the diagonal entires of the confusion matrix correspond to the estimation accuracy of each scaling factor using our CNN-based approach. Experiments show that our proposed approach can achieve 98.40% estimation accuracy which is equivalent to the identification rate of our CNN. Typically it can achieve higher than 99% on most scaling factors. Noticeably, our approach can detect 140% upscaled images with 100% accuracy. However, from Table 1 one can observe that the estimation accuracy decreases with low scaling factors. Specifically, when $s \leq 70\%$ our approach can achieve 96.68% with 70% downscaled images and at least 92.19% with 60% downscaled images.

Extracting resampling traces in downscaled images is very challenging problem since most of pixel value relationships are destroyed after an image is being downscaled. Specifically, our approach can estimate the scaling factor in 50% downscaled images with 95.89% accuracy. This result demonstrates that CNN can still extract good low-level pixel-value dependency features even in very challenging scenarios.

4.2.2 Estimation given arbitrary scaling factor. In our previous experiment, we showed that our CNN can distinguish between traces induced by different scaling factors in resampled images. In more realistic scenarios, the forger could use an arbitrary scaling factor. In this experiment, we assume that the investigator knows only an upper and lower bound on the scaling factor, i.e., $\Theta = [45\%, 155\%]$ is the parameter set and $\Phi = \{[45\%, 55\%), \cdots, [145\%, 155\%]\}$ is the set of all parameter subsets ϕ_k. Our estimate θ is the scaling factor denoted by s. Additionally, we assume that any $\theta \in \phi_k$ will be mapped to the centroid of ϕ_k using the operator $h(\cdot)$ defined in Section 2.1, i.e., if $s \in [t_k, t_{k+1})$ then $\hat{\theta} = \frac{t_{k+1}+t_k}{2}$. Each scaling interval will correspond to a class c_k. We use our CNN to distinguish between these scaling factor intervals. The output layer of CNN in Fig. 2 consists of 11 neurons.

We then built a training data that consisted of 732, 600 grayscale 256×256 patches. To do this, we randomly selected 7, 400 images from the Dresden database. Subsequently, we divided these images into 256×256 patches to generate grayscale images in the same manner described above. In order to generate the corresponding resampled images for each grayscale patch, we used the 'randint' command from the 'numpy' module in Python, which returns integers from the discrete uniform distribution, to compute scaling factor values that lie in the [45%, 155%] interval. We then selected

Table 3: Confusion matrix showing the parameter identification accuracy of our constrained CNN for JPEG compression manipulation with different quality factors (QF); True (rows) versus Predicted (columns).

Acc=98.90%	U	QF=50	QF=60	QF=70	QF=80	QF=90
U	**98.50%**	0.08%	0.19%	0.11%	0.36%	0.75%
QF=50	0.01%	**99.86%**	0.13%	0.00%	0.00%	0.00%
QF=60	0.01%	0.29%	**99.58%**	0.07%	0.05%	0.00%
QF=70	0.04%	0.23%	0.12%	**99.17%**	0.34%	0.11%
QF=80	0.05%	0.12%	0.54%	0.19%	**98.87%**	0.23%
QF=90	0.57%	0.12%	0.41%	0.60%	0.89%	**97.41%**

505 images not used for the training to similarly build our testing database which consisted of 49, 995 grayscale 256×256 patches.

We used our trained CNN to estimate the scaling factor interval of each testing patch in our testing dataset. In Table 2, we present the confusion matrix of our CNN used to estimate the different scaling factor intervals. Our experimental results show that our proposed approach can achieve 95.45% estimation accuracy. Typically it can achieve higher than 93% accuracy on most scaling factor intervals. From Table 2, one can notice that CNN can detect upscaled images using $s \in [125\%, 135\%)$ with 99.56% accuracy. Similarly to the previous experiment, the performance of CNN decreases with downscaled images when the scaling factor lies in intervals with small boundaries. Specifically, when $s < 95\%$ our approach can achieve 97.67% estimation accuracy with $s \in [85\%, 95\%)$ and at least 85.98% accuracy with $s \in [65\%, 75\%)$.

Similarly to the previous experiment, these results demonstrate again that even in challenging scenarios where images are downscaled with very small parameter values CNN can still extract good classification features to distinguish between the different used intervals. Noticeably, one can observe from Table 2 that CNN can determine resampled images using $s \in [45\%, 55\%)$ with 93.89% accuracy. Note that given that the chosen intervals are separate by just 1%, estimating an arbitrary scaling factor that lies in different intervals is more challenging than when the scaling factor estimate belongs to a fixed set of known candidates.

4.3 JPEG Compression: Quality factor estimation

JPEG is one of the most widely used image compression formats today. In this part of our experiments, we would like to estimate the quality factor of JPEG compressed images. To do this, we consider two practical scenarios where an investigator can estimate either a quality factor from a given known candidate parameter set or an arbitrary quality factor in more realistic scenario.

4.3.1 Quality factor estimation given known candidate set. In this experiment, we assume that the investigator knows that the forger used one of quality factor values in a fixed set. Here, this set is $\Theta = \{50, 60, 70, 80, 90\}$. Our estimate θ is the quality factor denoted by QF. In this simplified scenario, we approximate the quality factor estimation problem in JPEG compressed images by a classification problem. Thus, we assign each quality factor to a unique class c_k and the unaltered images class is denoted by c_0. The number of classes c_k's is equal to six which corresponds to the number of neurons in the output layer of CNN.

We built a training database that consisted of 777, 600 grayscale patches of size 256×256. First, we randomly selected 14, 400 images from the Dresden database. Next, we divided these images into 256×256 grayscale patches in the same manner described in Section 4.1. Each patch corresponds to a new image that has its corresponding tampered images created by the five different choices of JPEG quality factor.

To evaluate the performance of our proposed approach, we similarly created a testing database that consisted of 50, 112 grayscale patches. This is done by dividing 928 images not used for the training into 256×256 grayscale patches in the same manner described above. Then we applied to these grayscale patches the same editing operations.

We used our trained CNN to estimate the quality factor of each JPEG compressed patch in our testing dataset. In Table 3, we present the confusion matrix of our CNN-based approach used to estimate the different quality factors. The overall estimation accuracy on the testing database is 98.90%. One can observe that CNN can estimate the quality factor of JPEG compressed images with an accuracy typically higher than 98%. This demonstrates the ability of the constrained convolutional layer to adaptively extract low-level pixel-value dependency features directly from data. This also demonstrates that every quality factor induces detectable unique traces.

From Table 3, we can notice that the estimation accuracy of CNN decreases when the quality factor is high. More specifically, with $QF = 90$ images are 0.89% misclassified as JPEG compressed images with $QF = 80$ and 0.57% are misclassified as unaltered images. Similarly, with $QF = 80$ subject images are 0.54% misclassified as JPEG compressed images with $QF = 60$ and the unaltered images are 0.75% misclassified as JPEG compressed images with $QF = 90$.

4.3.2 Estimation given arbitrary quality factor. In the previous experiment, we experimentally demonstrated that CNN can distinguish between traces left by different JPEG quality factors. Similarly to the resampling experiments, we would like to estimate the JPEG quality factor in more realistic scenarios where the forger could use an arbitrary quality factor. we assume that the investigator knows only an upper and lower bound on the quality factor, i.e., $\Theta = [45, 100\%]$ is the parameter set and $\Phi = \{[45, 55), \cdots, [85, 95), [95, 100]\}$ is the set of all parameter subsets ϕ_k. Our estimate θ is the quality factor denoted by QF. Additionally, we assume that any $\theta \in \phi_k$ will be mapped to the centroid of ϕ_k using the operator $h(\cdot)$ defined in Section 2.1, i.e., if $QF \in [t_k, t_{k+1})$ then $\hat{\theta} = \frac{t_{k+1}+t_k}{2}$. We define the centroid of the inclusive interval $[95, 100]$ as 97. Each quality

Table 4: Confusion matrix showing the parameter identification accuracy of our constrained CNN for JPEG compression manipulation with different quality factors (QF) intervals; True (rows) versus Predicted (columns).

Acc=95.27%	QF=45-54	QF=55-64	QF=65-74	QF=75-84	QF=85-94	QF=95-100
QF=45-54	**96.76%**	3.23%	0.00%	0.00%	0.00%	0.01%
QF=55-64	2.39%	**95.20%**	2.32%	0.01%	0.00%	0.07%
QF=65-74	0.22%	2.20%	**94.49%**	3.03%	0.01%	0.05%
QF=75-84	0.19%	0.45%	2.83%	**94.46%**	1.93%	0.14%
QF=85-94	0.11%	0.49%	1.23%	2.54%	**94.01%**	1.62%
QF=95-100	0.07%	0.38%	0.53%	0.63%	1.68%	**96.71%**

Table 5: Confusion matrix showing the parameter identification accuracy of our constrained CNN for median filtering manipulation with different kernel sizes K_{size}; True (rows) versus Predicted (columns).

Acc=99.55%	U	K_{size} = 3×3	K_{size} = 5×5	K_{size} = 7×7	K_{size} = 9×9	K_{size} = 11×11	K_{size} = 13×13	K_{size} = 15×15
U	**99.97%**	0.00%	0.00%	0.02%	0.02%	0.00%	0.00%	0.00%
K_{size} = 3×3	0.02%	**99.92%**	0.03%	0.02%	0.02%	0.00%	0.00%	0.00%
K_{size} = 5×5	0.02%	0.02%	**99.86%**	0.10%	0.02%	0.00%	0.00%	0.00%
K_{size} = 7×7	0.02%	0.00%	0.08%	**99.60%**	0.27%	0.03%	0.00%	0.00%
K_{size} = 9×9	0.00%	0.00%	0.00%	0.03%	**99.68%**	0.29%	0.00%	0.00%
K_{size} = 11×11	0.00%	0.00%	0.00%	0.00%	0.26%	**99.36%**	0.38%	0.00%
K_{size} = 13×13	0.00%	0.00%	0.00%	0.00%	0.03%	0.50%	**98.82%**	0.66%
K_{size} = 15×15	0.00%	0.00%	0.00%	0.00%	0.02%	0.02%	0.70%	**99.26%**

factor interval will correspond to a class c_k. We use our CNN to distinguish between these quality factor intervals. The output layer of CNN in Fig. 2 consists of six neurons.

To train our CNN, we built a training database that consisted of $388, 800$ grayscale patches of size 256×256. To do this, we randomly selected $7, 200$ images from the Dresden database that we divided into 256×256 grayscale patches as described in Section 4.1. To generate for each grayscale patch its corresponding compressed images with quality factors that lie in the defined [45, 100] interval, similarly to the resampling experiments we used the 'randint' command from the 'numpy' module in Python to compute such quality factor values. Subsequently, we selected 928 images not used for the training to similarly build our testing database that consisted of $50, 112$ grayscale patches of size 256×256.

We used our trained CNN to estimate the quality factor interval of each JPEG compressed patch in our testing dataset. In Table 4, we present the confusion matrix of our CNN used to estimate the different quality factor intervals. The overall estimation accuracy on the testing database is 95.92%. One can observe that CNN can estimate the quality factor interval of JPEG compressed images with an accuracy typically higher than 94%. This demonstrates again the ability of the constrained convolutional layer to adaptively extract low-level pixel-value dependency features directly from data to distinguish between quality factor intervals.

From Table 4, we can notice that the estimation accuracy is high either with low or high interval boundaries. Specifically, our approach can noticeably achieve 96.76% estimation accuracy when subject images are compressed with $QF \in [45, 54]$ and 96.71% accuracy with $QF \in [95, 100]$. This is mainly because these two intervals are either only followed by an upper interval or only preceded by a lower interval. Estimating an arbitrary quality factor

that lies in different intervals is more challenging than when the quality factor estimate belongs to a fixed set of known candidates given that these intervals are chosen to be separate by $QF = 1$. Thus, when $55 \leq QF < 95$ intervals are misclassified as either a subsequent or preceding intervals (see Table 4).

4.4 Median Filtering: Kernel size estimation

Median filtering is a commonly used image smoothing technique, which is particularly effective for removing impulsive noise. It can also be used to hide artifacts of JPEG compression [35] and resampling [23]. This type of filter operates by using a sliding window, also called kernel, that keeps the median pixel value within the window dimension. When a forger applies a median filtering operation to an image, typically they choose an odd kernel size. Therefore, we assume that the investigator knows that the forger used one of kernel size values in a fixed set. Here, this set is $\Theta = \{3\times3, 5\times5, \cdots, 15\times15\}$. Our estimate θ is the kernel size denoted by k_{size}. In this simplified scenario, we approximate the filtering kernel size estimation problem in filtered images by a classification problem. Thus, we assign each choice of kernel size to a unique class c_k and the unaltered images class is denoted by c_0. The number of classes c_k's is equal to eight which corresponds to the number of neurons in the output layer of CNN.

We collected $15, 495$ images for the training and testing datasets. We then randomly selected $14, 800$ images from our experimental database for the training. Subsequently, we divided these images into 256×256 grayscale patches by retaining the green layer of the nine central blocks. As described above, each block will correspond to a new image that has its corresponding tampered images created

Table 6: Confusion matrix showing the parameter identification accuracy of our constrained CNN for gaussian blurring manipulation with different kernel sizes K_{size} and $\sigma = 0.3 \times ((K_{size} - 1) \times 0.5 - 1) + 0.8$; True (rows) versus Predicted (columns).

Acc=99.38%	U	$K_{size} = 3 \times 3$	$K_{size} = 7 \times 7$	$K_{size} = 11 \times 11$	$K_{size} = 15 \times 15$
U	**99.98%**	0.00%	0.00%	0.00%	0.02%
$K_{size} = 3 \times 3$	0.00%	**99.96%**	0.02%	0.00%	0.02%
$K_{size} = 7 \times 7$	0.00%	0.02%	**99.38%**	0.59%	0.02%
$K_{size} = 11 \times 11$	0.00%	0.00%	0.07%	**98.61%**	1.32%
$K_{size} = 15 \times 15$	0.00%	0.00%	0.00%	1.00%	**99.00%**

by median filtering manipulation using seven different kernel sizes. In total, our training database consisted of 1,065,600 patches.

We built our testing database in the same manner by dividing the 695 images not used for the training into 256×256 grayscale pixel patches. Then we edited these images to generate their tampered homologues. In total, our testing database consisted of 50,040 patches. Our constrained CNN is then trained to determine unaltered images as well as the kernel size used to median filter testing images.

We used our trained CNN to estimate the median filtering kernel size of each filtered patch in our testing dataset. In Table 5, we present the confusion matrix of our CNN used to estimate the different kernel sizes. Our proposed approach can achieve 99.50% accuracy. From Table 5, we can notice that CNN can determine the kernel size with an estimation accuracy typically higher than 99%. Noticeably, it can achieve 99.97% with unaltered images and at least 98.82% with 13×13 median filtered images. Additionally, one can observe that most of the off-diagonal entries of the confusion matrix are equal to zero. Thus, we experimentally demonstrated that the constrained convolutional layer can adaptively extract traces left by a particular kernel size of a median filtering operation.

4.5 Gaussian Blurring

Gaussian filtering is often used for image smoothing, in order to remove noise or to reduce details. Similarly to median filtering, this type of filter operates by using a sliding window that convolves with all the regions of an image and has the following expression

$$G(x, y) = \alpha \exp\left(-\frac{x^2 + y^2}{2\sigma^2}\right), \qquad (14)$$

where x and y are the kernel weight spatial locations where $G(0, 0)$ is the origin/central kernel weight, α is a scaling factor chosen such that $\sum_{x,y} G(x, y) = 1$, and σ^2 is the variance blur value. In this work, we experimentally investigate a set of two scenarios. First, we use CNN to estimate the filtering kernel size with size dependent blur variance. Subsequently, we fixed the kernel size and use our approach to identify the blur variance.

4.5.1 Kernel size estimation with size dependent blur variance. One of the most common ways to perform median blurring on images is to choose the kernel size with size dependent blur variance. That is, the blur variance is formally defined in programming libraries (e.g., OpenCV [17]) in terms of the kernel size as $\sigma^2 = \left(0.3 \times ((K_{size} - 1) \times 0.5 - 1) + 0.8\right)^2$. We assume that the investigator knows that the forger used one of kernel size values in a fixed set. Here, this set is $\Theta = \{3 \times 3, 7 \times 7, 11 \times 11, 15 \times 15\}$. Our

estimate θ is the kernel size denoted by k_{size}. In this simplified scenario, we approximate the smoothing kernel size estimation problem in filtered images by a classification problem. Thus, we assign each choice of kernel size to a unique class c_k and the unaltered images class is denoted by c_0. The number of classes c_k's is equal to five which corresponds to the number of neurons in the output layer of CNN.

We collected 15,920 images to perform the training and testing. To train CNN, we randomly selected 14,800 images for training and the rest 1,120 images were used for testing. Similarly to all previous experiments, images in the training and testing sets were divided into 256×256 blocks and the green layer of the central nine patches was retained. Each patch corresponds to a new image then we used the four different filtering kernel sizes to create their manipulated homologues. In total, we collect 666,000 patches for training and 50,400 for testing.

We used our trained CNN to estimate the smoothing kernel size of each filtered patch in our testing dataset. The confusion matrix of CNN to detect gaussian blur kernel size is presented in Table 6. Our proposed approach can identify the filtering kernel size with 99.38% accuracy. In particular it can identify unaltered images with 99.98% accuracy and it can achieve at least 98.64% detection rate with 11×11 filtered images. Furthermore, one can notice from Table 6 that the detection rate of the filtering kernel size decreases when the standard deviation blur $\sigma > 2$ which is equivalent of choosing a filtering kernel size bigger than 7×7. More specifically, the 11×11 filtered images are 1.32% misclassified as 15×15 filtered images. Similarly, the 15×15 filtered images are 1% misclassified as 11×11 filtered images. In what follows, we compare these results to the scenario when gaussian blurring is parameterized in terms of its variance σ^2 with a fixed filtering kernel size.

4.5.2 Variance Estimation with fixed kernel size. In this part, we use our approach to estimate the gaussian blur variance when the filtering kernel size is fixed to 5×5. To accomplish this, we assume that the investigator knows that the forger used one of blur standard deviation values in a fixed set. Here, this set is $\Theta = \{1, 2, 3, 4, 5\}$. Our estimate θ is the blur variance denoted by σ^2. In this simplified scenario, we approximate the blur variance estimation problem in smoothed images by a classification problem. Thus, we assign each choice of blur standard deviation σ a unique class c_k and the unaltered images class is denoted by c_0. The number of classes c_k's is equal to six which corresponds to the number of neurons in the output layer of CNN.

We collected 15,734 images from our Dresden experimental database. To train the CNN, we then randomly selected 14,800 images

Table 7: Confusion matrix showing the parameter identification accuracy of our constrained CNN for gaussian blurring manipulation with fixed kernel size (i.e., K_{size} = 5×5) and different σ; True (rows) versus Predicted (columns).

Acc=96.94%	U	$\sigma = 1$	$\sigma = 2$	$\sigma = 3$	$\sigma = 4$	$\sigma = 5$
U	**99.94%**	0.04%	0.00%	0.00%	0.00%	0.02%
$\sigma = 1$	0.01%	**99.90%**	0.08%	0.00%	0.00%	0.00%
$\sigma = 2$	0.00%	0.01%	**99.92%**	0.06%	0.01%	0.00%
$\sigma = 3$	0.00%	0.04%	0.12%	**97.87%**	1.70%	0.27%
$\sigma = 4$	0.01%	0.01%	0.02%	1.45%	**90.68%**	7.82%
$\sigma = 5$	0.02%	0.01%	0.01%	0.08%	6.54%	**93.33%**

for the training that we divided into 256×256 patches as described above. Then we generated their corresponding edited patches using the five possible parameter values. In total our training database consisted of 799, 200 patches. To evaluated our method in determining the gaussian blur variance σ^2, similarly we divided the 934 images not used for the training into 256×256 blocks then we generated their corresponding edited patches using the same editing operations. In total, we collected 50, 400 patches for the testing database.

We used our trained CNN to estimate the blur variance of each filtered patch in our testing dataset. In Table 7, we present the confusion matrix of our method. Our experimental results show that our proposed approach can determine the blur variance with 96.94%. From Table 7, we can notice from the confusion matrix of CNN that these results match the results presented in Table 6. In fact, when the standard deviation blur $\sigma \leq 2$, CNN can identify the parameter values with an accuracy higher than 99%. Noticeably, it can achieve 99.94% at identifying unaltered images and at least 99.90% accuracy with gaussian blurred images using a standard deviation blur $\sigma = 1$.

One can observe that similarly to the previous experiment, when $\sigma > 2$ the estimation accuracy significantly decreases and it can achieve at most 97.87% accuracy with gaussian blurred images using a standard deviation blur $\sigma = 3$. Note that in the size dependent blur variance experiment, the highest value of σ is equal to 2.6. Finally, these experiments demonstrate that CNN is able to adaptively extract good low-level representative features associated with every choice of the variance value.

4.6 Experimental results summary

In this section, we experimentally investigated the ability of our CNN-based generic approach to forensically estimate the manipulation parameters. Our experimental results showed that CNNs associated with the constrained convolutional layer are good candidates to extract low-level classification features and to estimate a particular manipulation parameter. We used the proposed CNN to capture pixel-value dependency traces induced by each different manipulation parameter in all our experiments. In a simplified scenario where a forensic investigator knows a priori a fixed set of parameter candidates, our CNN was able to perform manipulation parameter estimation with an accuracy typically higher than 98% with all underlying image editing operations.

Specifically, when the parameter value θ belongs to a fixed set of known candidates, CNN can accurately estimate resampling scaling factor, JPEG quality factor, median filtering kernel size and gaussian blurring kernel size respectively with 98.40%, 98.90%, 99.55% and 99.38% accuracy. This demonstrates also that our method is generic and could be used with multiple types of image manipulation. It is worth mentioning that when images are downscaled, scaling factor estimation is difficult [22]. Our proposed approach, however, is still able to determine the scaling factor in downscaled images with at least 92% accuracy.

When the parameter value θ is an arbitrary value in a bounded but countable set, our CNNs performance decreases. This is mainly because we consider a very challenging problem where parameter intervals are chosen to be separate by one unit distance, e.g. scaling factor interval [65%, 75%) followed by [75%, 85%) interval. Specifically, our generic approach can estimate the resampling scaling factor interval as well as the JPEG quality factor interval with an accuracy respectively equal to 95.45% and 95.27%. These results demonstrate the ability of CNN to distinguish between different parameter value intervals even when the distance between these intervals is very small.

Though we have demonstrated through our experiments that our proposed method can accurately perform manipulation parameter estimation, our goal is not necessarily to outperform existing parameter estimation techniques. It is instead to propose a new data-driven manipulation parameter estimation approach that can provide accurate manipulation parameter estimates for several different manipulations without requiring an investigator to analytically derive a new estimator for each manipulation.

5 CONCLUSION

In this paper, we have proposed a data-driven generic approach to performing forensic manipulation parameter estimation. Instead of relying on theoretical analysis of parametric models, our proposed method is able to learn estimators directly from a set of labeled data. Specifically, we cast the problem of manipulation parameter estimation as a classification problem. To accomplish this, we first partitioned the manipulation parameter space into an ordered set of disjoint subsets, then we assigned a class to each subset. Subsequently, we designed a CNN-based classifier which makes use of a constrained convolutional layer to learn traces left by a desired manipulation that has been applied using parameter values in each parameter subset. The ultimate goal of this work is to show that our generic parameter estimator can be used with multiple types of image manipulation without requiring a forensic investigator to make substantial changes to the proposed method. We evaluated the effectiveness of our generic estimator through a set of experiments using four different types of parameterized manipulation. The results of these experiments showed that our generic method can provide an estimate for these manipulations with estimation accuracies typically in the 95% to 99% range.

6 ACKNOWLEDGMENTS

This material is based upon work supported by the National Science Foundation under Grant No. 1553610. Any opinions, findings, and conclusions or recommendations expressed in this material are those of the authors and do not necessarily reflect the views of the National Science Foundation.

REFERENCES

[1] BAHRAMI, K., KOT, A. C., LI, L., AND LI, H. Blurred image splicing localization by exposing blur type inconsistency. *IEEE Transactions on Information Forensics and Security 10*, 5 (May 2015), 999–1009.

[2] BAYAR, B., AND STAMM, M. C. On the robustness of constrained convolutional neural networks to jpeg post-compression for image resampling detection. In *The 2017 IEEE International Conference on Acoustics, Speech and Signal Processing*, IEEE.

[3] BAYAR, B., AND STAMM, M. C. A deep learning approach to universal image manipulation detection using a new convolutional layer. In *Proceedings of the 4th ACM Workshop on Information Hiding and Multimedia Security* (2016), ACM, pp. 5–10.

[4] BAYAR, B., AND STAMM, M. C. Design principles of convolutional neural networks for multimedia forensics. In *International Symposium on Electronic Imaging: Media Watermarking, Security, and Forensics* (2017), IS&T.

[5] BENGIO, Y. Practical recommendations for gradient-based training of deep architectures. In *Neural Networks: Tricks of the Trade*. Springer, 2012, pp. 437–478.

[6] BIANCHI, T., ROSA, A. D., AND PIVA, A. Improved dct coefficient analysis for forgery localization in jpeg images. In *IEEE International Conference on Acoustics, Speech and Signal Processing (ICASSP)* (May 2011), pp. 2444–2447.

[7] CHEN, F., AND MA, J. An empirical identification method of gaussian blur parameter for image deblurring. *IEEE Transactions on signal processing 57*, 7 (2009), 2467–2478.

[8] CHEN, J., KANG, X., LIU, Y., AND WANG, Z. J. Median filtering forensics based on convolutional neural networks. *IEEE Signal Processing Letters 22*, 11 (Nov. 2015), 1849–1853.

[9] CHO, T. S., PARIS, S., HORN, B. K. P., AND FREEMAN, W. T. Blur kernel estimation using the radon transform. In *CVPR 2011* (June 2011), pp. 241–248.

[10] CONOTTER, V., COMESAA, P., AND PREZ-GONZLEZ, F. Forensic detection of processing operator chains: Recovering the history of filtered jpeg images. *IEEE Transactions on Information Forensics and Security 10*, 11 (Nov 2015), 2257–2269.

[11] COX, I. J., KILIAN, J., LEIGHTON, F. T., AND SHAMOON, T. Secure spread spectrum watermarking for multimedia. *IEEE Transactions on Image Processing 6*, 12 (Dec 1997), 1673–1687.

[12] FAN, Z., AND DE QUEIROZ, R. L. Identification of bitmap compression history: Jpeg detection and quantizer estimation. *IEEE Transactions on Image Processing 12*, 2 (2003), 230–235.

[13] FARID, H. Blind inverse gamma correction. *IEEE Transactions on Image Processing 10*, 10 (Oct 2001), 1428–1433.

[14] FRIDRICH, J., AND KODOVSKÝ, J. Rich models for steganalysis of digital images. *IEEE Transactions on Information Forensics and Security 7*, 3 (2012), 868–882.

[15] GLOE, T., AND BÖHME, R. The dresden image database for benchmarking digital image forensics. *Journal of Digital Forensic Practice 3*, 2-4 (2010), 150–159.

[16] GOLJAN, M., AND FRIDRICH, J. Camera identification from cropped and scaled images. In *Electronic Imaging* (2008), International Society for Optics and Photonics, pp. 68190E–68190E.

[17] ITSEEZ. Open source computer vision library. https://github.com/itseez/opencv, 2015.

[18] JIA, Y., SHELHAMER, E., DONAHUE, J., KARAYEV, S., LONG, J., GIRSHICK, R., GUADARRAMA, S., AND DARRELL, T. Caffe: Convolutional architecture for fast feature embedding. *arXiv preprint arXiv:1408.5093* (2014).

[19] KANG, X., STAMM, M. C., PENG, A., AND LIU, K. J. R. Robust median filtering forensics using an autoregressive model. *IEEE Transactions on Information Forensics and Security, 8*, 9 (Sept. 2013), 1456–1468.

[20] KANG, X., STAMM, M. C., PENG, A., AND LIU, K. R. Robust median filtering forensics using an autoregressive model. *IEEE Transactions on Information Forensics and Security 8*, 9 (2013), 1456–1468.

[21] KEE, E., JOHNSON, M. K., AND FARID, H. Digital image authentication from jpeg headers. *IEEE Transactions on Information Forensics and Security 6*, 3 (Sept. 2011), 1066–1075.

[22] KIRCHNER, M. Fast and reliable resampling detection by spectral analysis of fixed linear predictor residue. In *Proceedings of the 10th ACM Workshop on Multimedia and Security* (New York, NY, USA, 2008), MM&Sec '08, ACM, pp. 11–20.

[23] KIRCHNER, M., AND BOHME, R. Hiding traces of resampling in digital images. *IEEE Transactions on Information Forensics and Security 3*, 4 (2008), 582–592.

[24] KIRCHNER, M., AND FRIDRICH, J. On detection of median filtering in digital images. In *IS&T/SPIE Electronic Imaging* (2010), International Society for Optics and Photonics, pp. 754110–754110.

[25] PEVNY, T., BAS, P., AND FRIDRICH, J. Steganalysis by subtractive pixel adjacency matrix. *IEEE Transactions on Information Forensics and Security 5*, 2 (June 2010), 215–224.

[26] PEVNY, T., AND FRIDRICH, J. Detection of double-compression in jpeg images for applications in steganography. *IEEE Transactions on Information Forensics and Security 3*, 2 (June 2008), 247–258.

[27] PFENNIG, S., AND KIRCHNER, M. Spectral methods to determine the exact scaling factor of resampled digital images. In *Communications Control and Signal Processing (ISCCSP), 2012 5th International Symposium on* (2012), IEEE, pp. 1–6.

[28] POPESCU, A. C., AND FARID, H. Exposing digital forgeries by detecting traces of resampling. *IEEE Transactions on Signal Processing 53*, 2 (Feb. 2005), 758–767.

[29] QIU, X., LI, H., LUO, W., AND HUANG, J. A universal image forensic strategy based on steganalytic model. In *Proceedings of the 2nd ACM workshop on Information hiding and multimedia security* (2014), ACM, pp. 165–170.

[30] RUANAIDH, J. J. O., AND PUN, T. Rotation, scale and translation invariant spread spectrum digital image watermarking. *Signal processing 66*, 3 (1998), 303–317.

[31] SIMARD, P. Y., STEINKRAUS, D., AND PLATT, J. C. Best practices for convolutional neural networks applied to visual document analysis. In *ICDAR* (2003), vol. 3, pp. 958–962.

[32] STAMM, M. C., CHU, X., AND LIU, K. J. R. Forensically determining the order of signal processing operations. In *IEEE International Workshop on Information Forensics and Security (WIFS)* (Nov 2013), pp. 162–167.

[33] STAMM, M. C., AND LIU, K. J. R. Forensic detection of image manipulation using statistical intrinsic fingerprints. *IEEE Transactions on Information Forensics and Security 5*, 3 (Sept 2010), 492–506.

[34] STAMM, M. C., AND LIU, K. J. R. Forensic estimation and reconstruction of a contrast enhancement mapping. In *2010 IEEE International Conference on Acoustics, Speech and Signal Processing* (March 2010), pp. 1698–1701.

[35] STAMM, M. C., AND LIU, K. R. Anti-forensics of digital image compression. *IEEE Transactions on Information Forensics and Security 6*, 3 (2011), 1050–1065.

[36] STAMM, M. C., WU, M., AND LIU, K. J. R. Information forensics: An overview of the first decade. *IEEE Access 1* (2013), 167–200.

[37] THAI, T. H., COGRANNE, R., RETRAINT, F., ET AL. Jpeg quantization step estimation and its applications to digital image forensics. *IEEE Transactions on Information Forensics and Security 12*, 1 (2017), 123–133.

Recasting Residual-based Local Descriptors as Convolutional Neural Networks: an Application to Image Forgery Detection

Davide Cozzolino
DIETI
University Federico II of Naples
80125, Naples, Italy
davide.cozzolino@unina.it

Giovanni Poggi
DIETI
University Federico II of Naples
80125, Naples, Italy
poggi@unina.it

Luisa Verdoliva
DIETI
University Federico II of Naples
80125, Naples, Italy
verdoliv@unina.it

ABSTRACT

Local descriptors based on the image noise residual have proven extremely effective for a number of forensic applications, like forgery detection and localization. Nonetheless, motivated by promising results in computer vision, the focus of the research community is now shifting on deep learning. In this paper we show that a class of residual-based descriptors can be actually regarded as a simple constrained convolutional neural network (CNN). Then, by relaxing the constraints, and fine-tuning the net on a relatively small training set, we obtain a significant performance improvement with respect to the conventional detector.

KEYWORDS

Local descriptors, bag-of-words, CNN, image forgery detection

ACM Reference format:
Davide Cozzolino, Giovanni Poggi, and Luisa Verdoliva. 2017. Recasting Residual-based Local Descriptors as Convolutional
Neural Networks: an Application to Image Forgery Detection. In *Proceedings of IH&MMSec '17, June 20–22, 2017, Philadelphia, PA, USA, , 6 pages.*
DOI: http://dx.doi.org/10.1145/3082031.3083247

1 INTRODUCTION

Images and videos represent by now the dominant source of traffic on the Internet and the bulk of data stored on social media. Nowadays, however, such data may be easily manipulated by malicious attackers to convey some twisted and potentially dangerous messages in areas like politics, journalism, judiciary. For this reason, in the last few years there has been intense and growing activity on multimedia forensics, aiming at developing methods to detect, localize, and classify possible image manipulations.

Typical attacks consist in adding or deleting objects, using material taken from the same image (copy-move) or from other sources (splicing). As a consequence, many researchers have focused on detecting near-duplicates in the image or across a repository of images. More fundamentally, one may be interested in establishing whether the image under analysis is pristine or else has been subjected to some post-processing, since any form of manipulation may raise suspects and suggest deeper inquiry. In fact, most of the times, copy-moves and splicing are accompanied by various forms of elaboration aimed at removing the most obvious traces of editing. These include, for example, resizing, rotation, linear and non-linear filtering, contrast enhancement, histogram equalization and, eventually, re-compression.

A number of papers have been proposed to detect one or the other of such elaborations [13, 15, 16, 22, 25]. These methods, however, are sensitive to just some specific manipulations. A more appealing line of research is to detect *all* possible manipulations, an approach that has been followed in several papers [5, 10, 20, 26]. Notably, in the 2013 IEEE Image Forensics Challenge, the most effective techniques for both image forgery detection [6] and localization [7] used this approach, relying on powerful residual-based local descriptors. These features, such as SPAM (subtractive pixel adjacency matrix) [21] or SRM (spatial rich models) [11], inspired to previous work in steganalysis, are extracted from the so-called residual image. In fact, the noise residual, extracted through some high-pass filtering of the image, contains a wealth of information on the in-camera and out-camera processes involved in the image formation. Such subtle traces, hardly visible without enhancement, may reveal anomalies due to object insertion [8, 9] or allow detecting different types of image editing operations [4, 20, 26].

Very recently, inspired by impressive results in the closely related fields of computer vision and pattern recognition [17], the multimedia forensics community began focusing on the use of deep learning [3, 19], especially convolutional neural networks (CNN) [27]. Taking advantage of the lesson learnt from SPAM/SRM features, constrained CNN architectures have been proposed both for steganalysis [23] and manipulation detection [2], where the first convolutional layer is forced to perform a high-pass filtering.

In this paper we show that there is no real contraposition between residual-based features and CNNs. Indeed, these local features can be computed through a CNN with architecture and parameters selected so as to guarantee a perfect equivalence. Once established this result, we go beyond emulation, removing constraints on parameters, and fine-tuning the net to further improve performance. Since the resulting network has a lightweight structure, fine-tuning can be carried out through a small training set, limiting computation time and memory usage. A significant performance gain with respect to the conventional feature is observed, especially in the most challenging situations.

In the following we describe in more detail the residual-based local features (Section 2), recast them as a constrained CNN, to be further trained after removing constraints (Section 3), show experimental results (Section 4), and draw conclusions (Section 5).

2 RESIDUAL-BASED LOCAL DESCRIPTORS

Establishing which type of processing an image has undergone calls for the ability to detect the subtle traces left by these operations, typically in the form of recurrent micropatterns. This problem has close ties with steganalysis, where weak messages hidden in the data are sought, so it is no surprise that the same tools, residual-based local descriptors, prove successful in both cases. To associate a residual-based feature to an image, or an image block, the following processing chain has been successfully used in steganalysis [11, 21]:

(1) extraction of noise residuals
(2) scalar quantization
(3) computation of co-occurrences
(4) computation of histogram

In the following, we describe in some more depth all these steps, taking a specific model out of the 39 proposed in [11] as running example.

Extraction of noise residual. The goal is to extract image details, in the high-frequency part of the image, which enables the analysis of expressive micropatterns. As the name suggests, this step can be implemented by resorting to a high-pass filter. In [11] a number of different high-pass filters have been considered, both linear and nonlinear, with various supports. Here, as an example, we focus on a single 4-tap mono-dimensional linear filter, with coefficients $w = [1, \; 3, 3, \; 1]$. The filter extracts image details along one direction, but is applied also on the image transpose (assuming vertical/horizontal invariance) to augment the available data. Choosing a single filter rather than considering all models proposed in [11] is motivated not only by the reduced complexity but also by the very good performance observed in the context of image forgery detection [6, 20, 26].

Scalar quantization. Residuals are conceptually real-valued quantities or, in any case, high-resolution integers, so they must be quantized to reduce cardinality and allow easy processing. In [11] a uniform quantization is used with an odd number of levels (to ensure that 0 is among the possible outputs). Therefore, the only parameters to set are the number of quantization levels, L, and the quantization step Δ. In our example we set $L = 3$ and $\Delta = 4.5$.

Co-occurrences. The computation of co-occurrences is the core step of the procedure. In fact, this is a low-complexity means for taking into account high-order dependencies among residuals and hence gather information on recurrent micropatterns. Following [11] we compute co-occurrences on $N = 4$ pixels in a row, both along and across the filter direction. With these values, two co-occurrence matrices with $3^4 = 81$ entries are obtained. Of course, the image or block under analysis must be large enough to obtain meaningful estimates. All the co-occurrence N-dimensional bins are eventually coded as integers.

Feature formation. Counting co-occurrences one obtains the final feature vector describing the image. Neglecting symmetries, our final feature has length equal to 162. The final classification phase is performed by a linear SVM classifier.

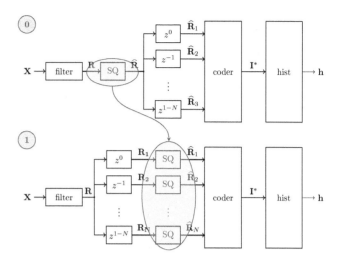

Figure 1: Basic processing scheme (0) for extracting the single model SRM feature, and equivalent scheme (1) with inverted order of scalar quantization (SQ) and n-pixel shifting (z^{-n}).

3 RECASTING LOCAL FEATURES AS CNN

We will now show that local residual-based features can be extracted by means of a convolutional neural network. Establishing this equivalence leaves us with a CNN architecture and a set of parameters that are already known to provide an excellent performance for the problem of interest. Then, given this good starting point, we can move a step forward and fine-tune the network through a sensible training phase with labeled data. Note that in this way we will carry out a joint optimization of both the feature extraction process and classification. In the following we will first move from local features to a Bag-of-Words (BoW) paradigm, and then proceed to the implementation by means of Convolutional Neural Networks.

3.1 From local features to Bag-of-Words

In Fig.1 (top) we show the basic processing scheme used to extract the single model SRM feature. Let X be the input image[1], R the residual image, and $\widehat{R}$ the quantized residual image. To compute the output feature, the input image is high-pass filtered, then the residual image is quantized, and N versions of it are generated, shifted one pixel apart from one another. For each pixel s, the values $\widehat{r}_{1,s}, \ldots, \widehat{r}_{N,s}$ are regarded as base-L digits and encoded as a single scalar i_s^*, finally, the histogram h of this latter image is computed. The scheme at the bottom of Fig.1 is identical to the former except for the inverted order of scalar quantization (SQ) and shifting. This inversion, however, allows us to focus on the two groups of blocks highlighted at the top of Fig.2.

The filter-shifter group can be replaced by a bank of N filters, all identical to one another except for the position of the non-zero weights. So, with reference to our running example, the n-th filter will have non-zero weights, [1, -3, 3, -1], only on the n-th row, and

---

[1]We use capital boldface for images, lowercase boldface for vectors, and simple lowercase for scalars. The value of image X at spatial site s, will be denoted by x_s.

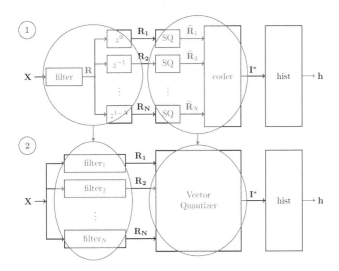

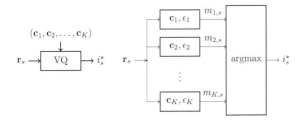

Figure 2: The cascade of filter and shifters of scheme (1) can be replaced by a bank of filters, while the bank of independent SQ's + coder can be replaced by product VQ. The resulting scheme (2) fits the Bag-of-Words paradigm.

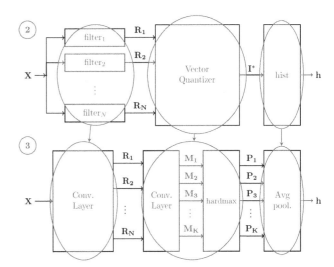

Figure 4: The whole scheme (2) can be converted in the CNN (3). The filter bank is replaced by a convolutional layer, VQ is replaced by convolutional-hardmax layers, the histogram can be computed through an average pooling layer.

3.2 From Bag-of-Words to CNN

We now show that the processing steps of Fig.2 can be all implemented through a CNN. First of all, the bank of linear filters used to extract noise residuals can be replaced by a pure convolutional layer, with neurons computing the residuals as

$$r_{n,s} = f(w_{n,s} * x_s + b_n) \qquad n = 1, \cdots, N \qquad (1)$$

with s used for image spatial location and n to identify neurons. The neuron weights coincide with filter coefficients, biases b_n are all set to zero, and the non-linearity $f(\cdot)$ is set to identity.

As for the vector quantizer, assuming the usual minimum distance hard-decision rule, it can be implemented by means of a convolutional layer followed by a hard-max layer. Let $\mathbf{r}_s$ be a vector formed by collecting a group of residuals at site s, and $\mathbf{c}_k$ the k-th codeword of the quantizer. Their squared Euclidean distance, $d_{k,s}^2$, can be expanded as

$$
\begin{aligned}
||\mathbf{r}_s - \mathbf{c}_k||^2 &= ||\mathbf{r}_s||^2 + ||\mathbf{c}_k||^2 - 2 < \mathbf{r}_s, \mathbf{c}_k > \\
&= ||\mathbf{r}_s||^2 - 2\epsilon_k - 2 < \mathbf{r}_s, \mathbf{c}_k > \qquad (2)
\end{aligned}
$$

with $|| \cdot ||^2$ and $< \cdot, \cdot >$ indicating norm and inner product, respectively. Hence, neglecting the irrelevant $||\mathbf{r}_s||^2$ term:

$$
\begin{aligned}
i_s^* &= \mathrm{argmin}_{k=1, \cdots, K} \; d_{k,s} \\
&= \mathrm{argmax}_{k=1, \cdots, K} \; (< \mathbf{r}_s, \mathbf{c}_k > + \epsilon_k) \\
&= \mathrm{argmax}_{k=1, \cdots, K} \; m_{k,s} \qquad (3)
\end{aligned}
$$

with $m_{k,s}$ interpreted as a matching score between the feature vector at site s and the k-th codeword.

This equivalence is depicted in Fig.3. The matching scores $m_{k,s}$ are computed through a convolutional layer, equipped with $K = L^N$ filters (remember that L is the number of quantization levels), one for each codeword, having weights $\mathbf{c}_k$, bias ϵ_k and, again, an identity as activation function. The best matching codeword is then selected through a hardmax processing.

Figure 3: A vector quantizer (left) can be implemented through a bank of filter followed by argmax (right).

zero weights everywhere else. Turning to the second group, the combination of N scalar quantizers can be regarded as a constrained form of vector quantization (VQ). More specifically, it is a product VQ, since the VQ codebook is obtained as the cartesian product of the N SQ codebooks. On one hand, product quantization is much simpler and faster than VQ. On the other hand, its strong constraints are potentially detrimental for performance. Its $K = L^N$ codewords are forced to lie on a truncated N-dimensional square lattice [12] and cannot adapt to the data distribution. Many of them will be wasted in empty regions of the feature space, causing a sure loss of performance with respect to unconstrained VQ.

However, the most interesting observation about the new structure at the bottom of Fig.2 is that it implements the Bag-of-Words (or also Bag-of-Features) paradigm. The filter bank extracts a feature vector for each image pixel, based on its neighborhood. These features are then associated, through VQ, with some template features. Finally, the frequency of occurrence of the latter, computed in the last block, provides a synthetic descriptor of the input image. The fact that filters and vector quantizer are largely sub-optimal impacts only on performance, not on interpretation. Needless to say, they could be both improved through supervised training.

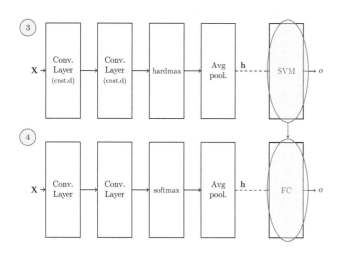

Figure 5: The constrained CNN of scheme (3) extracts the features which feed an external classifier. In scheme (4) this is replaced by an internal fully connected layer, and all constraints are removed. By fine-tuning on training data, all layers can be optimized jointly. The dashed lines are to remind that this net provides only half the feature, a twin net (not shown for clarity) provides the other half.

The evolution of the whole network is shown in Fig.4. As already said, the first filter bank is replaced by a convolutional layer. Then, the VQ is replaced by another convolutional layer followed by a hardmax layer. The former outputs K feature maps, $\mathbf{M}_k$, with the matching scores. The latter outputs K binary maps, $\mathbf{P}_k$, where $p_{k,s} = 1$ when the corresponding matching score $m_{k,s}$ is maximum over k, and 0 otherwise. Finally, the histogram computation is replaced by an average pooling layer operating on the whole feature maps, that is, $h_k = \sum_s p_{k,s}$. The resulting scheme is shown at the bottom of Fig.4.

This net computes only half the desired feature, the part based on across-filter co-occurrences. The twin half is computed similarly, and the complete feature is eventually fed to the SVM classifier, as shown in Fig.5 (top). In this network, weights and biases of the convolutional layers are all hard-wired to reproduce exactly the behavior of the residual-based local feature described in Section 2, thereby ensuring the good performance observed in the literature. We now proceed to remove all constraints and allow the net to learn on a suitable training set. First of all, the classifier itself can be implemented as part of the CNN architecture by including a fully connected layer at the end, obtaining the architecture of Fig.5 (bottom). Now, to exploit the full potential of deep learning, all parameters must be optimized by appropriate training, thereby overcoming all the impairing constraints mentioned before. Note that the learning phase allows us not only to optimize all layers, which could be done also in the BoW framework, but to optimize them *jointly*, taking full advantage of the CNN structural freedom. Moreover, the lightweight architecture of the network is instrumental to achieve good results even with a limited training set.

However, before proceeding with the training, it is necessary to replace the hard-max layer, with a soft-max layer that approximates it, so as to avoid non-differentiable operators. Given the input vector

Table 1: Image manipulations under test.

Manipulation	Parameters
Median Filtering	kernel: 7×7, 5×5, 3×3
Gaussian Blurring	st. dev: 1.1, 0.75, 0.5
Additive Noise (AWGN)	st. dev.: 2.0, 0.5, 0.25
Resizing	scale: 1.5, 1.125, 1.01
JPEG Compression	quality factor: 70, 80, 90

$\{m_{k,s}, k = 1, \ldots, K\}$, the soft-max computes the quantities

$$p_{k,s} = e^{\alpha m_{k,s}} / \sum_l e^{\alpha m_{l,s}} \qquad (4)$$

With the aim to preserve a close correspondence with the original descriptor, we should choose a very large α parameter, so as to obtain a steep nonlinearity. However, as said before, this is not really necessary, since our goal is only to improve performance. Hence, we select a relatively small value for α in order not to slow down learning. Likewise, to implement minimum distance VQ exactly, the biases in the second convolutional layer should depend on the filter weights, but there is no practical reason to enforce this constraint, and we allow also the biases to adapt freely.

Now, the final CNN can be trained as usual with stochastic gradient descent [17] to adapt to the desired task. It should be clear that a number of architectural modifications could be also tested starting from this basic structure, but this goes beyond the scope of the present paper, and will be the object of future research. We must underline that the equivalence between CNN and BoW has been noticed before in the literature, for example in [1, 18, 24].

4 EXPERIMENTAL ANALYSIS

To test the performance of the proposed CNN architecture we carry out a number of experiments with typical manipulations. Our synthetic dataset includes images taken from 9 devices, 4 smartphones (Apple iPhone 4S, Apple iPhone 5s, Huawei P7 mini, Nokia Lumia 925) and 5 cameras (Canon EOS 450D, Canon IXUS 95 IS, Sony DSC-S780, Samsung Digimax 301, Nikon Coolpix S5100). Each device contributes 200 images, and from each image non-overlapping patches of dimension 128×128 are sampled. We select at random 6 devices to form the training set, while the remaining 3 are used as a testing set. Therefore, the patches used for testing come from devices that are never seen in the training phase. For each pristine patch, the corresponding manipulated patch is also included in the set. Overall, our training set comprises a total of just 10800+10800 patches, quite a small number for deep learning applications. We consider 5 types of image manipulation: median filtering, gaussian blurring, AWGN noise addition, resizing, and JPEG compression, with three different settings for each case (see Tab.1) corresponding to increasingly challenging tasks. For example, JPEG compression with quality factor Q=70 is always easily detected, while a quality factor Q=90 makes things much harder.

In the proposed CNN the first convolutional layer includes 4 filters of size $5 \times 5 \times 1$ operating on the monochrome input (we use only the green band normalized in [0, 1]). In the second layer there

Table 2: Detection Accuracy for binary classification tasks.

Manipulation		Small Training Set			Large Training Set		
		Bayar2016 60 epochs	SRM+SVM	prop. CNN 15 epochs	Bayar2016 60 epochs	SRM+SVM	prop. CNN 15 epochs
Median Filtering	7x7	98.23	99.61	99.07	99.69	99.68	99.55
	5x5	96.66	99.67	99.47	99.78	99.68	99.60
	3x3	94.56	99.83	99.35	99.80	99.87	99.75
Gaussian Blurring	1.1	99.65	99.93	99.79	99.98	99.97	99.95
	0.75	98.52	99.90	99.82	99.94	99.77	99.93
	0.5	83.10	87.10	95.70	94.57	87.55	96.56
Additive Noise	2.0	97.08	99.94	99.95	99.56	99.94	99.94
	0.5	82.93	99.37	99.36	93.83	99.34	99.66
	0.25	51.83	85.06	88.81	80.28	84.01	90.79
Resizing	1.5	99.22	99.99	100.00	99.72	99.87	100.00
	1.125	91.06	98.94	99.56	97.02	96.00	99.78
	1.01	80.51	96.01	97.81	98.44	95.11	97.20
JPEG Compression	70	96.04	99.99	99.99	99.43	99.99	99.94
	80	77.01	99.73	99.37	98.12	99.94	99.86
	90	63.77	90.86	92.08	79.69	90.90	94.59

are 81 filters of size $1 \times 1 \times 4$. Filters are initialized as described in Section 3 and the α parameter of soft-max is set to 2^{16}. The code is implemented in Tensorfow and runs on a Nvidia Tesla P100 with 16GB RAM. We set the learning rate to 10^{-6}, with decay $5 \cdot 10^{-4}$, batch size 36 and Adam [14] optimization method, using the cross-entropy loss function. Together with the proposed CNN we consider also the basic solution, with the handcrafted feature followed by linear SVM, and the CNN proposed in Bayar2016 [2] based on the use of a preliminary high-pass convolutional layer.

Results in terms of probability of correct decision for each binary classification problem are reported in the left part of Tab.2 (small training set). With "easy" manipulations, *e.g.* JPEG@70, all methods provide near-perfect results and there is no point in replacing the SRM+SVM solution with something else. In the presence of more challenging attacks, however, the performance varies significantly across methods. After just 15 epochs of fine tuning, the proposed CNN improves over SRM+SVM of about 2 percent points for JPEG compression, resizing, and noising, and more than 8 points for blurring, while median filtering is almost always detected in any case. In the same cases, the CNN architecture proposed in [2] provides worse results, sometimes close to 50%, even after 60 epochs of training. Our conjecture is that a deep CNN is simply not able to adapt correctly with a small training set. In this condition a good hand-crafted feature can work much better. The proposed CNN builds upon this result and takes advantage of the available limited training data to fine-tune its parameters.

To carry out a fair comparison we also considered a case in which a much larger training set is available, comprising 460800 patches, that is more than 20 times larger than before. Results are reported in the right part of Tab.2. As expected the performance does not

change much for the SRM+SVM solution, since the SVM needs limited training anyway. For the proposed CNN, some improvements are observed for the more challenging tasks. As an example, for JPEG@90 the accuracy grows from 92.08 to 94.59. Much larger improvements are observed for the network proposed in [2], which closes almost always the performance gap and sometimes outperforms slightly the proposed CNN. Nonetheless in a few challenging cases, like the already mentioned JPEG@90 or the addition of low-power white noise, there is still a difference of more than 10 percent point with our proposal. It is also interesting to compare the two adjacent columns, proposed CNN at 15 epochs and the CNN architecture proposed in [2] at 60 epochs, which speak clearly in favor of the first solution, in terms of both complexity and performance.

The ability to reliably classify small patches may be very valuable in the presence of spatially localized attacks. This is the case of image copy-move or splicing, where only a small part of the image is tampered with. In these cases, a descriptor computed on small patches can more reliably detect manipulations, and even localize the forgery by working in sliding-window modality. Fig.6 shows two examples of forgery localization with a slightly blurred splicing and a resized copy-move, respectively. In both cases using the proposed CNN in sliding-window modality (block size equal to 128×128), a sharp heat map is obtained. The SRM+SVM solution also provides good results, but more false alarms are present. It is worth underlining again that the images used for these tests come from cameras that did not contribute to the training set.

5 CONCLUSIONS

Residual-based descriptors have proven extremely effective for a number of image forensic applications. Improving upon the current

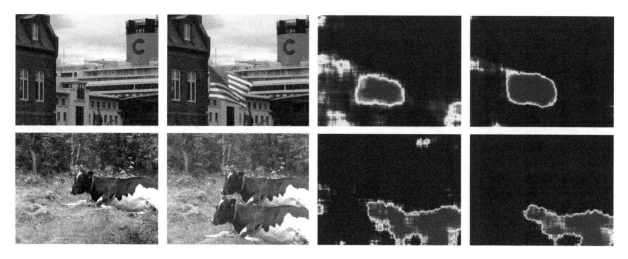

Figure 6: Top: splicing (blurred with st. dev. 0.5). Bottom: copy-move (resized with scale 1.125). From left to right: original image, forged image, SRM+SVM heat map, proposed CNN heat map. Images are of dimension 768×1024.

state of the art, however, is slow and costly, since the design of better hand-crafted features is not trivial. We showed that a class of residual-based features can be regarded as compact constrained CNNs. This represent a precious starting point to exploit the huge potential of deep learning, as testified by the promising early results. However, this is only a first step, and there is much room for improvements, especially through new architectural solutions. This will be the main focus of future work.

6 ACKNOWLEDGEMENT

This material is based on research sponsored by the Air Force Research Laboratory and the Defense Advanced Re search Projects Agency under agreement number FA8750-16-2-0204. The U.S. Government is authorized to reproduce and distribute reprints for Governmental purposes notwithstanding any copyright notation thereon. The views and conclusions contained herein are those of the authors and should not be interpreted as necessarily representing the official policies or endorsements, either expressed or implied, of the Air Force Research Laboratory and the Defense Advanced Research Projects Agency or the U.S. Government.

REFERENCES

[1] R. Arandjelovic, P. Gronat, A. Torii, T. Pajdla, and J. Sivic. 2016. NetVLAD: CNN architecture for weakly supervised place recognition. In *IEEE International Conference on Computer Vision*. 5297–5307.

[2] B. Bayar and M.C. Stamm. 2016. A Deep Learning Approach To Universal Image Manipulation Detection Using A New Convolutional Layer. In *ACM Workshop on Information Hiding and Multimedia Security*. 5–10.

[3] Y. Bengio, A. Courville, and P. Vincent. 2013. Representation Learning: A Review and New Perspectives. *IEEE Transactions on Pattern Analysis and Machine Intelligence* 35, 8 (2013), 1798–1828.

[4] M. Boroumand and J. Fridrich. 2017. Scalable Processing History Detector for JPEG Images. In *IS&T Electronic Imaging - Media Watermarking, Security, and Forensics*.

[5] H. Cao and A.C. Kot. 2012. Manipulation Detection on Image Patches Using FusionBoost. *IEEE Transactions on Information Forensics and Security* 7, 3 (june 2012), 992–1002.

[6] D. Cozzolino, D. Gragnaniello, and L. Verdoliva. 2014. Image forgery detection through residual-based local descriptors and block-matching. In *IEEE International Conference on Image Processing*. 5297–5301.

[7] D. Cozzolino, D. Gragnaniello, and L. Verdoliva. 2014. Image forgery localization through the fusion of camera-based, feature-based and pixel-based techniques. In *IEEE International Conference on Image Processing*. 5302–5306.

[8] D. Cozzolino, G. Poggi, and L. Verdoliva. 2015. Splicebuster: a new blind image splicing detector. In *IEEE International Workshop on Information Forensics and Security*. 1–6.

[9] D. Cozzolino and L. Verdoliva. 2016. Single-image splicing localization through autoencoder-based anomaly detection. In *IEEE Workshop on Information Forensics and Security*. 1–6.

[10] W. Fan, K. Wang, and F. Cayre. 2015. General-purpose image forensics using patch likelihood under image statistical models. In *IEEE International Workshop on Information Forensics and Security*. 1–6.

[11] J. Fridrich and J. Kodovský. 2012. Rich models for steganalysis of digital images. *IEEE Transactions on Information Forensics and Security* 7, 3 (june 2012), 868–882.

[12] R. M. Gray and D. L. Neuhoff. 1998. Quantization. *IEEE Transactions on Information Theory* 44, 6 (1998), 2325–2383.

[13] F. Huang, J. Huang, and Y.Q. Shi. 2010. Detecting double JPEG compression with the same quantization matrix. *IEEE Transactions on Information Forensics and Security* 5, 4 (dec 2010), 848–856.

[14] D.P. Kingma and J. Ba. 2015. Adam: A Method for Stochastic Optimization. In *International Conference on Learning Representations (ICLR)*.

[15] M. Kirchner. 2008. Fast and Reliable Resampling Detection by Spectral Analysis of Fixed Linear Predictor Residue. In *Proceedings of the Multimedia and Security Workshop*. 11–20.

[16] M. Kirchner and J. Fridrich. 2010. On Detection of Median Filtering in Digital Images. In *SPIE, Electronic Imaging, Media Forensics and Security XII*. 101–112.

[17] A. Krizhevsky, I. Sutskever, and G. E. Hinton. 2012. ImageNet Classification with Deep Convolutional Neural Networks. In *Conference on Neural Information Processing Systems*. 1097–1105.

[18] Z. Lan, S. Yu, M. Lin, B. Raj, and A.G. Hauptmann. 2015. Local handcrafted features are convolutional neural networks. *arXiv preprint arXiv:1511.05045* (2015).

[19] Y. LeCun, Y. Bengio, and G. Hinton. 2015. Deep Learning. *Nature* 521 (2015), 436–444.

[20] H. Li, W. Luo, X. Qiu, and J. Huang. 2016. Identification of Various Image Operations Using Residual-based Features. *IEEE Transactions on Circuits and Systems for Video Technology, in press* (2016).

[21] T. Pevný, P. Bas, and J. Fridrich. 2010. Steganalysis by subtractive pixel adjacency matrix. *IEEE Transactions on Information Forensics and Security* 5, 2 (2010), 215–224.

[22] A.C. Popescu and H. Farid. 2005. Exposing digital forgeries by detecting traces of resampling. *IEEE Transactions on Signal Processing* 53, 2 (2005), 758–757.

[23] Y. Qian, J. Dong, W. Wang, and T. Tan. 2015. Deep learning for steganalysis via convolutional neural networks. In *IS&T/SPIE Electronic Imaging*. 94090J–94090J.

[24] A. Richard and J. Gall. 2017. A bag-of-words equivalent recurrent neural network for action recognition. *Computer Vision and Image Understanding* (2017), 79–91.

[25] M.C. Stamm and K.J. Ray Liu. 2010. Forensic Detection of Image Manipulation Using Statistical Intrinsic Fingerprints. *IEEE Transactions on Information Forensics and Security* 5, 3 (september 2010), 492–506.

[26] L. Verdoliva, D. Cozzolino, and G. Poggi. 2014. A feature-based approach for image tampering detection and localization. In *IEEE Workshop on Information Forensics and Security*. 149–154.

[27] M.D. Zeiler and R. Fergus. 2014. Visualizing and Understanding Convolutional Networks. In *European Conference on Computer Vision*, Vol. 8689. 818–833.

Image Forensics Based on Transfer Learning and Convolutional Neural Network

Yifeng Zhan
Sun Yat-Sen University
School of Data and Computer Science
510006, Guangzhou, China
zhanyf3@mail2.sysu.edu.cn

Qiong Zhang
Sun Yat-Sen University
School of Data and Computer Science
510006, Guangzhou, China
zhangq39@mail.sysu.edu.cn

Yifang Chen
Sun Yat-Sen University
School of Data and Computer Science
510006, Guangzhou, China
chenyf79@mail2.sysu.edu.cn

Xiangui Kang
Sun Yat-Sen University
School of Data and Computer Science
510006, Guangzhou, China
isskxg@mail.sysu.edu.cn

ABSTRACT

There have been a growing number of interests in using the convolutional neural network(CNN) in image forensics, where some excellent methods have been proposed. Training the randomly initialized model from scratch needs a big amount of training data and computational time. To solve this issue, we present a new method of training an image forensic model using prior knowledge transferred from the existing steganalysis model. We also find out that CNN models tend to show poor performance when tested on a different database. With knowledge transfer, we are able to easily train an excellent model for a new database with a small amount of training data from the new database. Performance of our models are evaluated on Bossbase and BOW by detecting five forensic types, including median filtering, resampling, JPEG compression, contrast enhancement and additive Gaussian noise. Through a series of experiments, we demonstrate that our proposed method is very effective in two scenario mentioned above, and our method based on transfer learning can greatly accelerate the convergence of CNN model. The results of these experiments show that our proposed method can detect five different manipulations with an average accuracy of 97.36%.

KEYWORDS

Image Forensics, Steganalysis, Deep Learning, Transfer Learning

ACM Reference format:
Yifeng Zhan, Yifang Chen, Qiong Zhang, and Xiangui Kang. 2017. Image Forensics Based on Transfer Learning and Convolutional Neural Network.

This work was supported by NSFC (Grant nos. U1536204, 61379155, 61332012) and NSF of Guangdong province (Grant no. s2013020012788), Special funding for basic scientific research of Sun Yat-sen University (6177060230).

In *Proceedings of ACM IH&MMSec '17, Philadelphia, PA, USA, June 20-22, 2017*, 6 pages.
https://doi.org/http://dx.doi.org/10.1145/3082031.3083250

1 INTRODUCTION

Multimedia forensics has been an active research area during the last decade. Blind forensic techniques generally utilize statistical fingerprints to verify the authenticity of multimedia data without access to the original source. However, such imperceptible fingerprints may be destroyed by various manipulations. Some work has been done to expose the processing methods on digital images, such as median filtering [4], re-sampling [6], JPEG compression [3], contrast enhancement [5], and additive Gaussian noise.

There are a growing number of methods using CNN as the fundamental architecture. Since the first layer of neural networks tends to lose pixel dependency information during the training process, most of these methods use the features extracted from images by preprocessing layer as the input of CNN instead of the original images. Current preprocessing algorithms are not able to eliminate all image contents. Thus, the features extracted from images are usually highly data-dependent, which leads to poor generalization ability when these models are applied to different databases. Besides, CNN models need a large amount of data to train because of the huge learning capacity. In response to these issues, we apply transfer learning to two application scenarios, including the transfer learning between tasks and the transfer learning between databases. In this paper, we propose a new approach for training CNN models, which detects multiple image manipulations using transfer learning. To accomplish this goal, we need to train the CNN model proposed in [10] for steganalysis on Bossbase, then we transfer parameters from the steganalysis model to the image forensic model. With the transferred parameters, our forensic model can achieve almost perfect performance with a small amount of training data and much less training time. Another contribution of this paper is that we present the parameter transfer strategy for the forensic model on a different database. In the beginning, we need a well-performed forensic model trained on Bossbase. Then we retrain this model using a small amount of data from a new database, which only takes thousands of iterations.

In this paper, we present a comprehensive review of transfer learning and multimedia forensics based on CNN for the first time, and afterwards we discuss how we apply this powerful approach to image forensic tasks, *i.e.* what we can transfer and how we transfer it/them. Experimental results show that our method is very flexible and powerful in the generic image forensic tasks. Besides, the training models demonstrate the state-of-the-art performance on five forensic types as mentioned before.

2 RELATED WORK

Our proposed work is related to transferring parameters between CNN models, the application of CNN in image forensics and the concept of transfer learning are given as follows.

2.1 Multimedia Forensics using CNN

Plenty of multimedia forensic methods using CNN have been proposed. Generally, there are three types of applications used in multimedia forensic tasks. The first type is directly applying CNN to forensic tasks regardless of the original purpose of object recognition, *e.g.* a new approach for camera identification using CNN was proposed in [1]. The second type is extracting features from images with a hand-crafted algorithm before feeding into CNN. Since CNN does not consider the statistical properties that are important for multimedia forensic tasks, it tends to consider the original and the tampered images as the same because of the tiny difference between them. Based on this property, researchers have added a preprocessing layer at the front of CNN architecture in order to magnify the difference between the original and the tampered images. Chen proposed a new approach for median filtering detection by adding a preprocesing layer which improves the performance of CNN model by about 7.22%[4]. The third type is altering the architecture of CNN in order to fit multimedia forensic tasks. Take the method proposed in [2] for example, Bayar came up with a special convolution layer aiming to suppress image content and enlarge pixel dependencies, which proves to be very efficient in image manipulation detection.

2.2 Transfer Learning

Traditional machine learning algorithms use statistical models to make predictions on the future data that are trained on previously collected labeled or unlabeled data. Most of the algorithms assume that the distribution of the labeled and unlabeled data are the same. *Transfer learning*, on the contrary, allows the domains, tasks, and distributions used in training and testing to be different. The study of *Transfer learning* is motivated by the fact that people can intelligently apply previously learned knowledge to solve new problems faster or through better solutions. In the real world, we can find many examples of transfer learning, for instance, learning to recognize apples may help to recognize oranges. Similarly, in this scenario, learning to classify median filtered images might help to classify average filtered images. The approaches on transfer learning can be classified into different categories based on the varieties of knowledge being transferred[7]. In this paper, we choose the parameter transfer approach, in which the parameters of the layers between different tasks and databases are transferred.

3 THE PROPOSED SCHEME BASED ON CNN AND TRANSFER LEARNING

3.1 The CNN Model Used For Transfer

The CNN architecture we use in this paper is the scheme proposed in [9], where the customized deep CNN model can effectively capture useful statistical information for steganalysis. We briefly review the neural network architecture used for transfer learning in the following content.

The overall architecture contains one preprocessing layer which aims to enhance the weak stego noise, six layer groups and one classification module. The feature preprocessing layer is produced to feed to the first convolution layer, while the last layer of the convolutional module output a 256-D features to a fully-connected layer following an n-way softmax layer, which produces a distribution of n-class labels.

3.2 Parameter Transfer Between Tasks And Between Databases

3.2.1 Transfer Between Steganalysis and Forensic Tasks. In this scenario, we transfer parameters from a steganalysis model to a forensic model. We are interested in the answers to the following questions:

- *Which part of the steganalysis model should be transferred in order to boost the forensic model?*
- *How many layers should be transferred in order to obtain the best performance?*

To answer these questions, we use the standard transfer learning approach, which is to train a base network and then copy its first n layers to the first n layers of a target network[11]. The remaining layers of the target network are then initialized randomly and trained toward the target task. Transferring shallow layers of the base network is pretty standard in the transfer learning between different tasks, because shallow layers are more *general* than deep layers, which makes it more transferable.

Here we introduce some fundamental settings of our experiment described in Figure 1. In Figure 1(a), model S, a steganalysis network, is trained using the standard supervised backpropagation on the input S, which has been created for steganalysis using Bossbase. The labeled rectangles(e.g. W_S^1) represent the parameters learned from the corresponding convolution layer. W_S^P represent the parameters of preprocessing layer. Different colors indicate different dataset, on which different layers are originally trained. The thin, white, vertical bars between parameters represent the activations layer, batch normalization layer and pooling layer between the convolution layers, whose parameters are initialized and kept fixed before training. Figure 1(b) shows the forensic model with almost identical architecture as the steganalysis model except for the fully-connected layer. Here, the fully-connected layer of model F has 2 neurons in binary classification and 6 neurons in multiclass classification of this work. The input F is created for image forensics using Bossbase. Figure 1(c) shows the strategy of transferring parameters from the steganalysis model to the image forensic model, where the first n weight layers of the forensic model(in the example of Figure 2(c), $n = 3$) are copied from the steganalysis model, and the final $6 - n$ layers are randomly initialized. This entire network

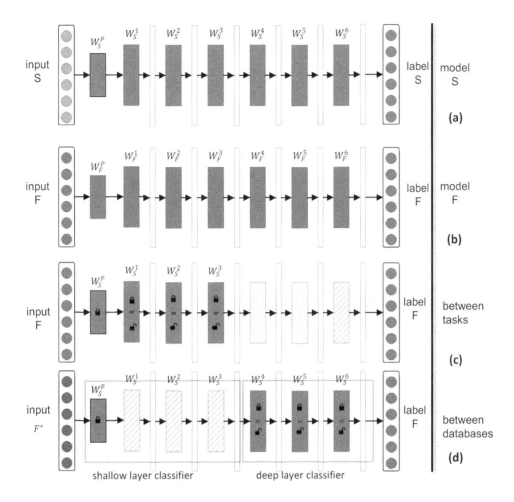

Figure 1: Overview of the experimental setting. (a) trained steganalysis model (b) untrained forensic model (c) parameter transfer between tasks (d) parameter transfer between databases

is trained on the Input *F*. We need to emphasize that in order to achieve good performance, the parameter W_S^P in the preprocessing layer is always the same in the target model. Experimental results demonstrate the effectiveness of our strategy in Section 4.2.

3.2.2 Transfer Between Different Databases. In this section, we discuss how to transfer parameters between two forensic models which are trained on different databases. The source and the target tasks are identical, while different training database are used.

When it comes to transfer learning in forensic tasks, labeling target domain data is no longer expensive, we only need to label it when we produce the target dataset. Thus, instead of using unlabeled target domain data, we fine tune the network using some labeled training data. According to [8], for the domain adaptation, we want to minimize the distance between domains, called Maximum Mean Discrepancy(MMD).

Not only do we need to minimize the distance between source and target domain representation, but we also need to train a strong classifier. In order to meet both of these criteria, our approach tends to minimize the loss by retraining the shallow layers which

have larger domain distribution distance compared to deep layers. Then use the output of the shallow layer classifier to train another classifier, the deep layer classifier. Our strategy sets numbers of fixed deep layers and randomly initializes the rest layers, then retrains the shallow layers in order to fit in the new domain. Figure 1(d) indicates that we use the first and the last 6-n of the network from model S and randomly initialize the rest, then the entire network is trained on a dataset F^* created from another database BOW; the upper $6 - n$ layers can be either kept locked or unlocked, while the parameter of the first layer, W_S^P, is always copied and kept fixed as in Section 3.2.1. Experimental results show the effectiveness of our strategy in Section 4.3.

4 EXPERIMENTAL RESULTS

4.1 Experimental Setup

We perform experiments of transfer learning between tasks on benchmark Bossbase database, which consists of a total of 10000 512×512 gray-scale images. The transfer learning between databases is tested on benchmark BOW database, which also consists of a

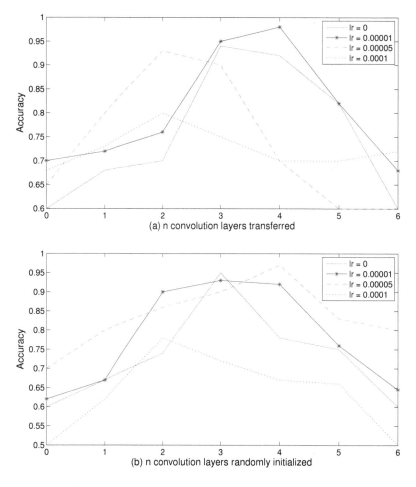

Figure 2: The performance of transfer learning related with the number of transferred layers (a) transfer between tasks (b) transfer between databases

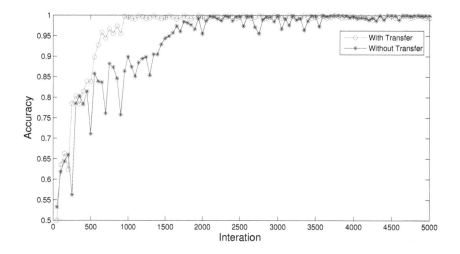

Figure 3: Test accuracy with and without transfer learning(JPEG 70 detection)

Table 1: Test Accuracy for Binary Classification On Bossbase.

Modification	JPEG(70)	JPEG(80)	JPEG(90)	MF(3×3)	MF(5×5)	CE($\gamma = 0.4$)
Accuracy	99.90%	99.90%	99.60%	99.90%	99.90%	83.60%
Modification	CE($\gamma = 2.0$)	Resampling($SF = 1.1$)	Resampling($SF = 1.5$)	AWGN($\sigma = 1$)	AWGN($\sigma = 2$)	
Accuracy	92.30%	98.60%	99.30%	99.90%	99.90%	

Table 2: Test Accuracy for Binary Classification On BOW.

Modification	JPEG(70)	JPEG(80)	JPEG(90)	MF(3×3)	MF(5×5)	CE($\gamma = 0.4$)
Accuracy	99.80%	99.80%	99.60%	99.40%	99.90%	83.50%
Modification	CE($\gamma = 2.0$)	Resampling($SF = 1.1$)	Resampling($SF = 1.5$)	AWGN($\sigma = 1$)	AWGN($\sigma = 2$)	
Accuracy	92.70%	98.40%	99.70%	99.90%	99.90%	

Table 3: Test Accuracy for Multiple Classification On Bossbase

Test/Prediction	Original	JPEG(70)	MF(3×3)	CE($\gamma = 0.4$)	Resampling($SF = 1.1$)	AWGN($\sigma = 2$)
Original	**98.90%**	0.69%	0.23%	0.02%	0.05%	0.11%
JPEG(70)	0.02%	**99.90%**	0.00%	0.06%	0.00%	0.02%
MF(3×3)	0.05%	0.00%	**99.90%**	0.03%	0.02%	0.00%
CE($\gamma = 0.4$)	15.40%	0.15%	0.25%	**83.20%**	1.00%	0.00%
Resampling($SF = 1.1$)	0.12%	0.05%	0.00%	0.11%	**99.60%**	0.12%
AWGN($\sigma = 2$)	0.00%	0.03%	0.02%	0.01%	0.04%	**99.90%**

Table 4: Test Accuracy for Multiple Classification On BOW

Test/Prediction	Original	JPEG(70)	MF(3×3)	CE($\gamma = 0.4$)	Resampling($SF = 1.1$)	AWGN($\sigma = 2$)
Original	**98.60%**	0.52%	0.50%	0.32%	0.00%	0.06%
JPEG(70)	0.04%	**99.90%**	0.00%	0.06%	0.00%	0.00%
MF(3×3)	0.21%	0.05%	**99.40%**	0.03%	0.25%	0.06%
CE($\gamma = 0.4$)	15.10%	0.50%	0.00%	**83.20%**	1.20%	0.00%
Resampling($SF = 1.1$)	0.02%	0.05%	0.27%	0.11%	**99.50%**	0.05%
AWGN($\sigma = 2$)	0.00%	0.02%	0.00%	0.01%	0.07%	**99.90%**

total of 10000 512×512 gray-scale images. The tampered images are created via different image manipulations.

- The JPEG images are created by JPEG compression using quality factors 70, 80 and 90, respectively.
- The median filtered(MF) images are filtered by 3×3 and 5×5 kernel, respectively.
- Resampled images are created by resampling (resizing) using bilinear interpolation, scaling factor(SF) are 1.1 and 1.5, respectively.
- Contrast Enhancement(CE) images are created by Gamma correction with $\gamma = 0.4$ and $\gamma = 2.0$.
- Gaussian Noise datasets are created by adding White Gaussian Noise(AWGN) with the standard deviation as 1.0 and 2.0, respectively.

The steganalysis model we use for parameter transfer is trained to detect S-UNIWARD at 0.4 bpp embedding rate on Bossbase. Stego images are generated through data embedding into the cover images. Hence, the dataset contains 10,000 pairs of images. 5,000 pairs are set aside for training, the rest 5,000 pairs are used as the testing dataset.

We run our experiments using one Nvidia Tesla K80 GPU, and the training parameters of the stochastic gradient decent are set as follows: *momentum* = 0.9, *decay* = 0.004, learning rate *lr* = 0.0001. We set the batch size for training and testing to be 50 images, and we use early stopping as a form of regularization to avoid overfitting. The training process can be stopped either by early stopping or by maximum iterations. The experiment of transfer learning between tasks is reported in Section 4.2. Section 4.3 presents the experiments of transfer learning between databases. We need to emphasize that the testing images of forensic task are not used in learning the steganalysis model , which ensures the reliability of the experimental results.

4.2 Transfer Between Tasks

The results of the first experiment are shown in Figure 2(a), which illustrate the performance of transfer learning related to the number of transferred layers. For simplicity, the accuracy in Figure 2(a) is calculated by averaging the test accuracy of all binary classification models after 1000 iterations. n indicates the number of convolution layers we transfer(W_S^P not included), lr is the learning rate of transferred layers. We can observe from Figure 2(a) that, with the same learning rate, the accuracy declines on both sides of the vertex. Base on this, we conclude that, with more transferred layers, the specificity of the transferred knowledge constrains the learning capacity for new tasks. With the decrease of the number of transferred layers, the performance also declines because of the deficiency of the transferred knowledge. For instance, in Figure 2(a), when the transferred layers are fixed *i.e. lr* = 0, the accuracy of the model is 0.6 if we don't transfer any parameters(*i.e. n* = 0), and the accuracy also drops to 0.6 with all parameters transferred(*i.e. n* = 6). The other lines in Figure 2(a) show the performance related to different learning rates for the transferred layers. As the learning rate increases, the peak accuracy increases; after reaching the peak accuracy, the bigger learning rate will cause rapid performance degradation.

After a series of experiments, we've selected eleven models for binary classification which achieves the highest accuracy in testing. These models are applied to detect the aforementioned image manipulations separately. We randomly select 2000 pairs of images(original and tampered) for the training process and use 5000 pairs of images in testing, and the experimental results prove that our model can indeed be well trained using only a small amount of data with transferred parameters. Table 1 records the accuracy of our models in the binary classification, except for CE detection(CE may be harder to be detected compared to some other image operations), and we can see that our models achieve almost perfect accuracies.

As for multiclass classification, we change the output neurons of the fully-connected layer from 2 to 6 in the CNN architecture before the training process, then we test our trained model on the dataset including five kinds of the forensic images. Therefore, there is a total of 60000 images used for training and testing, just as in the binary classification. Here, we select 20% of images as the training data, which are 12000 images, and we select 30000 images for testing. Table 3 summarizes the performance of our best model for the multiple classification, we can see from this table that our proposed model achieves an average accuracy of 97.25% in detecting the five types of image manipulations.

CNN with transfer learning converges faster compared to off-the-shelf CNN, because of the transferred knowledge. Figure 3 presents the learning curve of the JPEG 70 detection task as an example, obviously the CNN with transfer learning converges faster and has more stable test accuracy during the training process.

4.3 Transfer Between Databases

For the parameter transfer between two databases, we came up with a different strategy, which transfers parameters of deep layers and randomly initializes shallow layers, which can be shown in Figure 1(d). *n* means the number of the randomly initialized layers, as shown in Figure 2(b). From Figure 2(b), we can see that, with fixed parameters(*i.e. lr* = 0), the accuracy reaches the peak when *n* = 3, which means random initialization of the first 3 layers(starting from the first convolution layer) is the best setting. The accuracy drops on both sides of the vertex, implying that less randomly initialized shallow layers would decrease the learning capacity of the network,

while insufficient transferred layers could not provide enough prior knowledge for the task.

Table 2 and Table 4 respectively show the performance of our trained binary/multiclass classification model tested on BOW with the same experiment settings in Section 4.2. We can see that after the parameter transfer and retraining, our model performs as superior as in the model trained on Bossbase.

5 CONCLUSION

In this paper, we have proposed a transfer learning method for forensic tasks, which reveals the transferability between steganalysis and forensic models. We have also discussed the transfer learning strategy when we want to apply the forensic model to another database. Experimental results show the efficiency of parameter transfer in both cases. Our method can easily train a forensic model with a small amount of data and much less time. As for parameter transfer between databases, our method solve the problem of performance degression by fine-tunning the model with a small amount of labeled data from the new database. We can see that, the models trained by our method exhibit almost perfect performance, which indicates that initialization with transferred parameters not only can boost the training process of the forensic model, but also can improve the generalization performance of our forensic model. This approach could be a very useful technique for future knowledge transfer between different multimedia forensic tasks.

REFERENCES

[1] Luca Baroffio, Luca Bondi, Paolo Bestagini, and Stefano Tubaro. 2016. Camera identification with deep convolutional networks. *arXiv preprint arXiv:1603.01068* (2016).
[2] Belhassen Bayar and Matthew C Stamm. 2016. A deep learning approach to universal image manipulation detection using a new convolutional layer. In *Proceedings of the 4th ACM Workshop on Information Hiding and Multimedia Security*. ACM, (2016), 5–10.
[3] Chunhua Chen, Yun Q Shi, and Wei Su. 2008. A machine learning based scheme for double JPEG compression detection. In *Proceedings of the Pattern Recognition, 2008. ICPR 2008. 19th International Conference on*. IEEE, (2008), 1–4.
[4] Jiansheng Chen, Xiangui Kang, Ye Liu, and Z Jane Wang. 2015. Median filtering forensics based on convolutional neural networks. *IEEE Signal Processing Letters* 22, 11 (2015), 1849–1853.
[5] Yeong-Taeg Kim. 1997. Contrast enhancement using brightness preserving bi-histogram equalization. *IEEE transactions on Consumer Electronics* 43, 1 (1997), 1–8.
[6] Matthias Kirchner. 2008. Fast and reliable resampling detection by spectral analysis of fixed linear predictor residue. In *Proceedings of the 10th ACM workshop on Multimedia and security*. ACM, (2008),11–20.
[7] Sinno Jialin Pan and Qiang Yang. 2010. A survey on transfer learning. *IEEE Transactions on knowledge and data engineering* 22, 10 (2010), 1345–1359.
[8] Eric Tzeng, Judy Hoffman, Ning Zhang, Kate Saenko, and Trevor Darrell. 2014. Deep domain confusion: Maximizing for domain invariance. *arXiv preprint arXiv:1412.3474* (2014).
[9] Guanshuo Xu, Han-Zhou Wu, and Yun Q Shi. 2016. Ensemble of CNNs for Steganalysis: An Empirical Study. In *Proceedings of the 4th ACM Workshop on Information Hiding and Multimedia Security*. ACM, (2016), 103–107.
[10] Guanshuo Xu, Han-Zhou Wu, and Yun-Qing Shi. 2016. Structural Design of Convolutional Neural Networks for Steganalysis. *IEEE Signal Processing Letters* 23, 5 (2016), 708–712.
[11] Jason Yosinski, Jeff Clune, Yoshua Bengio, and Hod Lipson. 2014. How transferable are features in deep neural networks. In *Proceedings of Advances in neural information processing systems*. (2014), 3320–3328.

Author Index